"Parnell's Funeral and Other Poems" from "A Full Moon in March"

Manuscript Materials

PLAYS

The Countess Cathleen, edited by Michael J. Sidnell and Wayne K. Chapman
The Land of Heart's Desire, edited by Jared Curtis
The Hour-Glass, edited by Catherine Phillips
Deirdre, edited by Virginia Bartholome Rohan
"The Dreaming of the Bones" and "Calvary," edited by Wayne K. Chapman
The Words Upon the Window Pane, edited by Mary FitzGerald
The Herne's Egg, edited by Alison Armstrong
Purgatory, edited by Sandra F. Siegel
The Death of Cuchulain, edited by Phillip L. Marcus

POEMS

The Early Poetry, Volume I: "Mosada" and "The Island of Statues," edited by George Bornstein
The Early Poetry, Volume II: "The Wanderings of Oisin" and Other Early Poems to 1895, edited by George Bornstein
The Wind Among the Reeds, edited by Carolyn Holdsworth
"In the Seven Woods" and "The Green Helmet and Other Poems," edited by David Holdeman
Responsibilities, edited by William H. O'Donnell
The Wild Swans at Coole, edited by Stephen Parrish
Michael Robartes and the Dancer, edited by Thomas Parkinson, with Anne Brannen
The Winding Stair (1929), edited by David R. Clark
Words for Music, Perhaps, edited by David R. Clark
"Parnell's Funeral and Other Poems" from "A Full Moon in March," edited by David R. Clark
New Poems, edited by J. C. C. Mays and Stephen Parrish
Last Poems, edited by James Pethica

"Parnell's Funeral and Other Poems" from "A Full Moon in March"
Manuscript Materials

BY W. B. YEATS

EDITED BY
DAVID R. CLARK

Cornell University Press
ITHACA AND LONDON

The preparation of this volume was made possible in part
by a grant from the National Endowment for the Humanities.

First published 2003 by Cornell University Press

Printed in the United States of America

Library of Congress Cataloging-in-Publication Data

Yeats, W. B. (William Butler), 1865-1939.
Parnell's funeral and other poems from A full moon in March : manuscript materials / by W. B. Yeats ; edited by David R. Clark
p. cm. -- (The Cornell Yeats)
Includes bibliographical references.
ISBN 0-8014-4183-8
1. Yeats, W. B. (William Butler), 1865-1939. Full moon in March--Criticism, Textual. 2. Yeats, W. B. (William Butler), 1865-1939--Manuscripts. 3. Parnell, Charles Stewart, 1846-1891--Poetry. I. Clark, David R. II. Title.

PR5904.F8 2003
821'.8--dc21 2003048968

Cornell University strives to utilize environmentally responsible suppliers and materials to the fullest extent possible in the publishing of its books. Such materials include vegetable-based, low-VOC inks and acid-free papers that are recycled, totally chlorine-free, or partly composed of non-wood fibers. For further information, visit our website at www.cornellpress.cornell.edu.

1 3 5 7 9 cloth printing 10 8 6 4 2

THE CORNELL YEATS

The volumes in this series present all available manuscripts, revised typescripts, proof-sheets, and other materials that record the growth of Yeats's poems and plays from the earliest draftings through to the lifetime published texts. Most of the materials are from the archives of Senator Michael Yeats, now in the care of the National Library of Ireland, supplemented by materials held by the late Anne Yeats; the remainder are preserved in public collections and private hands in Ireland and around the world. The volumes of poems, with a few exceptions, follow the titles of Yeats's own collections; several volumes of plays in the series contain more than one play.

In all of the volumes manuscripts are reproduced in photographs accompanied by transcriptions, in order to illuminate Yeats's creative process—to show the poet at work. The remaining materials—such as clean typescripts and printed versions—are generally recorded in collated form in an apparatus hung below a finished text. Each volume contains an introduction describing the significance of the materials it includes, tracing the relation of the various texts to one another. There is also a census of manuscripts, with full descriptive detail, and appendixes are frequently used to present related materials, some of them unpublished.

As the editions seek to present, comprehensively and accurately, the various versions behind Yeats's published poems and plays, including versions he left unpublished, they will be of use to readers who seek to understand how great writing can be made, and to scholars and editors who seek to establish and verify authoritative final texts.

THE YEATS EDITORIAL BOARD

For my wife

Contents

Acknowledgments

Senator Michael Butler Yeats and the late Miss Anne Yeats have been most generous in allowing the use of manuscripts of W. B. Yeats from their own collections and those which they have given to the National Library of Ireland. This editor has a great debt of gratitude to the Yeats family, including Mrs. W. B. Yeats, outstanding since he began working with the Yeats manuscripts in 1957.

Among libraries, my principal debt is to the National Library of Ireland. I am also very grateful to the Henry W. and Albert A. Berg Collection, New York Public Library, Astor, Lennox, and Tilden Foundations; the Harry Ransom Humanities Research Center, University of Texas at Austin; the H. Lytton Wilson Collection of William Butler Yeats, Special Collections, Morris Library, Southern Illinois University at Carbondale; the Houghton Library at Harvard University; Special Collections and Archives, John J. Burns Library, Boston College; Special Collections, University of Chicago Library; the William Butler Yeats Microfilmed Manuscripts Collection in the Special Collections Department and University Archives, Frank Melville Jr. Memorial Library, State University of New York at Stony Brook; Manuscript Department, Louis Pound Wilson Library, University of North Carolina at Chapel Hill; as well as the Library and Media Center at Peninsula College Library, Port Angeles, Washington; and Special Collections and Archives, W. E. B. Dubois Library, University of Massachusetts at Amherst, and the staffs of all these libraries.

I am especially grateful to Jared Curtis, coordinating editor for the series, who also acted as editor, copy editor, and typesetter of this book, assistant editor Declan Kiely, and all the editorial board, especially Stephen Parrish and Richard J. Finneran, editor of the poems series. I also thank Henry Summerfield for helpful suggestions for revision, Tom Desmond, Isaac Gewirtz, David Garcia, George Mills Harper, Phillip L. Marcus, J. C. C. Mays, Dónall Ó Luanaigh, Katharine Salzmann, Jacqueline Stuhmiller, and my family, who got me books and read and reread my introduction.

David R. Clark

Sequim, Washington

Abbreviations

FMM	W. B. Yeats, *A Full Moon in March* (London: Macmillan, 1935).
KGCT'34	William Butler Yeats, *The King of the Great Clock Tower, Commentaries and Poems* (Dublin: Cuala Press, 1934).
KGCT'35	William Butler Yeats, *The King of the Great Clock Tower, Commentaries and Poems* (New York: Macmillan, 1935).
LM	*The London Mercury*, December 1934. "Supernatural Songs" is on pages 110–113.
P	*Poetry: A Magazine of Verse* 45, no. 3 (December 1934).
SB	William Butler Yeats Microfilmed Manuscripts Collection, in the Special Collections and Archives, Frank Melville Jr. Memorial Library, State University of New York (SUNY), Stony Brook. Whereas most transcriptions are of the originals, a few are of photocopies in this collection.

Census of Manuscripts

BC Notebook and diary, June–December 1934, containing drafts of "Supernatural Songs" and other poems. An octavo volume, with a mock medieval binding. In its one-hundred-plus pages of cream-colored laid paper without watermark, each page 24.1 cm by 15.8 cm, the notebook contains drafts of "Alternative Song for the Severed Head," "Two Songs Rewritten for the Tune's Sake," "A Prayer for Old Age," and all the "Supernatural Songs" except "A Needle's Eye" and "Meru." It is 17.2 cm wide by 25 cm high and, at the thickest point, 3.5 cm thick. The mock hinge design tooled onto upper and lower leather boards has a five-petalled flower design on the spine that is replicated on each of the "hinges." The inside front and back covers and the fly leaves are decorated with small brown flowers on green stalks. The verso of the front (or first) endpaper is inscribed in Yeats's hand "W. B. Yeats / Savile Club / 69 Brook Street / London" and underneath that, in Mrs. Yeats's hand, "or Riversdale / Rathfarnam / Dublin / Ireland." Yeats moved to Riversdale, his last home, in 1932. Yeats Collection, John J. Burns Library, Boston College.

Chicago(1) Proof pages of eight *Supernatural Songs* that Yeats sent to Morton Zabel, then editor of *Poetry* magazine, on October 1, 1934. An accompanying letter of that date explains, "What I send you is part of a book called 'The King of the Great Clock Tower, Commentaries and Poems' of which my sister will publish at the Cuala Press an edition limited to 400 copies in the middle of December." The "Supernatural Songs" are pages 38–44 of a proof for that book, with a few holograph corrections. The poems are "1 RIBH AT THE TOMB OF BAILE AND AILLINN," "2 RIBH PREFERS AN OLDER THEOLOGY" ["RIBH DENOUNCES PATRICK"], "3 RIBH CONSIDERS CHRISTIAN LOVE INSUFFICIENT," "4 HE AND SHE," "5 THE FOUR AGES OF MAN," "6 CONJUNCTIONS," "7 A NEEDLE'S EYE," "[unnumbered] MERU." "Commentary on *Supernatural Songs*" begins on page 44 and ends on page [45]. The colophon states that the book was finished in the last week of October. The poems appeared in *Poetry* in December 1934. Box 3, folder 24, of the Morton Dauwen Zabel Papers at the University of Chicago Library.

Chicago(2) Corrected proofs of Yeats's "Three Songs to the Same Tune" from *The King of the Great Clock Tower*, which appeared in *Poetry* for December 1934. Morton Dauwen Zabel Papers at the University of Chicago Library.

***FMM*-HRC** Unbound corrected pages for a proposed Scribner edition, c. 1937–1939. In the Harry Ransom Humanities Research Center, University of Texas, Austin, Yeats, W. B., Works, Collected Poetry and Prose, volume 2 (folder 1 of 5). Above the printed "PARNELL'S FUNERAL" is printed in pencil, probably in Mrs. Yeats's hand, "Poems (1933 to 1937)." The group consists of loose pages 45–[70] of *A Full Moon in March*, paginated 319–344 in heavy pencil, canceled in green, and repaginated 175–200 in green. There are corrections by Yeats on pages 56 and 63. On page 56, in the first line of the song from *A Pot of Broth*, the phrase "That blonde girl there" is altered in pencil to "A bright haired slut." On page 63, line 2 of the second poem of "Supernatural Songs" is revised in black ink.

Houghton "Ribh denounces Patrick." Typescript (carbon copy), one page, undated. Titled "RIBH PREFERS AN OLDER THEOLOGY." Cream-colored, wove paper stock, no watermark, 25.3 cm by 20.2 cm. Houghton Library, Harvard University, bMS Eng 338.12 (9).

HRC "Three Songs to the Same Tune." Typescript in Harry Ransom Humanities Research Center, University of Texas, Austin, black (i.e., gray) ribbon copy in six leaves of blue-gray paper 26.1 cm high by 17.9 / 20.5 cm wide. Watermark Swift Brook / Bond; no chain lines. Revised in Yeats's hand in pencil and ink; also the pages renumbered. Accompanied by a two-page typescript note (ribbon copy), revised and signed in pencil, these pages measuring 25.4 cm high by 20.4 cm wide, with the watermark Swift Brook / Bond and no chain lines; also marked up by the printer. Included with this is Yeats's covering typed letter, signed, to *The Spectator*, dated February 18, 1934. Shelfmark: MS / (Yeats,WB) Works. "Three songs to the same tune."

MBY 545 Large manuscript book bound in white vellum, formerly in Michael Yeats's collection under number 545, now in other private hands. "Begun Nov 23 1930 at 42 Fitzwilliam Square, Dublin" and continued through 1933, this notebook contains a variety of verse and prose. The notebook is unfoliated; small neat page numbers are penciled at top center on each page, probably by Curtis Bradford, whose index (see entry below), presumably based on his own pagination, locates the following relevant material: on pages 304–317, 319–335, Yeats develops the essay on "Modern Ireland" that leads to "Parnell's Funeral." On pages 334–336, 338, 342, 366, 368–369, and 374–375 are manuscripts of "Parnell's Funeral," and on pages 356–367 are "Historical Notes" to that poem. On pages 379, 380, and 381 Yeats has developed "Meru." The transcriptions have been made from the SUNY Stony Brook photocopies: "Parnell's Funeral" from SB 21.5.193–195, 197, 209, 211, and 213; "Meru" from SB 21.5.192.

MBY 545 Index Typed index to MBY 545. Prepared by Curtis Bradford. The entry for page 379 contains the germ of "Meru" transcribed by Bradford. Films of this index are at Houghton Library, Harvard University, and at the Yeats Archive, Melville Library, SUNY Stony Brook, SB 21.5.11-14.

MBY 673 Letters from William Butler Yeats in Michael Yeats's collection. I have seen only photocopies of these. Certain letters to Olivia Shakespear contain poems and comment. These are transcribed from the photocopy of MBY 673 in the William Butler Yeats Archive at SUNY Stony Brook, but alternative transcriptions may be found in *The Letters of W. B. Yeats*, ed. Allan Wade (London: Rupert Hart-Davis, 1954). Letter 1 was written from Riversdale: July 24 [postmark July 25, 1934], with information leading to "The Four Ages of Man," quoting the "just written" "Ribh denounces Patrick," and telling of "another poem in my head" that becomes "Ribh at the Tomb of Baile and Aillinn." (This letter is transcribed from SUNY Stony Brook reel 3, bound volume 4, page 58 [in short form, SB 3.4.58]; see also *Letters*, pp. 823–825.)

Letter 2, written July 25, [1934], explains further about "The Four Ages of Man" (see *Letters*,

p. 825). Letter 3 of August 7 [postmark August 9, 1934] quotes a version of "The Four Ages of Man" (which is transcribed from SB 3.4.56; see also *Letters*, pp. 826–827). And letter 4 of August 25 [postmark August 28, 1934] quotes versions of "Conjunctions" and "He and She" (transcribed from SB 3.4.47–49; see also *Letters*, pp. 827–829).

NLI 8769 *The King of the Great Clock Tower*, in prose. Thirteen numbered leaves of three-hole notebook paper, ruled with blue lines 5 mm apart, measuring 20.3 cm by 16.4 cm, watermarked WALKER'S / LOOSE / LEAF MADE IN GT. BRITAIN. Contains holograph drafts of the opening of *The King of the Great Clock Tower*. On pages 11 and 12 are three stanzas of the song of the severed head, here untitled, beginning "Images ride,—I heard a man say—," followed by twelve unnumbered leaves (the last one blank) of large three-hole notebook paper, same blue lines, same watermark, but measuring 22.9 cm by 18.1 cm and containing the introduction and notes to *The King of the Great Clock Tower* and "Contents," with page references apparently to page proofs listing "A Full Moon in March," "The King of the Great Clock Tower," "I A Parnellite at Parnell's Funeral," "II After Forty Years." List closes with "Three Songs to the Same Tune" and "Supernatural Songs." Contains also a two-page preface signed "WBY / May."

NLI 30,004 Page 276 of *The Spectator* for February 23, 1934, "Three Songs to the Same Tune," corrected in pencil, probably by Mrs. Yeats, perhaps as a preliminary to typing it for a submission. The next printing after February 23, 1934, is in *Poetry*, December 1934.

NLI 30,020 Final page proofs of *The King of the Great Clock Tower, Commentaries and Poems* [1934], including ["The Severed Head"], "A Parnellite at Parnell's Funeral," "Three Songs to the Same Tune," "Ribh considers Christian Love insufficient," . . . up through "Meru"; pages numbered 1–45 (NLI $30{,}020_2$), with an added set of earlier marked pages numbered 25–32 and 41–[45] (NLI $30{,}020_1$).

NLI 30,111 One-page manuscript in ink in Yeats's hand of "Meru" under the title "The Summing Up" on typing paper measuring 25.2 cm by 20.2 cm and watermarked SWIFT BROOK / BOND.

NLI 30,167 "Whence had they Come?" No title. One-page typescript (in elite, black or gray type) on white typing paper with line and chain marks, measuring 26 cm by 20.2 cm and watermarked EXCELSIOR / FINE / BRITISH MAKE / DCM SH.

NLI 30,178 One-page typescript, elite, black (gray) ribbon copy of "What Magic Drum?" No title. Same typewriter and type of paper as NLI 30,167.

NLI 30,519 One-page fragment of manuscript from a draft of "Ribh in Ecstasy" in ink in Yeats's hand on three-hole notebook paper, ruled with blue lines and measuring 22.8 cm by 18.1 cm, watermarked WALKER'S / LOOSE / LEAF / MADE IN GT BRITAIN. SUNY Stony Brook, subgroup I, series I, subseries A, box 4, folder 75.

NLI 30,521 One-page autograph manuscript, dated August 1934, of draft of postscript to "Commentary on Three Songs" with a draft of "Church and State," on three-hole notebook paper, identical to that of NLI 30,519. Untitled.

NLI 30,546 and **NLI 30,547** Companion notebooks beautifully bound in brown vellum. The size of each, overall, is 22.5 cm wide, 27.3 cm high, and 2.2 cm thick. The cover of each is framed by three gilt lines on four sides and a small gilt rosette at each corner where the lines meet. **NLI 30,546** has on the spine in gilt letters "W. B. / YEATS / PROSE." The endpapers have a swirling design in gray, white, brown, yellow, and black. The leaves, measuring 20.3 cm by 26.3 cm, are white unlined paper watermarked BASKERVILLE / VELLUM / WOVE / [design], without line or chain marks. The prose volume contains entries of around 1933, notes on "Three Songs to the Same Tune," a note on *The King of the Great Clock Tower*; and a prose draft, 3^r, leading to "Ribh considers Christian Love insufficient." The draft is in blue-black ink. The date of the draft is October 17, [1933]. Transcribed from photocopy at SUNY Stony Brook. **NLI 30,547**, the companion notebook to NLI 30,546, has on the spine "W. B. / YEATS / POETRY." On its first ten leaves (ten rectos, seven versos) the notebook contains poems from *A Full Moon in March*, including two drafts of the second part of "Parnell's Funeral," thirteen drafts of what was printed as "Three Songs to the Same Tune," which was revised for *Last Poems* as "Three Marching Songs" (see W. B. Yeats, *Last Poems: Manuscript Materials*, ed. James Pethica [Ithaca: Cornell University Press, 1997], pp. xiv–xv, 148–187), and a draft of the rewritten song on Paistin Finn from *The Pot of Broth*.

NLI 30,795 An autograph, signed, pencil draft, untitled, of "Church and State" on the back of the last page of a ten-page typescript of the "Commentary on 'At Parnell's Funeral.'" The paper measures 25.8 cm by 20.3 cm, watermarked SWIFT BROOK / BOND.

NYPL(1) Autograph manuscript, signed, of "Septimus' Song" from *The Player Queen*. Single sheet of cream-colored, laid paper stock, watermarked WALKER'S / LOOSE / LEAF. Lined (narrow, blue) notepaper with double red line at top of page and measuring 22.8 cm by 18.0 cm. Three holes on left-hand side; all corners of the sheet are rounded. Black ink autograph on recto with one line of black ink and several lines written in pencil on verso. Berg Collection, New York Public Library.

NYPL(2) One holograph correction to a line in "Three Songs to the Same Tune" in a copy of *The King of the Great Clock Tower* (1935), page 34. Berg Collection, New York Public Library.

O'Shea 2039A A draft of "A Needle's Eye" in pencil under the title "A Crowded Cross" written facing the last flyleaf in volume 2 of Emanuel Swedenborg, *The Principia*, trans. James R. Rendell and Isaiah Tansley (London: Swedenborg Society, 1912), reproduced under item 2039A in Edward O'Shea, *A Descriptive Catalog of W. B. Yeats's Library* (New York: Garland Publishing, 1985), p. 271.

SIU(1) Two corrected carbon typescript pages containing "Somebody at Parnell's Funeral," signed "W. B. Yeats, April 9, 1933." The sheets are white, with no watermark, and measure 20.3 cm by 25.3 cm. The typescript includes only the first part of the poem, consisting of four stanzas. The first stanza has seven verses, while the other three have eight. There are significant holograph corrections in ink, and, on the first page, three lines have been entirely handwritten. Collection 76, box 1, folder 10. H. Lytton Wilson Collection of William Butler Yeats, Morris Library, Southern Illinois University at Carbondale.

SIU(2) Carbon typescript with holograph revisions of "Three Songs to the Same Tune." The usual description is that the typescript is divided into a "Second Version" and a "Third Version." However, the "First Version" is present also, occupying the last page; but because it has no title it has been thought to be an extension of the "Third Version." The "Second Version" consists of three stanzas of six lines rhyming ABCBDD, each followed by a chorus of four lines rhyming ABBA, on the rectos of two foolscap (16 in. by 13 in.) sheets of white paper, without watermark, 40.5 cm by 33.0 cm, corrected in ink. There are a few corrections on sheet one, none on sheet two. The "Third Version" consists of three stanzas of six verses each, followed by the same chorus as in the "Second Version," on one foolscap sheet. This third sheet is heavily corrected, the third stanza having five holograph lines, one canceled, substituted for the first four lines. The fourth foolscap sheet contains what would have been the "First Version" but is untitled. It consists of three stanzas of six verses each, with only two corrections, followed by the usual chorus of four lines. On the back of the third sheet is a prose note of six holograph lines, unrelated to the poem, comprising a rough draft of the note at the end of Yeats's "Initiation upon a Mountain," *The Criterion* 13, no. 53 (July 1934): 537–556. Collection 76, box 1, folder 11. H. Lytton Wilson Collection of William Butler Yeats, Morris Library, Southern Illinois University at Carbondale.

Times A manuscript, fair copy, in Yeats's hand, of the second of "Two Songs Rewritten for the Tune's Sake," a song from *The Player Queen*, provides the frontispiece for a pamphlet, *WILLIAM BUTLER YEATS, Aetat. 70*, which is reprinted from *The Irish Times* of June 13, 1935. The pamphlet of sixteen pages includes appreciations by Yeats's friends and colleagues: named are Francis Hackett, Sean O'Faolain, F. R. Higgins, Denis Johnston, Aodh de Blacam, and Andrew E. Malone. The front cover has a picture of W. B. Yeats, seated. Transcribed from a copy of the pamphlet in the Berg Collection, New York Public Library.

UNC The poem "Parnell's Funeral," part of "A Poem and a Commentary," is on two loose sheets measuring 26.5 cm high by 20.3 cm wide. The carbon typescript is corrected in black ink, stamped "8839" in red ink, and copyedited in blue and graphite pencil. The top left of each sheet was damaged by previous attachment. The verso of each sheet is stamped "Received JUL 10 1934 J. B. LYON COMPANY" in red ink. The first sheet had further date stamping in red and blue. The "Commentary" part is in a paper pamphlet binding. There is one unnumbered leaf followed by ten numbered leaves. There is no text on any verso. Each recto of the "Commentary" is also stamped "8839" in red ink. The verso of leaf ten has stamping as above for the first leaf of "Parnell's Funeral." Typescript, edits, and copyediting as above. The "Commentary" bears an autograph note "corrected April 1934." Cover of binder penned in black ink and copyedited in blue and graphite pencil. Watermarked Swift Brook Bond. Location: RBC Yeats—call number PR5904 .P37 1934. Wilson Library of the University of North Carolina at Chapel Hill.

Introduction

The manuscripts of *Parnell's Funeral and Other Poems* presented in this book were written from spring 1933 through December of 1934.[1] This introduction will relate events of Yeats's life to what the manuscripts show about the chronological order of his writing these poems, followed by comments on each poem and its manuscripts in the order in which the poems appear in *A Full Moon in March* (1935).

Events of the early 1930s provide a background. A positive influence was Yeats's meeting with Shri Purohit Swami at Sturge Moore's, June 6, 1931. Yeats persuaded the swami to write an account of his life, *An Indian Monk*, which he read in manuscript in February 1932. The introduction by Yeats is dated September 5, 1932, the book being published in November.[2] The swami then translated his master Bhagwan Shri Hamsa's *The Holy Mountain, Being the Story of a Pilgrimage to Lake Manas and of Initiation on Mount Kailas in Tibet*. Yeats's introduction appeared first in *The Criterion*, July 1934, and the book was published in September.[3] The poems in "Supernatural Songs" were much influenced by the swami's work.

A negative influence was Lady Gregory's decline, which began in July 1931 and ended with her death May 22, 1932. Yeats stayed with her at Coole Park much of the autumn, winter, and spring of 1931–1932. The full flow of Yeats's poetry diminished, and in the preface to *The King of the Great Clock Tower* he gives reasons. "Perhaps Coole Park where I had escaped from politics, from all that Dublin talked of, when it was shut, shut me out from my theme; or did the subconscious drama that was my imaginative life end with its owner?"[4]

In July 1932 the Yeatses moved from Fitzwilliam Square and resettled at Riversdale, Rathfarnum, Yeats's last home. Then began his last tour of the United States from October 1932 to January 22, 1933. On his return, politics occupied him again. He tangled successfully with the new administration, De Valera's, which considered censoring the Abbey Theatre. Yeats had his fling with O'Duffy and his fascist Blueshirt movement in the summer of 1933. By February 1934 he was disillusioned with both the Blueshirts and fascism generally.[5]

---

[1]So the group is called in *The Poems*, ed. Richard J. Finneran, 2d ed. (New York: Scribner, 1997; so also the 1st ed., 1989). The 1997 edition is cited henceforth as *The Poems*. The same group, with "Three Songs to the Same Tune,"which is postponed to the "Additional Poems" section of *The Poems* (1989, 1997), is called "From A Full Moon in March" in *The Poems of W. B. Yeats* (London: Macmillan, 1949), volume 2, hereafter cited as *Poems* (1949).

[2]Shri Purohit Swami, *An Indian Monk*, introduction by W. B. Yeats (London: Macmillan, 1932).

[3]Bhagwan Shri Hamsa, *The Holy Mountain*, introduction by W. B. Yeats, trans. Shri Purohit Swami (London: Faber and Faber, 1934). Hereafter cited as *Holy Mountain*.

[4]*KGCT'34*.

[5]Elizabeth Cullingford, *Yeats, Ireland and Fascism* (New York: New York University Press, 1981). See p. 212 and all of chapter 11, "Blueshirts."

The order of composition of the poems starts with "Parnell's Funeral" (see pp. xxv, 3). Yeats worked up this poem on many later pages of the large manuscript book bound in white vellum "Begun Nov 23 1930 at 42 Fitzwilliam Square, Dublin" and continued through 1933. A near-final draft of "Parnell's Funeral" dated "April 1933" is on page 375, and in a letter to Olivia Shakespear dated "April" [postmark 1933] Yeats says, "I have been in a dream finishing a poem, the first I have done in perhaps a year. I have written nothing in verse since Lady Gregory's death."[6] "Meru" follows in the notebook and is probably near to the same date (see pp. xlvii, 242). It occupies pages 379–381 of the 386-page notebook. The prose germ of "Meru" appears on page 379 and may be dated perhaps, like "Parnell's Funeral," some time near April 1933. "Meru," unnumbered, is the last poem in the series of only eight "Supernatural Songs," when that collection was published in *The King of the Great Clock Tower* (1934).

The two companion notebooks NLI 30,546 ("Prose") and NLI 30,547 ("Poetry") are probably next. NLI 30,546 contains the prose germ dated "Oct 17" [1933] of "5. Ribh considers Christian Love insufficient" from "Supernatural Songs," the poem being written elsewhere almost a year later (see pp. xxxvii, 170). NLI 30,547 contains two drafts of the second part of "Parnell's Funeral" and versions of "Three Songs to the Same Tune." This latter poem was included by Mrs. Yeats in the section "From A Full Moon in March" in *The Poems* (1949). But it is omitted from that group in Richard Finneran's *The Poems* (1997). Because it was much revised to "Three Marching Songs" of *Last Poems and Two Plays* (1939), it is now regarded as superceded and is relegated to the "Additional Poems" section of *The Poems*. The manuscripts are, however, included in this book, since they are a part of *A Full Moon in March* (1935) (see pp. xxvii, 46). "A Needle's Eye" may have been written next (see pp. xlvi, 240). It is neither in MBY 545 nor in the notebook at Boston College that contains most of the rest of the poems in *A Full Moon in March.* It is written, undated, opposite the back flyleaf in a book of Swedenborg (O'Shea 2039A). Since it was printed in time to be part of the "Supernatural Songs" in *The King of the Great Clock Tower* (1934), finished by the Cuala Press in the last week of October, it may well have preceded the Boston College notebook, or been contemporaneous with the first half of it.

Worried about his creativity, Yeats "wrote the prose dialogue of *The King of the Great Clock Tower*" that he "might be forced to make lyrics for its imaginary people" (*KGCT'34*, p. [1]). Fearing that his prime as a poet was over, he submitted this play to Ezra Pound for his judgment. Pound's response was negative and rough, but Yeats had his own solution to his worry about age. On April 5, 1934, he had the Steinach rejuvenation operation. On May 10 he wrote to Olivia Shakespear, "It is too soon to know whether I have benefitted by the operation but I feel as if my blood pressure was down—I am not irritable and that is a new event" (*Letters*, p. 822). Although apparently merely a vasectomy, the operation eventually convinced him that he was a renewed man. One result was his late philandering with younger women. His acquaintance with Margot Collis (or Margot Ruddock) began in June 1934, that with Ethel Mannin in late December 1934, that with Dorothy Wellesley in June of the next year, and that with Edith Shackelton Heald in April 1937. None of these intimate affairs developed in time to influence the poems in the volume *The King of the Great Clock Tower*, but the summer was full of poetry writing for that book.

When in June he and Mrs. Yeats went to Rapallo to close up their flat, he had with him the notebook now in the John J. Burns Library, Boston College.[7] The first entry is "Rapallo. June.

---

[6]*The Letters of W. B. Yeats*, ed. Allan Wade (London: Rupert Hart-Davis, 1954), pp. 808–809. Hereafter cited as *Letters*.

[7]Hereafter cited as BC.

1934. Gave 'Clock Tower' to Ezra [Pound] to read. He condemned it 'nobody language'. At first I took his condemnation as [a] confirmation of my fear that I am now too old. I have ~~hardly~~ written little verse for three years. But 'nobody language' is something I can remedy. I must write in verse but first [in] prose to set structure" (BC, 1^r). Yeats first mentioned the prose play *The King of the Great Clock Tower* in a letter of November 11 [1933], when he gave an early version of its verses for the opening of the curtain (*Letters*, p. 817). This prose version, revised, was in rehearsal July 25 [1934] (*Letters*, p. 826). But the early part of the notebook at Boston College contains a new rewriting, first in prose then in verse, in which at first the King assumes the name and character of O'Rourke of Breffny.

There seems no reason to doubt that Yeats composed the poems in the notebook in the order in which they appear there. The order is inconsistent. Ideally it would be leaves 1^r, 1^v, 2^r, 2^v, 3^r, 3^v and so on. But Yeats usually wrote on the right-hand page first and then added or corrected or substituted on the facing left-hand page, so that the order becomes 1^r, 2^r, 1^v, 3^r, 2^v, 4^r, 3^v and so on. Occasionally the verso was left blank, and occasionally a portion of a play or a note on some other subject would interrupt the sequence.

The first poem, on leaf 4^v, is a draft of what becomes "Alternative Song for the Severed Head in *The King of the Great Clock Tower*" (see pp. xxx, 94). This poem was dropped from the play when Yeats changed the latter from prose to verse, and the inclusion of the poem in the volume *The King of the Great Clock Tower* as an "Alternative Song" is an act of salvage. After it comes "A Prayer for Old Age" on leaves 7^v and 8^r (see pp. xxxii, 112). Then on BC, 12^v Yeats begins the "Supernatural Songs." First are drafts of what became "2. Ribh denounces Patrick" (see pp. xxxiv, 132; I give the final numbers of the poems, which is not the order of their composition). This poem is dated by a July 24 [1934] letter in which he says he has "just written" it. In the same letter he says that he has in his head plans for what becomes "1. Ribh at the Tomb of Baile and Aillinn" (*Letters*, p. 824). The first draft of this is at 16^r (see pp. xxxiii, 122). "9. The Four Ages of Man," started on 17^v, is mentioned as "written yesterday" in a letter of August 7 [1934] (see pp. xliv, 230; see also *Letters*, p. 826). Somewhere along in here comes "Church and State," of which one manuscript (NLI 30,521) is dated "August 1934" (see pp. xxxii, 118). Next, on 18^v, comes "5. Ribh considers Christian Love insufficient," eight months after its prose germ in the notebook NLI 30,546 (see pp. xxxvii, 170). Poem "10. Conjunctions," appears on 19^r and is quoted in a letter of August 25 [1934], where it is said to have been written "some days" before (see pp. xlv, 231; see also *Letters*, pp. 827–828). On 22^v comes "6. He and She," the last poem written before the letter of August 25 [1934] (see pp. xxxviii, 190; see also *Letters*, pp. 828–829).

Yeats had now done all the poems included in *The King of the Great Clock Tower* (1934). There were only eight "Supernatural Songs" at that time. On 25^v he started the new play, eventually titled *A Full Moon in March*, with the song beginning "Every loutish lad in love," telling Margot Collis, in a letter of November 13 [1934], that it is "partly addressed" to her.[8] The progress of his affair with Margot Collis is indicated by the modes of address in his letters: On September 3 and 24 she is "Dear Miss Collis," on October 5, 11, and 30 she is "My dear Margot," and on November 13 she is "My dearest" (*Ah, Sweet Dancer*, pp. 19–24).

On 26^v Yeats formally planned the new play, although with the old title *The Great Clock Tower*. On the bottom of 27^v, under the heading "Oct 24," he jots a schedule for the week of October 21–27, including "Thursday. Group theatre men come here at 7:30[.] Margot to be asked[.]"

---

[8] *Ah, Sweet Dancer, W. B. Yeats, Margot Ruddock, A Correspondence*, ed. Roger McHugh (London: Macmillan, 1970), p. 25. Hereafter cited as *Ah, Sweet Dancer*.

From October 20 through the winter of 1934–1935 Yeats met off and on with people associated with the Group Theatre—Rupert Doone, Ashley Dukes, T. S. Eliot—in the hope that there could be a Group Theatre production of some of his plays and that Margot Collis might act in them.[9] There are many drafts of *A Full Moon in March*, and then, starting on 33^{v}, a love poem, "Margot," which he sends to her in a letter of November 26 [?27] (*Ah, Sweet Dancer*, pp. 33–34).[10]

On leaves 35 and 36 he works on "Two Songs Rewritten for the Tune's Sake" (see pp. xxxi, 99), revisions of songs from *The Pot of Broth* (1902) and *The Player Queen* (1922). On 36^{v} begins "8. Whence had they Come?" (see pp. xliii, 224) and on 38^{r} "7. What Magic Drum?" (see pp. xl, 206). On 40^{v} he returns to work on the verse version of *The King of the Great Clock Tower*.

Starting on BC, 46^{v} and finishing on BC, 49^{r} is a love poem, which gives us the date, "Dec 27" [1934].

r}
~~Portrae~~} ~~aed~~

I

{yed
Portra{ed before his eyes
Implacably lipped,
It seemed that she moved;
It seemed that he ~~clas~~ clasped her knees.
What man so worshipped
When Artemis roved?

II

He sat worn out & she
Kneeling seemed to him
Pitiably frail;
Loves anxiety
Made his eyes dim
Made his breath fail

III

There suffered he
~~He suffered all~~ heart ache,
Driven by Love & dread
Alternate will [~~—?—~~],
A winding pathway took.
In love's levelling bed
All gyres lie still.
Dec 27

---

[9]See Michael J. Sidnell, *Dances of Death: The Group Theatre of London in the Thirties* (London: Faber and Faber, 1984), pp. 115–116, 266–269.

[10]There is a photograph opposite p. 80 in *Ah, Sweet Dancer*.

On BC, 48ᵛ are "3. Ribh in Ecstasy" and "4. There" (see pp. xxxv, 154, 168), which are finished in the remaining pages. These two begin as one poem and then separate. A few lines of *The Player Queen* are on 52ʳ, and the notebook ends on 52ᵛ with a "comment on E Mannins Stories." When he prepared the volume *A Full Moon in March* in December 1934, four poems were inserted into the "Supernatural Songs"—"3. Ribh in Ecstasy," "4. There," "7. What Magic Drum?" and "8. Whence had they Come?" The time frame for this group of poems is therefore April 1933 to December 1934. The preface to *A Full Moon in March* is dated May 30, 1935, and the book was published on November 22, 1935.

It would be insufficient to furnish the reader only with the commentary necessary to an edition of these manuscripts. The pages that follow provide more interpretation than is usual in this series. But critics have little dealt with most of these poems. As astute a reader as Helen Vendler comments on the "riddling expression" of the "Supernatural Songs" and confesses having "avoided them for years, as too difficult."[11] Therefore, the poems here require independent analysis, along with material from Yeats's letters and commentary, to be properly introduced to the reader.

Parnell's Funeral

Considering the poems, not in the order of their composition, but in their order in the book *A Full Moon in March* (1935), first again is "Parnell's Funeral" (see pp. 2–45). Yeats wrote, "I rhymed a passage from a lecture I had given in America" (preface, *KGCT'34*). The lecture was probably "Modern Ireland: An Address to American Audiences 1932–1933." The second section of the lecture is the one most relevant to the poem.

> I stood on Kingstown Pier, now Dun Laoghaire pier, a little after six, awaiting the mail boat. I was there to meet a friend and it [was] accident that I saw the arrival of Parnell's body. My friend, more tireless than I, accompanied the body to Glasnevin and told me that evening of the stars that fell in the broad daylight as the body was lowered into the grave; and a few years later the Irish historian, Standish O'Grady, was to write: "I state a fact; it was witnessed by thousands. While his followers were committing Charles Parnell's remains to the earth, the sky was bright with strange lights and flames." [12]

This incident is used in the first stanza of the first draft of "Parnell's Funeral," which, slightly edited, goes as follows:

> They
> We stand under the Glasnevin tomb

[11]Helen Vendler, "New Wine in Old Bottles, Yeats's *Supernatural Songs*," *Southern Review* 27, no. 2 (April 1991): 399. Hereafter cited as "New Wine."

[12]"Modern Ireland: An Address to American Audiences 1932–1933," transcribed by Curtis Bradford in *Irish Renaissance: A Gathering of Essays, Memoirs, and Letters from* The Massachusetts Review, ed. Robin Skelton and David R. Clark (Dublin: Dolmen Press, 1965), p. 14. Hereafter cited as *Irish Renaissance*.

> The coffin is ~~lowered~~ lowering, the ~~sov~~ [?shovel] of earth falls upon the lid
> Somebody ~~cries he has~~ whispers it falls on a murdered man
> Slowly a star falls invisible in daylight
>
> ~~Those thousands lift their~~ bowed heads a moment
> ~~Glasnevin's tomb [?takes/likes] the air light~~ What arrow flew [. . . ?]

With the arrow, Yeats switches from the lecture to a vision of his own, which is also old material. He had written about it ten years before in *Autobiographies*, in the sixth section of "The Stirring of the Bones" and in notes on "The Vision of an Archer."[13] The draft goes on, as he begins to make a second stanza:

> The child sat in the [?branched] [?olive] tree
> The centaur guarding the tree
> The mother [?Marker] bent her bow
> Drew the bow string to her ear. (MBY 545, p. 368)

Here is part of the note on "The Woman who shot the Arrow": "She was, it seems, the Mother-Goddess, whose representative priestess shot the arrow at the child, whose sacrificial death symbolized the death and resurrection of the Tree-spirit, or Apollo" (*Au*, p. 486). Parnell, whose burial is noticed by shooting stars, is equated with a dead god.

Yeats begins to make a third stanza, in which Parnell's death marks a historical change. At first he begins to create new material: "Another angel & [?an] other age" (MBY 545, p. 368, l. 30), but perhaps these words remind him of the lines beginning "An age is the reversal of an age," in the same verse form, which he had published at least a year before. He goes into a flurry of revision to accommodate this stanza to the new poem, yet he finally returns to the original stanza, unaltered except in punctuation from its first appearance in 1932.[14] There, in the introduction to *Fighting the Waves*, the stanza capped a passage describing the severe effect of Parnell's death on politics and writing in Ireland. The words with which the stanza ends, "when we devoured his heart," give both the brutal reality of the death, caused by the people of Ireland, and its relevance to a ritual of sacrifice. "Ten years later," Yeats reminds us in "Modern Ireland," "when St. Gaudens designed the memorial that stands now in O'Connell Street, he set round its base the ox heads and wreaths that commemorate the sacrificial victims of classical Rome" (*Irish Renaissance*, p. 15).

The fourth stanza is new, not resurrected like the others. It can be seen to grow in strength through five drafts. It rejects nationalist political rhetoric as "a lie / Bred out of the contagion of the throng" (*The Poems*, p. 285). Parnell, in contrast, was a solitary.

> Leave nothing but the nothings that belong
> To this bare soul, let all men judge that can
> Whether it be an animal or a man. (*The Poems*, p. 286)

---

[13]*Autobiographies*, ed. William H. O'Donnell and Douglas N. Archibald (New York: Scribner, 1999), pp. 279ff., 485ff.; first published in *The Dial*, July 1923. Hereafter cited as *Au*.

[14]"Fighting the Waves / Introduction," *Wheels and Butterflies* (London: Macmillan, 1934), p. 72. This introduction was first published in *The Dublin Magazine* (April–June 1932).

The last line of this stanza was once "How much of it is pack and how much man" (MBY 545, p. 338). Again, "Whether it be all pack or half a man," and "Whether I am all brute or half a man" (MBY 545, p. 334). "Animal" accordingly means one of the mob; "man" a solitary. The second part of "Parnell's Funeral" develops this contrast. "One sentence I unsay" (*The Poems*, p. 286) refers to "when we devoured his heart," the merely negative meaning of which is "we killed Parnell." What he unsays is the positive meaning: to gain the greatness of the sacrificed one. Had de Valera, Cosgrave, O'Duffy eaten Parnell's heart they would have gained his nobility, but they did not. They, by implication, were animals, he a man. "Through Jonathan Swift's dark grove he passed, and there / Plucked bitter wisdom that enriched his blood" (*The Poems*, p. 286).

Three Songs to the Same Tune

Discussion of "Three Songs to the Same Tune" (see pp. 46–93) is inevitably mixed up with Yeats's interest in the Blueshirts, an Irish fascist organization, for whom these marching songs were originally conceived. Critics try to convince us that Yeats was or was not a fascist at the time of writing them. Conor Cruise O'Brien tells us that the "political man" Yeats, "had his cautious understanding with Fascism."[15] Elizabeth Cullingford, on the other hand, shows "the inappropriateness of the label 'fascist'" for Yeats (Cullingford, p. viii). These two authors' works will give the reader some of the background of "Three Songs to the Same Tune."

Although the songs were started for the Blueshirts, as they developed Yeats wished to disentangle them from that or any contemporary group. He changed the order of the poems and revised their content. Most of the manuscripts, written in 1933, are found in a leather-bound, gilt-decorated notebook labeled "W. B. / YEATS / POETRY" (NLI 30,547). In *A Full Moon in March* (1935) the three songs are in the following order: (I) beginning "Grandfather sang it under the gallows"; (II) beginning "Justify all those renowned generations"; and (III) beginning "The soldier takes pride in saluting his Captain." The songs we shall therefore call (I) Grandfather, (II) Justify, and (III) Soldier. The versions in this book are presented in the order in which they seem to have been written, which is the order of the notebook pages (with slight variations), followed by those manuscripts and publications whose short titles are SIU(2), HRC, the *Spectator*, NLI 30,004, Chicago, *Poetry*, *KGCT'34*, *KGCT'35, and FMM* (see the census, above).

Yeats began on 2^r and 1^v of the notebook with (II) Justify. On 3^r and 2^v he turned to (III) Soldier. Then on 4^r and 4^v he went back to work on (II) Justify. Not until 5^r did he work on (I) Grandfather. On 6^r, 5^v, and 6^v he worked on (III) Soldier; on 8^r on (II) Justify; on 7^v on (III) Soldier and (II) Justify; and on 7^r on (III) Soldier. In the typescript from Southern Illinois University he began with (III) Soldier, then followed with (I) Grandfather, (II) Justify. In the typescript in the Harry Ransom Humanities Research Center (HRC), he followed this revised order, but then in holograph made changes and adopted a new order: (II) Justify, (I) Grandfather, (III) Soldier.

In this new order, the songs were published in the *Spectator* for February 23, 1934, page 276. A letter to the *Spectator* dated February 18, 1934, accompanied the poems:

> If you care for the enclosed poems and preliminary note I would be greatly obliged if The Spectator could publish them as soon as possible. A great deal has happened about them here. They were to have been sung from the Abbey Theatre

[15]Conor Cruise O'Brien, "Passion and Cunning: An Essay on the Politics of W. B. Yeats," in *In Excited Reverie*, ed. A. Norman Jeffares and K. G. W. Cross (London: Macmillan; New York: St. Martin's Press, 1965), pp. 207–278.

> stage tomorrow night but at the last moment I have been compelled to withdraw them. The situation both between the Government and the IRA and between the Blueshirts and the IRA has become too acute. For certain reasons I am very anxious to have them published immediately and in some paper that has no connection with Irish parties.
>
> I have gone through the typescript very carefully and you need not send me proofs if that will enable you to get them into the next number of the Spectator.
>
> Please notice that all three poems have the same chorus, I give the chorus in full at the end of the first verse of the first song, after that I merely put its first words "Those fanatics etc." It is really a poem for singing and getting its whole quality from that chorus. (HRC)

Yeats's "certain reasons" for wanting immediate publication probably related to his desire to distinguish clearly between his songs and those the Blueshirts marched to.

The HRC typescript of the poems is, but for one line and two punctuation points, exactly what came out in the *Spectator*. By that time a note indicated that he was eager *not* to be associated with the Blueshirts.

> In politics I have but one passion and one thought, rancour against all who, except under the most dire necessity, disturb public order, a conviction that public order cannot long persist without the rule of educated and able men. That order was everywhere their work, is still as much a part of their tradition as the Iliad or the Republic of Plato; their rule once gone, it lies an empty shell for the passing fool to kick in pieces. Some months ago that passion laid hold upon me with the violence which unfits the poet for all politics but his own. While the mood lasted it seemed that our growing disorder, the fanaticism that inflamed it like some old bullet embedded in the flesh, was about to turn our noble history into an ignoble farce. For the first time in my life I wanted to write what some crowd in the street might understand and sing; I asked my friends for a tune; they recommended that old march "O'Donnell Abu." I first got my chorus "Down the fanatic, down the clown," then the rest of the first song. But I soon tired of its rhetorical vehemence, thought that others would tire of it unless I found some gay playing upon its theme, some half-serious exaggeration and defence of its rancorous chorus, and therefore I made the second version. Then I put into a simple song a commendation of the rule of the able and the educated, man's old delight in submission; I wrote round the line "The soldier takes pride in saluting his captain" thinking the while of a Gaelic poet's lament for his lost masters "My fathers served their fathers before Christ was crucified." I read my songs to friends, they talked to others, those others talked, and now companies march to the words "Blueshirt Abu"' and a song that is all about shamrocks and harps or seems all about them because its words have the peculiar variation upon the cadence of "Yankee Doodle" Young Ireland reserved for that theme. I did not write that song: I could not if I tried. Here are my songs. Anybody may sing them, choosing "clown" and "fanatic" for himself, if they are singable—musicians say they are but may flatter—and worth singing. (HRC)

Although Yeats says, "I first got my chorus 'Down the fanatic, down the clown', then the rest of the first song," the manuscripts show that the version in the revised HRC papers was the third arrangement and that the quoted line of the chorus is part of that revision. It was revised from "Tyrant, fanatic, clown," which appears in earlier versions. Later the order was changed again, in Mrs. Yeats's hand on a copy of page 276 of the *Spectator* (NLI 30,004), perhaps preparatory to her retyping the songs according to instructions from Yeats. This revised order was (I) Grandfather, (II) Justify, and (III) Soldier. The remaining publications—*Poetry* (December 1934), *The King of the Great Clock Tower* (1934) and (1935) and *A Full Moon in March* (1935)—all preserve this same order. In the typescripts and publications each of the songs has had its turn at being first of the three.

Although the *Spectator* publication is accompanied by a note that says Yeats has rewritten the songs to avoid "rhetorical vehemence," preferring "some gay playing upon [their] theme, some half-serious exaggeration," it is essentially not much different from the first drafts in NLI 30,547 and begins, like them, with (II) Justify. The *Spectator* version as revised in Mrs. Yeats's hand (NLI 30,004), however, crosses out the refrain in II:

> [Those fanatics all that we do would undo:
> Down the fanatic, down the clown,
> Down, down, hammer them down,
> Down to the tune of O'Donnell Abu.

In the margin she writes "Fierce young woman." She means that the new refrain is to be included here, as it is in *Poetry* and the other following publications:

> "Drown all the dogs," said the fierce young woman,
> "They killed my goose and a cat.
> Drown, drown in the water butt,
> Drown all the dogs," said the fierce young woman.

A letter of February 28, 1934, recounts the incident that gave Yeats these lines.

> Next door is a large farm-house in considerable grounds. People called ________[16] live there, "blue shirts" of local importance, and until one day two weeks ago they had many dogs. "Blue shirts" are upholding law, incarnations of public spirit, rioters in the cause of peace, and George hates "Blue shirts."' She was delighted when she caught their collie-dog in our hen-house and missed a white hen. I was going into town and she said as I started "I will write to complain. If they do nothing I will go to the police." When I returned in the evening she was plunged in gloom. Her letter sent by our gardener had been replied to at once in these words: "Sorry, have done away with collie-dog"—note the Hitler touch—a little later came the gardener. In his presence Mrs. ________ had drowned four dogs. . . . I tried to console George—after all she was only responsible for the death of the collie and so on. But there was something wrong. At last it came. The white hen had returned. Was she to write and say so? I said "No; you feel a multi-murderess and if you write, Mrs. ________ will feel she

[16]The family, named Weldon, was several times the source of conflict for the Yeatses (Ann Saddlemyer, *Becoming George, The Life of Mrs. W. B. Yeats* [Oxford: Oxford University Press, 2002], pp. 459, 495).

is." "But she will see the hen." "Put it in the pot." "It is my best layer." However I insisted and the white hen went into the pot. (*Letters*, pp. 820–821)

A "Commentary on the Three Songs" accompanies the version printed in *Poetry*, and is reprinted with slight variations in *The King of the Great Clock Tower* (1934 and 1935). It complains that the "upper class cares nothing for Ireland except as a place for sport, that the rest of the population is drowned in religious and political fanaticism":

> [T]he mob reigned. If that reign is not broken our public life will move from violence to violence, or from violence to apathy; our Parliament disgrace and debauch those that enter it; our men of letters live like outlaws in their own country. It will be broken when some government seeks unity of culture not less than economic unity, welding to the purpose museum, school, university, learned institution. . . .
>
> If any Government or party undertake this work it will need force, marching men (the logic of fanaticism, whether in a woman or a mob is drawn from a premise protected by ignorance and therefore irrefutable); it will promise not this or that measure but a discipline, a way of life; that sacred drama ["of its own history"] must to all native eyes and ears become the greatest of the parables. There is no such government or party today; should either appear I offer it these trivial songs and what remains to me of life.
>
> *April 1934*
>
> P.S. Because a friend belonging to a political party wherewith I had once some loose associations, told me that it had, or was about to have, or might be persuaded to have, some such aim as mine, I wrote these songs. Finding that it neither would nor could, I increased their fantasy, their extravagance, their obscurity, that no party might sing them.
>
> ["Church and State," untitled, follows here.]
>
> *August, 1934*
>
> *William Butler Yeats*
>
> (*Poetry*, December 1934, pp. 132–134)

Alternative Song for the Severed Head in *The King of the Great Clock Tower*

An untitled version of "Alternative Song for the Severed Head" (see pp. 94–98) in an early draft of *The King of the Great Clock Tower*, NLI 8769, pp. 11–12, shows what Yeats was revising when he wrote BC, 4^{v}. In the latter, which is really the only manuscript to deal with here, he tries out "That roaring man [?Conglures] / The ablest knight upon a time" and then drops him. Whoever Conglures is, if that name is right, he does not appear in later versions.

The remarkable revision is that from

> How can a phantom ride among these
> Grip the saddle tight with your knees
> Images ride among images (NLI 8769, ll. 18–20)

to

~~He~~ That King that made the people stare
Because he had feathers instead of hair
And all the rest are waiting there. (BC, 4^{v}, ll. 6–8)

This becomes, saving the feather for the climactic line,

And all alone comes riding there
The King that could make his people stare,
Because he had feathers instead of hair (*Life and Letters* [London] 11 [November 1934]: 145),

which gives a tremendous lift to the end of the poem.

Two Songs Rewritten for the Tune's Sake

Of the four versions of the song from *The Pot of Broth* (see pp. 99–104), the first is the one with which Yeats starts, *Plays in Prose and Verse* (New York: Macmillan, 1924), pp. 34–35. Then in BC, 35^{r}, he lists "Various suggested burdens for 'Paistin.'" The next to the last is "Tomorrow night I shall break in the door" (l. 15), which is the principal revision given in *A Full Moon in March*:

Aro, aro,
To-morrow night I will break in the door. (*FMM*, pp. 56–57)

In *Poems* (1949) Mrs. Yeats, probably using after his death some note of her husband's, changes this:

Oro, oro!
To-morrow night I will break down the door.[17]

Either revision is striking. There is in the Harry Ransom Humanities Research Center of the University of Texas at Austin a copy of *A Full Moon in March* (1935) with a revision in Yeats's hand of the first line of this song.

A bright haired slut
~~That blond girl there~~ is my heart's desire. . . .

This may be an exciting revision, but Yeats has forgotten the play for a moment. The song is meant by the Tramp to flatter Sibby, the proud, stupid, romantic "woman of the house," who would certainly not accept "slut." Included here also is the version in *Plays in Prose and Verse* of "O would that I were an old beggar," from *The Player Queen* (see pp. 109–111). Yeats revises this by expanding it from eight to twelve lines, making it more lyrical, full of personality, and down-to-earth.

[17] *The Poems of W. B. Yeats* (London: Macmillan, 1949), vol. 2.

A Prayer for Old Age

Looking at the first draft of "A Prayer for Old Age" (see pp. 112–117), BC, 7^v, one might guess that the original poem went something like this:

I had great dread of thinking thoughts
    In the mind alone
He who sings the song aright
    Thinks in his back bone.

The thoughts that make a wise old man
    And can be praised of all
O what am I that I should not seem
    For the songs sake a fool

I pray to god & god I know
    Will grant all men what he can
That I may seem though I die old
    A foolish passionate man[.]

In revising, Yeats immediately generalized the first line to "God guard me from those thoughts men think" and in BC, 8^r, line 8, discovered "marrow-bone." He evidently decided that he could not, in this secular age, use "I pray" without apology, so he excuses himself by blaming fashion (lines 13–14, 17–20, and in the final poem). The prayer that he may seem "A foolish passionate man" ends all versions.

On 1^r, the first page of the Boston College notebook—the date is June 24—he records submitting his play to Ezra Pound and being rebuffed. On BC, 7^r, only six pages later, he starts this poem. The fact that it immediately follows Yeats's attempt to put the prose *The King of the Great Clock Tower* into verse and precedes his working out on BC, 9^v, 10^r, and 10^v the preface, in which he relates the Pound incident, supports A. N. Jeffares's perception that the poem was provoked by Pound's didactic condemnation of the play. Jeffares points to Yeats's statement "We only believe in those thoughts which have been conceived not in the brain but in the whole body."[18]

Church and State

"Church and State" (see pp. 118–121) was written in August of 1934 and first published in a postscript to the "Commentary on the Three Songs" (*KGCT'34*, p. 38). Yeats was reflecting on his flirtation with the Blueshirts in 1933. "Church and State" seems to proclaim his disillusionment with fascism. The first draft, NLI 30,795, is already close to the final poem. One notes, however, that the rhetorical question

---

[18]*Essays and Introductions* (New York: Macmillan, 1961), p. 235; A. Norman Jeffares, *A New Commentary on the Poems of W. B. Yeats* (Stanford: Stanford University Press, 1984), pp. 348–349. (See also note 29, p. xlvii, below.)

What are the church & the state
But the mob that howls at the door (NLI 30,795, ll. 10–11)

is more definite than the real question used in the final poem:

What if the Church and the State
Are the mob that howls at the door! (*KGCT'34*, p. 38)

Nevertheless the exclamation point, used instead of a question mark, strongly implies the answer "Yes, they are!" And the last two lines assume that this answer is accepted.

Supernatural Songs
1. Ribh at the Tomb of Baile and Aillinn

When Yeats worked on any of the "Supernatural Songs," he seems to have done the preliminary work in his head. In the manuscripts there are few ideas explored only to be rejected. Most of the drafts seem used only to find the best manner of saying what he already desired to say. Sometimes he discovers a word or phrase that gives a particular tone yet does not make a basic change.

The first of the "Supernatural Songs," "Ribh at the Tomb of Baile and Ailinn" (see pp. 122–131) in its final version is well summarized by the prose sketch in a letter to Olivia Shakespear (*Letters*, p. 824). The written poem does not change the situation there described, nor alter the tone, only intensify it. He begins "I have another passage in my head." What does not change from sketch to final poem is the ironic—almost Wildean—situation. A monk accepts the brilliant union of the souls of two lovers and does not marvel at the miracle but uses their light as a sort of lamp to read his breviary by. His use does not change from sketch to poem, and the simple line "I turn the pages of my holy book" is the same in all drafts.

There is one idea that Yeats starts to develop in the manuscript and then drops. We hear of Baile and Aillinn that

~~They were not of one faith & yet at death~~
Their bodies were [?transfigured]
~~transformed after their death~~
The
~~Yet~~ miracle ~~they share that form after their death~~
that gave them such a death
Transfigured to pure substance what had once
Been bone & sinew~~,~~ ~~not of one faith fold~~
~~Born so to speak within another~~ fold
~~They grew angelical.~~ (BC, 16^{r}, ll. 16–22)

What Yeats had in mind is unclear, whether the difference is between Baile and Aillinn, who were not of one "fold," or between both of them and what they were after death. "They were not of one faith" makes it seem the former. But what could that mean? Was one Christian and the other pagan? Is there any basis for such a division in the old story? In any case Yeats drops the idea, and it appears in no other draft.

Another change is in the word that describes Ribh's eyes, from "pure" (BC, 17^r, l. 17; BC, 18^r, l. 22) to "aquiline" (Chicago[1], l. 24), where the control of tone is marvelous: "Pure" has a pious ring; "aquiline" lacks that and adds the power of an eagle's sight.

2. Ribh denounces Patrick

"Ribh denounces Patrick" (see pp. 132–153) is written in triplets. Leaf 13^r attempts the first two stanzas, already deciding on three lines rhyming with "man" or "son" and three with "said," the middle line of each triplet longer than the first and third. Leaf 14^r attempts the third and fourth stanzas, rhyming with "kind" and "three."

"A Trinity that is wholly masculine" is the final description of Patrick's mistaken creed. Ribh has used angry words for it in 13^r. "At those mail gods I spit" or "I spit upon the three man god" or "His three male gods make a cat laugh" (ll. 2, 3, and 4). In 12^v Ribh defies the deity: "On the creator of one son I spit—." All of this spitting is rejected. Even Yeats dared not spit upon the Trinity in Ireland. He saved his saliva for less dangerous opponents, the dancers of Degas in the prologue to *The Death of Cuchulain.*

The great thing worked on in these early drafts and perfected in line 3 of BC, 14^v is the line about the serpent with mirror scales. Lines 3–7 of BC, 14^r already play with "the mirror scales" and "the mirroring serpent scales" that are "mans increase." These are also "the mirroring serpent scales" in BC, 13^v. In BC, 14^v, line 3, we have the perfect line, which grasps in simplicity the culmination of a great evolution of symbolism:

> The mirror scaled serpent is multiplicity[.]

This is a symbol that comes from the tree of life and from Blake, and this line could be what Blake sought and never quite found. We might expect one of his serpents to achieve scales that mirror multiplicity, but there is no such symbolism. Daniel Albright refers to *John Sherman* (1891), in which a room "glimmers like the strange and chaotic colours the mystic Blake imagined upon the scaled serpent of Eden."[19] But Blake so far as we know never combined the image of the serpent with the image of mirrors. Nor did Yeats before this, and it is a brilliant collocation. To Yeats, "[T]he naturalistic movement, Stendahl's mirror dawdling down a lane" seems related to "Locke's mechanical philosophy."[20] A mirror-scaled serpent would at all times reflect his surroundings in infinitesimal details. "Gaze no more in the bitter glass" warns "The Two Trees." "For all things turn to barrenness / In the dim glass the demons hold, / The glass of outer weariness / Made when God slept in times of old" (*The Poems*, pp. 44–45). Only in Yeats do the scales mimic multitudinous actuality. The remarkable directness and simplicity of this six-beat line contrast with the cumbrous length, eight beats, of line 11, which ends up "But all that run in couples, on earth, in flood or air, share God that is but three" (*The Poems*, p. 290).

The Tree of Life may be imagined as an actual tree, or, as Yeats explains, the cabalistic tree, "a geometrical figure made up of ten circles or spheres called Sephiroth joined by straight lines" (*Au*, p. 282). In the unfallen universe the serpent was controlled. (See the lowest category in figures 5, 6, and 8 of Kathleen Raine, *Yeats, The Tarot and the Golden Dawn* [Dublin: Dolmen

---

[19]W. B. Yeats, *The Poems*, ed. Daniel Albright (London: Everyman's Library, 1992), p. 761.

[20]*W. B. Yeats: Later Essays*, ed. William H. O'Donnell, with assistance from Elisabeth Bergmann Loiseaux (New York: Scribner, 1994), p. 108. Hereafter cited as *Later Essays*.

Press, 1972]). In the universe that we know, the serpent has escaped control and ranges freely through the tree, standing for Nature. (Compare figure 12 in Raine.) The adept may follow the ascent of the brazen serpent, or Nature, through the tree, rising slowly toward the top. This "Way of the Serpent" is itself a way in which the soul escapes the tree and achieves salvation. It is shown in Raine's illustrations 9, 10, and 11. Or, if saint or sage, the adept may renounce experience, shoot along the path Samekh, from Yesod to Tiphareth, from moon to sun, the path of "deliberate effort" attributed to Sagittarius (*Au*, p. 282). This is "the burning bow," the figure in "The Phases of the Moon," line 119 (*The Poems*, p. 168). At any time the supernatural may strike down in the opposite direction, with inspiration or revelation, as the lightning strikes the tower in the tarot card (figures 41 a, b, and c, and 42 of Raine).

As Yeats wrote to Olivia Shakespear, "The point of the poem is that we beget and bear because of the incompleteness of our love" (*Letters*, p. 824). "The mirroring serpents scales [?coiled] through [his] embraces wind" (BC, 13ᵛ, l. 10) so that the conflagration of love sinks to reproduction. As the serpent in the sephirothic tree rises at the fall and puts everything under his power, so the mirror-scaled serpent here condemns couples to have children rather than to beget and bear themselves. Otherwise the conjoining of the sexes would be a flame, as with Baile and Aillinn, or like Godhead begetting Godhead.

> Gods creatures do not couple to increase their kind
> But when the conflagration of their passion sinks, damped by the body or the mind
> Then juggling nature mounts, her coils through their embraces wind.
>
> (BC, 14ᵛ, ll. 7–9)

3. Ribh in Ecstasy, and

4. There

"Ribh in Ecstasy" and "There" (see pp. 154–169) start as one poem. However, there are two motives struggling in that one poem. One is to express ecstasy, the other to comment on it. These motives finally separate the poem into two. However, in the process, "Ribh in Ecstasy" becomes a dramatization rather than simply an expression.

The first nine lines in BC, 48ᵛ are the expression of a romantic ego. All verbs are in the present tense. One verb is omitted—"All ages [go] by"—increasing the speed. There is one speaker and one moment. These lines are in prose, and whereas at first they may be taken as an immediate expression—like Pascal's "Fire, fire!"—the last lines, which are discursive, are circled and clued into the beginning, making the whole more discursive and less expressive.

> All circles are joined
> The teeth are in the tale [?]. All ages by in a
> moment. (BC, 48ᵛ, ll. 7–9)

Lower on the page are lines 10–25, rhyming in iambic pentameter couplets and entitled "The Mystic." In line 11 the action is "now," but "now" is canceled, the action being put not off but away to "there," "There" becoming the title of poem 4:

can there
[?go] Nothing but Soul t Soul ~~can now~~ avail. (BC, 48^{v}, l. 11)

The tense remains the present:

Godhead & godhead in their sexual spasm met
~~Beget & bare themselves~~ Create themselves. (BC, 48^{v}, ll. 17–18)

"~~Eden & judgment pass before his mind~~" (BC, 48^{v}, l. 14). The two are apparently simultaneous. But now a moment of time intrudes:

Soul ah dizzy soul forget . . .
[~~cry~~ life
cry That ~~sound~~, & common [?daily] resume. (BC, 48^{v}, ll. 18, 21)

Yeats perhaps felt that he could not express ecstasy except by contrasting it with "common [?daily] life."

There is no sweetness but the trump of doom
Forget it all & common life resume. (BC, 48^{v}, ll. 23–24)

In the first lines of 50^{r} the "There" poem practically takes over and becomes quite Miltonic in line 6, when "A sound as though some angel host prevails" is heard. At the same time Yeats develops the lines that best express ecstasy, working against the regularity of the poem:

on a
Godhead ~~in~~ god head in ^ sexual spasm ~~get~~ beget . . .
Godhead. (BC, 50^{r}, ll. 8, 15)

This is a trochee and wins out over Yeats's various attempts to introduce an iamb, as in BC, 48^{v}, line 17, "Create themselves[.]" The trochee makes an even more abrupt caesura, expressing strong excitement, and afterward comes, following timeless with timebound—"what shadow [passed *rev to*] falls?" These words are little changed in the final poem.

All signs of the "There" poem disappear from the second poem in BC, 51^{r}, lines 9–22. Opposite it in the notebook, BC, 51^{v} is devoted entirely to "There," so it is here that the definite division of the two poems takes place. Other changes make a new and different poem of "Ribh in Ecstasy." For the first time "you," a person to whom Ribh is talking, is introduced.

What matter that you understood
~~You heard me speaking? Understood~~ no word?
Doubtless
~~Doubtless~~ I spoke or sang what I had heard
In
~~Mere~~ broken sentences. My soul had found
All happiness in its own cause or ground (BC, 51^{r}, ll. 9–12)

This is all new. The poem has become Ribh's side of a dialogue with some unnamed person. Instead of the romantic ego expressing ecstasy, he has become a dramatic character, explaining and justifying his strange behavior. Yeats, the old dramatist, having begun with an emotion to express, now creates a character to express it and a situation in which it is expressed. Next follow the lines that remain the most important in the poem, the tumbling lines that express Ribh's ecstasy, "Godhead on godhead in a sexual spasm begot / Godhead," followed by "Some shadow fell" (BC, 51ʳ, ll. 13–14). Yeats tries to finish the poem, canceling and then restoring two elaborate lines:

> My soul forgot; . . .
> Those amorous cries had vanished with its ground
> And must resume the common daily round (BC, 50ᵛ, ll. 9, 11–12),

which are changed to

> Soul that forgot
> Those amorous cries that out of quiet come
> Must mechanical day & night resume (BC, 50ᵛ, ll. 13–15)

and again simplified:

> My soul forgot
> Those amerous cries that out of quiet come
> And must the common round of day resume. (NLI 30,519, ll. 6–8)

Thus the poem is now Ribh's explanation to someone that he has had the ecstatic experience and sunken from it afterwards. From a romantic expression of ecstasy, the poem has become the presentation of a character remembering ecstasy and telling us about it.

A by-product of the writing of "Ribh in Ecstasy" is "There," which contains no hint that the speaker has been in paradise or experienced ecstasy. The little poem is all-encompassing, but is not even claimed for Ribh as his speech. It is really gnomic.

5. Ribh considers Christian Love insufficient

"Ribh considers Christian Love insufficient" (see pp. 170–189) is one of the great poems of the series. Apparently it started from words Mrs. Yeats repeated when she was in a trance, " 'hate god.' " In Yeats's report, "We must hate all ideas concerning god that we possess, that if we did not absorption in god would be impossible" (NLI 30,546, 3ʳ). "Love is of God & comes unsought" (BC, 20ʳ, l. 2). Hatreds are "purges of the soul" (BC, 20ʳ, l. 14). Leaf BC, 20ʳ develops the first lines of the final poem and BC, 21ʳ the ending lines. Leaf BC, 20ᵛ gives the striking couplet in the middle, which does not change much from then on:

> Such thoughts are garments & the soul's a bride
> That cannot in such trash and tinsel hide. (BC, 20ᵛ, ll. 5–6; see ll. 15–16)

Much of the work from then on is to provide a setting for these lines. Leaves 22ʳ and 21ᵛ work on the whole poem, including the magnificent conclusion, which we then are given in the Chicago(1) draft:

> At stroke of midnight soul cannot endure
> A bodily or mental furniture,
> What can she take until her Master give!
> Where can she look until He make the show!
> What can she know until He bid her know!
> How can she live till in her blood He live! (Chicago[1])

There seems nothing strange to the final poem in any of these drafts except in 19^{v}, where Yeats develops, and drops, an image of hounds and hunting. The lines seem almost like a parody of "The Hound of Heaven" by Francis Thompson, whom Yeats has called a great poet.[21]

> Why do I hate man woman or event
> ~~How do they snap my trap, what [?stench] or~~ scent
> ~~Compels my [?hounds] to follow where they~~ pass
> ~~Born from the confusion in my mind~~—
> ~~Con~~
> What hound lives [?snared] by those whose scent
> ~~Lures that I cannot put them from my mind~~
> [?Lures] (BC, 19^{v}, ll. 1–8)

6. He and She

Of "He and She" (see pp. 190–205) Yeats reported to Olivia Shakespear, "I have written a lot of poetry of a personal metaphysical sort. Here is one on the soul—the last written. . . . It is of course my centric myth" (*Letters*, pp. 828–829). The moon moves through twenty-eight phases in each month. These movements are those of Yeats's system in *A Vision*, in which a soul inhabits twenty-eight incarnations, phases two to fourteen leading to absolute subjectivity in phase fifteen, and phases sixteen to twenty-eight leading back to absolute objectivity in phase one. In its last phases the moon "sidles up" toward the sun and at its nearest point is dark. Yeats "saw in the changes of the moon all the cycles: the soul realising its separate being in the full moon, then, as the moon seems to approach the sun and dwindle away, all but realising its absorption in God, only to whirl away once more."[22] In 1930 he commented, "I am always, in all I do, driven to a moment which is the realisation of myself as unique and free, or to a moment which is the surrender to God of all that I am. . . . Could those two impulses, one as much a part of truth as the other, be reconciled, or if one or the other could prevail, all life would cease."[23]

This carefully constructed poem can be read on three levels: Moon and sun, woman and man, the soul and God. The movement of moon versus sun stands for a woman's relation to man. *But*

---

[21]*W. B. Yeats, A Vision* (London: Macmillan, 1962), p. 250.

[22]*The Collected Works of W. B. Yeats,* vol. 2: *The Plays*, ed. David R. Clark and Rosalind E. Clark (New York: Scribner, 2001), p. 700.

[23]*Explorations*, sel. Mrs. W. B. Yeats (London: Macmillan, 1962), p. 305.

the relation of the sexes is used as a metaphor of the soul's relation to God. Through the ages the moon has often been associated with woman because it was thought to control the menstrual cycle. The Greek goddesses were lunar deities. Female shyness, in Yeats's perhaps antiquated view, increases near to the male, but woman declares her own unique personality when seemingly independent of him. Yet the moon is caught up in its orbit, and its "brightness" is really not its own. So, in this perhaps chauvinistic metaphor, femaleness is meaningless without the male. " 'His light had struck me blind / Dared I stop' " (*The Poems*, p. 292). But the moon does not stop, and from crescent to half and half to whole the "scared moon" trips away brighter and brighter until at full moon it is both farthest from the sun and at its brightest. The sidling up is the end of the lunar cycle, after which "away must she trip" toward increasingly subjective phases, so that " 'The greater grows my light / The further that I fly.' " All created beings flee the creator into their full individuality—"I am I am I"—and then lose that individuality as they sink back into the undifferentiated.

The first draft, BC, 23^{r}, introduces the paradox that her individuality (her, the soul's, the woman's, the moon's) depends on her increasing use of his light (his, God's, the man's, the sun's). Yeats plays with the idea that "she thought the light her own" (BC, 23^{r}, l. 2, right) but only in this first draft, and even that contains the line "Though that light's but his light." The moon, as she gets farther from the sun, reflects more of his light, and thus becomes more herself, the moon. Thus "I am I am I" is full of paradox. It contains the great "I am." "And God said unto Moses, I AM THAT I AM: and he said, Thus shalt thou say unto the children of Israel, I AM hath sent me unto you" (Exodus 3:14). In "I am I am I" the great "I am" becomes the individual created person. As St. Paul says, "But by the grace of God I am what I am . . . yet not I but the grace of God which was with me" (I Corinthians 15:10).

Not until the fifth and sixth drafts (BC, 25^{r} and BC, 24^{v}) does Yeats generalize this insight to all creation:

> [And all creation shivers
> At the sweet
> All creation shivers
> With that swee cry (BC, 25^{r}, ll. 15–18)

and

> She
> 4 ~~And~~ sings as the moon sings
> 5 I am I, am I.
> The
> 6 ~~And~~ greater grows my light
> that
> ~~that~~ off
> 7 The further ~~off~~, I fly
> Till A
> 8 ~~And~~ all creation shivers
> 9 With that sweet cry[.] (BC, 24^{v}, 4–9)

The darkness of the moon—"His light had struck me blind / Dared I stop" (*The Poems*, p. 292)—is paralleled by the "blindness" experienced in sexual arousal according to Sappho's classic description—"Mine eyes cannot see."[24] This has its religious parallel in the shock of revelation, as in St. Paul's vision of Christ—"Suddenly there shined about him a light from heaven: And he fell to earth" (Acts 9:3–4), "And he was three days without sight" (Acts 9:9). Similarly, her tripping away has its religious parallel in the soul's flight from God, as Jonah "fled from the presence of the Lord" (1:10) or the speaker of Francis Thompson's "The Hound of Heaven" "fled Him down the nights and down the days." At the beginning and the end of the soul's cycle the soul has disappeared in objectivity, while at its fifteenth phase it is bright with complete subjectivity. The moon metaphor, however, implies that the soul's uniqueness, the uniqueness with which all parts of the creation "shiver," depends on God, is a reflection of God's sunlike light, or "stands in God's unchanging eye," as "22. Words for Music Perhaps" puts it (*The Poems*, p. 273).

The manuscripts show no other organization than is sketched above. The evolution is toward concentrated and eloquent expression. There are few significant rejected ideas. Drafts 1 (23^r), line 19, and 2 (22^v), line 12, consider but reject the line "He would have the whole of her," which states what might be true in the psychology of the sexes, but does not work for sun and moon nor for God and the soul. God, we might think, does not want our uniqueness consumed in Himself but perpetually renewed through our "repining restlessness," as George Herbert says, using a figure that also depends on alternating movement ("The Pulley," l. 17).

In BC, 26^r the title "Bride and [Bride]-Groom" recalls the magnificent imagery of Psalms 19: 5, where the sun is "as a bridegroom coming out of his chamber," but Yeats drops that title for the more general "He and She," perhaps not wishing to confuse and multiply imagery, nor to rival the moon itself as central image. Moreover he had already used the bride image in poem 5, "Ribh considers Christian Love insufficient."

7. What Magic Drum?

"What Magic Drum?" (see pp. 212–223) has been called "perhaps Yeats's obscurest poem"[25] and "the strangest poem he ever wrote" ("New Wine," p. 408). Scholars and critics from T. R. Henn on have thrown such blinding light on the poem as to leave some readers in the dark. Perhaps a review of the manuscripts may give a better idea of what the literal level of the poem is. The speaker is a man who is caressing a woman. In the first stanza he sublimates desire into a motherly tenderness for her. Whether or not because of an actual age difference, she seems to him like a child. (A concordance will show how often in his poems Yeats, like others of his generation, applies the word "child" to a grown woman.) The second stanza is in a mirroring but opposite mood. The "gyre has turned" (BC, 39^r, l. 17). Both mirror and gyre are images from the manuscripts. The motherly tenderness gives way to a surge of male desire. From sublimation and sublimity he turns to deepest animal involvement and engages the woman in an act of oral sex. "Primordial motherhood" and the male "beast" may, with the child, have trinitarian significance, but the first two persons are aspects of the one speaker. There are only two people in the poem, speaker and "child," and they are making love, love which in two stanzas runs the gamut from the sublime to the animal. The point is that the second kind of love is just as holy as the first and, as Yeats says elsewhere, is "contrapuntal" to it ("The Lady's Third Song," l. 10, *The Poems*, p. 306). They are opposing gyres in a sphere.

---

[24]*The Portable Greek Reader*, ed. W. H. Auden (New York: Viking, 1948), p. 501.

[25]Dennis E. Smith and F. A. C. Wilson, "The Source of Yeats's 'What Magic Drum?'" *Papers on Language and Literature* 9, no. 2 (spring 1973): 197–201.

In draft 1 (BC, 38^{r}) the sexual "pleasure" from which the speaker refrains is qualified as "deliberate" (38^{r}, l. 1). In other words he enjoys the peaceful moment without acting. "But now his body moves" (l. 7). A mood that is mirror image yet opposite, "The joyous mirror of another joy" (l. 14), takes over. "[P]assion has begun" (l. 15). The first occurrence of the mouth and tongue images definitely points to sexual behavior: "Down & around those dark declivities travel his mouth & tongue" (l. 16). In the poem "Parting" a woman says to her lover, "I offer to love's play / My dark declivities" (l. 16, *The Poems*, p. 278). One will not find "dark declivities" in an anatomy book, yet the context is clearly sexual. Just as the speaker's first mood is ascribed to the mother out of the "ancient woods" (l. 5), so his alternate but mirroring mood is ascribed to a forest beast: "What comes from the great [forest] what beast has licked its young" (l. 17).

Draft 2 (BC, 37^{v}) concentrates on the first stanza. Line 1 suggests that "pleasure" is postponed, but only for "a while." There is no "beast" in this craft. The "mother from ancient forest" (l. 3) is not actively involved but "looks down" benignly—figuring forth the speaker's own physical tenderness combined with sublimation of desire. He "has held back . . . passion" (l. 5) lest "It bring the man" (l. 6) in him so that he will "forget what child . . . / Drinks joy," that is, lest he cease to see his lover as a child and himself as mother. Both "mother" and "man" are clearly aspects of the speaker.

In the second stanza of draft 3 (39^{r}, top of page) "passion has begun" (l. 5). Draft 4 (39^{r}, bottom) explicitly refers to Yeats's system: "The passionate gyre has turned" (l. 17). With the turning of the gyre "the mother & the child are gone" (l. 17) and we have the male beast licking a woman's body: "Down limb & breast along her glimmering belly" (l. 18). "That" is changed in line 18 to "her," clear in the original manuscript, the only instance in the drafts or the poem where the female gender of the "child" is indicated.

Draft 5 (38^{v}, top) perfects the next-to-last line: "Down limb & breast, [along *rev to*] or down that glimmering belly move his mouth & sinewy tongue" (l. 8). The "dark declivities," which are the route of this downward movement, are now specified as "limb," "breast," and "belly." In this draft the speaker "checks his passion" because of the force of that "secret symbol" (l. 2), the child upon a maternal breast. He does not want the "Ancient Mother" to "vanish from his veins" because she will "take the child" with her (l. 4), which probably means that he would no longer be able to regard his beloved only with the gentle physical tenderness of a mother. But the "great cathedral gong" sounds (l. 6). The "starlit dome" awaits (l. 7), and a beast from "The ancient forest . . . has licked its young" (l. 9). Desire has awaked; a new gyre has started; yet it is a mirroring one. Though bestial, it is possessive and loving. Just as Yeats took "dark declivities" from "Parting" in draft 2, so he takes the "great cathedral gong" and "the starlit dome" from "Byzantium" (ll. 4–5, *The Poems*, p. 252). In that poem a moonlit dome represents phase fifteen of Yeats's system and a starlit dome phase one. Clearly with the coming of the male beast a new cycle begins. As in "The Second Coming," the "rough beast" replaces mother and child as symbol (l. 21, *The Poems*, p. 190). It is a holy moment, a supernatural moment, and yet, on the literal level, a sexual consummation.

In BC, 38^{v}, drafts 5 and 6 are the first to introduce the "garden." In draft 5 the garden (l. 6) is distinguished from the cathedral on the one hand and from the forest on the other. In draft 6 (BC, 38^{v}, bottom) "Byzantium" is gone. The "great cathedral gong" has become "the magic gong" (l. 13) so that it can go back a few thousand years before the building of Santa Sophia. Primeval "cries among the garden trees" (l. 13) replace "the starlit dome." In BC, 38^{v}, bottom, there are only garden and forest, and the forest is "holy" (l. 15). The garden is not definitely Edenic, but it suggests a human realm within the holy forest from which "Ancient Mother" (l. 11) and male beast alternately come. Note that in draft 6 the "Ancient Mother" possesses the speaker's limbs and that he dare not move lest she "in alarm rise up" (l. 11). But he does move, this new phase beginning, as Yeats wrote in "Nineteen Hundred and Nineteen," "to the barbarous clamour of a gong" (l. 58, *The Poems*, p. 212). Yet the male beast is in his way as tender as the mother.

Draft 7 (BC, 39^{v}, top) is the first dated, a sign that the poem seemed to Yeats finished. "Dec" (l. 7) can only refer to the year 1934. Yeats was possibly about to indicate the day of the month, when he suddenly started tinkering again, the poem not finished after all. The version "What beast of the sacred forest came to lick its young?" (l. 7) is interesting in its definite assignment of a new purpose that makes "That Ancient Mother leave" the speaker's limbs and breaks the "rest" of the "child" (l. 2).

In draft 8 (BC, 39^{v}, bottom) the garden imagery returns—"Amid the starlit garden foliage" and "Under the starlit garden foliage sounds the magic gong" (l. 16)—with echoes of "Ribh at the Tomb of Baile and Aillinn," "Though somewhat broken by the leaves, that light" (l. 26, *The Poems*, p. 290). Yeats cannot determine here whether the gong "rings," "sounds," "booms," or perhaps "sings" (l. 16).

In draft 9 (40^{r}) the garden foliage symbolism is developed and perfected. It is first "slumbering" (l. 6), then "star obliterating" (l. 7), recalling "Byzantium," then "slumbering" again (l. 7), and finally "light obliterating" (l. 5), more pointedly recalling "Ribh at the Tomb of Baile and Aillinn." The lines were written in the order 6, 7, 5. Further to exorcise "Byzantium" and other echoes and to get a more primitive note, Yeats defies exact rhyme and substitutes "drum" for "gong" (l. 7). "Mother" is abstracted to "motherhood" (l. 2) to make clear that an aspect of the speaker himself is meant, and then Yeats finds the right word, "Primordial" (l. 3), to go with it. The sound and rhythm of "Primordial Motherhood" back up the meaning, and Yeats has created another of those wonderful phrases that one can roll around one's teeth. The reader's facial muscles are alerted, ready to respond to the phrase "mouth & sinewy tongue" (l. 8).

Draft 10 (NLI 30,178) is the typescript that accords with the published poem in all but punctuation.

8. Whence had they Come?

According to "Whence had they Come?" (see pp. 224–229), in individual lives and in movements of history, human beings unconsciously act out roles that are given them by some mysterious "dramatist."

The first line of the first draft (BC, 36^{v}), canceled, begins "Love is a [sacred] drama." A sacred drama, like that which, in the last two lines of the poem, heaved through the body of Rome when Charlemagne was conceived, takes place in the lives of the girl and boy, the impassioned man, and the flagellant. The events in their lives are in small what the birth of Charlemagne is in large, all performing what the unknown drama maker causes.

"Love is ~~a Sacred Drama~~" is followed by a semicolon in BC, 37^{r}, and thus "Eternity is passion," which is substituted for it, is perhaps also separated from "girl & boy / . . . Cry at the onset of their [?sexual] joy/ For ever & for ever." In BC, 37^{v} "Eternity is passion" is followed only by a comma, and the "girl or boy" clause provides an example of eternity's being passion. In NLI 30,167 and in *A Full Moon in March* the semicolon follows "forever," thus making lines 1–3 all one idea. At the semicolon occurs the return to wakeful reality. Draft 2 (BC, 37^{r}) cancels "Love is a Sacred Drama," and "sacred drama" is put off to line 20. "What sacred drama *in* her body heaved" in BC, 37^{r} becomes "What sacred drama *through* her body heaved" in BC, 37^{v} and all later versions.

For the first phrase in BC, 37^{r} Yeats substitutes first "Love is a thing of [?Art]" and then "Eternity is passion." This latter is an ambiguous statement that stays put in the finished poem. Does it mean that what we flatter by calling it "Eternity" is merely the intensity of a momentary passion, or that, beyond time, love is an orgasm without end, as in "Ribh in Ecstasy"? Or both, one in time, the other in eternity? Boy, girl, and impassioned man are helpless before the unknown power. In BC, 36^{v} and BC, 37^{r} the impassioned man is given more space than in the final poem.

> the grown man
> And ~~grown men~~ when eye [?entangles] eye
> Speaks out an [?unknown] ecstasy
> Sentences that he has never thought
> And must fulfil or make his whole life naught. (BC, 37^{r}, ll. 7–10)

Yeats perhaps felt it was a mistake to enlarge the man's role over the flagellant's when the lash was so important in the poem.

Rome is the passive, beaten receiver of the unknown's seed:

> What lay upon her, what seed had she received
> When world transforming Charlemagne was conceived. (BC, 36^{v}, ll. 20–21)

The lash, "that cruel symbol" (36^{v}, l. 16), beats down not only the flagellant's loins but also "frigid Rome." In 36^{v} it is all in one sentence:

> The flagalant, lashing those beloved loins
> ~~R[?e]~~ Has never heard what dramatist ~~joins~~ enjoins . . .
> That cruel symbol, at what bidding came
> The hand & lash that beat down [?frigid] Rome. (BC, 36^{v}, ll. 12–13, 16–17)

One assumes that the loins are the flagellant's own, but it is possible here that they are another's, in which case the flagellant is not a penitent but a sexual deviant. Although unlikely, this goes better with beating "down [?frigid] Rome." But Yeats apparently does not want this ambiguity, so he changes "beloved" to "submissive" from then on. This is not enough, so that ultimately, in the typescript NLI 30,167 and in *A Full Moon in March*, although in none of the three autograph drafts, "Flagellant" is capitalized. If the capitalization is not an error, perhaps this Flagellant was a penitent in one of the organized medieval groups or brotherhoods of that name.

The poem presents a series of passionate actors, the boy and girl, the "exultant man," the flagellant, and whoever possesses "frigid Rome." The line "The hand and lash that beat down frigid Rome" occurs in all drafts and the finished poem. "Frigid" means not just "averse to sexual intercourse" but "*abnormally* averse to sexual intercourse." Certainly the boy and girl and the exultant man are not "frigid." One assumes that the unfrigid flagellant is trying to conquer desire, beating himself into frigidity. But Rome is "frigid," until frigidity is beaten out of her. The word expresses her complete disinterest and unwillingness, which is savaged by the unknown power. Rome, what was left of her at that time (A.D. 747), had no intention of giving birth to "world-transforming Charlemagne." But the eternal "hand and lash" determined it.

9. The Four Ages of Man

A letter to Olivia Shakespear, July 24 (postmark July 25, 1934), gives us the thought process that went into "The Four Ages of Man" (see pp. 230–235):

> My dear Olivia, . . .Yes that book [unidentified] is important. Notice this symbolism

Waters under the earth		
	The bowels etc.	*Instinct*
The Earth		
The water	=The blood and the sex organ.	*Passion*
The Air	=The lungs, logical thought	*Thought*
The Fire	=	*Soul*

> They are my four quarters. The Earth before 8, the Waters before 15, the Air before 22, the Fire before 1. (See *A Vision* [1925 edition], page 86 [actually p. 36].) Note that on page 85 of *A Vision* [actually p. 35] the conflict on which we now enter is "against the intellect" [Yeats does not quote exactly but rephrases "16. The Table of the Quarters" on p. 35]. The conflict is to restore the body. . . .

The Earth	=	Every early nature-dominated civilization
The Water	=	An armed sexual age, chivalry, Froissart's chronicles
The Air	=	From the Renaissance to the end of the 19th Century.
The Fire	=	The purging away of our civilization by our hatred. (on these two I have a poem). (*Letters*, pp. 823–825)

Which two? Air and Fire? What poem? Possibly "5. Ribh considers Christian Love insufficient"? "Hatred" in that poem purges away our misconceptions of God. Yeats followed this letter with one on July 25 [1934] that corrects the pages but mixes up everything else: "My dear Olivia, I muddled the explanation and the quotation from my own book. It is from page 35 (not 85) and it is there written that in the last quarter of a civilization (the quarter we have just entered,) the fight is against body and body should win. You can define soul as 'that which has value in itself,' or you can say of it 'it [is] that which we can only know through analogies'" (*Letters*, p. 825).

We are not surprised that he writes on August 7 [1934], "Yesterday I put into rhyme what I wrote in my last letter." Then he quotes "The Four Ages of Man" and adds the following comment:

> They are the four ages of individual man, but they are also the four ages of civilization. You will find them in that book you have been reading [unidentified]. First age, *earth*, vegetative functions. Second age, *water*, blood, sex. Third age, *air*, breath, intellect. Fourth age, *fire*, soul etc. In the first two the moon comes to the full—resurrection of Christ and Dionysus. Man becomes rational, no longer driven from below or above. My two plays [*The King of the Great Clock Tower* and *The Resurrection*] . . . both deal with that moment—the slain god, the risen god. . . .

> The poem in this letter is one of a group of philosophical poems I am writing for the new Cuala book. (*Letters*, pp. 826–827)

The "New Cuala book" is *The King of the Great Clock Tower* (1934).

10. Conjunctions

On August 25 [1934] Yeats wrote to Olivia Shakespear about "Conjunctions" (see pp. 236–239):

> I was told, you may remember, that my two children would be Mars conjunctive Venus, Saturn conjunctive Jupiter respectively; and so they were—Anne the Mars-Venus personality. Then I was told that they would develop so that I could study in them the alternating dispensations, the Christian or objective, then the Antithetical or subjective. The Christian is the Mars-Venus—it is democratic. The Jupiter-Saturn civilization is born free among the most cultivated, out of tradition, out of rule.
>
> Should Jupiter and Saturn meet,
What a crop of mummy wheat!
>
> The sword's a cross; thereon He died:
On breast of Mars the goddess sighed.
>
> I wrote those lines some days ago. George said it is very strange but whereas Michael is always thinking about life Anne always thinks of death. Then I remembered that the children were the two dispensations. Anne collects skeletons. She has asked leave to go to the geological museum to draw skeletons. She buries little birds and beasts and then digs them up when worms and insects have eaten their flesh. She has a shelf of very white little skeletons. She has asked leave to go to the geological museum to draw skeletons. Then she loves tragedies, has read all Shakespeare's, and a couple of weeks ago was searching reference books to learn all about the poison that killed Hamlet's father. When she grows up she will either have some passionate love affair or have some close friend that has—the old association of love and death.
>
> . . . When George spoke of Michael's preoccupation with Life as Anne's with death she may have subconsciously remembered that her spirits once spoke of the centric movement of phase I as the kiss of Life and the centric movement of phase 15 (full moon) as the kiss of Death. (*Letters,* pp. 827–829)

11. A Needle's Eye

Yeats's "A Needle's Eye" (see pp. 240–241) inevitably refers to Jesus's words in the New Testament: "It is easier for a camel to go through the eye of a needle, than for a rich man to enter into the kingdom of God." Mark goes on, "And they were astonished out of measure, saying among themselves, Who then can be saved? And Jesus looking upon them saith, With men it is impossible, but not with God: for with God all things are possible" (Mark 10:25–27).

The perpetual miracle of creation, impossible for man, is constant for God. Not only camels but all things, "all of history [and prehistory] becomes an expanding gyre streaming out of an unknowable and minute point of origin" ("New Wine," p. 412). "All the stream that's roaring by / Came out of a needle's eye."

There are only two versions of this small poem. The version written on a flyleaf of Swedenborg's *The Principia* has a puzzling title, "A Crowded Cross." A needle's eye appears also in Yeats's "Veronica's Napkin" and there also has to do with a cross.

> The Heavenly Circuit; Berenice's hair;
> Tent-pole of Eden; the tent's drapery;
> Symbolical glory of the earth and air!
> The Father and His angelic hierarchy
> That made the magnitude and glory there
> Stood in the circuit of a needle's eye.
>
> Some found a different pole, and where it stood
> A pattern on a napkin dipped in blood. (*The Poems*, p. 243)

The "tent-pole of Eden" is not crowded but takes its part in a spacious design. The "different pole," however, takes its chances in the flux of which it is a part. The title "A Crowded Cross" gets the cross into the poem, which otherwise has no reference to it. Since all things come out of the needle's eye, the cross, individual and unique as it is, is overwhelmingly crowded. In "A Crowded Cross" it is the needle's eye that goads things on, whereas in the version sent to *Poetry* it is "Things unborn" and "things that are gone" that goad it [the stream] on "*From* needle's eye."

What goes into and comes from an ordinary needle's eye is thread. In Indian thought, the thread strings all things together and to their first cause. This symbolism finds its best expression in the Upanishads, in which the thread (*sutra*) is said in fact to link "this world to the other world and to all beings."[26] As the Yeats-Purohit translation puts it,

> He said: "Do you know that thread wherein this world, the next world and all beings are strung? . . . Do you know who controls this world, the next world and all beings from within? . . . Who knows thread and controller, knows Spirit, knows the world, knows the gods, knows all beings, knows all knowledge, knows the Self, knows everything. . . . Life is that thread whereon this world, the next world, and all beings are strung. We say that when a man is dead his limbs are unstrung; everything is strung on life. . . . He who lives on earth, apart from earth, whom earth does not know; whose body is earth; controlling earth from within; is your own Self, the immortal, the controller. . . . He who lives in sky, wind, heaven, quarters, sun, moon, stars, air, darkness, light; apart from them; whom sky, wind, heaven, quarters, sun, moon, stars, air, darkness, light do not know; whose body is sky, wind, heaven, quarters, sun, moon, darkness, light; controlling them from within; is your own Self, the immortal, the controller. Thus He lives in all gods."

---

[26]Jean Chevalier and Alain Gheerbrant, *The Penguin Dictionary of Symbols*, trans. John Buchanan Brown (New York, 1996), p. 991.

The mysterious needle's eye is the controller of the thread in Yeats's poem. In the Upanishad it is explicitly the self. "Invisible, He sees; inaudible, He hears; unthinkable, He thinks; unknowable, He knows. None other can see, hear, think, know. He is your own Self, the immortal; the controller; nothing else matters."[27]

> The symbolism of the uniting thread applies to both the macrocosm and the events of man's individual life. The thread passing through the sphere of the pearl or precious stone [or a needle's eye?] is an *axis mundi*, and with the circular form of the bead depicts a cycle of manifestation. . . . The Thread of Brahma is the symbol of Mount Meru, the world axis, and in the human microcosm is the median canal.[28]

So perhaps the needle's eye leads to "Meru."

12. Meru

"Meru" (see pp. 242–253) refers to Mount Meru,

> [i]n Hindu mythology, a golden mountain that stands in the centre of the universe and is the axis of the world. . . . As the world axis, Mount Meru reaches down below the ground, into the nether regions, as far as it extends into the heavens. All of the principal deities have their own celestial kingdoms on or near it.[29]

In Yeats's own account,

> [t]o Indians, Chinese and Mongols, mountains from the earliest times have been the dwelling-places of the Gods. Their kings before any great decision have climbed some mountain, and of all these mountains Kailās, or Mount Meru, as it is called in the *Mahābhārata* was the most famous. . . . Thousands of Hindu, Tibetan and Chinese pilgrims, Vedāntin, or Buddhist, or of some older faith, have encircled it, some bowing at every step, some falling prostrate, measuring the ground with their bodies; an outer ring for all, an inner and more perilous for those called by the priests to its greater penance. On another ring, higher yet, inaccessible to human feet, the Gods move in adoration. Still greater numbers have known it from the *Mahābhārata* or from the poetry of Kalidās, known that a tree covered with miraculous fruit rises from the lake at its foot, that sacred swans sing there, that the four great rivers of India rise there, with sands of gold, silver, emerald and ruby, that at certain seasons from the lake—here Dattātreya is himself the speaker—springs a golden Phallos. Mānas Sarowar, the lake's full name, means "The great intellectual Lake," and in this Mountain, this Lake, a dozen races find the birth-place of their Gods and of

---

[27]*The Ten Principal Upanishads*, trans. Shree Purohit Swami and W. B. Yeats (1937; rpt., London: Faber and Faber, 1938), pp. 140–142.

[28]"Thread," J. C. Cooper, *An Illustrated Encyclopaedia of Symbols* (London: Thames and Hudson, 1978). This reference to the "Thread of Brahma" gives a further meaning to the marrow-bone or the substance of the spinal cord in "A Prayer for Old Age."

[29]*The New Encyclopaedia Britannica*, vol. 8 (Chicago: Encyclopedia Britannica, 1991), p. 44.

> themselves. We too have learnt from Dante to imagine our Eden, or Earthly Paradise, upon a mountain, penitential rings upon the slope.[30]

Mount Kailas, over 22,000 feet, is in Tibet. It has three peaks, which traditionally are, to the Hindus, the homes of Brahma, Vishnu, and Shiva. In speaking of the "Hermits upon Mount Meru or Everest / Caverned in night under the drifted snow," Yeats has in mind Bhagwan Shri Hamsa's account of his suffering in a vigil on the holy mountain. "The first night I experienced terrible hardships. Bitter cold, piercing winds, incessant snow, inordinate hunger and deadly solitude combined to harass the mind; the body became numb and unable to bear the pangs. Snow covered me up to my breast and, till after midnight, I was fighting desperately with my mind"[31] This "deadly solitude" relates to Yeats's early perception that "All civilization is held together by the suggestions of an invisible hypnotist—by artificially created illusions. The knowledge of reality is always in some measure a secret knowledge. It is a kind of death" ("Estrangement," section 33, February 12, 1909; *Au*, p. 356).

It is perhaps no accident that "A Needle's Eye" comes just before "Meru," where it stood before the four poems were added that changed the series from eight to twelve ("3. Ribh in Ecstasy," "4. There," "7. What Magic Drum?" and "8. Whence had they Come?"). These four were simply inserted, 3 and 4 after "Ribh Prefers an Older Theology" ("Ribh denounces Patrick"), and 7 and 8 after "He and She." "A Needle's Eye" comes just before "Meru" in both sequences, perhaps because the two are related, Meru being the ultimate symbol of which the needle's eye may be a suggestion.

In the first poem of "Supernatural Songs," the love of two spirits transfiguring "to pure substance what had once / Been bone and sinew" makes a light where the old hermit Ribh may read in the pitch dark night his holy book. "Natural and super-natural with the selfsame ring are wed," declares Yeats in poem 2, "Ribh denounces Patrick." Supernatural is natural and natural supernatural. In poem 3, "Ribh in Ecstasy," Ribh comes back to the "common round of day" after a vision in which he knows "Godhead on Godhead in sexual spasm" begets "Godhead." In poem 4, "There," "all the gyres converge in one," natural converging with supernatural. In poem 5, "Ribh considers Christian Love insufficient," "thought" and all "bodily or mental furniture" disappear in the reality of God's living in the soul's blood. Poem 6, "He and She," gives us the relations of moon and sun, woman and man, the soul and god, explained in a heavenly bodies metaphor, as in Yeats's system. Poem 7, "What Magic Drum?" gives us a woman and man relating in grossest animality. Poem 8 asks "Whence had they Come?" about the Hand and Lash (my capitals) that whip individuals and historical movements into shape. Poem 9 traces "The Four Ages of Man" through four quarters that repeat one of the moon's orbits. Poem 10, "Conjunctions," the most personal and impersonal of the poems, present the poet's bodily children, but impersonally, by their horoscopes, as they represent the primary and antithetical of all cycles. Poem 11 perhaps presents the thread of life as it comes through "A Needle's Eye." And poem 12 presents "Meru," the holy mountain, the axis of the world, unity, the "Thread of Brahma," where one comes "Into the desolation of reality," and a new, untenanted, dawn.

---

[30]Introduction to *Holy Mountain*, pp. 19–20. The introduction also appears in *Later Essays,* pp. 139–155.
[31]*Holy Mountain*, p. 179.

"Supernatural Songs" ends "Parnell's Funeral and Other Poems," giving us a group of twenty-one poems, eighteen of which are called songs—"Three Songs to the Same Tune," "Alternative Song for the Severed Head," "Two Songs Rewritten for the Tune's Sake," and the twelve "Supernatural Songs" themselves. "A Prayer for Old Age" is "a lasting song." "Church and State" is presented as a "song" that is not "cowardly" and appears in *The King of the Great Clock Tower* (1934) as a postscript to "Commentary on Three Songs." Only "Parnell's Funeral" itself is un-songlike, a declaration made by a Parnellite at Parnell's funeral. Long ago at the Cheshire Cheese the Rhymers' Club had taken "delight in poetry that was, before all else, speech or song, and could hold the attention of a fitting audience like a good play or a good conversation" (*Au*, p. 234). In "Parnell's Funeral and Other Poems" too Yeats wanted a direct lyrical urge. Moving "Three Songs to the Same Tune" into a section of "additional poems," as is done now in volumes of Yeats's collected poems, is appropriate, since Yeats revised it and retitled it "Three Marching Songs" for *Last Poems and Two Plays (1939)*. Nevertheless, leaving out these poems emasculates "Parnell's Funeral and Other Poems." With "Three Songs" included, however, even poems like "Meru" that lack lyricism are caught up in the music, and the whole group unites to sing out what the hermits know:

> That day brings round the night, that before dawn
> His glory and his monuments are gone.

Transcription Principles and Procedures

In the present volume, the growth of the eighteen poems in the group "Parnell's Funeral and Other Poems" is recorded from the earliest recoverable drafts through the form the poems took in *A Full Moon in March* (1935). From that point onward, the record can be traced in the indispensable Allt and Alspach variorum edition.[1]

Beneath the first transcription of each poem—normally the first draft—are listed under *found in* the manuscripts in which that poem appears, and under *published in* the magazine or book publication of the poem prior to *A Full Moon in March.* Beneath the *last* transcription of each poem—normally the one closest to the final version—appears an *apparatus criticus* showing variants (from the revised form of the text) that appear in manuscripts or typescripts not transcribed and in proofs or printed texts up through *A Full Moon in March.* In the *apparatus*, the proof copies I have called Chicago(1) and Chicago(2), and magazine and book publication are abbreviated as follows:

Chicago(1)	Corrected proofs of "Supernatural Songs," from the *The King of the Great Clock Tower* (Dublin: Cuala Press, 1934), sent by Yeats to *Poetry* (Chicago).
Chicago(2)	Corrected proofs of Yeats's "Three Songs to the Same Tune," from *The King of the Great Clock Tower* (Dublin: Cuala Press, 1934), sent by Yeats to *Poetry* (Chicago).
DM	*The Dublin Magazine*
FMM	*A Full Moon in March* (1935)
FMM-HRC	A copy of A *Full Moon in March* (1935) now in the Harry Ransom Humanities Research Center, University of Texas, Austin.
KGCT'34	*The King of the Great Clock Tower* (1934)
KGCT'35	*The King of the Great Clock Tower* (1935)
LM	*The London Mercury*
P	*Poetry* (Chicago)
S	*The Spectator* (London)
Times	A pamphlet reprinted from *The Irish Times* of June 13, 1935.
Wheels'34	*Wheels and Butterflies* (1934)
Wheels'35	*Wheels and Butterflies* (1935)

[1]*The Variorum Edition of the Poems of W. B. Yeats*, ed. Peter Allt and Russell K. Alspach (New York: Macmillan, 1957).

Omitted from the record are variants of single versus double quotation marks, "and" and "&," type style, spacing, underlining, and punctuation in titles and in speaker identifications.

In the *apparatus*, the following abbreviations are used:

del	deleted or deletion
punct	punctuation
quotes	quotation marks
rev	revised or revision

As earlier volumes of the Cornell Yeats have indicated, Yeats's manuscripts are impossible to transcribe with absolute fidelity. His hand was almost always difficult to read, especially when he was writing for his eye alone and with a carelessness reflecting the excitement of literary creation. He left the endings of many words unfinished or represented by a vague line, formed letters carelessly or inconsistently, was a poor and erratic speller, and punctuated unsystematically.

The photo-facsimiles in this book will enable the interested reader to *see* what Yeats wrote. The task of the editor is to present a transcription in which the often highly obscure documents are *read*, and this inevitably requires a certain amount of interpretive "translation." The principles in accordance with which that process has been carried out and the conventions used in presenting the resultant text are listed below.

1. Where there is no reasonable doubt what word Yeats intended, even though letters may seem to be missing or run together at the end of it, that word is generally transcribed in full. In many cases, Yeats's actual spelling is difficult or impossible to determine, and in such cases the standard spelling is given. On the other hand, Yeats's spelling is preserved when it is clear, even if it is incorrect.
2. Yeats frequently broke words at unusual points, or broke words not normally divided. Such words are joined in the transcriptions unless the width of the break approximates the spacing Yeats normally left between words, indicating that he thought the word in question to be actually two words or one needing hyphenation (though he himself rarely inserted hyphens).
3. Symbols used for illegible words and editorial conjectures are as follows:

[?]	a totally undeciphered word
[? ? ?]	several undeciphered words
[~~?~~]	an undeciphered word that was canceled
[?word]	a conjectural reading
[?world/?would]	equally possible conjectural readings

4. Overwritings are shown thus: ha$\begin{cases}\text{s}\\ \text{ve}\end{cases}$ = "have" emended to "has."
5. Cancellation of single lines or of words within a line is indicated by horizontal cancellation lines. (These lines are straight even where Yeats's were wavy.) Even when it seems likely that Yeats meant to cancel an entire phrase or line, no word that he did not at least partially cancel is canceled in the transcriptions. Cancellation of entire passages is indicated by a vertical bracket in the left margin.
6. Yeats's "stet" marks are preserved, as are his underscorings to indicate italics. Caret

symbols that Yeats placed just below the line are raised to line level. There are throughout the drafts certain obscure marks or blots, which may have been made accidentally. In cases where their significance has not been determined, they are silently omitted.

7. In the transcriptions of typescript material, minor and obvious typing errors such as strikeovers may not be recorded; but all holograph corrections of typescripts are indicated.

8. Spacing and relative position of words and lines approximate the originals insofar as printed type can reproduce handwritten and typescript material.

9. The following typographical conventions have been used to represent physical features of the texts:

roman	ink
italic	pencil
boldface	typescript or print

"Parnell's Funeral and Other Poems" from "A Full Moon in March"

Transcriptions

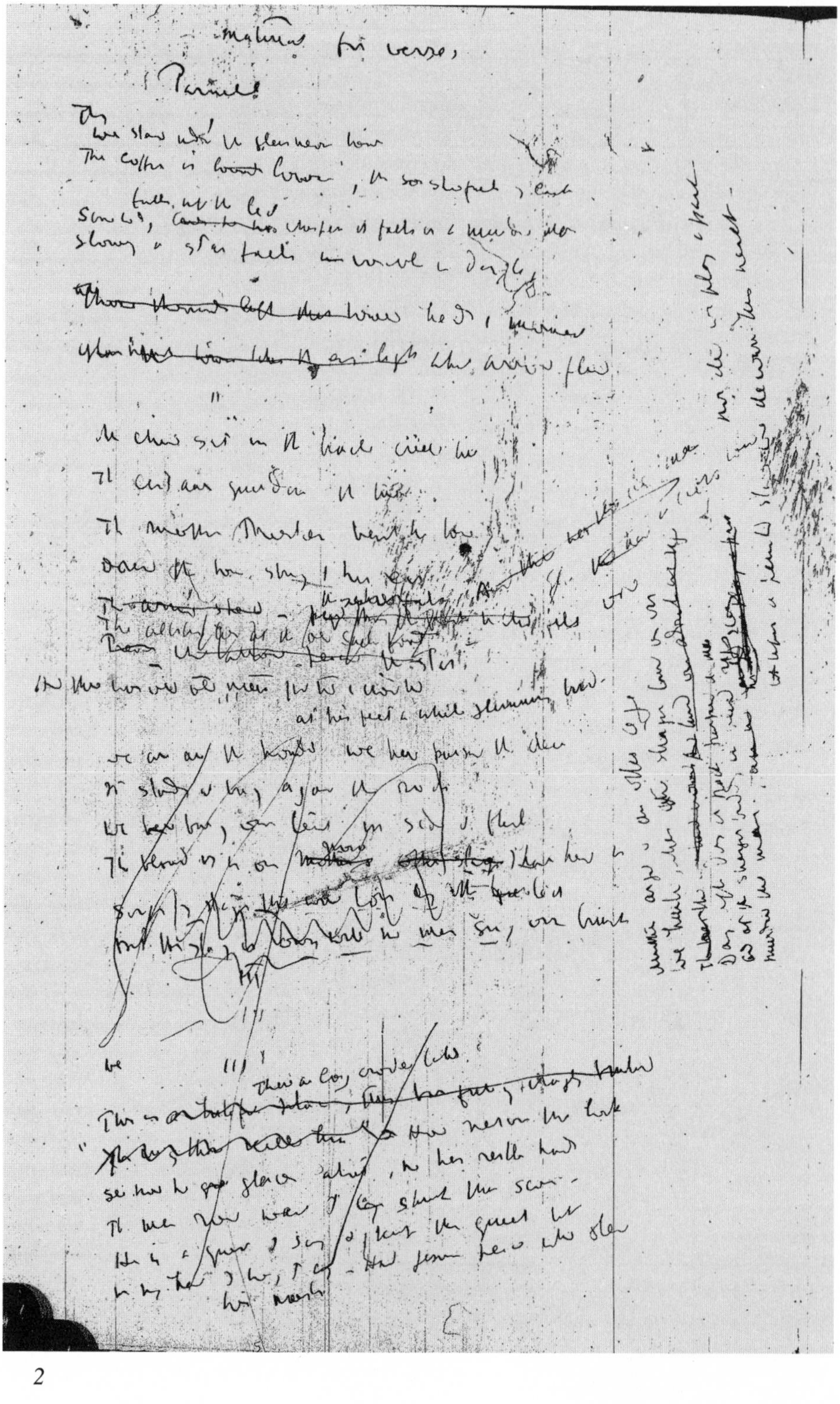
Materials for verse
Parnell

PARNELL'S FUNERAL

[MBY 545, p. 368]

1 material for verse
2 Parnell
They I
3 We stand under the Glasnevin tomb
4 The coffin is ~~lowered~~ lowering, the ~~sov~~ [?shovel] of earth
falls upon the lid
5 Somebody ~~cries he has~~ whispers it falls on a murdered man
6 Slowly a star falls invisible in daylight

7 ~~Those thousands lift their~~ bowed heads a moment
8 ~~Glasnevins tomb [?takes/likes] the air light~~ What arrow flew
II
9 The child sat in the [?branched] [?olive] tree
10 The centaur guarding the tree
11 The mother [?Marker] bent her bow
12 Drew the bow string to her ear
~~And there was the old man~~
~~the child fals~~ ~~She~~ ~~who had a cross bow~~
13 ~~The arrow she [?]~~ – [?~~pierced through the brest the child~~ fell]
The albatross lies at the old [?Sachems] foot
14 ~~[?Pierced] What arrow pearced the star~~
15 And there were old old men that had a cross bow

---

found in MBY 545, pp. 368, *transcribed above, and below* 335, 342, 366, 369, 336, 338, 334, 374, 375
SIU(1), pp. 1 and 2 *transcribed below*
UNC, pp. 1 and 2 *transcribed below*
NLI 30,547, 9^r, 10^r *transcribed below*
NLI $30{,}020_2$
published in *The Dublin Magazine*, April–June 1932
Wheels and Butterflies (1934)
The Spectator, October 19, 1934, p. 570 *transcribed below*
The King of the Great Clock Tower (1934)
Wheels and Butterflies (1935)
The King of the Great Clock Tower (1935)
A Full Moon in March (1935)

P. 368 is transcribed from SB 21.5.211.

[MBY 545, p. 368 continued]

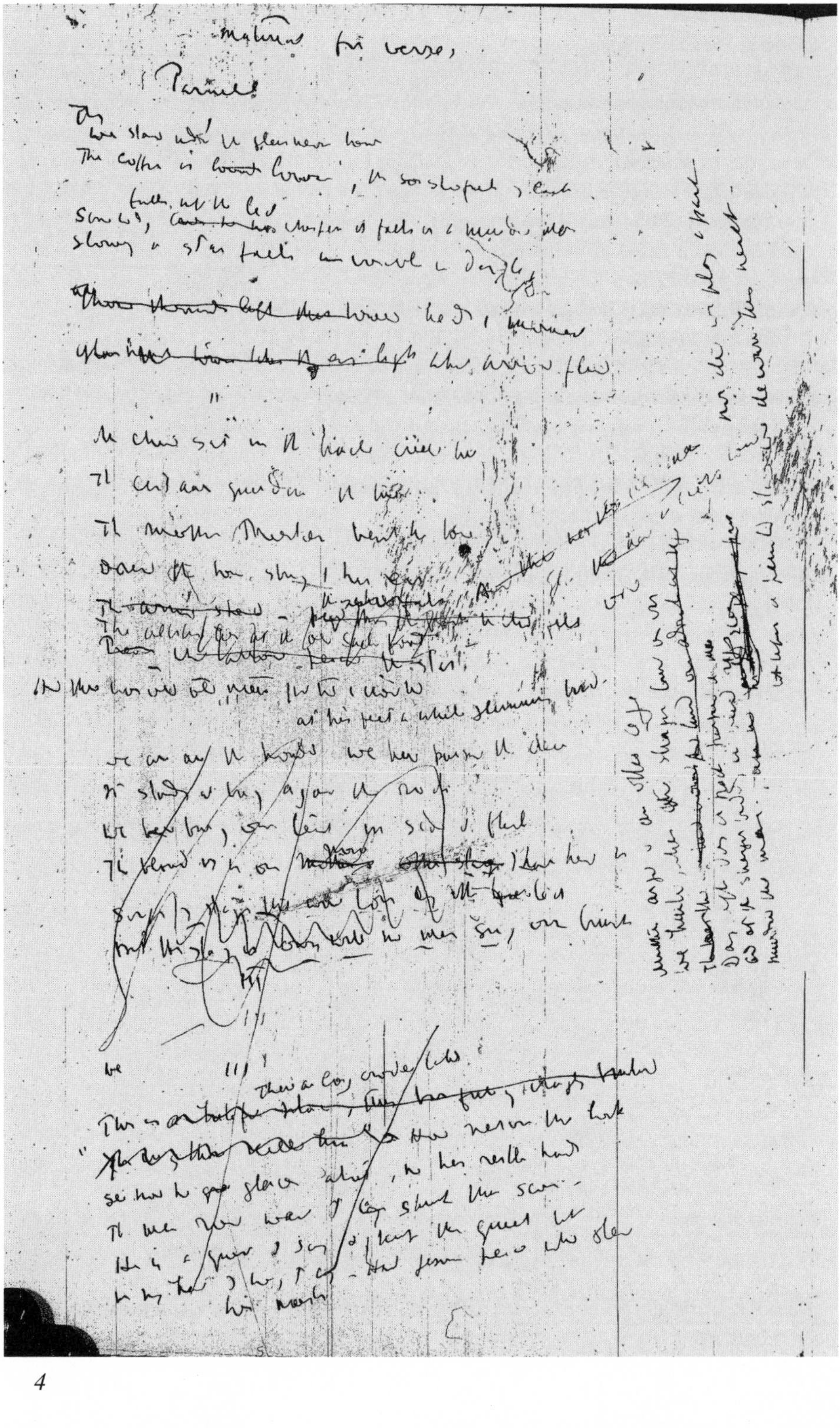

[MBY 545, p. 368 continued]

III at his feet a white glimmering bird
We are the hounds We have pursued the deer
It standing at bay against the rock
We ~~ber~~ bury our teeth in side of flesh
Mary
The [?blood] is [?not] our [~~?Mother s~~] ~~Other stags~~ I have had in
Singing stags that were torn by [?] [~~?~~——] teeth
But that stage is over will no more sing our [?friends]
III
III
be III
There are long crowded lights
This is ~~a hateful place, this has feeling [?wrongly] [?brutal]~~
" ~~For one of those kills him" [?]~~ How nervous the look
See how he ~~gre~~ glares about, he has neither hand
The men round want to ~~cry~~ shout their scorn –
He is a [?guest] I say & keep them quiet but
In my heart I long to cry - Had Jesus peace who slew
his master

Another angel & [?an] other age
We hunting when the stranger tarred us on
~~To kill~~ the we ~~had brothers And tarred on about our rage~~
Day after day our pack [?pursued] the man
And at the strangers bidding in blind rage
Murdered the man ~~upon no [?painted] stage~~ Nor did we play a part
~~Nor did we play a part~~
[~~?~~] Upon a painted stage we devoured his heart –

29 For "Jesus" read "Judas"?

[MBY 545, p. 335]

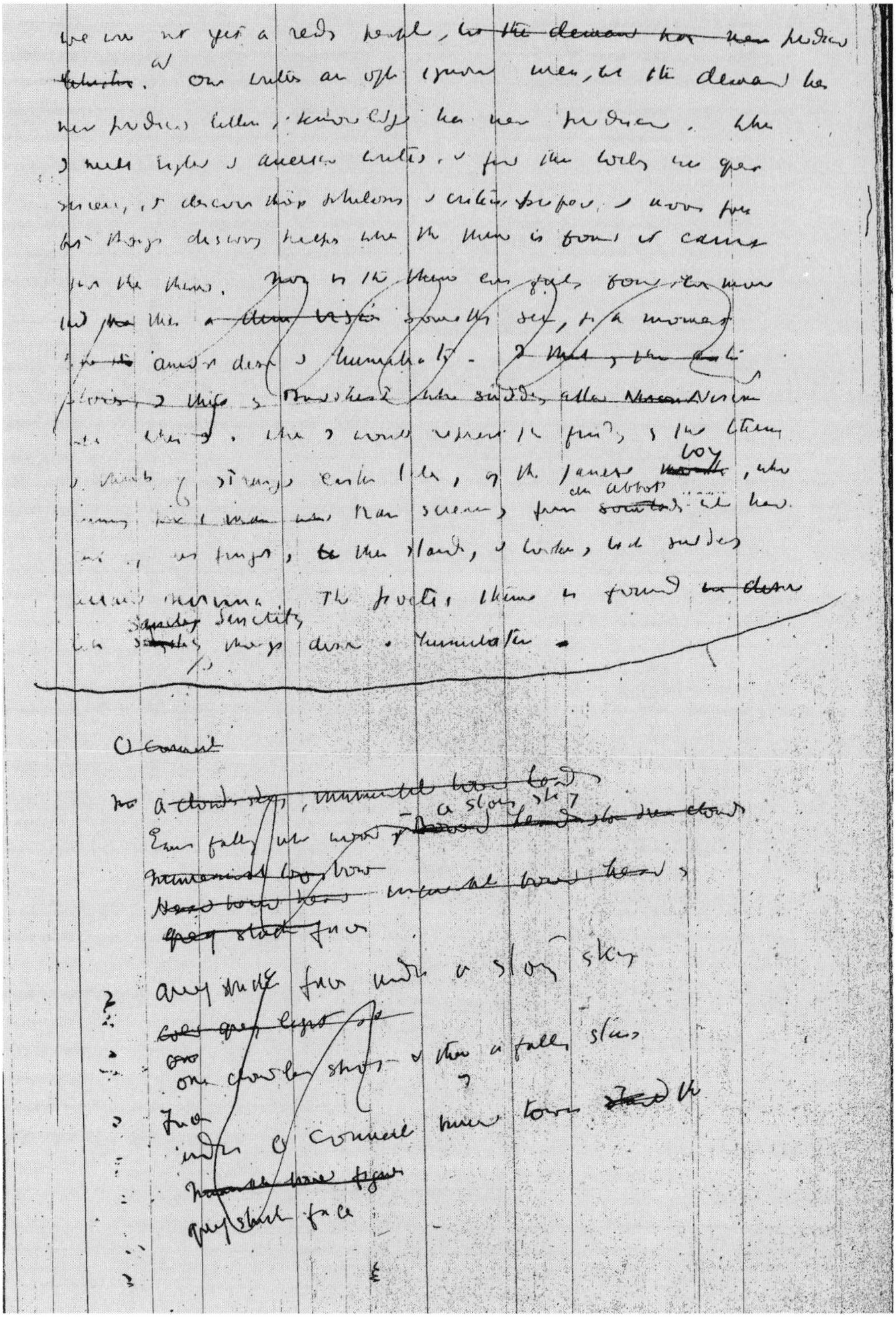

[MBY 545, p. 335]

1 ~~O Connel~~

2 ~~In~~ ~~A cloudy day, innumerable bowed heads~~
—a stormy sky
3 Evening falling upon [?wood] [?] ~~bowed heads storm driven clouds~~
4 ~~Innumerable bow~~ bow
5 ~~Head bowed head~~ ~~innumerable bowed heads~~
6 ~~grey [?stricken]~~ faces

7 Grey [?stricken] faces under a stormy sky
8 ~~Cold grey light~~
9 ~~one~~
10 one cloudless spot & then a falling star
11 Faces
12 under O Connells [?] tomb ~~stand~~ the
13 ~~Innumerable bowed figures~~
14 Grey stricken faces

Above the text is a version of the last paragraph of a Yeats lecture. See "Modern Ireland[:] An Address to American Audiences 1932–1933," transcribed and edited by Curtis Bradford, in *Irish Renaissance: A Gathering of Essays, Memoirs, and Letters from* The Massachusetts Review, ed. Robin Skelton and David R. Clark (Dublin: Dolmen Press, 1965), p. 25. For p. 335 of MBY 545, see SB 21.5.193.

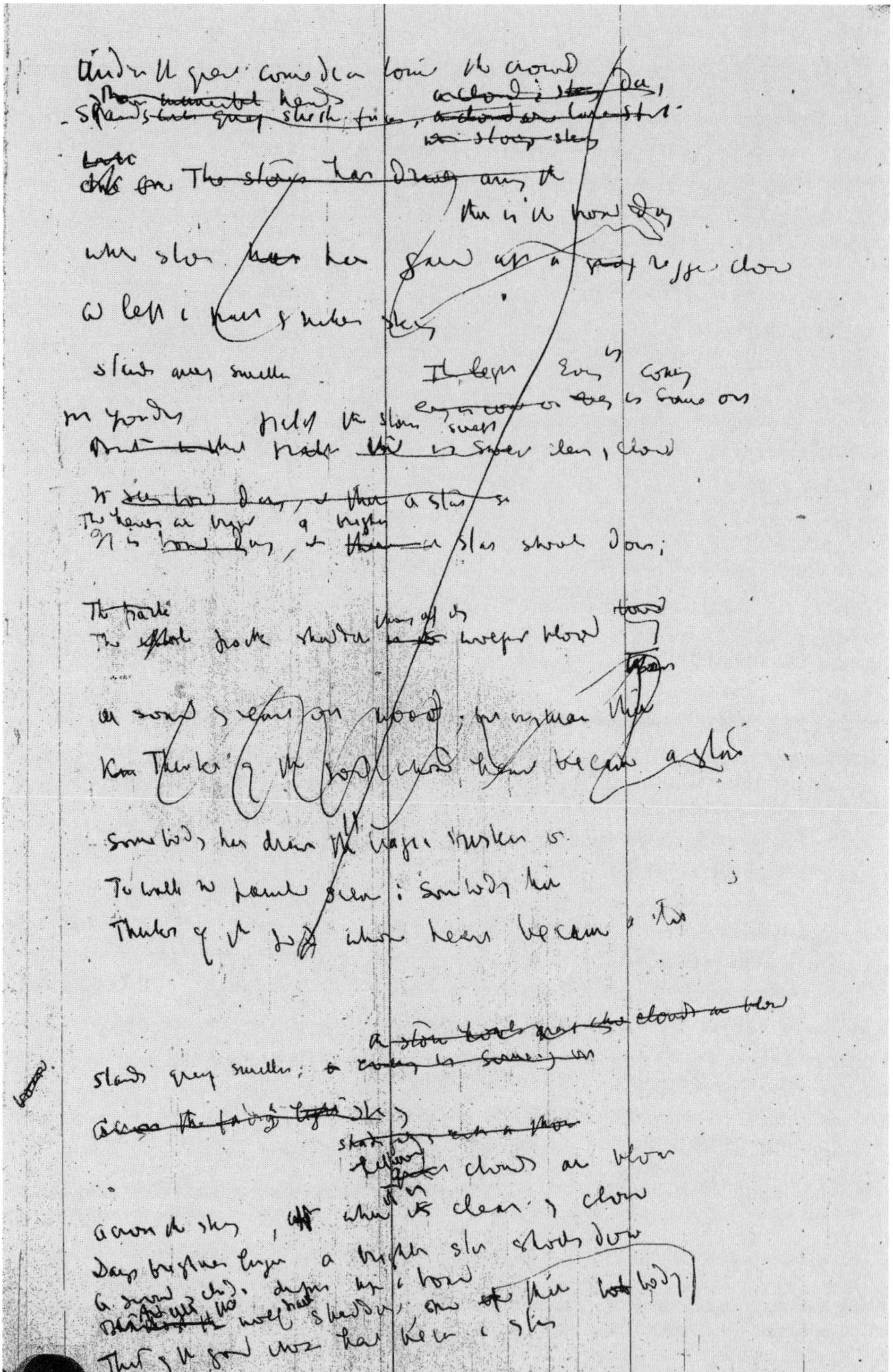

[MBY 545, p. 342]

1 Under the great comedian's tomb the crowd.
~~[?Bowed] innumerable~~ heads ~~a cloudy sky~~ day
2 Stands ~~with grey [?stricken] faces, a cloud one bare spot~~
~~was stormy sky~~
[?~~With~~]
3 ~~One One~~ ~~The storm has driven away the~~
There is the broad day
4 When storm ~~has~~ has [?gathered] up a ~~grey~~ ragged cloud
5 And left a path of [?] sky
is
6 Stands away [?] [~~? ?~~] Evening coming
~~evening comes~~ or ~~evening~~ is ~~come~~ out
In yonder half the storm swept
7 ~~But in that~~ ~~half that is swept~~ clean of cloud
8 It ~~seems broad day, & there a star so~~
The heavens are bright a brighter
9 It is ~~broad d~~ay, ~~& there a~~ star shoots down;
10 [?~~bowed~~]
~~The pack~~ [?] of its
11 The ~~whole~~ pack shudders ~~in its~~ [?woeful] blood
12 [?them]
13 A sound of earth on wood; but every man there
14 [~~?~~] Thinks of the god whose heart became a star
II
15 Somebody has drawn the tragic buskin on
16 To walk [?no] painted scene; somebody here
17 Thinks of the god whose heart became a star

~~The storm howls great where clouds are blown~~
18 Stands grey [?]; ~~as evening is coming on~~
19 ~~Across the fading light sky~~
20 ~~[? ?] as though~~
billowed
21 ~~great~~ clouds are blown
it is
22 Across the sky, [~~?~~] where ~~its~~ clear of cloud
23 Days brightness lingers a brighter star shoots down
24 A sound of clods [?dropping] upon a board
And all [?] [?half]
25 ~~But though the~~ wolf shudders, none ~~of~~ their [~~?~~] body
26 That of the god whose heart became a star

For p. 342, see SB 21.5.197.

[MBY 545, p. 366]

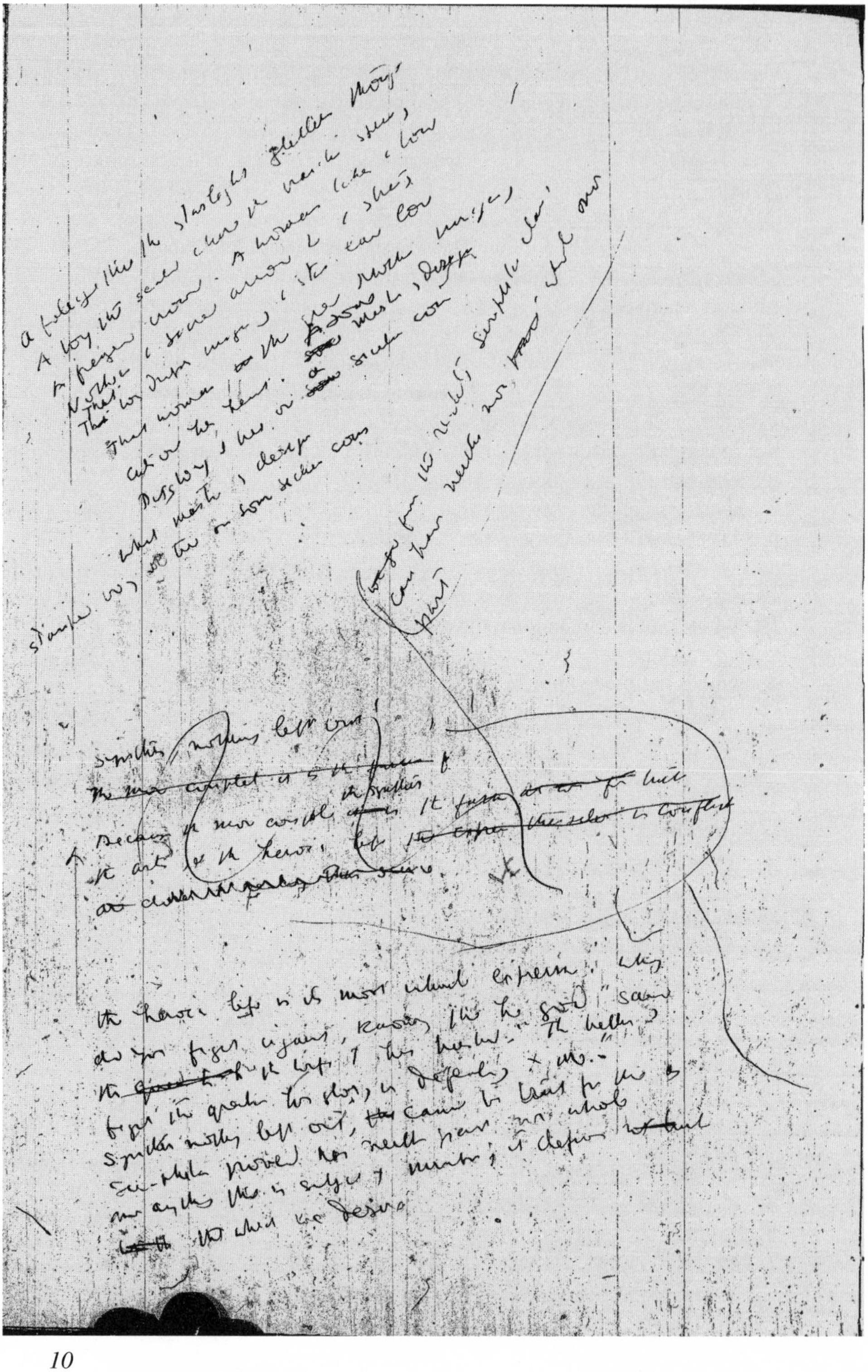

[MBY 545, p. 366]

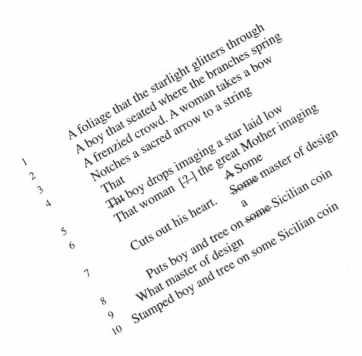

A foliage that the starlight glitters through
A boy that seated where the branches spring
A frenzied crowd. A woman takes a bow
Notches a sacred arrow to a string
That
~~Tht~~ boy drops imaging a star laid low
That woman [?-] the great Mother imaging
~~A~~ Some
Cuts out his heart. ~~Some~~ master of design
a
Puts boy and tree on ~~some~~ Sicilian coin
What master of design
Stamped boy and tree on some Sicilian coin

The text appears above a prose passage, apparently unpublished, that continues on p. 367. For p. 366, see SB 21.5.209.

[MBY 545, p. 369]

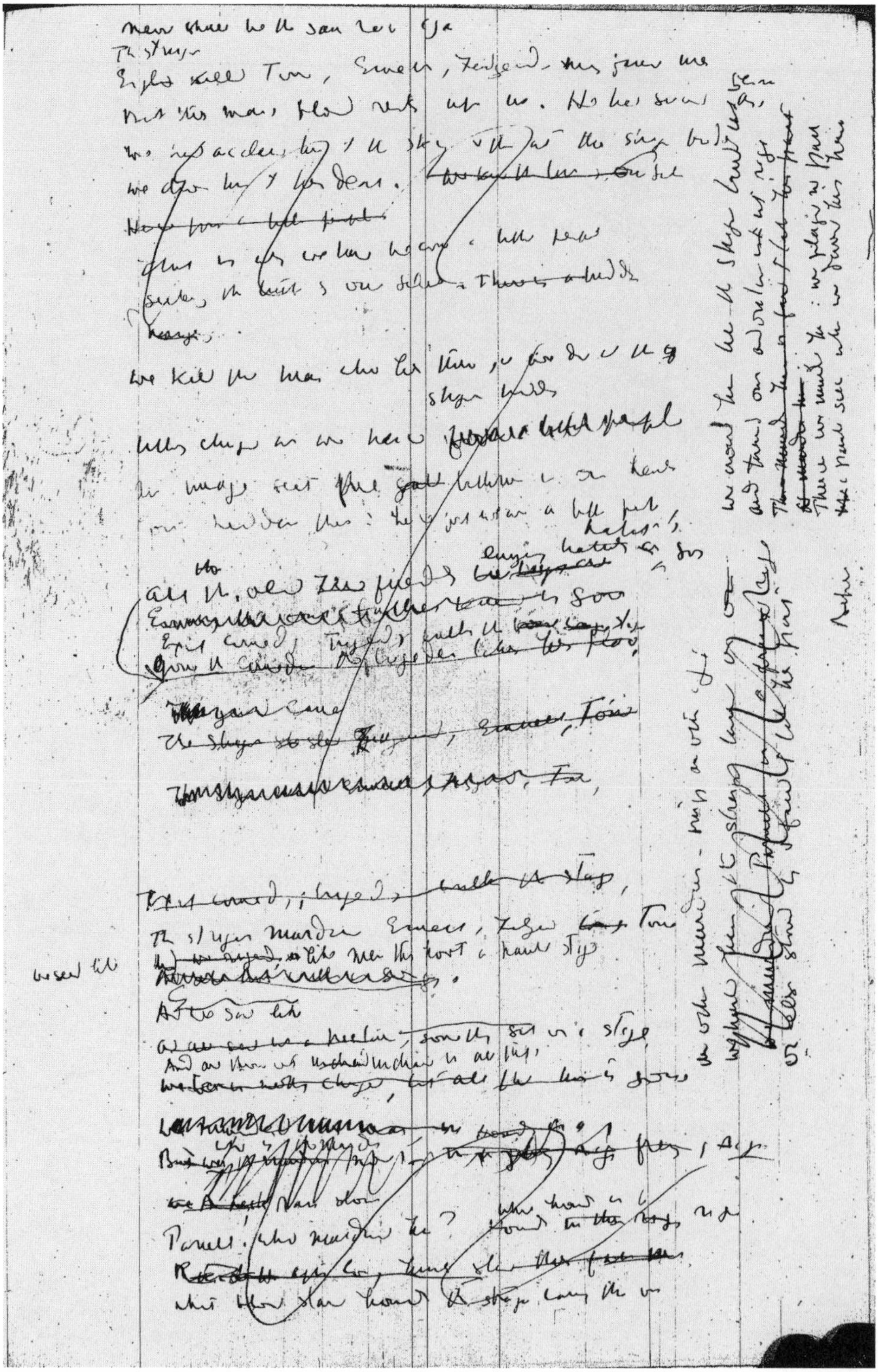

[MBY 545, p. 369]

1 Never shall be the same, never again
The stranger
2 ~~England~~ killed Tone, Emmett, Fitzgerald, [?]
[?]
3 But this man's blood rests upon us. He had [?served] [?us]
4 We had acclaimed him to the sky & then at the strangers bidding
5 We drove him to his death. ~~We [?killed him] our~~selves.
6 ~~Henceforth a bitter people~~
7 That is why we have become a bitter people
8 [?Seeking] the truth of our selves. ~~There is a h~~idden
9 ~~[?]~~

10 We killed that man who lies there, & we did at the ~~[?]~~ strangers bidding
11 Bitterness changed us we were hence~~forth a bitter pe~~ople —
12 An image [?set] the ~~gall~~ bitterness in our hearts
13 [?Long] [?hidden] this; henceforth we are a bitter people,
habit s
~~[?]~~ [? laying] [?~~habits~~] are gone
14 All the old ~~Fri~~ friendly [?] ~~ways are~~
15 ~~[?] once father killing his Son~~
Exit comedy. Tragedy walks the ~~board~~ ~~[?]~~ stage
16 ~~Gone the comedian. The tragedian take his place.~~
17 ~~Fitzgerald, Tone~~
18 ~~The stranger slew Fitzgerald, Emmet, Tone~~

19 ~~The stranger sle murdered Emmett, Fitzgerald, Tone.~~

For p. 369, see SB 21.5.211.
14 For "laying" read "laughing"?

[MBY 545, p. 369 continued]

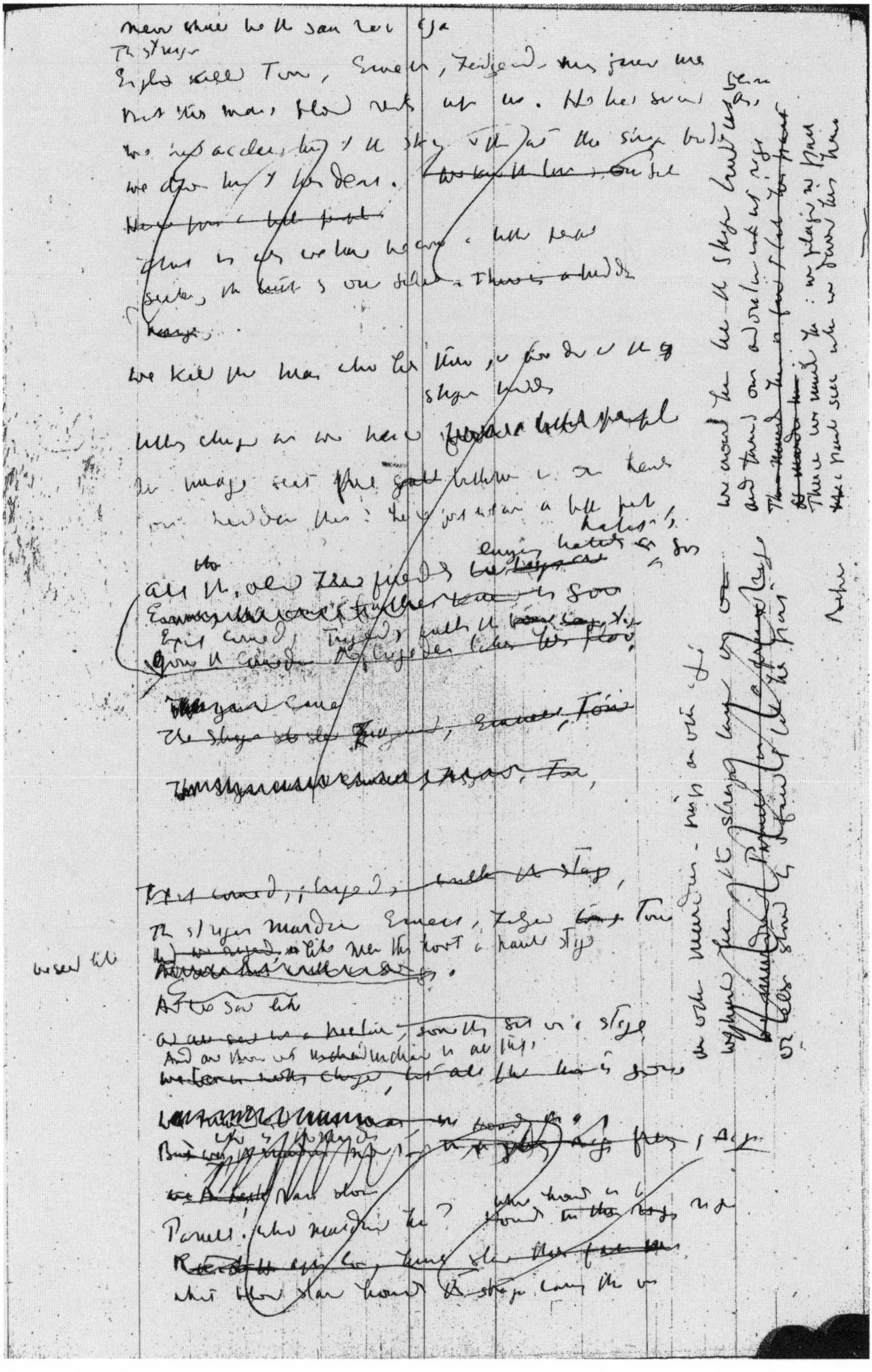

[MBY 545, p. 369 continued]

~~Exit comedy; tragedy walks the stage,~~
The stranger murdered Emett, Fitzgerald. ~~Tone~~ Tone
We seemed like ~~And we regard, [?]~~ like men that [?hont] a [?haunted] stage.
~~And are but [?]~~
~~And we sound like~~
~~And all [?seemed] but a picture, some thing set~~ on a stage
And are those [?] ~~unchanged~~ unchanged in all that's
~~We [?are] in nothing changed, but all that [?] is~~ gone

~~We murdered this man, [?]~~
Who is the murder Heads in a
~~But were the murderes now~~ – ~~[?]~~
~~we [?A] pack~~ ran down
What hounds in [?]
Parnell: who murdered him? Hounds ~~in their rage~~ rage
~~[?] We after long hunt~~ slew ~~this fated man~~
What blood star hounds the stranger tarring them on

[?An] other murder - brings an other age
We [?hunted him. The stranger tarred us ~~on~~
~~We murdered Parnell in a [?frenzied]~~ rage
Or else stood by & [?feared] to take his part

We [?] him till the stranger [?tarred] us on
And turned our adoration into rage
~~Then murdered him or feared to take his part~~
~~And murdered him~~
Thence we [?murdered] him: we played no part
Before ~~Upon~~ a painted [?scene] when we devoured his heart.

32 For "star" read "starved"?

[MBY 545, p. 336]

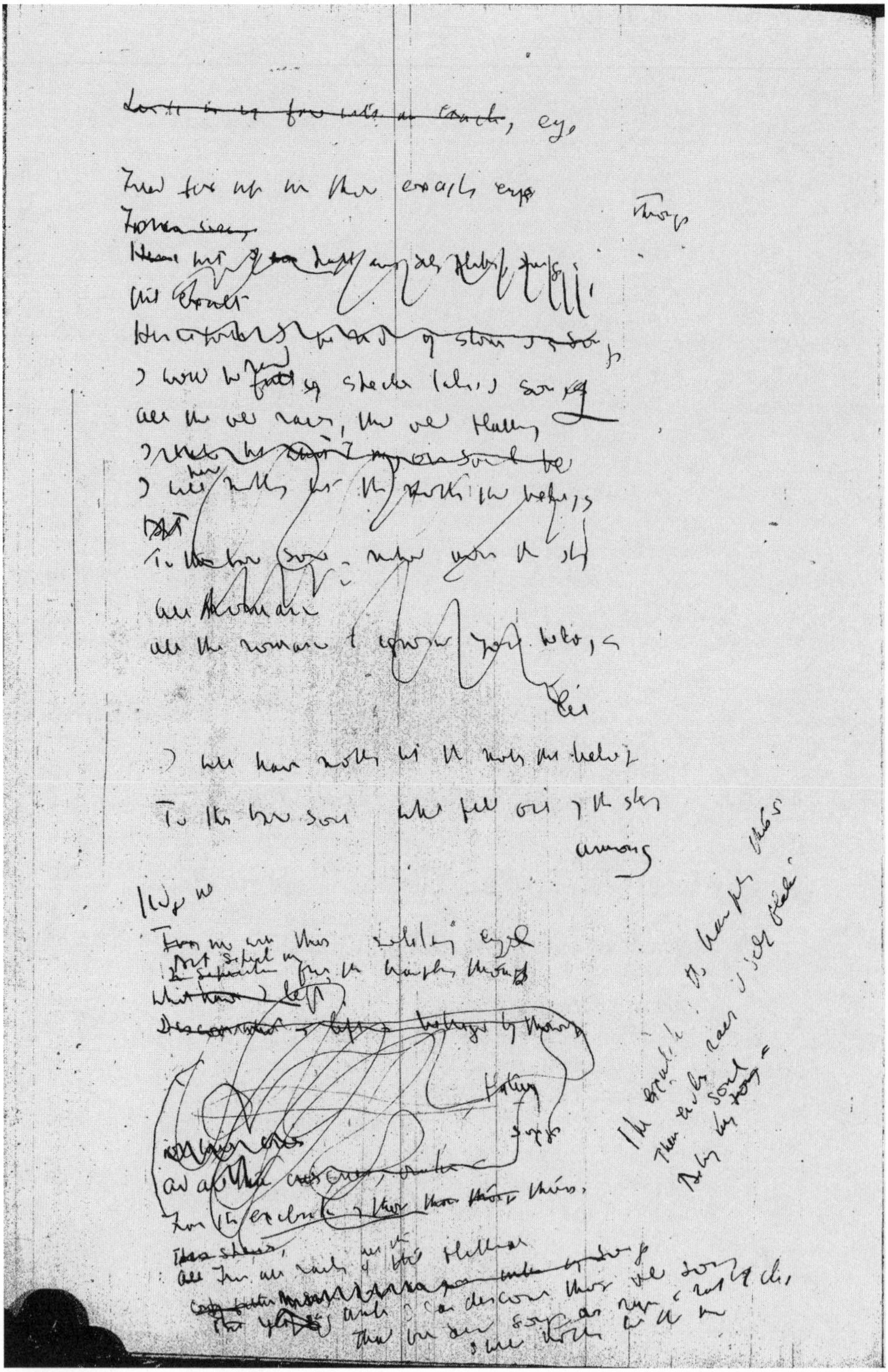

[MBY 545, p. 336]

~~Look in my face with an exacting~~ eye

[?Friend] fix upon me those exacting eyes [?Throngs]
~~Forever [?weary]~~
Hence forth I [?] [?putt] [?away] self flatery, songs
That exalt
Hen~~ceforth I be rid of [?storm] and of s~~ongs
rid
I would be ~~full of~~ [? ?] song
All the old [?railing], that old flattery
~~I write but what to my own soul be~~
have
I will nothing but the nothing that belongs
[?~~But~~]
To this bare soul - naked under the sky
All roman
All the romance to [?ignore] you belongs
lie
I will have nothing but the nothing that belongs
To this bare soul What fell out of the sky
among
Judge me
~~Turn~~ me with this solitary eye
But separate me
~~In separation~~ from the trampling throng
What ~~have I le~~ft
~~Discover what [?] left - betrayed by [?~~throngs]

Flatery
~~or low cries~~ song
And all their ~~cries~~ cries, [?]
For the exuberance of those ~~those~~ [?~~thongs~~] [?thiers],
~~[? ?]~~
all that
~~All~~ From all railing & ~~that~~ flattery
~~[?] unless by~~ songs
But ~~Yet [?]~~ Until I can discover those old songs
That [?] such songs as rhyme a rat to die
I wish nothing but the no

The exultation of the trampling throng
Then livelier [?railing] and self flatery
soul
Betray my ~~song~~ [?]

For p. 336, see SB 21.5.194.

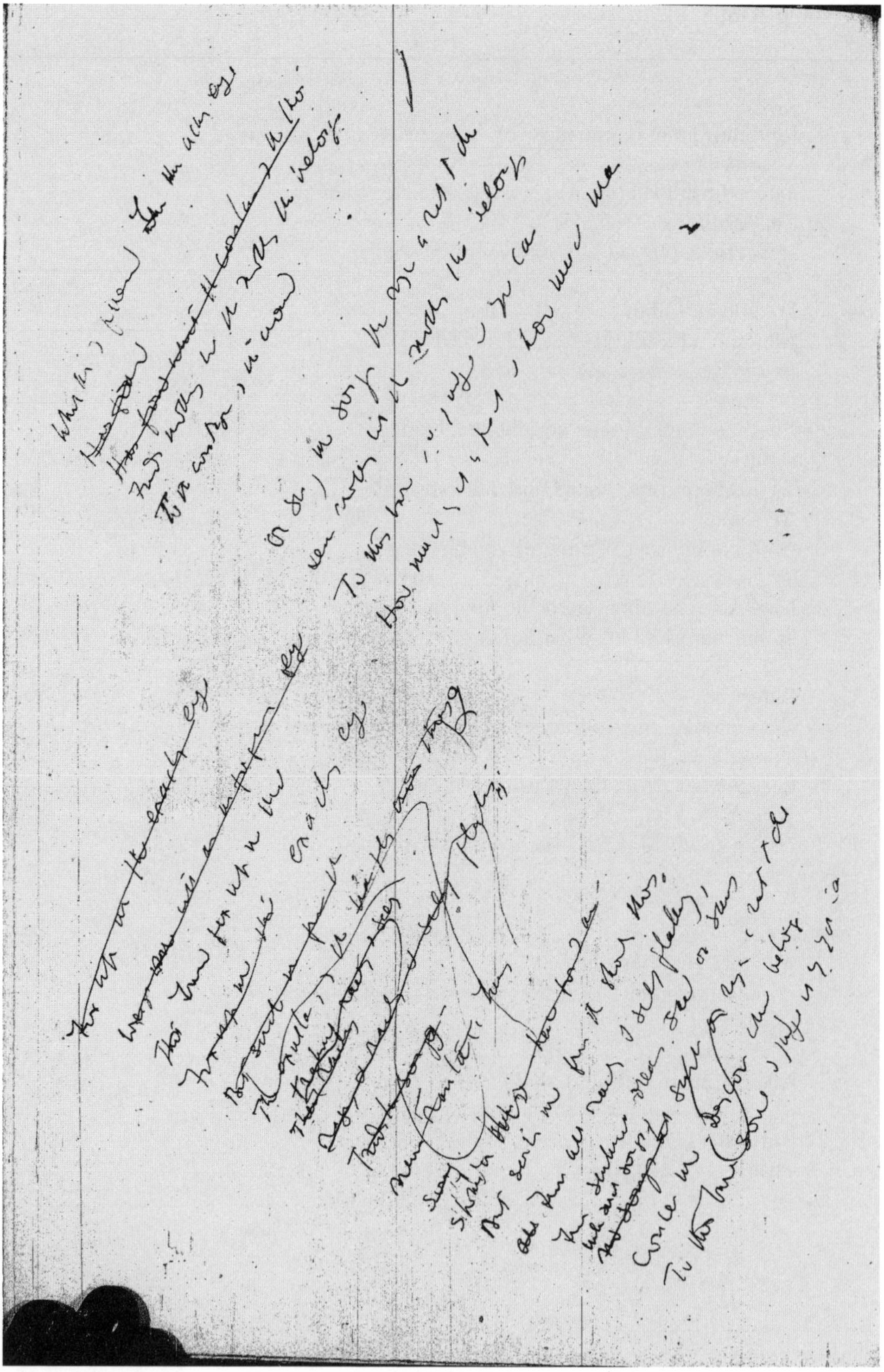

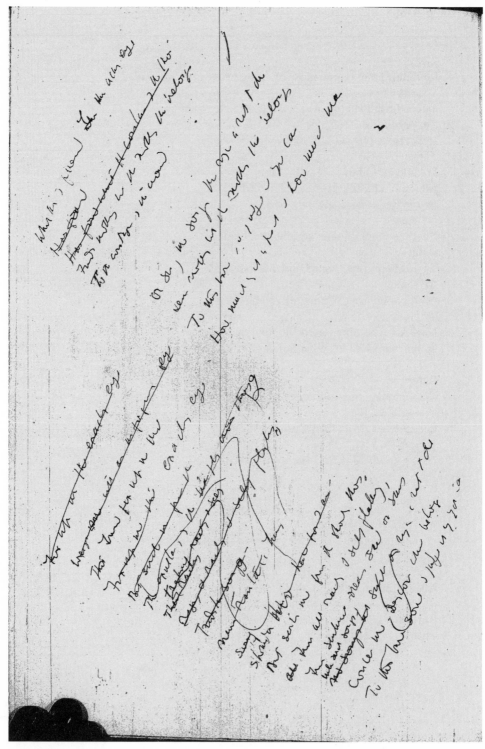

[MBY 545, p. 338]

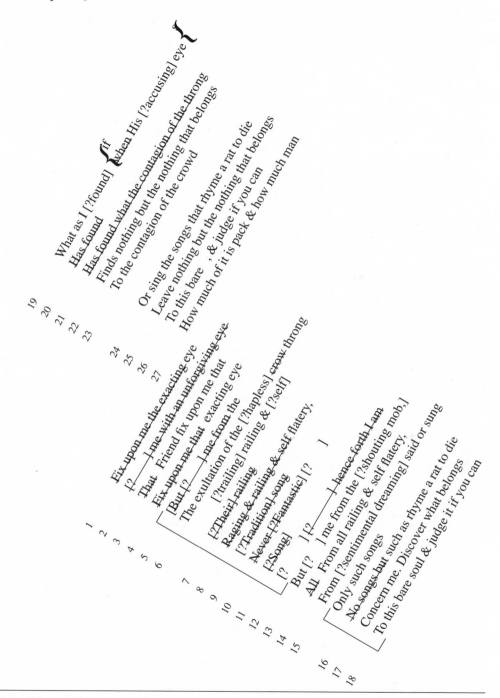

~~Fix upon me the exacting eye~~
[? ~~] me with an unforgiving eye~~
~~That~~ Friend fix upon me that
~~Fix upon me that~~ exacting eye
~~[But [?] me from the~~
The exultation of the [?hapless] ~~crow~~ throng
[?trailing] railing & [?self]
~~[?Their] railing~~
~~Raging & railing & self~~ flatery,
~~[?Tradition] song~~
~~Never [?Fantastic]~~ [?
[?Song]
[?
[?   ] ~~hence forth I am~~
But [?   ] [?   ] me from the [?shouting mob,]
~~All~~ From all railing & self flatery,
From [?sentimental dreaming] said or sung
Only such songs
~~No songs but~~ such as rhyme a rat to die
Concern me. Discover what belongs
To this bare soul & judge it if you can

What as I [?found] {if / ~~when~~ His [?accusing] eye}
~~Has found~~
~~Has found what the contagion of the throng~~
Finds nothing but the nothing that belongs
To the contagion of the crowd

Or sing the songs that rhyme a rat to die
Leave nothing but the nothing that belongs
To this bare   , & judge if you can
How much of it is pack & how much man

For p. 338, see SB 21.5.195.
15 Yeats writes "areas" no doubt meaning "arias."

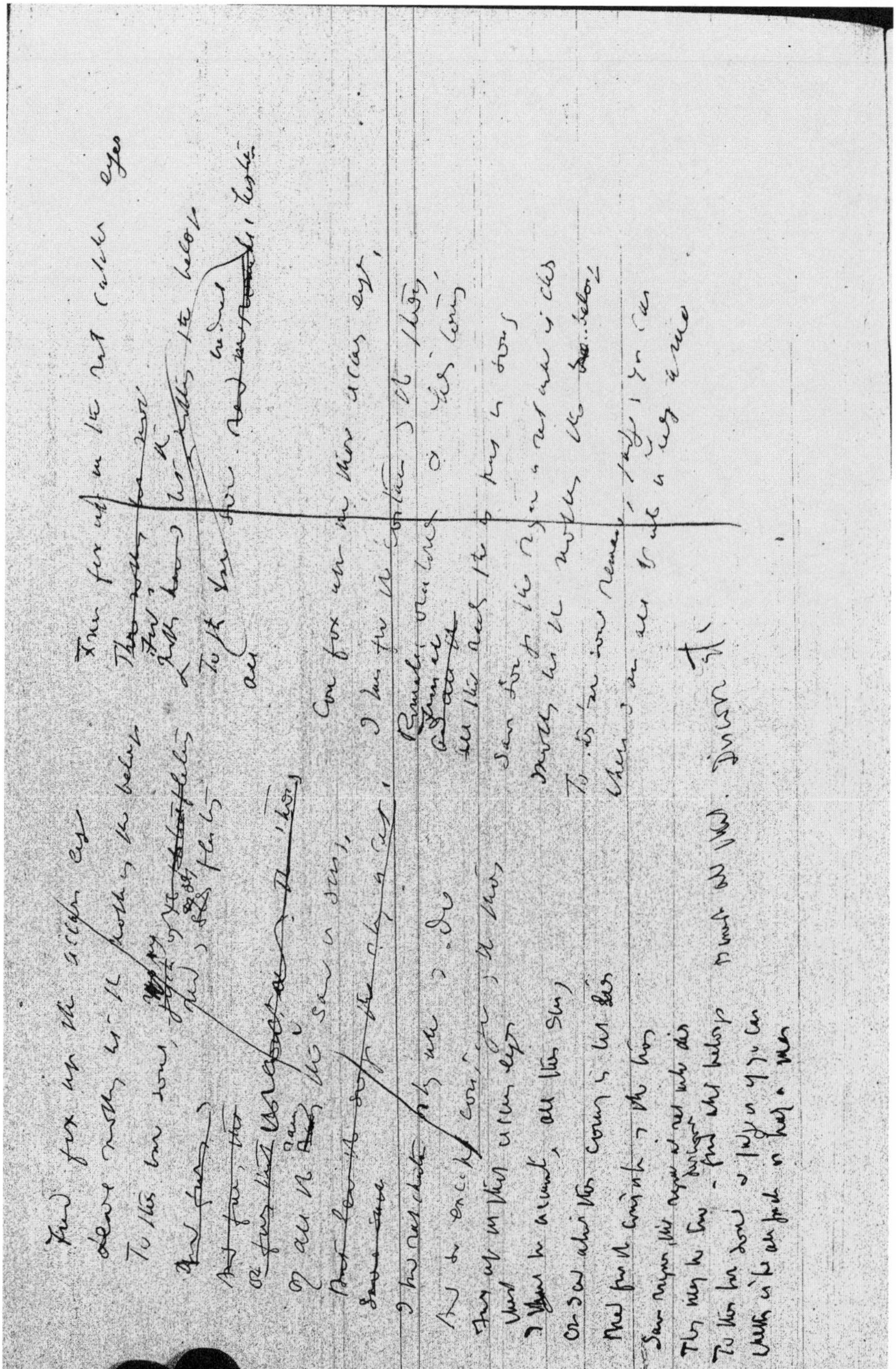

[MBY 545, p. 334]

1 [?Friend] fix upon the accusing eye
2 Leave nothing but the nothing that belongs
~~[?   ]~~
3 To this bare soul, ~~[?   ] of the flatery flatery~~
~~[?]~~ self
rid of the ~~self~~ flatery

4 ~~And fury of~~
5 ~~And fury that~~
6 ~~or fury that is contagion of the throng~~
[?raing]   [?I]
7 of all the ~~[?   ]~~ that   said or sung,
8 ~~But leave the songs that [?   ]~~
9 ~~Save such~~
10 I [?know] rat [?catchers] only when I die
11 And so excape contagion of the throng
12 Fix upon me those accusing eyes
[?thirst]
13 I ~~[?thirst]~~ for accusation, all thats sung
14 Or said about this country is but lies
15 Bred from the contagion of the throng
16 Save rymes, that ryme at rat who dies
discover
17 They may be true—find what belongs   Discover all that. Discover etc.
18 To this bare soul & judge it if you can
19 Whether it be all pack or half a man

For p. 334, see SB 21.5.193.
7 Perhaps "raing" was meant to be "railing" as in 29.

[MBY 545, p. 334 continued]

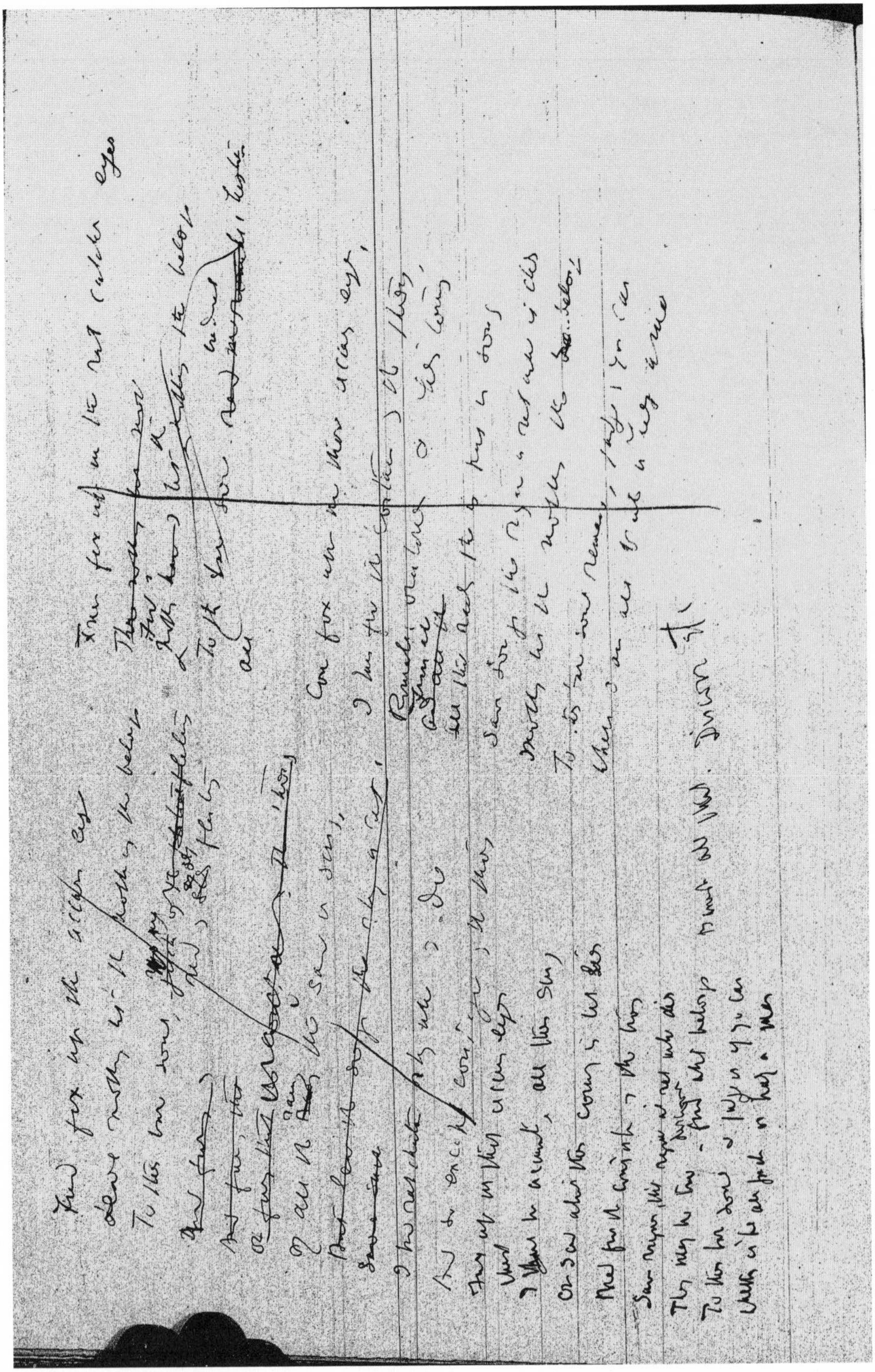

[MBY 545, p. 334 continued]

[?Then] fix upon me the rat catcher eyes
~~There nothing but noth~~
 [?Find]   the
Nothing ~~have I~~ but ^ nothing that belongs
                              [?   ]
To this bare soul.   ~~rid me romantic~~ histories
All

Come fix upon me those accusing eyes,
I [?   ][?from] the contagion of the throng
Romantic victories & histories
    From all
~~And all the~~
All that [?railing] that is put in song
Save songs that ryme a rat until it dies
Nothing but the nothing that ~~[?]~~ belongs
To this bare soul remains, judge if you can
Whether I am all brute or half a man

[MBY 545, p. 374]

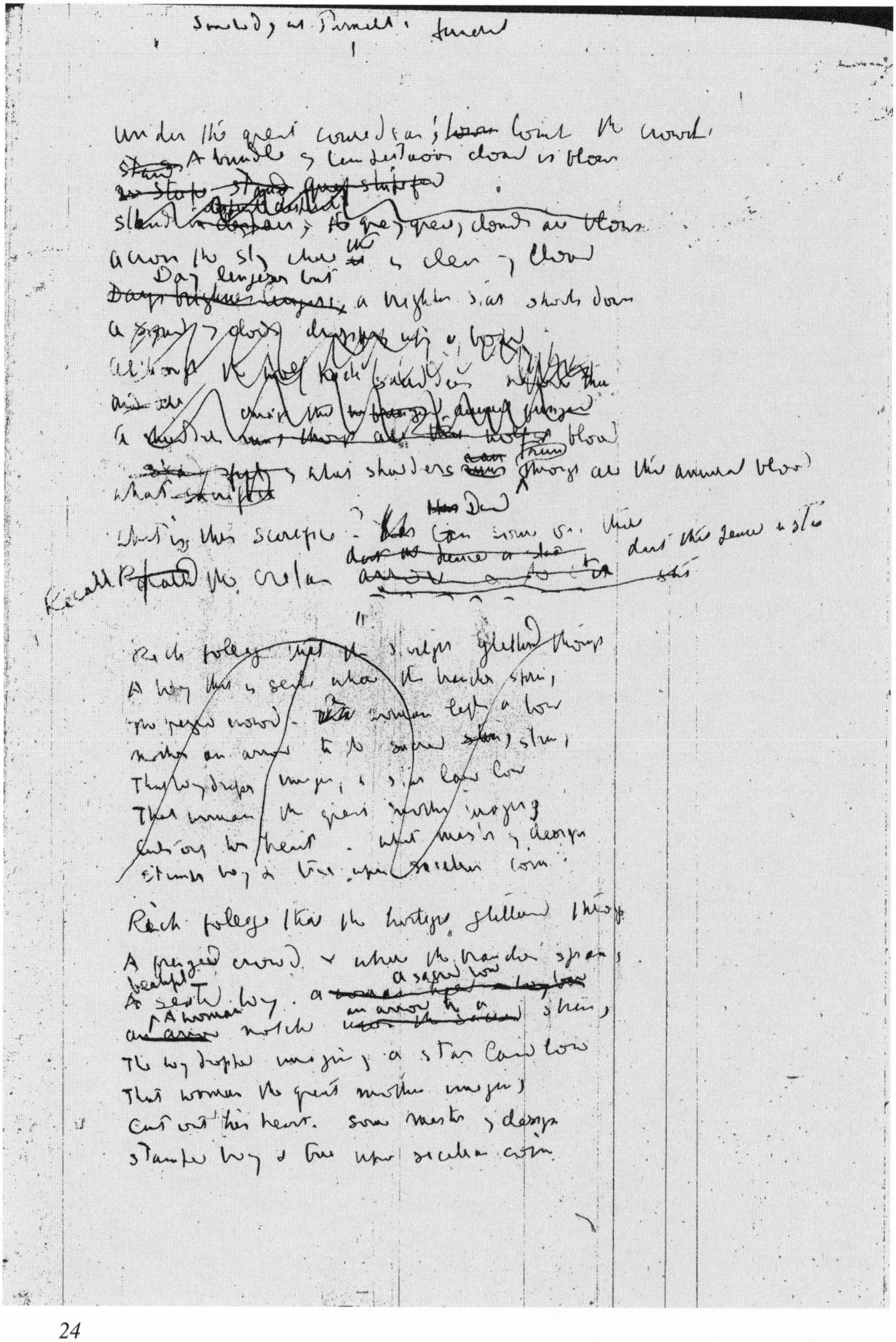

[MBY 545, p. 374]

Somebody at Parnell's Funeral
I

1 Under the great comedian's town tomb the crowd.
2 ~~Stands~~ A bundle of tempestuous cloud is blown
3 ~~In stupe~~ ~~Stands~~ ~~grief stupified~~
~~desperate~~ desperate
4 Stands ~~in despair~~, ~~the~~ grey [?growing] clouds are blown
that
5 Across the sky Where ~~it~~ is clear of cloud
Day lingers but
6 ~~Days brightness lingers~~, a brighter star shoots down
7 A sound of clods dropping upon a board,
8 Although the wolf pack shudders [?] [?]
9 And all
through that ~~[?]~~ ~~fren~~zied animal frenzied
10 A shudder runs ~~through all their wolfish~~ blood
s ~~ran~~ (run)
~~[?] [?]~~ What shudder } ~~runs~~ ^ through all that animal blood
11 What sacrifice
~~Has~~ Did
12 What is this sacrifice? ~~Has~~ Can some one there
~~dart that pierced a star~~ dart that pierced a star
13 Recall ~~Recalled~~ the Cretan ~~arrow & the star~~
stet

For p. 374, see SB 21.5.213.

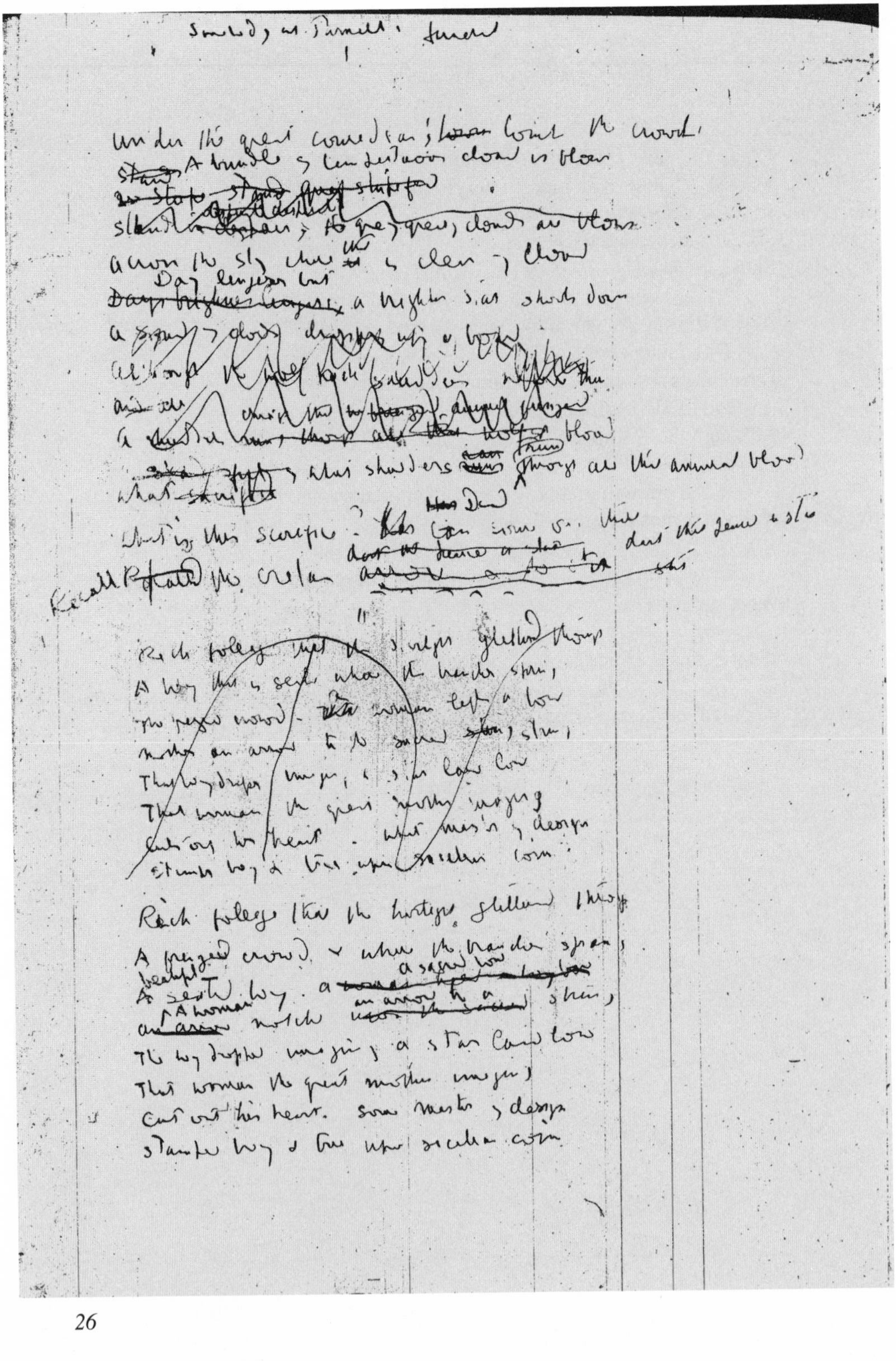

Scenes at Parnell's funeral

Under the great comedian's tomb the crowd.
A bundle of tempestuous cloud is blown
About the sky where that is clear of cloud
Day lingers but a brighter star shoots down
What shudders run through all the animal blood
What is this sacrifice? Can someone there
Recall the Cretan barb that pierced the star

Rich foliage that the starlight glittered through
A frenzied crowd, & where the branches sprang
A beautiful seated boy, a sacred bow
A woman, an arrow on a string,
The boy dropped imaging a star came low
That woman the great mother imaging
Cut out his heart. Some master of design
Stamped boy & tree upon Sicilian coin

[MBY 545, p. 374 continued]

II

Rich foliage that the starlight glittered through
A boy that is seated where the branches spring
A
The frenzied crowd – ~~That~~ woman lifts a bow
Notches an arrow to the sacred ~~sting~~ string
That boy drops imaging a star laid low
That woman the great mother imaging
Cuts out his heart. What master of design
Stamps boy & tree upon Sicilian coin

Rich foliage that the [?   light] glittered through
A frenzied crowd & where the branches sprang
beautiful   A sacred bow
A^seated boy.   ~~A woman held a boy bow~~
A woman   an arrow on a
~~An arrow~~ notched ~~upon the sacred~~ string
The boy dropped imaging a star laid low
That woman the great mother imaging
Cut out his heart. Some master of design
Stamped boy & tree upon Sicilian coin

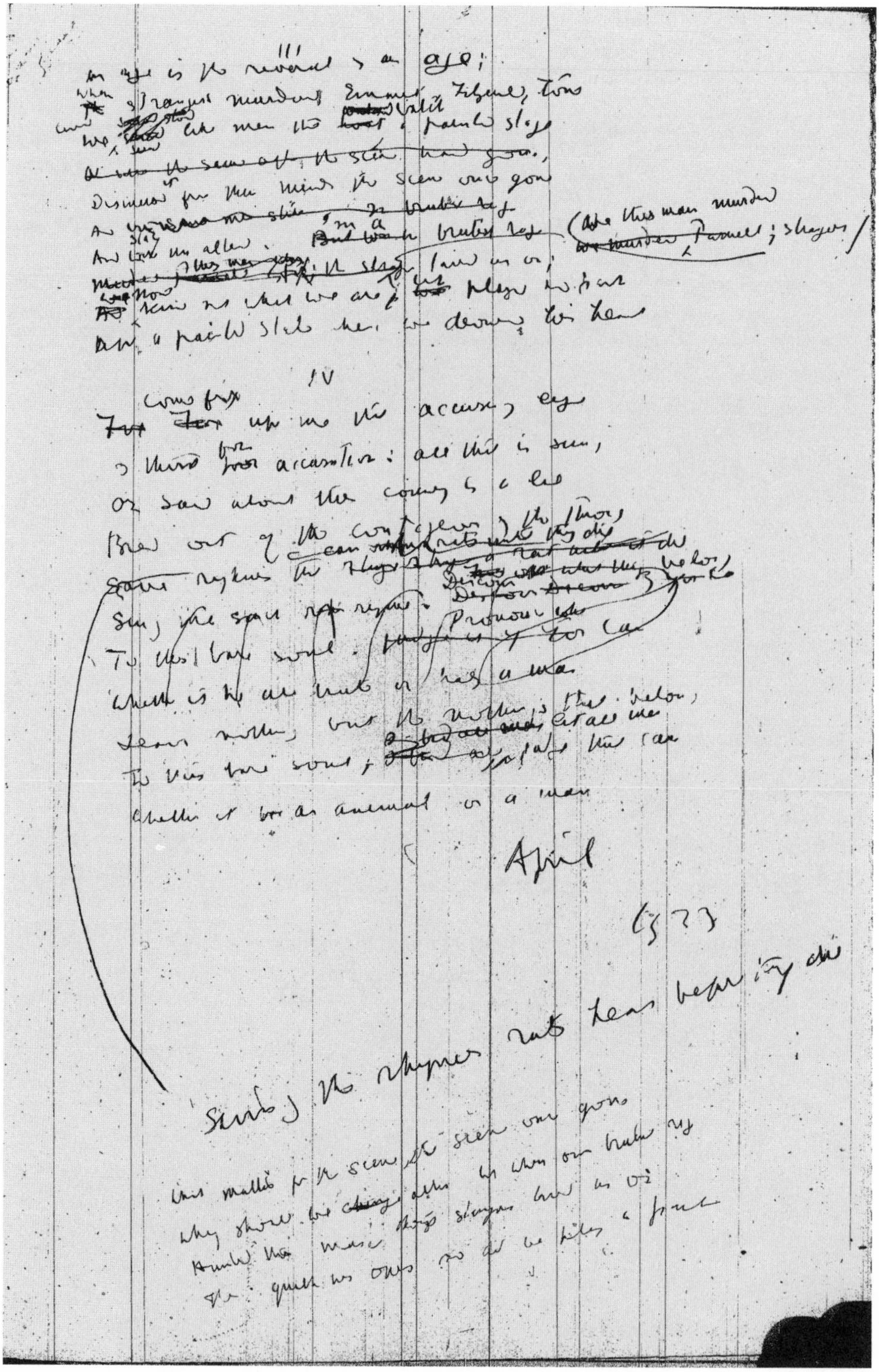

[MBY 545, p. 375]

III

1 An age is the reversal of an age;
When
2 ~~The~~ strangers murdered, Emmet, Fitzgerald, Tone
lived [~~?stand~~] stood [~~?watched~~] watch
3 We ^ ~~stood~~ like men that [~~?host~~] a painted stage
[?seemed]

4 ~~And were the scene after the scene had gone.~~
it
5 Dismissed from their minds the scene once gone
6 And were ~~the same men still. In brutish rage~~
stay In a
7 And ~~were~~ unaltered. ~~But were~~ in brutish rage | Was this man murdered
~~this man when~~ ~~we murdered Parnell~~; strangers
8 ~~Murdered Parnell [?Stran] ; the stranger~~ ^ tarred us on;
~~We~~ Now but
9 And ^ know not what we are; ~~we~~ played no part
10 Upon a painted [?stage] when we devoured his heart

IV

Come fix
11 ~~Fix~~ ~~Fix~~ upon me that accusing eye
for
12 I thirst [~~?four~~] accusation: all that is sung

For p. 375, see SB 21.5.213.

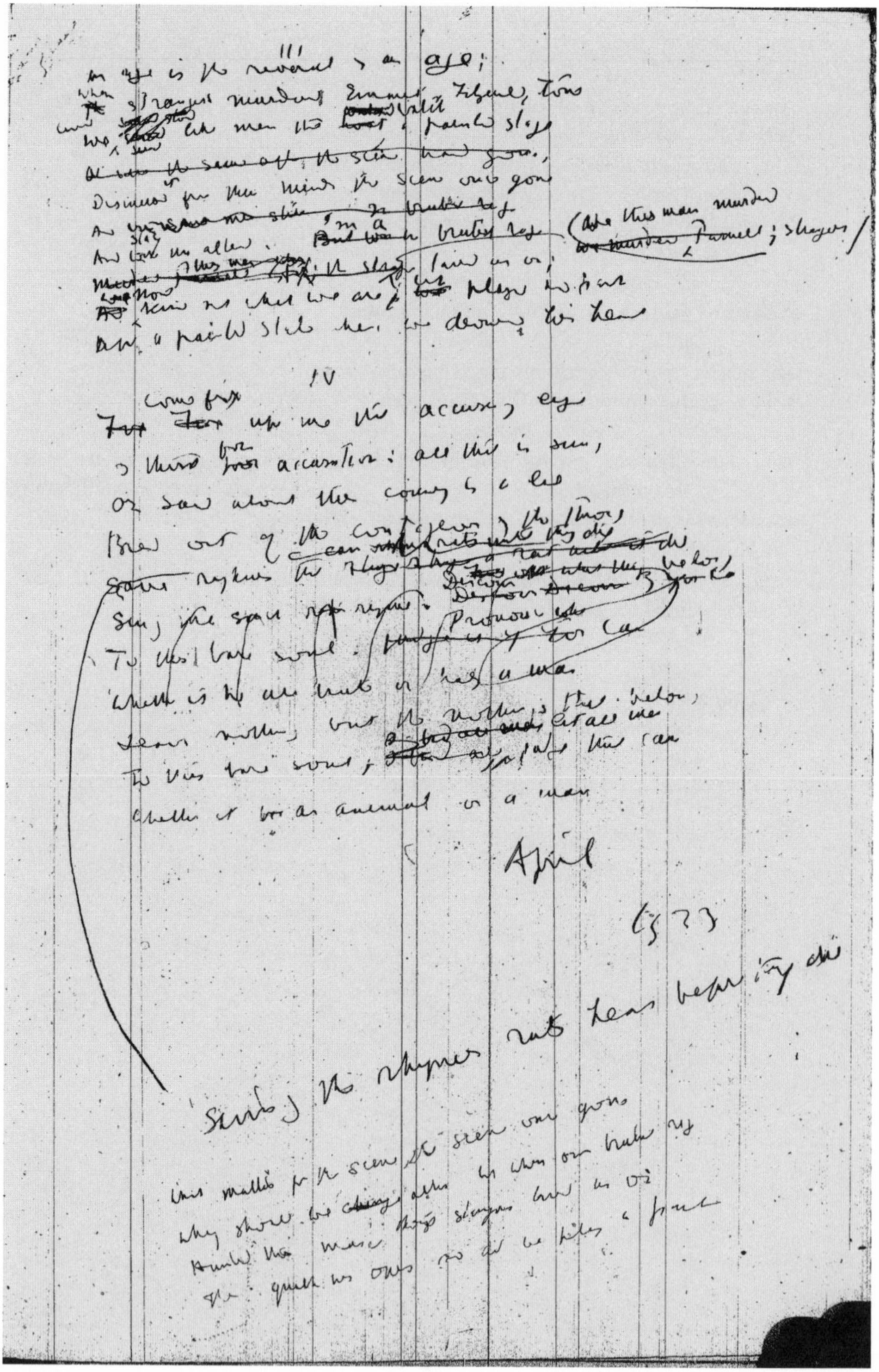

[MBY 545, p. 375 continued]

13 Or said about this country is a lie
14 Bred out of the contagion of the throng
~~can [?rhyme] rats until~~ they die
15 Save ryhmes that ~~[?rhyme] [?try] a rat until it die~~
~~[?]~~ ~~[?]~~ what things belong
Discover
16 Sing the [?same ripe] rhyme. ~~Discover~~ Discover ~~[?]~~
Pronounce who
17 To this bare soul. ~~Judge it if you~~ can
18 Whether it be all brute or half a man
19 Leave nothing but the nothing that belongs
~~I bid all men~~ let all men
20 To this bare soul; ~~I bid all~~ judge that can
21 Whether it be an animal or a man

April
1933

22 Saving the ryhmes rats hear before they die

23 What matter for the scene the scene once gone
24 Why should we ~~change~~ alter but when our brutish rage
25 Hunted this man though strangers tarred us on
26 The guilt was ours nor did we play a part

22 Line 22 is clued into line 15.

Somebody At Parnell's Funeral.

Under theGreat Comedian's tomb the crowd;
A bundle of tempestuous cloud is blown
About the sky, where that is clear of cloud
Brightness remains; a brighter star shoots down;
What shudders run through all that animal blood?
What is this sacrifice? Can someone there
Recall the Cretan [illegible] that pierced a star? barb/

Rich foliage that the starlight glitters through,
A frenzied crowd, and where the branches sprang
A beautiful seated boy; a sacred bow;
and an arrow on
A woman ~~notched an arrow to~~ a string;
A pierced/ [illegible] boy
~~The boy dropped.~~ imaging a star laid low;
That woman the Great Mother imaging
Cut out his heart. Some master of design
Stamped boy and tree upon Sicilian coin.

An age is the reversal of an age:
when
~~The~~ strangers murdered Emmet, Fitzgerald, Tone;
We lived like men that watch a painted stage,/ O
what matter for the scene,
~~Dismiss it from their minds~~ the scene once gone,/ [illegible] //
It had not touched our lives, but popular rage
~~And stay unaltered. In a brutish rage~~
Hysterica passio, dragged this quarry down.
Tarred
~~We this man murdered; strangers [illegible]~~ us on;
None shared our guilt nor did we play a
~~Now know not what we are, yet played~~ no part
Upon a painted stage when we devoured his heart.

[SIU(1), p. 1]

Somebody At Parnell's Funeral.

Under theGreat Comedian's tomb the crowd;
A bundle of tempestuous cloud is blown
r
About the sky, whe e that is clear of cloud
Brightness remains; a brighter star shoots down;
What shudders run through all that animal blood?
What is this sacrifice? Can someone there
barb
Recall the Cretan ~~barb~~ that pierced a star? barb/

ed
Rich foliage that the starlight glitters through,
A frenzied crowd, and where the branches sprang
A beautiful seated boy; a sacred bow;
and an arrow on
A womn ~~notched an arrow to~~ a string;
A
A pierced ~~That~~ ~~a pierced~~ boy
~~**The boy dropped,**~~ **imaging a star laid low;**
That woman the Great Mother imaging
Cut out his heart. Some master of design
Stamped boy and tree upon Sicilian coin.

An age is the reversal of an age :
When
~~**The**~~ **strangers murdered Emmet, Fitzgerald, Tone;**
d
We live like men that watch a painted stage,
what matter for the scene,
~~**Dismiss it from their minds**~~ **the scene once gone,** !/
It had not touched our lives, but popular rage
~~**And stay unaltered. In a brutish rage**~~
Hysterica passio, dragged this quarry down.
tarred
~~**We this man murdered; strangers fired us on**~~**;**
None shared our guilt nor did we play
~~**Now know not what we are, put played**~~ **no part**
Upon a painted stage when we devoured his heart.

[SIU(1), p. 2]

2

Come, fix upon me that accusing eye,
I thirst for accusation, all that is sung
Or said about this country is a lie
Bred out of the contagion of the throng
Saving the rhyme rats hear before they die;
Leave nothing but the nothings that belong
To this bare soul, let all men judge that can
Whether it be an animal or a man.

WBYeats
Apr 9
1938

[SIU(1), p. 2]

Come, fix upon me that accusing eye,
I thirst for accusation, all that is sung
Or said about this country is a lie
Bred out of the contagion of the throng
Saving the rhyme rats hear before they die;
Leave nothing but the nothings that belong
To this bare soul, let all men judge that can can
Whether it be an animal or a man.

WB Yeats
April 9
1933

Lines 16–23 were first published in "Introduction to 'Fighting the Waves,'" *The Dublin Magazine*, April–June 1932. Apparently Yeats revised these lines here and in the previous draft and then returned to the version originally published.

[UNC, p. 1]

To run across 2 facing pages

(Irish Review) 39

A POEM AND A COMMENTARY — 30 pt Italic Caps

William Butler Yeats — 14 pt

A PARNELL'S FUNERAL — 24 pt Caps

Set poem (4 stanzas) in Futura, spaced to fill page.

2 line initial 30 pt Italic

12 pt Vogue Bold

Under the Great Comedian's tomb the crowd;
A bundle of tempestuous cloud is blown
About the sky, where that is clear of cloud
Brightness remains; a brighter star shoots down;
What shudders run through all that animal blood?
What is this sacrifice? Can someone there
Recall the Cretan barb that pierced a star?

Rich foliage that the starlight glittered through,
A frenzied crowd, and where the branches sprang
A beautiful seated boy; a sacred bow;
A woman and an arrow on a string;
A pierced boy, imaging a star laid low;
That woman the Great Mother imaging
Cut out his heart. Some master of design
Stamped boy and tree upon Sicilian coin.

8839

[UNC, p. 1]

~~SOMEBODY AT~~ PARNELL'S FUNERAL

Under the Great Comedian's tomb the crowd;
A bundle of tempestuous cloud is blown
About the sky, where that is clear of cloud
Brightness remains; a brighter star shoots down;
What shudders run through all that animal blood?
What is this sacrifice? Can someone there
Recall the Cretan barb that pierced a star?

Rich foliage that the starlight glittered through,
A frenzied crowd, and where the branches sprang
A beautiful seated boy; a sacred bow;
A woman and an arrow on a string;
A pierced boy imaging a star laid low;
That woman the Great Mother imaging , ,
Cut out his heart. Some master of design
Stamped boy and tree upon Sicilian coin.

---

title untitled DM, Wheels'34, Wheels'35 **A PARNELLITE AT PARNELL'S FUNERAL** *KGCT'34, KGCT'35*
1 crowd. *FMM*
3 sky; *FMM*
11 woman, and *Spectator, KGCT'34, KGCT'35, FMM*
12 boy, image of . . . low. *Spectator, KGCT'34, KGCT'35, FMM*
13 woman, the *Spectator, KGCT'34, KGCT'35, FMM*

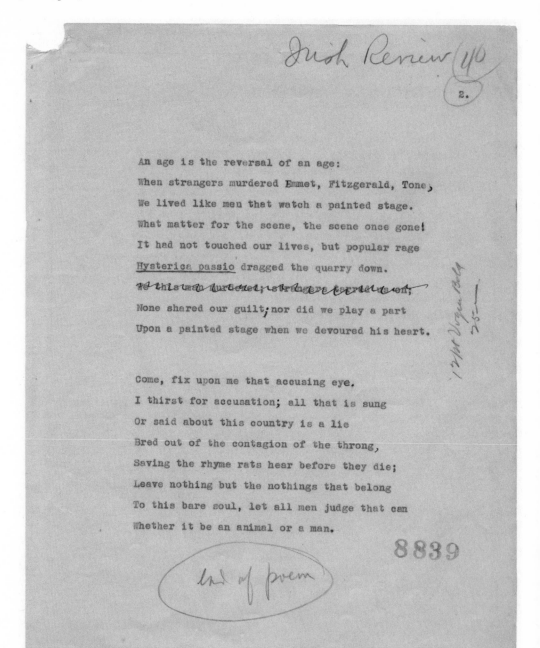

Irish Review (40)

2.

An age is the reversal of an age:
When strangers murdered Emmet, Fitzgerald, Tone,
We lived like men that watch a painted stage.
What matter for the scene, the scene once gone!
It had not touched our lives, but popular rage
<u>Hysterica passio</u> dragged the quarry down.
~~We this man [illegible]; strangers [illegible]~~
None shared our guilt; nor did we play a part
Upon a painted stage when we devoured his heart.

Come, fix upon me that accusing eye.
I thirst for accusation; all that is sung
Or said about this country is a lie
Bred out of the contagion of the throng,
Saving the rhyme rats hear before they die;
Leave nothing but the nothings that belong
To this bare soul, let all men judge that can
Whether it be an animal or a man.

8839

End of poem

[UNC, p. 2]

An age is the reversal of an age:
When strangers murdered Emmet, Fitzgerald, Tone ,
We lived like men that watch a painted stage.

!
What matter for the scene, the scene once gone:}
It had not touched our lives, but popular rage
Hysterica passio dragged the quarry down.
~~**We this man murdered; strangers tarred us on;**~~

;
None shared our guilt,} nor did we play a part
Upon a painted stage when we devoured his heart.

Come, fix upon me that accusing eye,
I thirst for accusation; all that is sung
Or said about this country is a lie
Bred out of the contagion of the throng ,
Saving the rhyme rats hear before they die;
Leave nothing but the nothings that belong
To this bare soul, let all men judge that can
Whether it be an animal or a man.

---

16 age; *DM*, *Wheels'34*, *Wheels'35*

17 Tone; *Spectator*, *KGCT'34*, *KGCT'35*, *FMM*

19 gone: *Spectator*, *KGCT'34*, *KGCT'35*, *FMM*

20 lives; but popular rage, *DM*, *Wheels'34*, *Wheels'35* lives. But *Spectator KGCT'34*, *KGCT'35*, *FMM* rage. *Spectator*, *FMM*

21 passio, dragged this quarry *DM* *passio*, dragged this quarry *Wheels'34*, *Wheels'35* this quarry *Spectator*, *KGCT'34*, *KGCT'35*, *FMM*

25 eye. *FMM*

26 accusation. All that was sung, *Spectator*, *KGCT'34*, *KGCT'35*, *FMM*

27 All that was said in Ireland is a lie *Spectator*, *KGCT'34*, *KGCT'35, FMM*

28 throng *Spectator*, *KGCT'34*, *KGCT'35*

29 die. *Spectator*, *KGCT'34*, *KGCT'35*, *FMM*

[NLI 30,547, 9r]

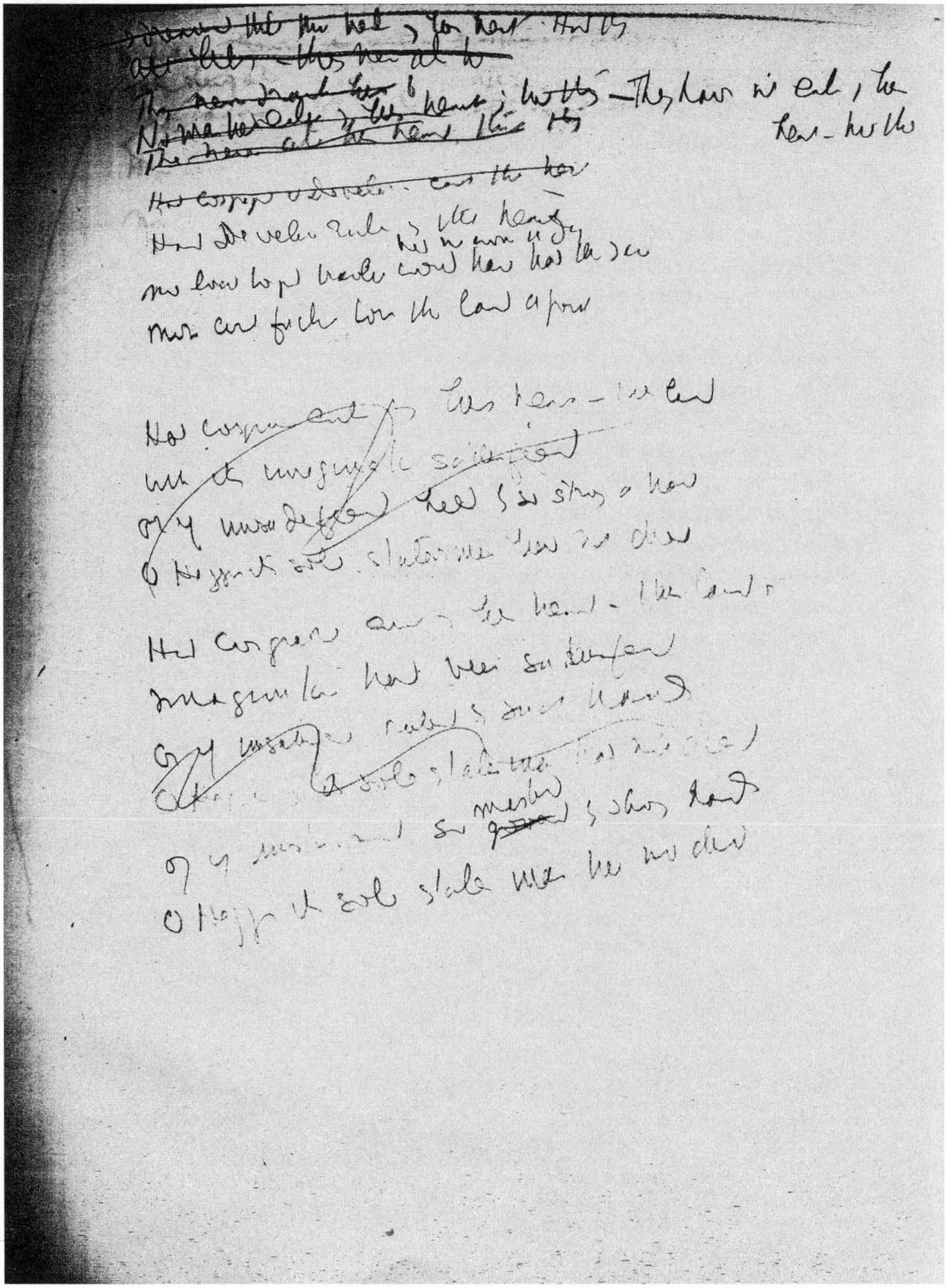

[NLI 30,547, 9r]

1 ~~*I dreamed that they had of his heart. Had they*~~
2 ~~*All lies they never ate h*~~
3 ~~*They never drank his b*~~
4 ~~*No man has eaten of his heart*~~; ~~*had they*~~ — *They have not eaten of his heart – had they —*
5 ~~*They never ate his heart that they*~~

6 ~~*Had Cosgrave & Develera eaten that hear*~~*t*
De
7 *Had {d Velera eaten of that heart*
had not won the day
8 *No loud tongued brawler could have had the* [?*say*/?*sway*]
9 *Nor civil factions torn the land apart*

10 *Had Cosgrave eaten of his heart — the land*
11 *With its imagination satisfied*
12 *Or if unsadified held by so strong a hand*
13 *O Higgins its sole statesman had not died*

14 *Had Cosgrave eaten of his heart - this lands*
t
15 *Imagination had been sad} isfied*
16 *Or if unsatisfied ruled by such hands*
17 *O Higgins its sole statesman had not died*
mastered
18 *or if unsatisfied so* ~~*governed*~~ *by strong hands*
19 *O Higgins its sole state man had not died*

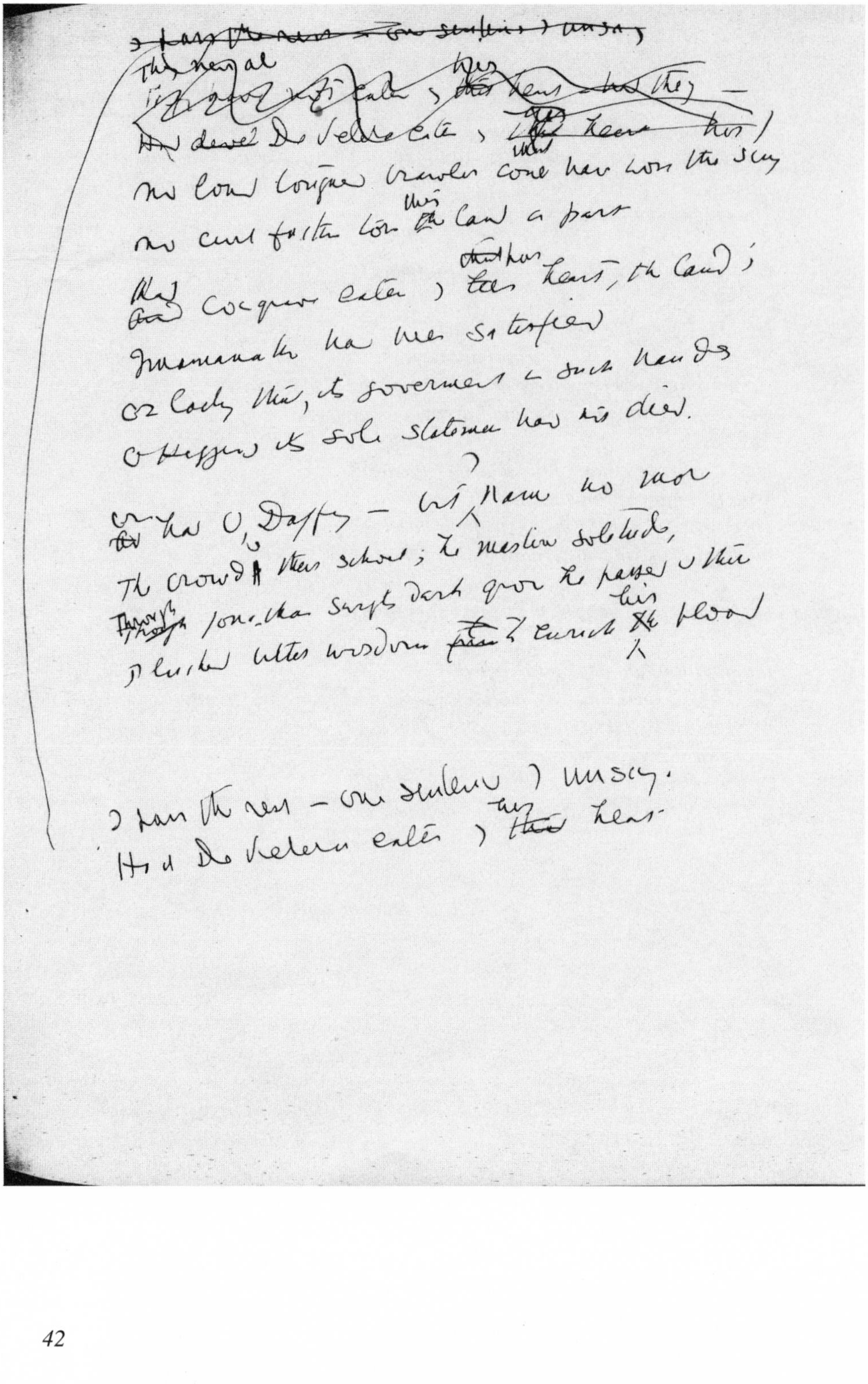
~~I pass the [illegible] — one sentence I unsay~~
They have all
~~Had [illegible] eaten [illegible] heart [illegible]~~ —
~~Had~~ Had de Valera eaten, ~~that~~ that heart ~~his~~ /
No loud tongue crawler come have won the sky
No civil faction torn this land apart
~~Had~~ Had Cosgrave eaten ~~that~~ that his heart, the land;
Imagination had been satisfied
Or lacking that, its government in such hands
O'Higgins its sole statesman had not died.

Or had O'Duffy — but I name no more
The crowd their school; the master solitude,
~~Through~~ Through Jonathan Swift's dark grove he passed & there
Plucked bitter wisdom ~~from~~ that enriched ~~the~~ his blood

I pass the rest — one sentence I unsay.
Had de Valera eaten ~~that~~ that heart

[NLI 30,547, 10r]

~~I pass the rest — one sentence I unsay~~
They never ate
his
They have not eaten of ~~that~~ heart — had they —
~~his~~
Had ~~devel~~ De Velera eaten of ~~that heart his~~ /
~~that~~
No loud tongued brawler could have won the [?sway]
their
No civil factions torn ~~the~~ land a part

Had ~~that~~ his
~~And~~ Cosgrave eaten of ~~his~~ heart, the land's
Imagination had been satisfied
Or lackng that, its government in such hands
O Higgins its sole statesman had not died.

Or I
~~and~~ had O Duffy — but ^ name no more
's
The crowd~~s~~ their school; he mastered solitude,
Through
~~Though~~ Jonathan Swifts dark grove he passed & there
~~to~~ his
Plucked bitter wisdom ~~from~~ to enrich ~~the~~ blood
^

I pass the rest — one sentence I unsay.
his
Had De Velera eaten of ~~that~~ heart

Lines 15–16 are clued in to replace lines 1–4.

[*The Spectator*, October 19, 1934, p. 570]

Forty Years Later

I pass the rest—one sentence I unsay—
Had de Valera eaten Parnell's heart
No loose lipped demagogue had won the day,
No civil rancour torn the land apart.

Had Cosgrave eaten Parnell's heart, the land's
Imagination had been satisfied,
Or lacking that, government in such hands
O'Higgins its sole statesman had not died.

Had even O'Duffy—but I name no more—
Their school the crowd, his master solitude,
Through Jonathan Swift's dark grove he passed and there
Plucked bitter wisdom that enriched his blood.

---

title *untitled in Commentary on a Parnellite at Parnell's Funeral KGCT'34, KGCT'35* II [*as the first part of this poem (above) is* I] *FMM*

1 The rest I pass, one sentence I unsay. *KGCT'34, KGCT'35, FMM*

2 Parnell's *rev from* of his *NLI* $30,020_2$

4/5 *no break between lines 4 and 5 KGCT'34, KGCT'35*

5 Parnell's *rev from* of his *NLI* $30,020_2$

9 name *rev from* naem *NLI* $30,020_2$

10 a crowd, . . . solitude; *KGCT'34, FMM* a crowd, his master's solitude; *KGCT'35*

11 passed, and *KGCT'34, KGCT'35, FMM*

[NLI 30,547, 1r]

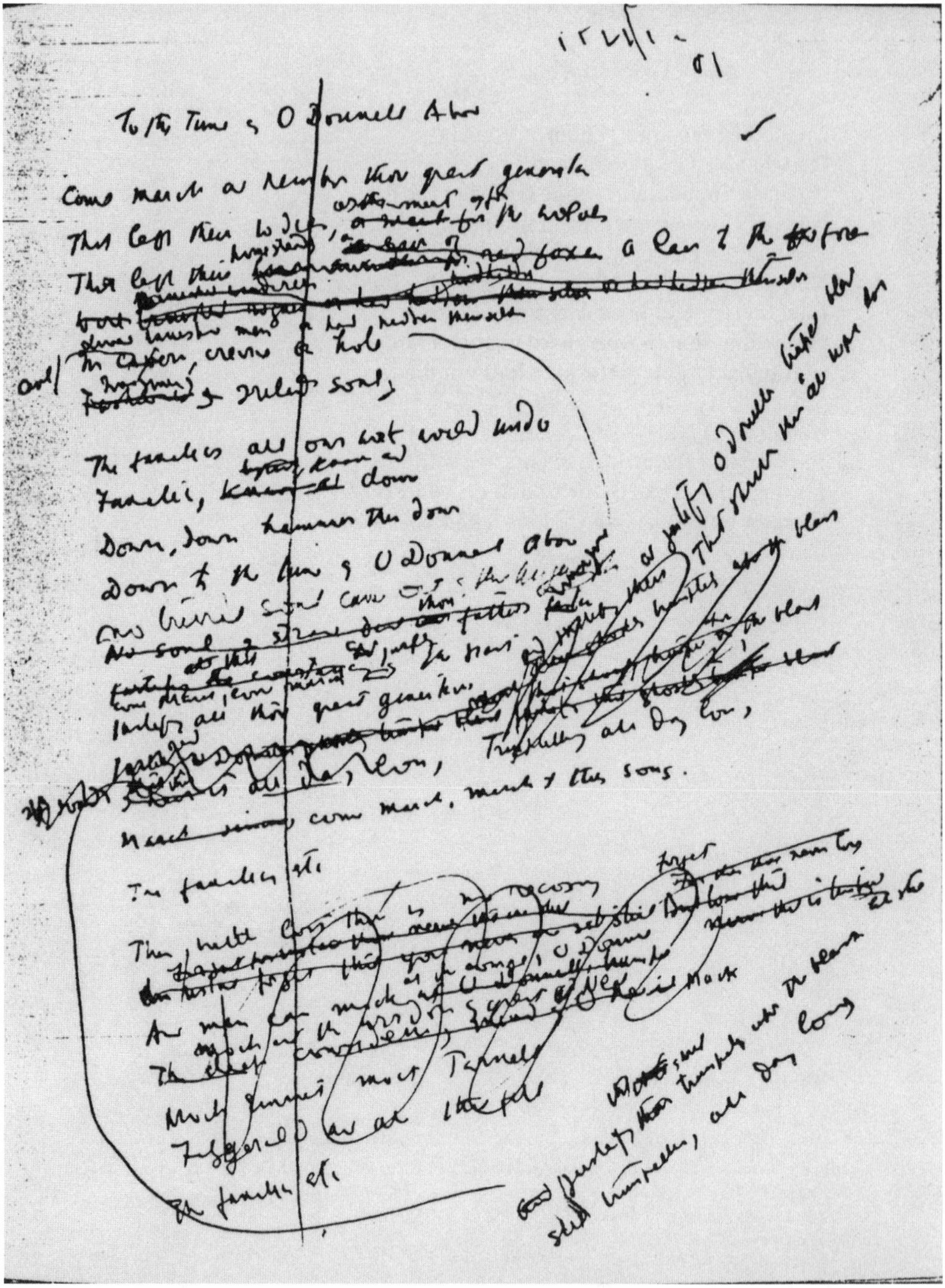

THREE SONGS TO THE SAME TUNE

[NLI 30,547, 1r]

To the Tune of O Donell Abou

1 Come march and remember those great generations
as ~~the~~ meat ~~of~~ for
2 That left their bodies, ~~as meat~~ for the wolves
homesteads ~~the lair of~~
3 That left their ~~houses as a [?den] for red foxes~~ a lair to the ~~fox~~ foxes
~~banished wanderers~~ ^~~had hidden~~
4 ~~Were banished rogues or had hidden themselves~~ ~~or had hidden themselves~~
Lived banished men or had hidden themselves
cave
5 In ~~cavern~~, crevice or hole
Imagining
6 ~~Fashioned by~~ Irelands soul;

7 The fanatics all our work would undo
~~tryant~~, knave and
8 Fanatic, ~~knave and~~ clown
9 Down, down hammer them down
10 Down to the tune of O Donnel Abou
No trivial soul came out of that anguish
those imagine
11 ~~No soul of straw did our fathers fashion~~
all that ~~[?]~~ justify
12 ~~Justify the constanc~~y of the past
13 Come march, come march and
14 Justify all those great generations

and justify O Donnells trumpet blast
That shrills [?] all [?] [?]
And justify their upon
~~Those ghostly~~ trumpets upon the blast
~~March~~ That ghostly trumpet ~~on~~ the blast

found in NLI 30,547, 1r, 2r, 1v, 3r, 2v, 4r, 4v, 5r, 6r, 5v, 6v. 8r, 7v, 7r *transcribed above and below*
HRC *transcribed below*
SIU(2) *transcribed below*
NLI 30,004
Chicago(2)
NYPL(2)
NLI $30{,}020_1$
NLI $30{,}020_2$

published in *The Spectator*, February 23, 1934 *transcribed below*
Poetry (Chicago), December 1934
The King of the Great Clock Tower (1934)
The King of the Great Clock Tower (1935)
A Full Moon in March (1935)

Pages are arranged according to the probable order of composition.
11 Entire line is canceled in pencil.

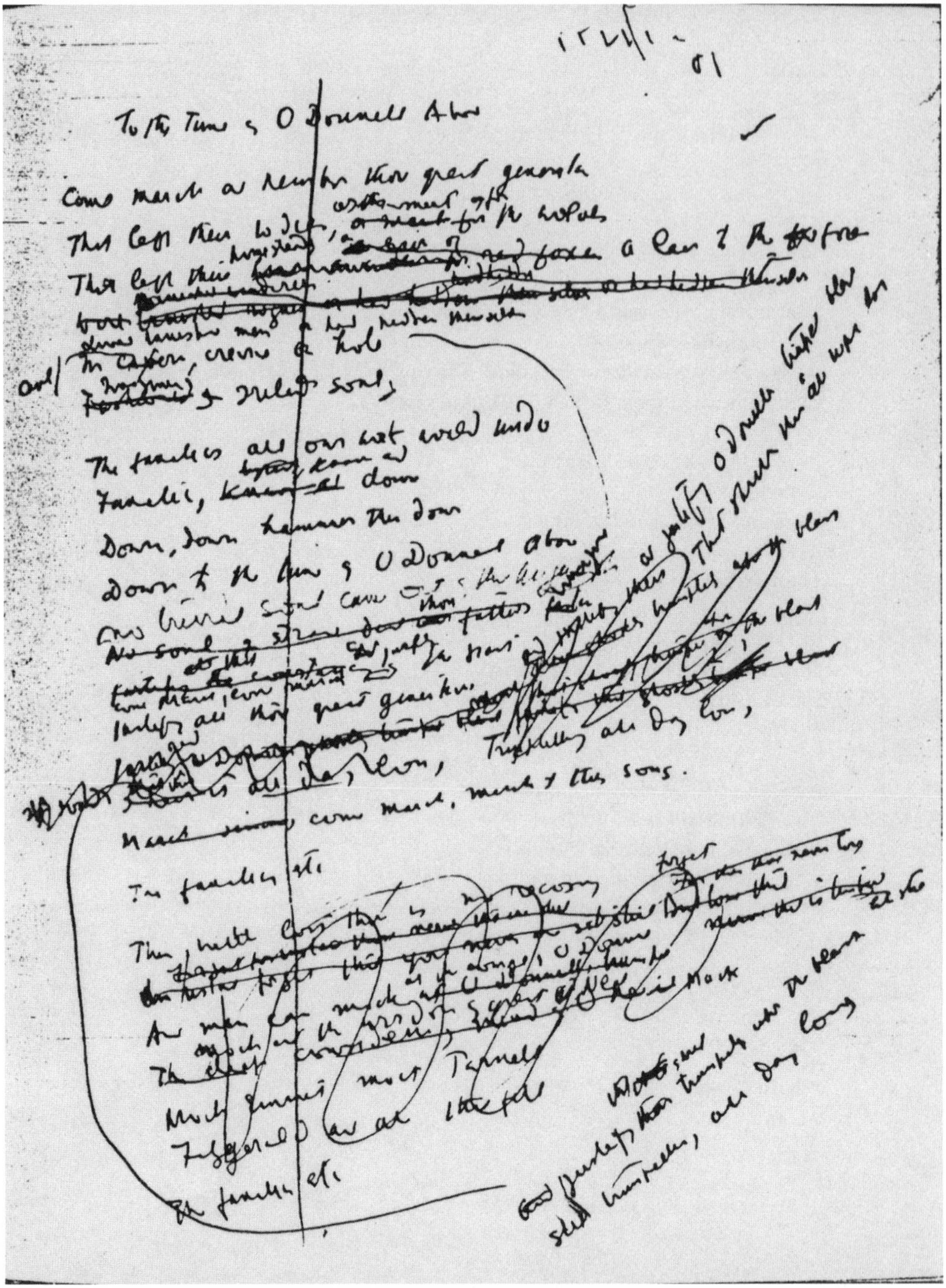

To the Tune of O Donnell Abu

Down, down hammer them down

Down to the tune of O Donnell Abu

The families etc

[NLI 30,547, 1r continued]

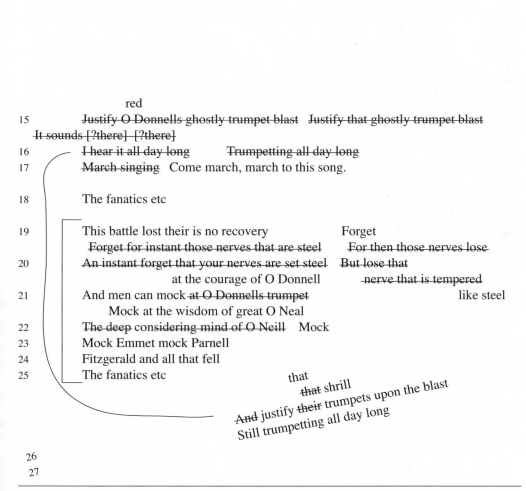

red
~~Justify O Donnells ghostly trumpet blast~~ ~~Justify that ghostly trumpet blast~~
~~It sounds [?there] [?there]~~
~~I hear it all day long~~ ~~Trumpetting all day long~~
~~March singing~~ Come march, march to this song.

The fanatics etc

This battle lost their is no recovery Forget
~~Forget for instant those nerves that are steel~~ ~~For then those nerves lose~~
~~An instant forget that your nerves are set steel~~ ~~But lose that~~
at the courage of O Donnell ~~nerve that is tempered~~
And men can mock ~~at O Donnells trumpet~~ like steel
Mock at the wisdom of great O Neal
~~The deep~~ con~~sidering mind of O Neill~~ Mock
Mock Emmet mock Parnell
Fitzgerald and all that fell
The fanatics etc

that
~~that~~ shrill
~~And~~ justify ~~their~~ trumpets upon the blast
Still trumpetting all day long

26–27 These lines are clued in to line 16.

[NLI 30,547, 2r]

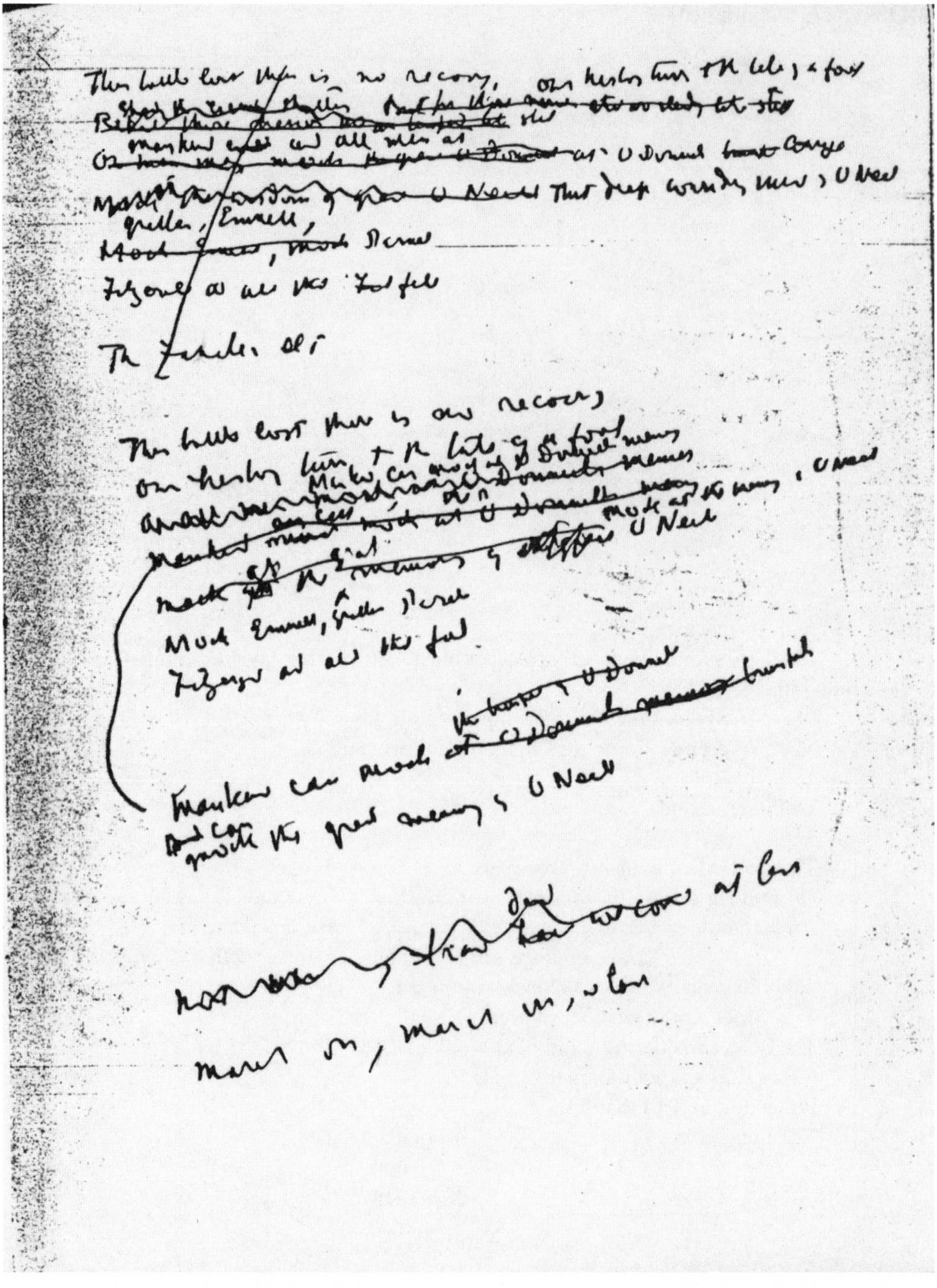

[NLI 30,547, 2r]

1 This battle lost there is no recovery,
our [?history] turns to the tale of a fool
~~Should the enemy shatter~~ ~~But for those nerves that are steady like steel~~
2 ~~[?Recall] those nerves that are tempered like steel~~
Mankind could and all men at
3 ~~Or men may mock the great O Donnel~~ at O Donnels ~~trumpet~~ courage
~~at~~
4 ~~Mock the wisdom of great O Neill~~ That deep considering mind of O Neil
Grattan, Emmett
5 ~~Mock Emmet, mock~~ Parnell
6 Fitzgerald and all that ~~Fit~~ fell
7 The Fanatics etc

8 This battle lost there is no recovery
9 Our history turns to the tale of a fool
Mankind can mock at O Donnells memory
10 ~~As all men mock, at O Donnels memory~~
~~[?can] [?call]~~ the [?]
11 ~~Mankind must mock at O Donnells memory~~
~~at~~ ~~great~~ Mock at the memory of O Neal
12 ~~Mock [?] at the~~ ^ ~~memory of the great~~ O Neil
13 Mock Emmett, Grattan Parnell
14 Fitzgerald and all that fell

~~the trumpet of O Donnel~~
15 Mankind can mock ~~at O Donnels memory trumpets~~
And can
16 Mock the great memory of O Neill

~~did~~
17 ~~Not men of straw have we come~~ at last
18 March on, march on, at last

[NLI 30,547, 1^{v}]

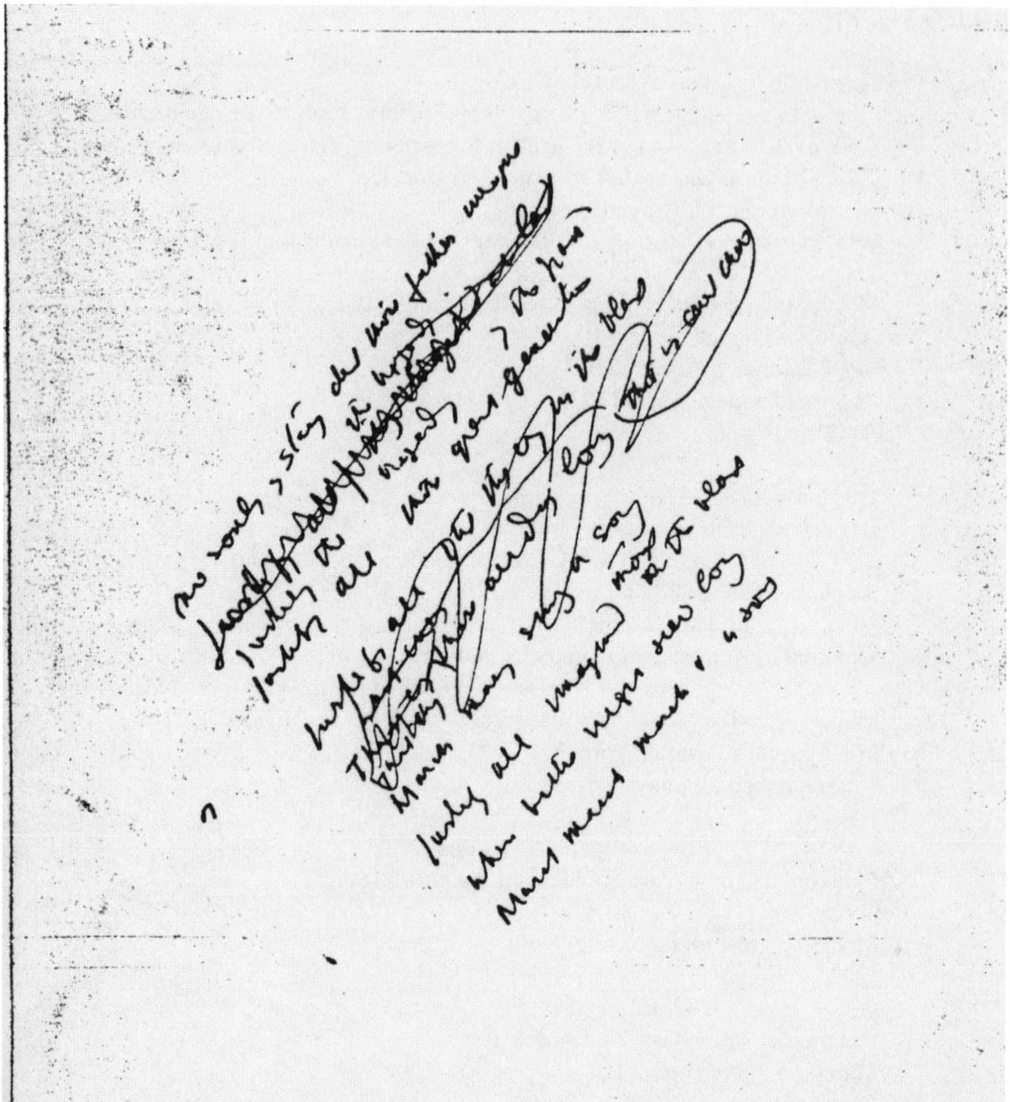

[NLI 30,547, 1v]

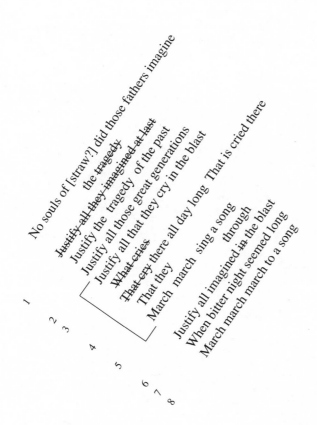

No souls of [straw?] did those fathers imagine
the ~~tragedy~~
~~Justify all they imagined at last~~
Justify the tragedy of the past
Justify all those great generations
Justify all that they cry in the blast
~~What cries~~
~~That cry~~ there all day long That is cried there
That they
March march sing a song
through
Justify all imagined ~~in~~ the blast
When bitter night seemed long
March march march to a song

1 What looks like "No souls of story" here is "No soul of straw" in 1r.
4 "That is cried there" is clued in to the beginning of the line.

[NLI 30,547, 3r]

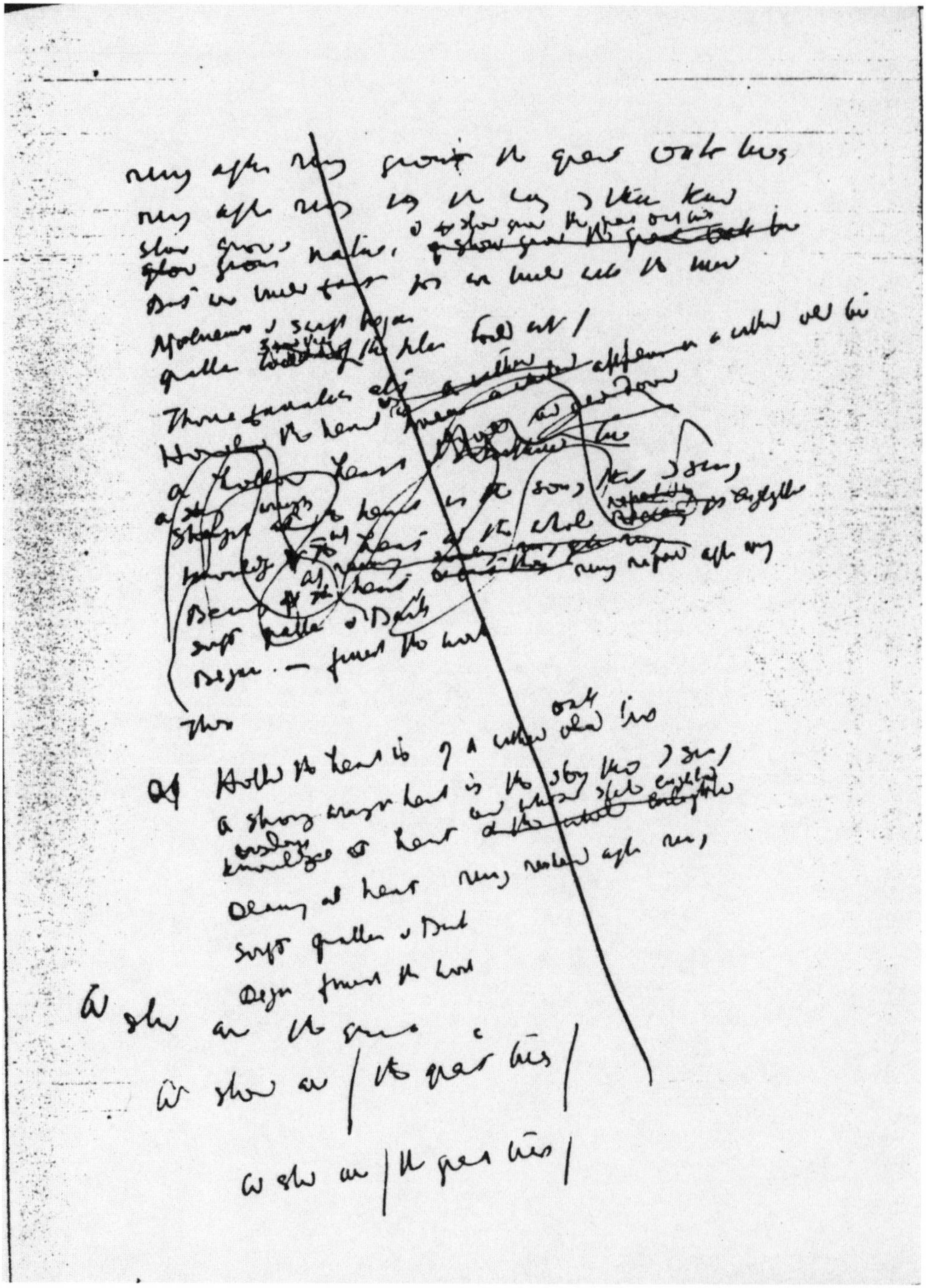

[NLI 30,547, 3r]

ring after ring grow the great oak trees
{s
ring after ring i{n the way of their kind
Slow grows & [~~?gr~~] slow grow the great oak trees
~~Glow~~ grows nature, ~~[?&] slow grow the great oak trees~~
But we build fast for we build with the mind
Molyneux & Swift began
~~[?]~~
Grattan ~~toiled at~~ the plan toiled at /
Those fanatics etc
is ~~a withered~~
Hollow the heart of ~~means a withered~~ ~~appears as~~ a withered old tree

an old and old [?down]
A hollow heart & a withered tree
A str [?wrought] ^
Strength at the heart is the song that I sing
at ~~refreshed by~~
Knowledge ~~at the~~ heart and the whole ~~receives is~~ enlightened
at ~~[?]~~ ~~spreading ring after ring~~
Beauty ~~at the~~ heart ~~[?& at the]~~ ring [?] after ring
Swift Grattan & Burke
Began — finish the work
Then

oak
[~~?~~] Hollow the heart is of a withered ~~old~~ tree
A strong wrought heart is the story that I sing
Wisdom and whole state enlightened
~~Knowledge~~ at heart ~~& the whole enlightened~~
Beauty at heart ring [?] after ring
Swift Grattan & Burke
Began finish the work

And slow are the great
And slow are / the great trees /
And slow are / the great trees /

[NLI 30,547, 2v]

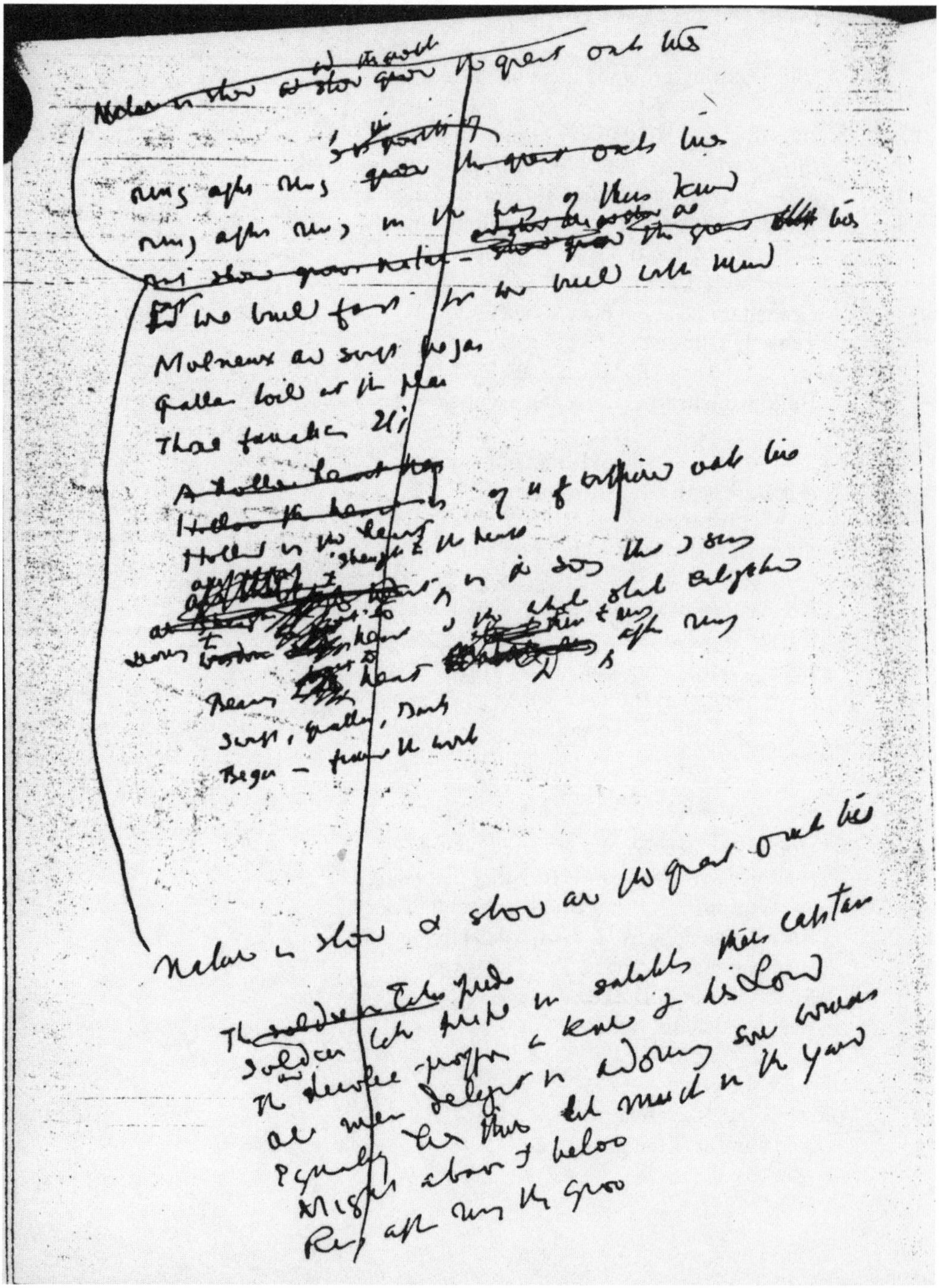

[NLI 30,547, 2v]

~~and the growth~~
~~Nature is slow and slow grow the great~~ oak trees
the
~~'s is growth of~~
ring after ring ~~grow the great oak~~ trees
ring after ring in the way of their kind
~~and slow are~~ ~~and slow~~ are
~~But slow grows nature~~ – ~~slow grow the great oak~~ trees
But
~~And~~ we build fast for we build with mind
Molyneux and Swift began
Grattan toiled at the plan
Those fanatics Etc

~~A hollow heart has~~
~~Hollow the heart~~ is of a f withered oak tree
Hollow is the heart
~~All might~~ strength to the heart
~~All strength to~~
~~Al~~ ~~Strength to the heart~~ ^ is the song that I sing
Learning to [~~? ?~~] to
~~Wisdom to the~~ heart & the whole state enlightened
[~~?~~] to ~~[?] to~~ their [?] ring
Beauty ~~to the~~ heart ~~[? ?] ring~~ after ring
Swift, Grattan, Burke
Began — finish the work

Nature is slow & slow are the great oak trees

The ~~soldier takes~~ pride
Soldiers take pride in saluting their captain
and
The devotee proffers a knee to his Lord
All men delight in adoring some woman
Equality lies there like muck in the yard
Might above to below
Ring after ring they grow

4 Lines 1 and 17 are clued in to line 4.

[NLI 30,547, 4r]

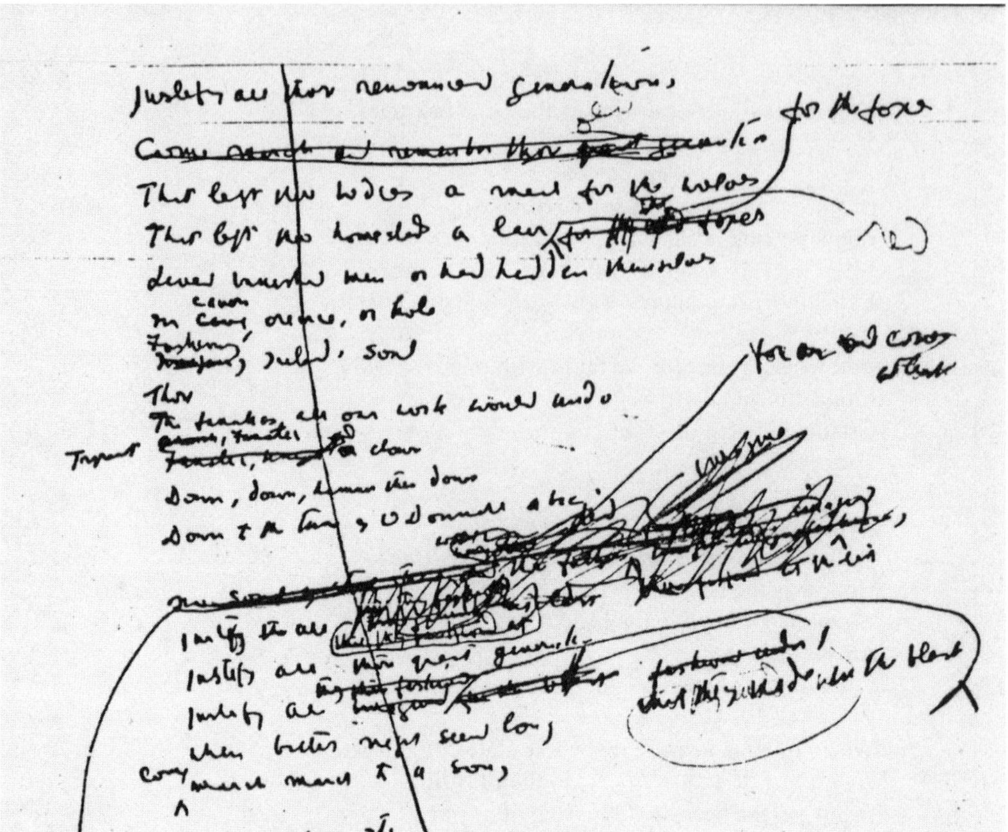

[NLI 30,547, 4r]

Justify all those renowned generations
old
~~Come march and remember those great generations~~ for the foxes
That left their bodies a meal for the wolves
the
That left their homesteads a lair ~~for the red foxes~~ red
Lived banished men or had hidden themselves
cavern
In ~~cave~~, crevice, or hole
Fashioning
~~[?Imagining]~~ Irelands soul for an end comes
Those
~~The~~ fanatics all our work would undo at last
Tyrant ~~Anarch~~, Fanatic
~~and~~
~~Fanatic, knave or~~ clown
Down, down, hammer them down
Down to the tune of O Donnell abu
~~[?] [?did]~~ ~~imagine~~
~~[? ? ?]~~ ~~[? ? ?] imagined~~
~~No soul of [?star / ?story] straw did those fathers imagine imagine fashion~~ ,
what they fashioned
Justify ~~the~~ all ~~[? ?] fashioned at last there fashioned at~~ the last
(~~that they fashioned at~~)
Justify all those great generations
~~they their fashioned~~
Justify all ~~imagined in the blast~~ ~~fashioned under~~
that they made in the blast
When bitter night seemed long
Come
March march to a song

6–7 The clause "for an end comes / at last"—in ink over pencil—is clued into line 12.
11 The arrow connects line 11 to line 25 (see p. 61).
13 The clause "that they fashioned at" is canceled in pencil.
14 The clause "that they made in the blast," which attaches to line 14, is ink over pencil and circled with pencil.

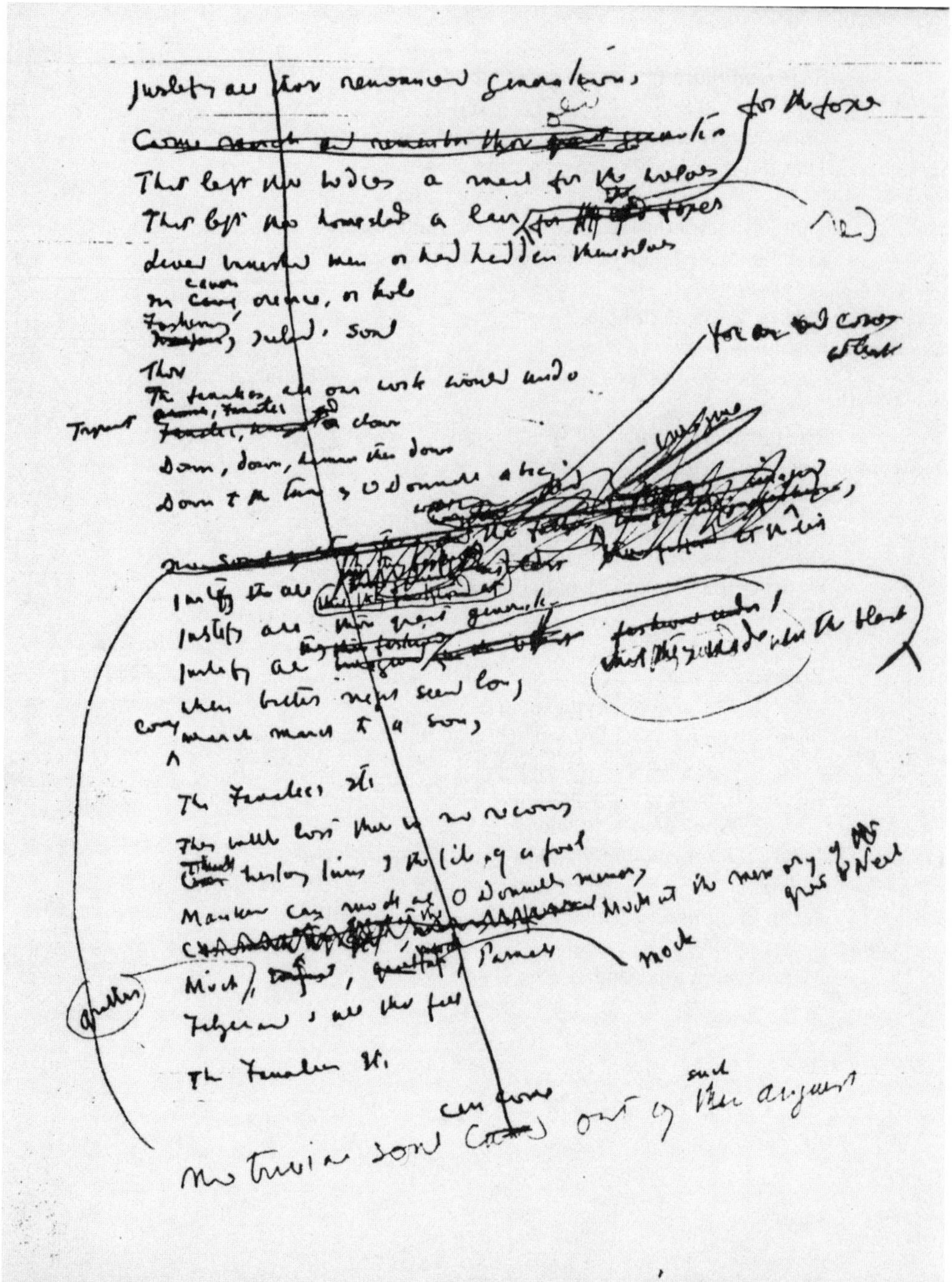

[NLI 30,547, 4r continued]

The Fanatics Etc
This battle lost there is no recovery
That
~~Our~~ history turns to the tale of a fool
Mankind can mock at O Donnells memory
~~at~~ ~~great at the~~
~~Can mock the great, memory of O Neal~~ Mock at the memory of that
^ great O Neil
~~Mock~~
Grattan Mock, ~~Emmet~~, ~~Grattan~~, Parnell mock
Fitzgerald and all that fell
The Fanatics Etc
can come such
No trivial soul ~~cried~~ out of ~~their~~ anguish

---

22 At the beginning of the line, "Grattan" is clued in pencil to follow "Mock".

25 Line 25 is clued in to line 11 by pencil (see p. 59, above).

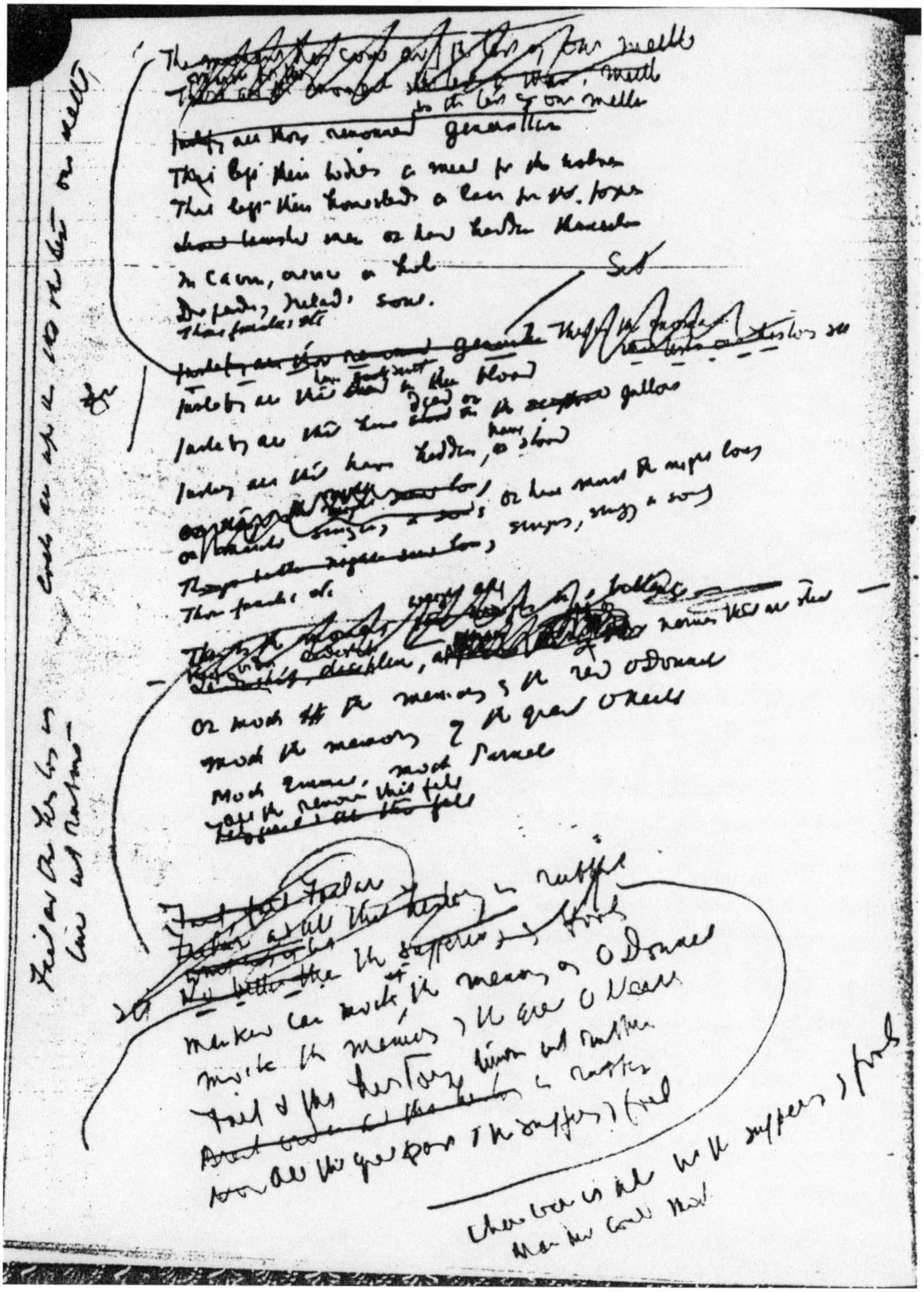

[NLI 30,547, 4ᵛ]

Events are upon us that shall test our mettle

The moment has come and the test of our mettle
March for this
1 ~~These are~~ the moments ~~[?] that test a mans mettle~~
is the test of our mettle
2 Justify all those renowned generations
3 That left their bodies a meal for the wolves
4 That left their homesteads a lair for the foxes
5 ~~Lived banished~~ men or had hidden themselves
6 In cavern, crevice or hole
7 Defending Irelands soul. [?Stet]
8 Those fanatics Etc

9 ~~In~~/ ~~Justify all those renowned generations~~ ~~This is the moment~~
~~that tests our history~~ stet
have ~~sank~~ sunk
10 Justify all that ~~choked~~ in their blood
died on
11 Justify all that have ~~stood on~~ the ~~scaffold~~ gallows
have
12 Justify all that have hidden, ~~or~~ stood
~~night~~
13 ~~Or thought the night seemed long~~
14 ~~or marched singing a song~~ or have march the night long
15 ~~Though bitter night seemed long~~ singing, singing a song
16 Those fanatics etc

---

1 Line 1 is clued in pencil to line 9. The line in pencil up the right margin near the top is a revision of line 1.

9 The "*Stet*" above (line 7) is clued to "generations" (line 9). The stet marks in line 9 are in pencil, as are the sentence "~~This . . . history~~ stet" and its stet marks.

[NLI 30,547, 4v continued]

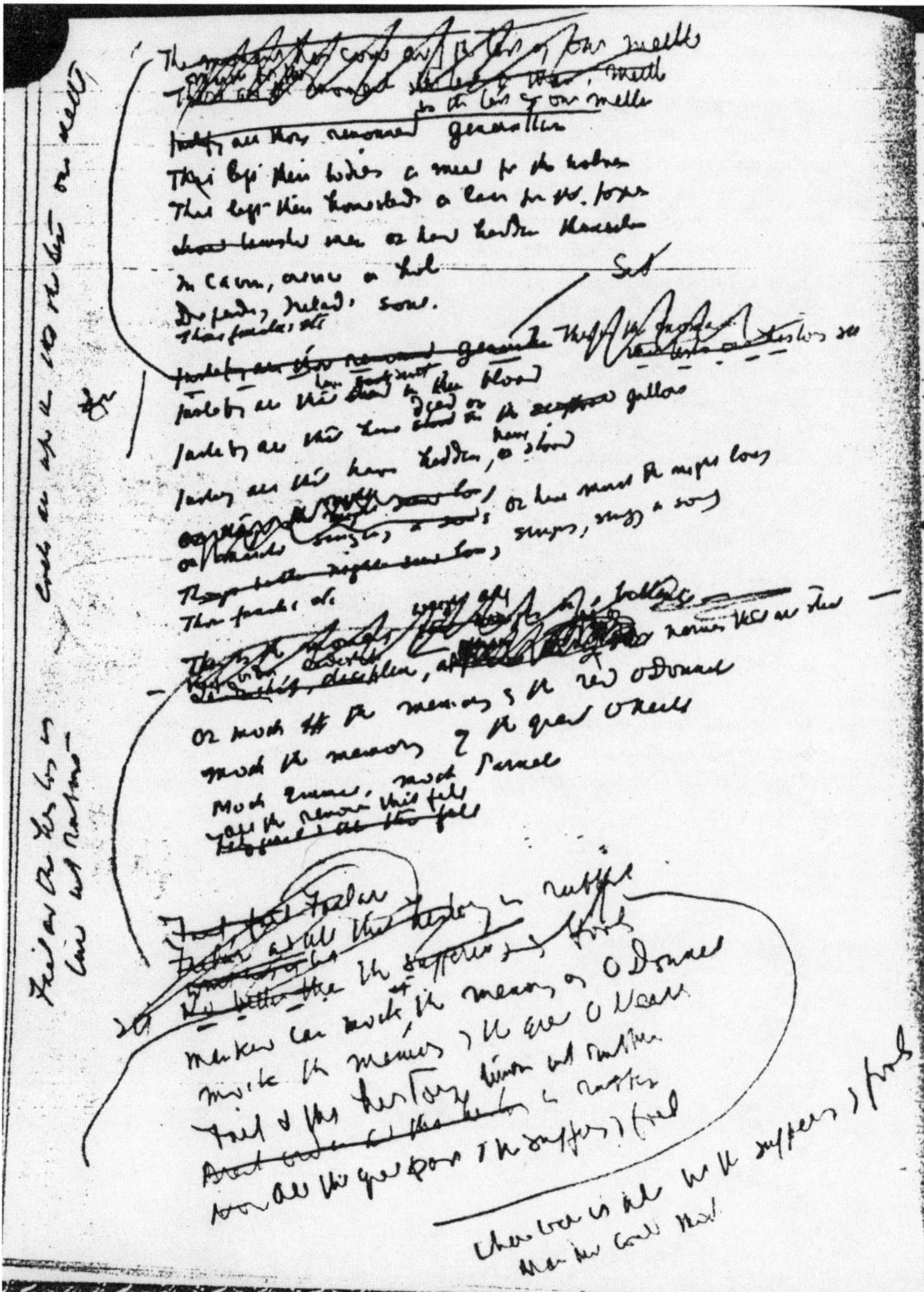

[NLI 30,547, 4[v] continued]

weighs all
17 This is the moment ~~that weighs~~ in a ballance --
—Keep order, leadership — [~~? ?~~] [~~? ? ?~~]
18 ~~Leadership, discipline,~~ [~~? ?]~~ ~~nerves~~ that ~~are steel~~ nerves that are steel —
Fail and that history [?]
turns out rubbish
19 Or mock ~~at~~ the memory of the red O Donnell
20 Mock the memory of the great O Neill
21 Mock Emmet, mock Parnell
All the renown that fell
22 ~~Fitzgerald all that fell~~

23 ~~Fail, fail~~ Failure
24 Failure and all that history is rubbish
25 ~~What was it~~ but
26 stet No better than the suffering of fools
~~it~~
27 Mankind can mock, the memory of O Donnell
28 Mock the memory of the great O Neill
Fail & that history turns out rubbish
29 ~~Break order and that history~~ is rubbish
30 ~~How~~ All the great past the suffering of fools

31 What was it all but the suffering of fools
32 Mankind could mock

17–18 These lines are canceled in pencil.
23 The line, in pencil, running up the left margin, goes with line 23 and following, which are clued in to line 17.
31–32 These lines are clued in pencil to line 24.

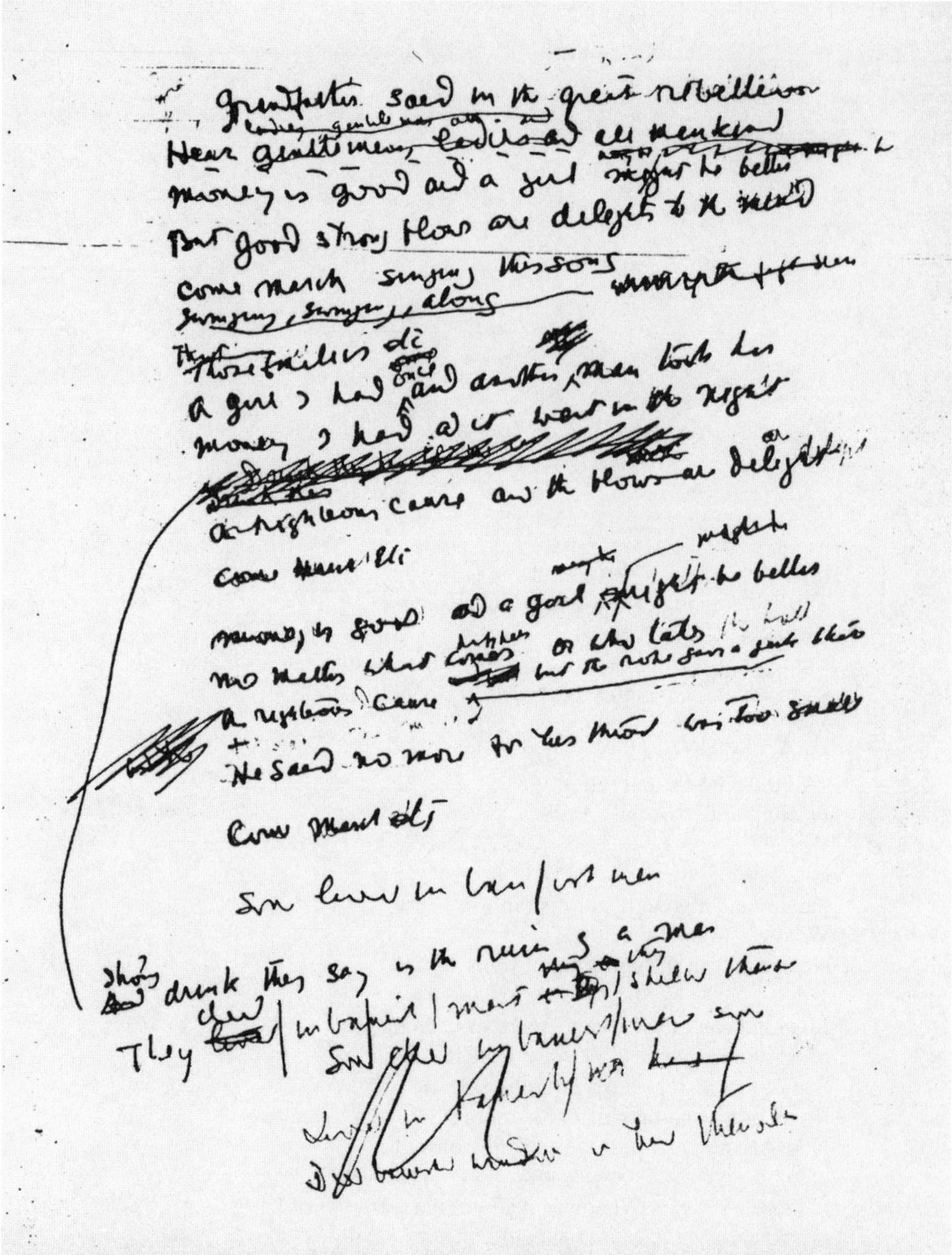
Grandfather said in the great rebellion
Hear gentlemen, ladies and all mankind
Money is good and a girl might be better
But good strong blows are delights to the mind
Come march singing this song
Singing, singing along
Those failures etc
A girl I had once and another man took her
Money I had and it went in the night
On righteous cause and the blows are delights
Come march etc
Money is good and a good might be better
No matter what comes or who lets
A righteous cause
He said no more for his throat was too small
Come march etc

[NLI 30,547, 5[r]]

Grandfather said in the great rebellion
~~ladies, gentlemen all – and~~
~~Hear gentlemen, ladies and~~ all mankind
~~may be~~ ~~might be~~
Money is good and a girl ~~might~~ be better
But good strong blows are delights to the mind
Come march singing this song
Swinging, swinging, along ~~what if the [?fight] [?seem]~~
That
~~Those~~ fanatics etc
~~once~~ ~~man~~
once ~~[?]~~
A girl I had ^ and another ^ man took her
Money I had and it went in the night
~~Drink they have told me can~~
~~Drink they~~
~~[?] the~~ are
A righteous cause and the blows are delight
Come march Etc
~~may be~~ ~~might be~~
Money is good and a girl might be better
happens
No matter what comes or who takes the fall
~~and but~~ but the rope gave a jerk there
A righteous cause & [~~? ? ? ? ? ? ?~~]
~~And he~~ [~~? ? ?~~]
He said no more for his throat was too small
Come march Etc

Some lived in ban/ ish men

Strong
~~And~~ drink they say is the ruin of a man
died ~~they or~~ they
They ~~lived~~/ in ba/ nish/ ment ~~or they~~/ sheltered themselves
Some died in banish/ ment some
Lived in banish/ ment ~~hid~~/
Died banished withdrew or hid themselves

The draft is in ink over pencil, except where in pencil only.
10 Line 19 is clued in to line 10.
15 Illegible penciled words were canceled by erasure.

[NLI 30,547, 6r]

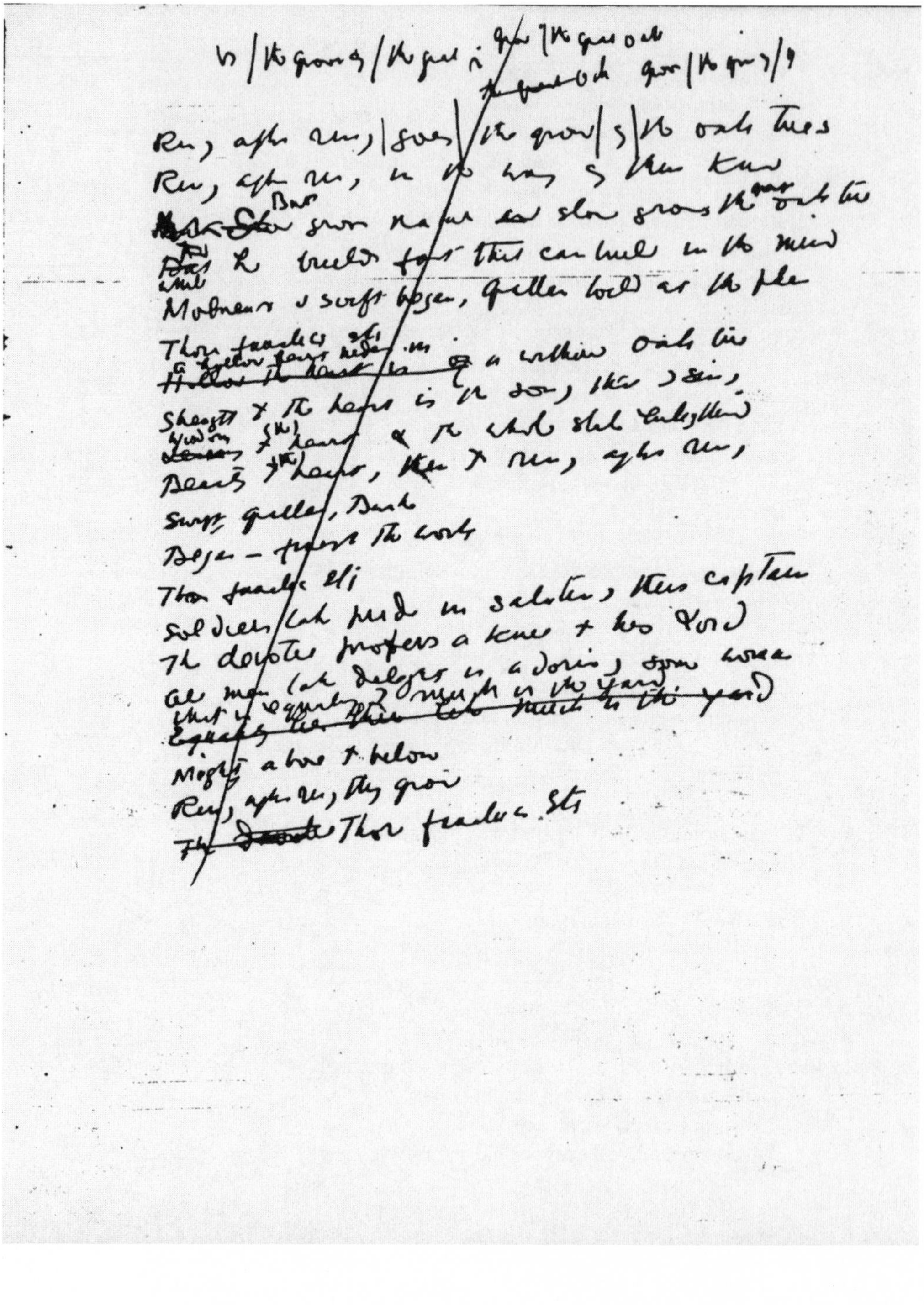

[NLI 30,547, 6r]

grows / the great oak
1 is/ the growth of/ the great^.
~~the great~~ oak grows / the grow of / of
2 Ring after ring / goes / the growth / of / the oak trees
3 Ring after ring in the way of their kind
But
{~~S~~ ~~great~~
4 ~~But~~ {~~slow~~ grows nature ~~and~~ slow grows the oak tree
~~And~~
5 ~~But~~ he builds fast that can build in the mind
While
6 Molyneux & Swift began, Grattan toiled at the plan
7 Those fanatics etc
A hollow heart hides in
8 ~~Hollow the heart is of~~ a withered oak tree
9 Strength to the heart is the song that I sing
Wisdom (the)
10 ~~Learning~~ to heart & the whole state enlightened
the
11 Beauty to heart, then to ring after ring
12 Swift, Grattan, Burke
13 Began – finish the work
14 Those fanatics Etc.
15 Soldiers take pride in saluting their captain
f}
16 The devotee prop}ers a knee to his Lord
17 All men take delight in adoring some woman
What is equality? Muck in the yard.
18 ~~Equality lies there like muck in the yard~~
19 Might, above to below
20 Ring after ring they grow
21 ~~The devotee~~ Those fanatics Etc

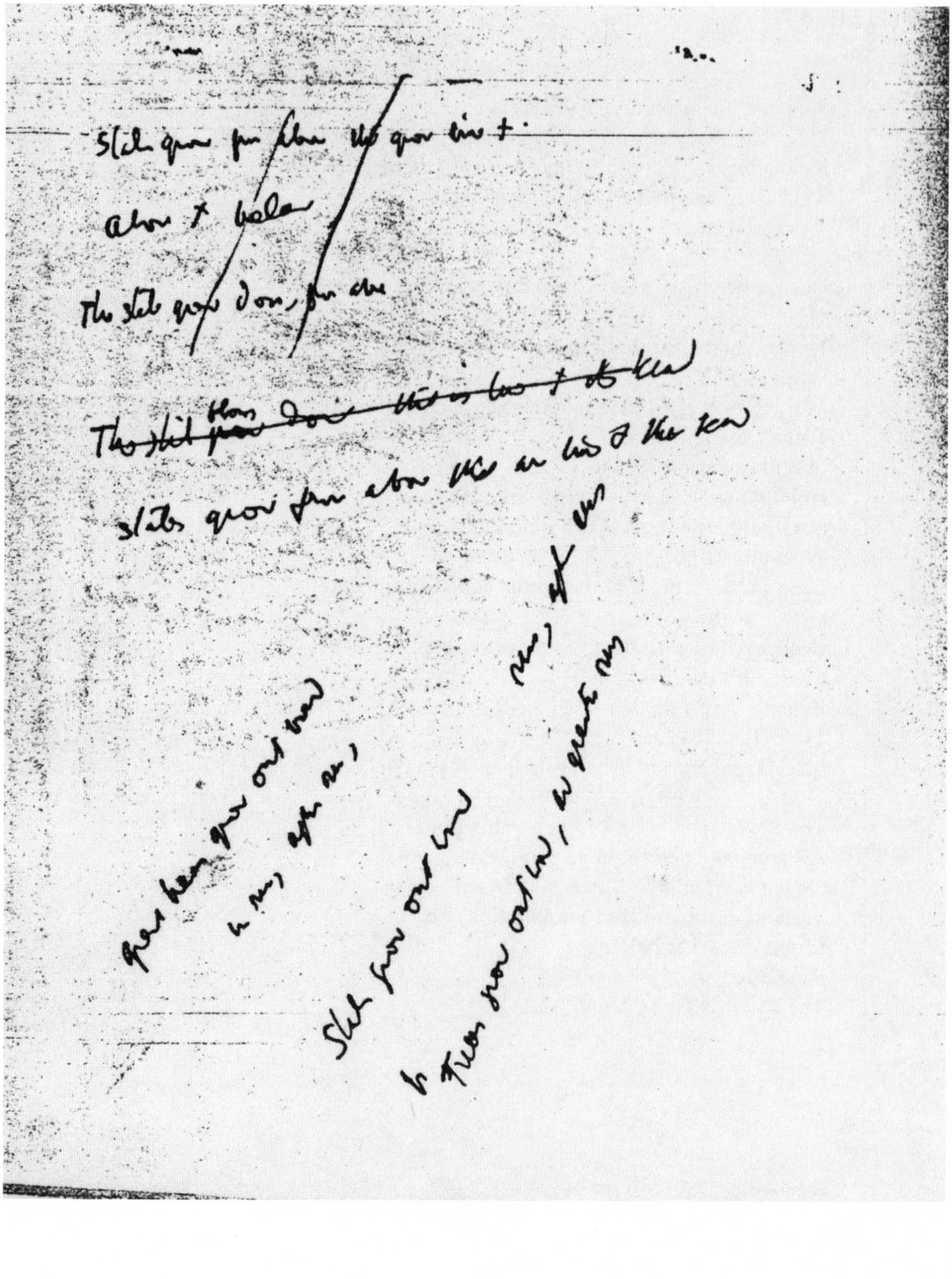

[NLI 30,547, 5ᵛ]

States grow from above that grow true to
Above to below
The state grows down, from above

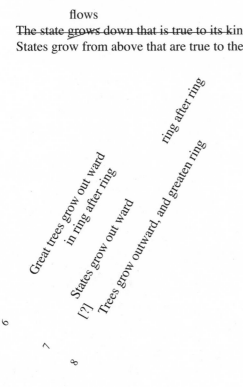

flows
~~The state grows down that is true to its kind~~
States grow from above that are true to their kind

Great trees grow out ward
in ring after ring
States grow out ward
ring after ring
[?] Trees grow outward, and greaten ring

[NLI 30,547, 6v]

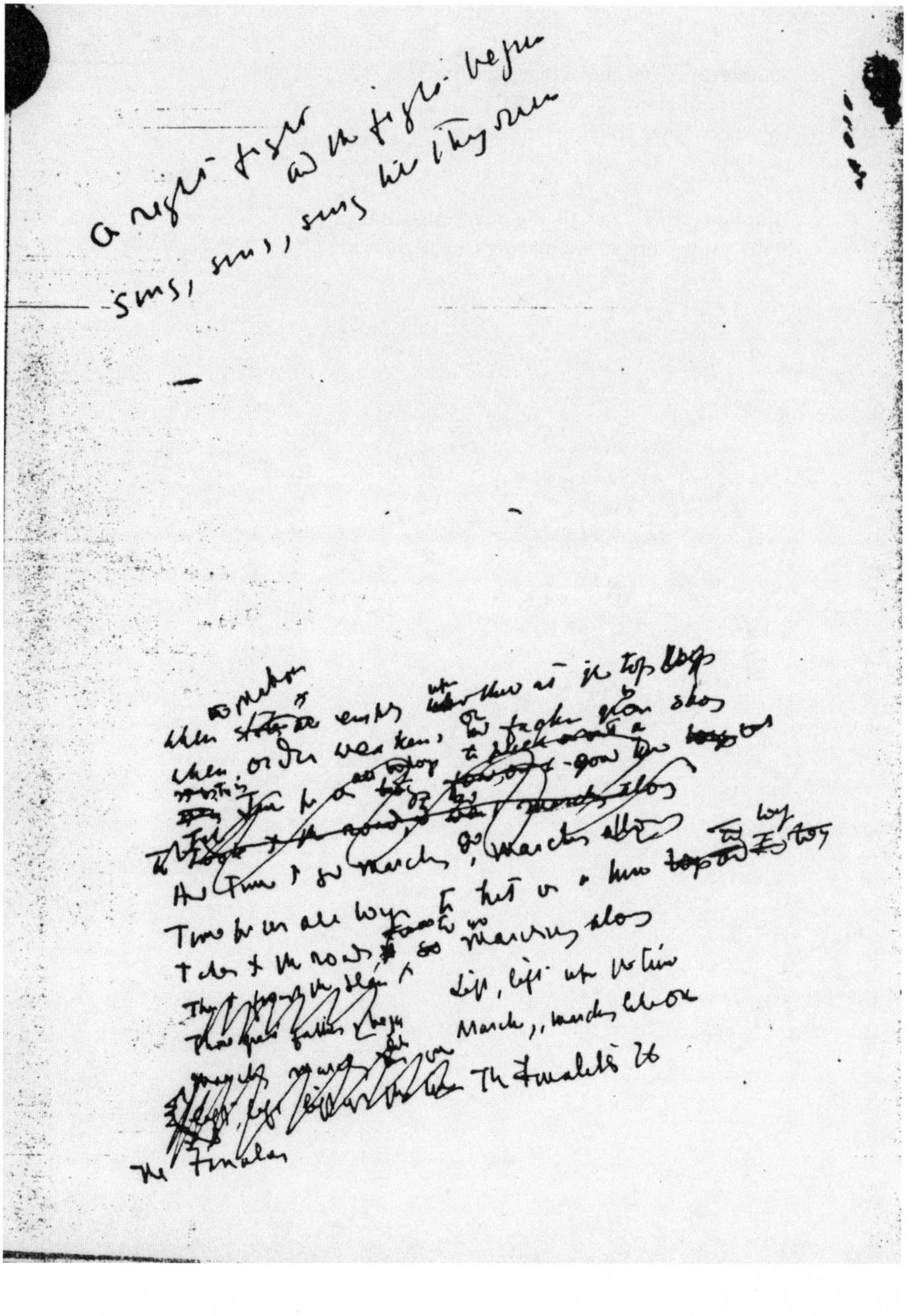

[NLI 30,547, 6v]

A right fight
And the fight begun

Sing, sing, sing till they run

the nation is up
When ~~states are~~ empty ~~upon~~ there at the top ~~top~~
or is
When order weakens ~~and~~ faction ~~grows~~ strong
~~It is~~ Time
{T all ~~be~~ boys to pick [~~?a~~] out a
It is {time for the ~~boys~~ ~~find out a~~ good tune [?] ~~boys~~ out
Take to go
~~To~~ ~~Took to the road, & went marching al~~ong
go
And Time to go marching , marching allong
~~to~~ boy
Time for us all boys to hit on a tune ~~boys and to boy~~
[~~?~~] to go
Takes to the roads ~~&~~ ^ go marching along
~~Then to finish the plan~~
~~Those great fathers began~~
~~like~~
~~Marching marching as one~~
~~lift, lift up the tune~~

Lift, lift up the tune
Marching, marching like one

The Fanatics Etc

The Fanatics

---

4 Canceled in pencil are "states" and the second "top".
13 Line 13 was clued to follow line 14; the arrow was then canceled.

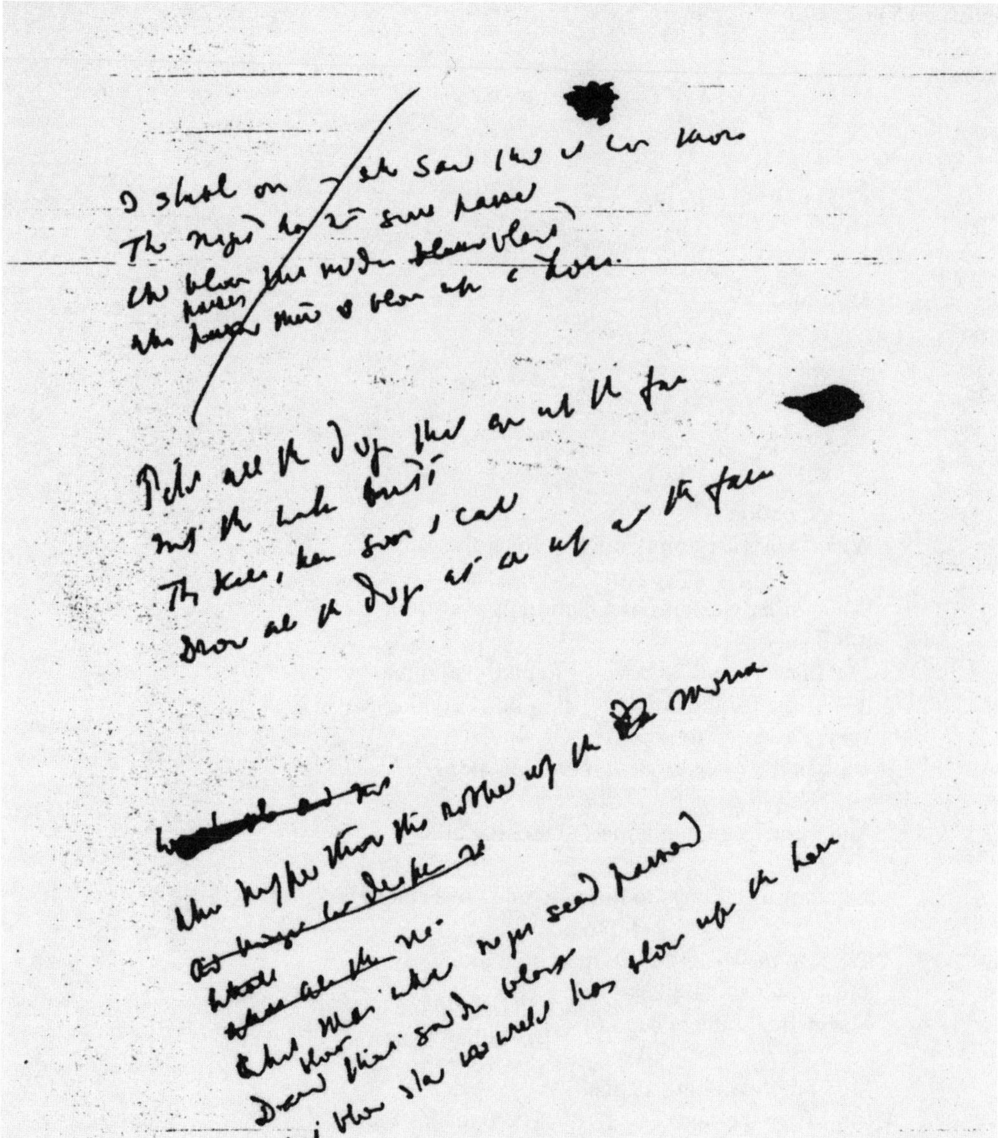

[NLI 30,547, 8[r]]

[~~?~~]
I stumble on — she said that it was morn
The night has not sure passed
Who blows that sudden [~~?blass~~] blast
passes
Who ~~passed~~ there & blows upon a horn

Pitch all the dogs that are upon the farm
Into the water bath
They kill, her goose & cat
Drown all the dogs at the up at the farm

[~~? ? ? ?~~]
What happened there that [?robbed] up the [?] morn
~~And brought [?] deeper [?]~~
~~Whole~~
~~What all the~~ [?]
What man when night seemed passed
blow
Drew that sudden blast
What blood stad ~~wre~~ wretch has blown upon the horn

Lines 1–4 and 9–16 seem to be from a different, unidentified, poem.
16 For "stad" read "starved"?

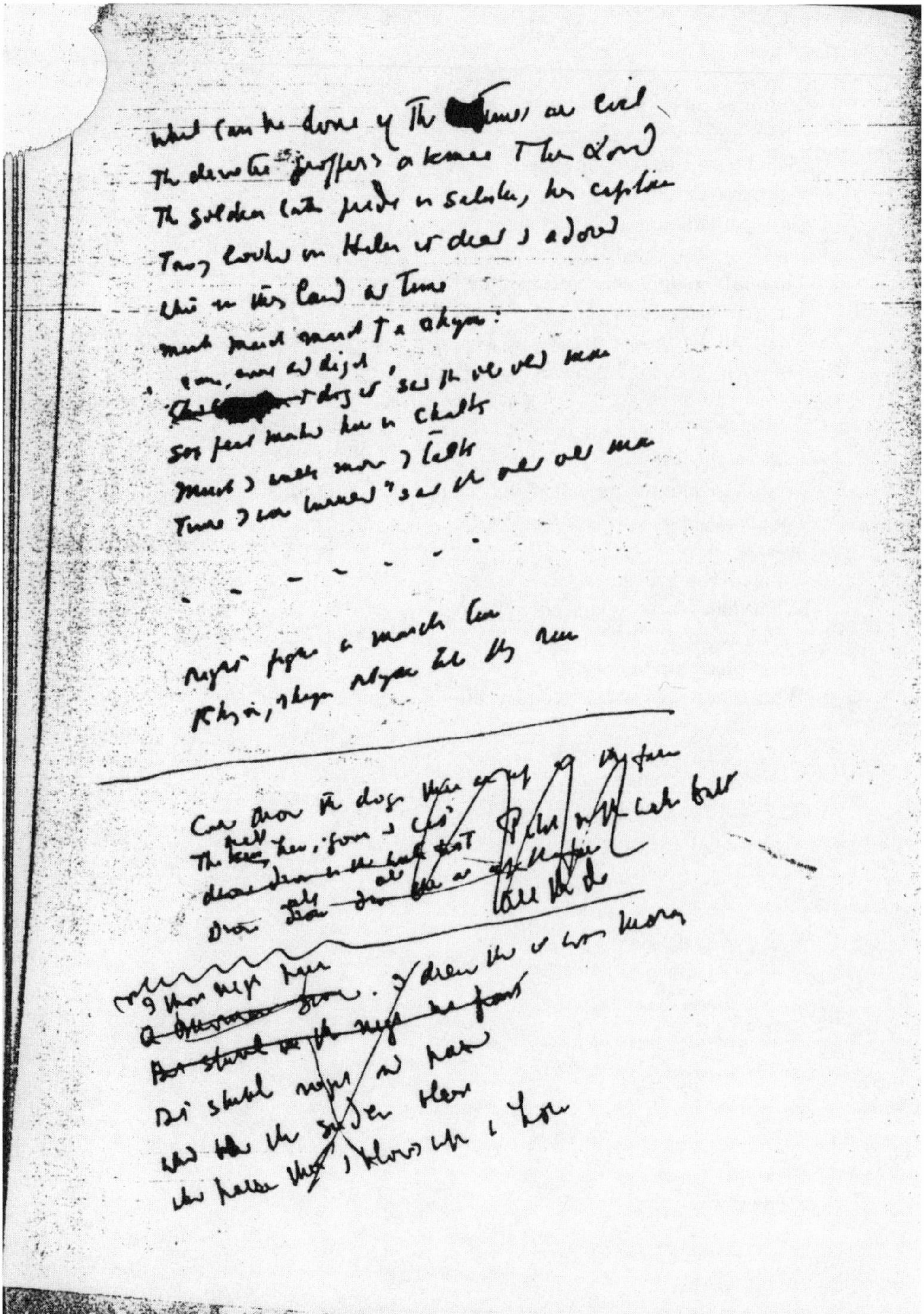

[NLI 30,547, 7v]

1 What can be done if the ~~[?]~~times are evil
2 The devotee proffers a knee to his Lord
3 The soldier takes pride in saluting his captain
4 Troy looked on Helen it died & adored
5 What in this Land and Time
6 March march march to a rhyme:
Come, come and dig it
7 ‘ ~~Who [? ?] to dig~~ it’ said the old old man
8 Six feet marked here in chalk
9 Much I walk more I talk
10 Time I were buried” said the old old man

— — — — — — —

11 right fight [?in] march time
12 Rhyme, rhyme rhyme till they run

---

kill
13 Come drown the dogs there are up at the farm
14 They ~~kill~~ her goose & cat
15 ~~drown drown in the water bath~~ Pitch in the water bath
all all
16 ~~Drown drown drown there at upon the farm~~
all the do

I [?thought] high [?]
17 ~~A moment gone~~. I dreamed that it was morn
18 ~~But stumble on the night has past~~
19 But stumble night [?and] passed
20 Who blew that sudden blast
21 Who passes there & blows upon t horn

[NLI 30,547, 7r]

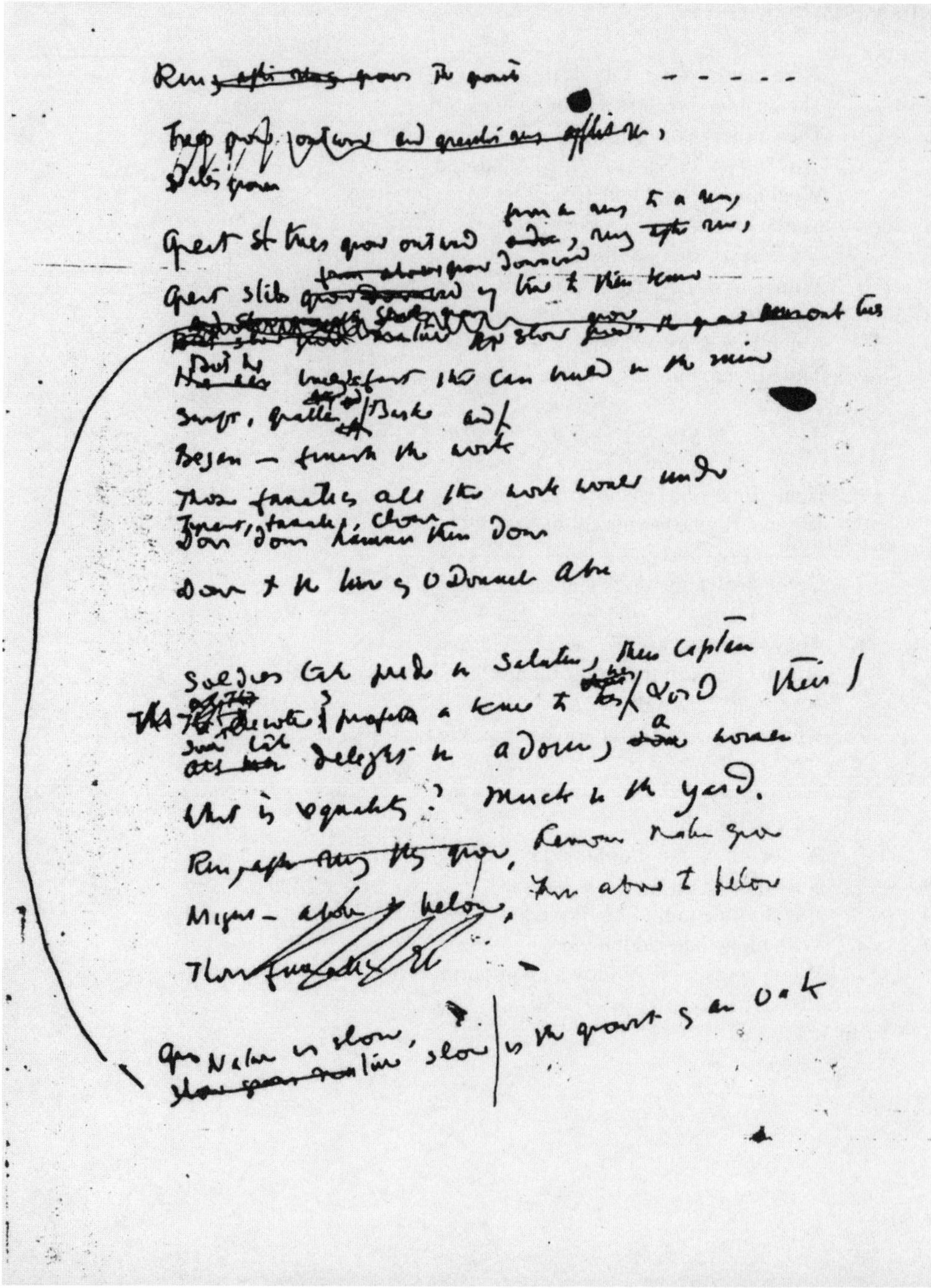

[NLI 30,547, 7r]

1 Ring ~~after ring grows~~ The growth — — — — —

2 Trees grow outward and greaten ring after ring
3 States grown
from a ring to a ring
4 Great ~~st~~ trees grow outward ~~adding~~ ring ~~after~~ ring
~~from above~~ grow downward
5 Great states ~~grow downward~~ if true to their kind
And ~~Slow grow~~ the ~~Slowly~~ grows grow
6 ~~But slow grow Nature~~ And slow ~~grows~~ the great ~~trees~~ oak trees
But he s
7 ~~He can~~ build fast that can build in the mind
~~Flood and~~
8 Swift, Grattan, Burke and
9 Began — finish the work
10 Those fanatics all the work would undo
11 Tyrant, fanatic, clown
12 Down down hammer them down
13 Down to the tune of O Donnel Abu

14 Soldiers take pride in saluting their captain
~~All the~~ his
D s r ~~their~~
15 ~~The~~ ~~The~~ devotee ~~s~~ proffe rs a knee to ~~his~~ Lord their/
Some take a
16 ~~All men~~ delight in adoring ~~some~~ woman
17 What is equality? Muck in the yard.
18 Ring ~~after ring they grow,~~ Renowned nations grow
19 ~~Might — above to below,~~ From above to below
20 ~~Those fanatics Etc~~

~~Gr~~ Nature is slow,
21 ~~Slow grows Nat~~ure slow / is the growth of an Oak

4 Probably Yeats started to write "state" and got as far as "st."
6 Line 21 is clued in to line 6.
18–20 The cancel marks in these lines are in pencil.

[HRC, 1^{r} and 3^{r}]

[1^{r}]

THREE SONGS TO THE SAME TUNE

[3^{r}]

Third Song ~~5~~ 6
~~**FIRST VERSION**~~

~~1.~~

Soldiers take pride in saluting their Captain,
The devotee proffers a knee to his Lord,
Some take delight in adoring a woman.
What's equality? – Muck in the yard:
Historic
~~**Conquering**~~ **nations grow**
From above to below.

Etc
Those fanatics ~~**all that work would undo;**~~
Down the
~~**Tyrant,**~~ **fanatic, clown** Down
Down, down, hammer them down
Down to the tune of O'Donnell Abu!

~~2.~~

When Nations are empty up there at the top,
When order has weakened or faction is strong,
Time for us all Boys, to hit on a tune Boys, /lc /lc
;
Take to the roads and go marching along.
~~**Lift, lift, lift up the tune**~~ Strong song and a swinging step.
~~**Marching, marching like one.**~~ What's there, there at the top?
Strong song and a swinging step.
What/s there, there at the top.

After the title on 1^{r}, the first and second sheets of the typescript contain the note, "In politics . . . and worth singing" (see the introduction, pp. xxviii–xxix). On 3^{r} the marks under the revised title signal all capitals.

[HRC, 2r and 3r]

[2r]

6 2.

Etc

Those fanatics all that work would undo:
Tyrant, fanatic, clown ,
Down, down, hammer them down
Down to the tune of O'Donnell Abu!

3. 7

Soldiers take pride in saluting their captain,
Where are the captains that govern mankind?
What happens a tree that has nothing within it?
O marching wind, O a blast of the wind
Marching, marching along .
Lift, lift; lift up the song.
Lifting, lifting its song.

Etc

Those fanatics all that work would undo . STET
Tyrant, fanatic, clown
Down, down, hammer them down
Down to the tune of O'Donnell Abu!

[3r]

3.

Song
SECOND ~~VERSION~~
///
~~1.~~

Grandfather said in the great Rebellion:
Hear gentlemen, ladies and all mankind,
Money is good and a girl might be better,
But good strong blows are delights to the mind.
Come march, singing this song,
Swinging, swinging along.

etc

Those fanatics ~~all that work would undo~~
Tyrant, fanatic, clown
Down, down, hammer them down
Down to the tune of O'Donnell Abu!

[HRC, 3^{r} and 4^{r}]

[3^{r} continued]

~~2.~~

A girl I had ,\\ ~~once~~ but she followed another;
Money I had and it went in the night;
I had, and it brought me to sorrow;
Strong drink ~~they say is the ruin of a man,~~
good strong
But a ~~righteous~~ cause and the blows are delight.
Come march, singing this song,
Swinging, swinging along.

[4^{r}]

4.

etc
~~we do~~
Those fanatics ~~all that work would undo;~~
Down the
~~Tyrant,~~ fanatic, ~~clown~~ down the clown,
Down, down, hammer them down
Down to the tune of O'Donnell Abu!

~~3.~~ 7

Money is good , and a girl might be better
No matter what happens or who takes the fall ,
But a good strong
~~A righteous cause~~ – ~~but~~ the rope gave a jerk there.
He said no more for his throat was too small.
Come march, singing this song
Swinging, swing along.

~~we do~~
Etc **Those fanatics ~~all that work would undo,~~**
Down the down the
~~Tyrant,~~ fanatic,^ clown,
Down, down hammer them down
Down to the tune of O'Donnell Abu!

[HRC, 5r and 6r]

[5r]

1
~~5.~~

First Song
~~THIRD VERSION~~

~~1.~~ 7

generationes
Justify all those renowned ~~generations~~ ^ ;
~~March in good order and keep to your order.~~
They left their bodies to fatten the wolves,
They left their homesteads to shelter the foxes,
Fled to far countries, or sheltered themselves
In cavern, crevice or hole,
Defending Ireland's soul.
we do
Those fanatics all that ~~work~~ would undo;
~~Dow~~ Down the
~~Tyrant,~~ fanatic, ~~clown,~~ down the clown,
Down, down, hammer them down ,
Down to the tune of O'Donnell Abu~~!~~ .

~~2.~~ 7

Justify all those renowned generations
Justify all that have sunk in their blood ,
Justify all that have died on the scaffold ,
Justify all that have fled or have stood,
Or have marched the night long,
Singing, singing a song.

Those fanatics etc

[6r]

~~6.~~ 2

Down fanatics Etc
we do
Those fanatics all that ~~work~~ would undo; ^
Down the
~~Tyrant,~~ fanatic, ~~clown,~~ Down the clown,
Down, down, hammer them down
Down to the tune of O'Donnell Abu!
Those fanatics Etc

[HRC, 6r continued]

~~3.~~ ~~1~~ 7 [?~~Stet~~]

Fail , and that history turns into rubbish,
All that great past to a trouble of fools;
Those that come after shall mock O'Donnell,
Mock at the memory of both O'Neills,
Mock Emmet~~t~~, mock Parnell,
All the renown that fell.

Etc
Those fanatics ~~all that work would undo;~~
Down the
~~Tyrant,~~ fanatic, ~~clown,~~ down the clown,
Down, down, hammer them down
Down to the tune of O'Abu!

[SIU(2), 1r and 2r]

[1r]

Soldiers take pride in saluting their Captain,
The devotee proffers a knee to his Lord,
Some take delight in adoring a woman.
What's equality? – Muck in the yard:
Victorious Historic
Conquering **~~Renowned~~ ~~Nations~~ grow**
/ **~~From above~~ to below** .
Those fanatics all that work would undo
Tyrant, fanatic, clown
Down, down, hammer them down
Down to the tune of O'Donnell Abu!

When Nations are empty up there at the top ,
When order has weakened or faction is strong ,
Time for us all Boys, to hit on a tune Boys,
Take to the roads and go marching along.
Lift, lift, lift up the tune
Marching, marching like one .
Those fanatics all that work would undo
etc etc . . . .

Soldiers take pride in saluting their captain,
Where are the captains that govern mankind?
What happens a tree that has nothing within it?
O O
~~A~~ marching wind, ~~and~~ a blast of the wind
Marching, marching along,
Lifting, lifting its song.
Those fanatics all that work would undo
etc. etc. . . . .

[2r]

~~Second Version~~

Grandfather said in the great Rebellion;
Money is good and a girl might be b

SECOND VERSION

Grandfather said in the great Rebellion:

In line 2 of the aborted start to "Second Version" the words "Money is good" were canceled by the typist with Xs.

[SIU(2), 2^{r} and 3^{r}]

[2^{r} continued]

2 **Hear gentlemen, ladies and all mankind**
3 **Money is good and a girl might be better**
4 **But good strong blows are delights to the mind**
5 **Come march, singing this song**
6 **Swinging, swinging, along**

7 **Those fanatics all that work would undo**
8 **Tyrant, fanatic, clown,**
9 **Down, down hammer them down**
10 **Down to the tune of O'Donnell Abu!**

but she followed another;
11 **A girl I had once ~~and another man took her~~**
12 **Money I had and it went in the night** ;
Strong
13 **~~And~~ drink they say is the ruin of a man** ,
But
14 **A righteous cause and the blows are delight**
15 ^**Come march, singing this song**
16–20 **etc., etc.,**

[3^{r}]

<u>**Second Version**</u>

21 **Money is good and a girl might be better**
22 **No matter what happens or who takes the fall**
23 **A righteous cause – but the rope gave a jerk there**
24 **He said no more for his throat was too small**
25 **Come march, singing this song,**
26 **etc., etc.,**

[SIU(2), 4r]

6 Copies

THIRD VERSION

March in good order and keep to your order
~~There is a moment to test a mans mettle~~;
1 ~~**Justify all those renowned generations**~~
They to fatten
2 ~~**That**~~ **left their bodies** ~~**a meal for**~~ **the wolves** ,
They to shelter
3 ~~**That**~~ **left their homesteads** ~~**a lair for**~~ **the foxes** ,
Fled to far countries, or sheltered
4 ~~**Lived banished men, or had hidden**~~ **themselves**
5 **In cavern, crevice or hole**
6 **Defending Ireland's soul** .
7 **Those fanatics all that work would undo** ;
8 **Tyrant, fanatic, clown,**
9 **Down, down, hammer them down**
10 **Down to the tune of O'Donnell Abu!**

~~This is the moment that weighs in the balance;~~
11 ~~**Justify all those renowned generations**~~ Stet
have sunk
12 **Justify all that** ~~**sank**~~ **in their blood**
^
scaffold
13 **Justify all that have died on the** ~~**gallows**~~
~~that [?fled], or have~~
14 **Justify all that have** ~~**hidden or**~~ **stood** , fled or have
15 **Or have marched the night long**
16 **Singing, singing a song**

17 **Those fanatics all that work would undo**
18–20 **etc. etc.**

[SIU(2), 4ʳ continued]

                                   that   the
21 **This is the moment ~~weighs~~ all in ~~a~~ balance** ;
22 **Keep order, leadership, nerves that are steel**
23 **Or mock the memory of the Red O'Donnell**
          at
24 **Mock ^ the memory of the great O'Neill** s
25 **Mock Emmett, mock Parnell**
26 **All the renown~~ed~~ that fell.**

27 **Those fanatics all that work would undo**
28–30 **etc. etc.**

Fail and that history turns into rubbish,
                                                   of
All that great past to a trouble ^ fools;
~~Mankind can mock at the red O'Donnell~~
Those that succeed us shall mock at O Donnell,
Mock at the memory of both O Neills,

[The Spectator, February 23, 1934, p. 276]

THREE SONGS TO THE SAME TUNE

FIRST SONG

Justify all those renowned generations;
They left their bodies to fatten the wolves,
They left their homesteads to shelter the foxes,
Fled to far countries, or sheltered themselves
In cavern, crevice or hole,
Defending Ireland's soul.

Those fanatics all that we do would undo;
Down the fanatic, down the clown,
Down, down, hammer them down,
Down to the tune of O'Donnell Abu.

Justify all those renowned generations,
Justify all that have sunk in their blood,
Justify all that have died on the scaffold,
Justify all that have fled or have stood,
Or have marched the night long,
Singing, singing a song.

Those fanatics [all that we do would undo;
Down the fanatic, down the clown,
Down, down, hammer them down,
Down to the tune of O'Donnell Abu.]

In *FMM* the refrains are in italics. In *The Spectator*, a note follows the title in column one (see introduction, pp. xxviii–xxix, above), and the verses are all in column two. Also in *The Spectator*, "Those fanatics, &c." is substitued for the refrain in "First Song" at lines 17 and 27, in the "Second Song" at lines 7, 17, and 27, and in "Third Song" at lines 7 and 17. I have supplied the full refrain, in brackets, so as to note variants.

subtitle II *rev from* First *NLI 30,004* II *P, Chicago(2), KGCT'34, KGCT'35, FMM*

3 shelter] fatten *P, Chicago(2), KGCT'34, KGCT'35, FMM*

5 crevice or] crevice, *P, Chicago(2), KGCT'34, KGCT'35, FMM*

7–10 *canceled, replaced by the note* Fierce young woman *in Mrs. Yeats's hand, NLI 30,004*
"Drown all the dogs," said the fierce young woman,
"They killed my goose and a cat.
Drown, drown, in the water butt,
Drown all the dogs," said the fierce young woman. *P; so Chicago(2), KGCT'34, KGCT'35, FMM but* 7, 10 dogs' said *KGCT'34, KGCT'35* 9 water-butt *FMM*

14 stood,] stood *P, Chicago(2)* fled or] fled or *rev to* fled, that *NLI 30,020$_2$* fled, that *KGCT'34, KGCT'35, FMM* or *rev to* stood *rev to* or *NLI 30,020$_1$*

15 long,] long *P, Chicago(2)* Stood or marched the night long *KGCT'34, KGCT'35, FMM*

17–20 *canceled NLI 30,004*
"Drown all the dogs," said the fierce young woman,
"They killed my goose and a cat.
Drown, drown in the water butt,
Drown all the dogs," said the fierce young woman. *P; Chicago(2), so KGCT'34, KGCT'35, FMM but* 17, 20 dogs' *Chicago(2), KGCT'34, KGCT'35* 19 water-butt *FMM*

[*The Spectator*, February 23, 1934, p. 276 continued]

Fail, and that history turns into rubbish,
All that great past to a trouble of fools;
Those that come after shall mock O'Donnell,
Mock at the memory of both O'Neills,
Mock Emmet, mock Parnell,
All the renown that fell.

Those fanatics [all that we do would undo;
Down the fanatic, down the clown,
Down, down, hammer them down,
Down to the tune of O'Donnell Abu.]

SECOND SONG

Grandfather said in the great Rebellion:
Hear gentlemen, ladies and all mankind,
Money is good and a girl might be better,
But good strong blows are delights to the mind.
Come march, singing this song,
Swinging, swinging along.

Those fanatics [all that we do would undo;
Down the fanatic, down the clown,
Down, down, hammer them down,
Down to the tune of O'Donnell Abu.]

---

23 mock] mock at *P, Chicago(2), KGCT'34, KGCT'35, FMM* O'Donnell,] O'Donnell *Chicago(2), KGCT'34, KGCT'35*

25 Parnell,] Parnell: *P, Chicago(2), KGCT'34, KGCT'35, FMM*

27–30 "Drown all the dogs," said the fierce young woman,
"They killed my goose and a cat.
Drown, drown in the water butt,
Drown all the dogs," said the fierce young woman. *P; so Chicago(2), KGCT'34, KGCT'35, FMM but* 27, 30 dogs' *Chicago(2), KGCT'34, KGCT'35* 29 water-butt *FMM*

---

subtitle First I *NLI 30,004* I *P, Chicago(2), KGCT'34, KGCT'35, FMM*

1 Grandfather sang it under the gallows *P, Chicago(2), KGCT'34, KGCT'35; so FMM but* gallows:

2 "Hear . . . mankind *P, Chicago(2), KGCT'34, KGCT'35* 'Hear, . . . mankind: *FMM*

3 better,] better *P, Chicago(2), KGCT'34, KGCT'35*

4 mind." *P, Chicago(2), KGCT'34, KGCT'35, FMM*

5–6 There, standing on the cart
He sang it from his heart. *P, Chicago(2), KGCT'34, KGCT'35, FMM*

7 Those fanatics, &c. *canceled and replaced by the note* repeat – No II / Chorus *in Mrs. Yeats's hand NLI 30,004*

8 clown; *P, Chicago(2), KGCT'34, KGCT'35, FMM*

In NLI 30,004, in the title, the words "First I" are in Mrs. Yeats's hand.

[*The Spectator*, February 23, 1934, p. 276 continued]

A girl I had, but she followed another;
Money I had and it went in the night;
Strong drink I had, and it brought me to sorrow;
But a good strong cause and the blows are delight.
Come march, singing this song,
Swinging, swinging along.

Those fanatics [all that we do would undo;
Down the fanatic, down the clown,
Down, down, hammer them down,
Down to the tune of O'Donnell Abu.]

Money is good, and a girl might be better
No matter what happens or who take the fall,
But a good strong cause—the rope gave a jerk there,
He said no more for his throat was too small.
Come march, singing this song,
Swinging, swinging along.

Those fanatics [all that we do would undo;
Down the fanatic, down the clown,
Down, down, hammer them down,
Down to the tune of O'Donnell Abu.]

THIRD SONG

Soldiers take pride in saluting their Captain,
The devotee proffers a knee to his Lord,

---

11 "A . . . another, *P, Chicago(2), KGCT'34, KGCT'35, FMM*
12 night, *P, Chicago(2), KGCT'34, KGCT'35, FMM* had, *FMM*
13 sorrow, *P, Chicago(2), KGCT'34, KGCT'35, FMM*
14 and blows are delight." *P, Chicago(2), KGCT'34, KGCT'35, FMM*
15 All there caught up the tune: *P, Chicago(2), KGCT'34, KGCT'35, FMM*
16 "On, on, my darling man." *P, Chicago(2), KGCT'34, KGCT'35, FMM*
17 &c. *canceled and* repeat *written in by Mrs. Yeats NLI 30,004*
18 clown; *P, Chicago(2), KGCT'34, KGCT'35, FMM*
21 "Money is good and *P, Chicago(2), KGCT'34, KGCT'35, FMM* better, *FMM*
22 or] and *P, Chicago(2), KGCT'34, KGCT'35, FMM*
23 cause"— . . . there *P, Chicago(2), KGCT'34, KGCT'35, FMM*
24 No more sang he . . . small; *P, Chicago(2), KGCT'34, KGCT'35; so FMM but* he,
25 But he kicked before he died; *P; so Chicago(2), KGCT'34, KGCT'35, FMM but* died, died; *rev to* died, *NLI 30,020*$_2$
26 He did it out of pride. *P, Chicago(2), KGCT'34, KGCT'35, FMM*
27 Those fanatics, &c. *canceled and* repeat *written in by Mrs. Yeats NLI 30,004*
28 clown; *P, Chicago(2), KGCT'34, KGCT'35, FMM*

---

subtitle III *P, Chicago(2), KGCT'34, KGCT'35, NYPL(2), FMM*
1 The soldier takes . . . his Captain, *P, Chicago(2), KGCT'34, KGCT'35, FMM*

[*The Spectator*, February 23, 1934, p. 276 continued]

Some take delight in adoring a woman.
What's equality?—Muck in the yard:
Historic Nations grown
From above to below.

Those fanatics [all that we do would undo;
Down the fanatic, down the clown,
Down, down hammer them down,
Down to the tune of O'Donnell Abu.]

When Nations are empty up there at the top,
When order has weakened or faction is strong,
Time for us all boys, to hit on a tune boys,
Take to the roads and go marching along;
Lift, every mother's son,
Lift, lift, lift up the tune.

Those fanatics [all that we do would undo;
Down the fanatic, down the clown,
Down, down, hammer them down,
Down to the tune of O'Donnell Abu.]

Soldiers take pride in saluting their captain,
Where are the captains that govern mankind?

---

3 Crowds back a mare that is bred of the best *rev to* Some back a mare thrown from a thoroughbred *NLI 30,020*$_1$ Some back a mare thrown from a thoroughbred *P, Chicago(2), FMM; so KGCT'34, KGCT'35 but* thorough-bred,

4 Troy looked on Helen, it died and adored; *P, KGCT'34, KGCT'35*
backed its Troy,
Troy looked on Helen, it died and adored; *NYPL(2), Chicago(2)*
Troy backed its Helen; Troy died and adored; *FMM*

5–6 Great nations, blossom above;
A slave bows down to a slave. *P, Chicago(2), KGCT'34, KGCT'35, FMM*

7 Those fanatics, &c. *canceled NLI 30,004*

7–10 Who'd care to dig'em," said the old, old man,
"Those six feet marked in chalk;
Much I talk, more I walk;
Time I were buried," said the old, old man. *P; so Chicago(2), KGCT'34, KGCT'35, FMM but* 7 dig'em said 9 walk; 10 buried' said *Chicago(2); KGCT'34, KGCT'35 as Chicago(2) but* walk, 8 chalk? *FMM*

11 Nations] nations *Chicago(2), KGCT'34, KGCT'35, FMM*

13 Time for us all to pick out a good tune, *P, Chicago(2), KGCT'34, KGCT'35, FMM*

14 along. *P, Chicago(2), KGCT'34, KGCT'35, FMM*

15 March, march—How does it run— *P, Chicago(2), KGCT'34, KGCT'35; so FMM but* run?—

16 O any old words to a tune. *P, Chicago(2), KGCT'34, KGCT'35, FMM*

17 dig'em *rev to* dig for e'm *NLI 30,020*$_2$

17–20 Who'd care to dig'em," said the old, old man,
"Those six feet marked in chalk;
Much I talk, more I walk,
Time I were buried," said the old, old man. *P; so Chicago(2), KGCT'34, KGCT'35, FMM but* 17 dig'em' said 20 buried' said *Chicago(2), KGCT'34, KGCT'35* 18 chalk? 19 walk; *Chicago(2), KGCT'34, FMM*

21 Captain, *KGCT'35, FMM*

[*The Spectator*, February 23, 1934, p. 276 continued]

What happens a tree that has nothing within it?
O marching wind, O a blast of the wind
Marching, marching along.
Lift, lift, lift up the song.

Those fanatics all that we do would undo;
Down the fanatic, down the clown,
Down, down, hammer them down,
Down to the tune of O'Donnell Abu.

---

23 happens to a *KGCT'35*
24 wind, *P, Chicago(2), KGCT'34, KGCT'35, FMM*
25 along, *P*
26 March, march, lift . . . song; *P, Chicago(2), KGCT'34, KGCT'35, FMM*
27–30 Who'd care to dig'em," said the old, old man,
"Those six feet marked in chalk;
Much I talk, more I walk;
Time I were buried," said the old, old man. *P; so Chicago(2), KGCT'34, KGCT'35, FMM but* 27 dig'em said 29 walk; 30 buried' said *Chicago(2); KGCT'34, KGCT'35 as Chicago(2) but* walk, 28 chalk? *FMM*

[NLI 8769, pp. 11 and 12]

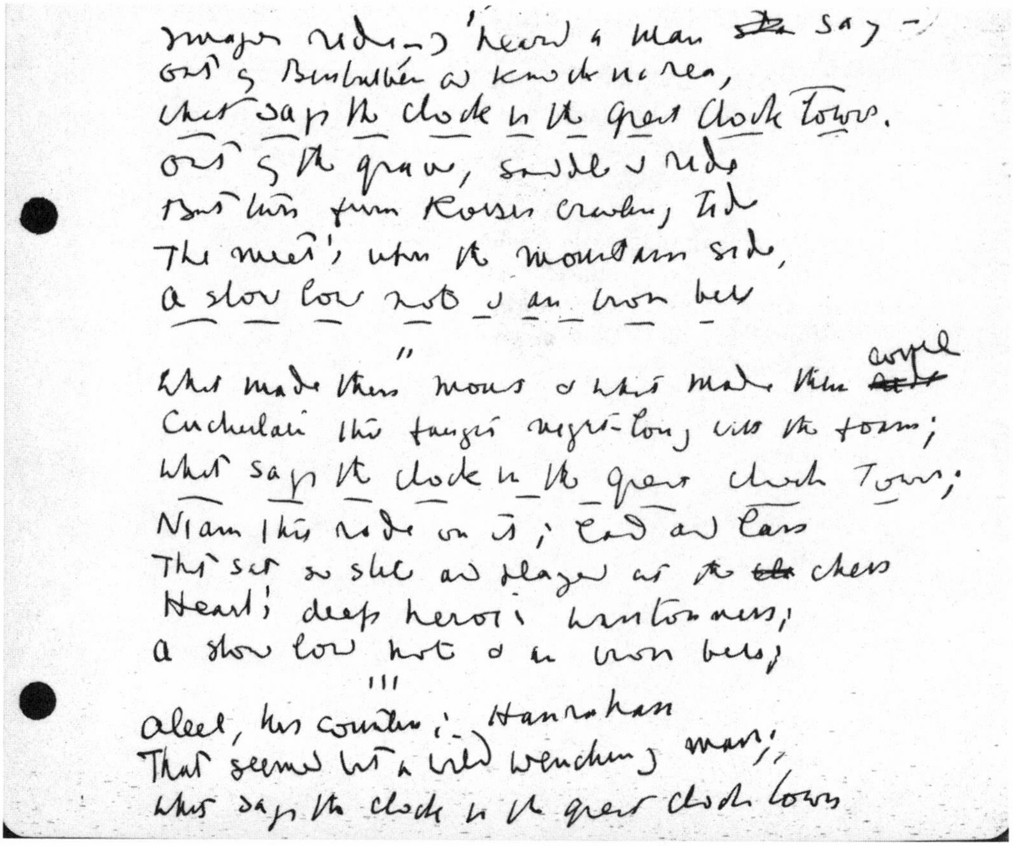

Images riding I heard a man say —
Out of Ben Bulben and Knocknarea,
What says the clock in the great clock tower.
Out of the grave, saddle & ride
But turn from horses crawling till
The meet; upon the mountain side,
A slow low note & an iron bell

II

What made them mount & what made them couple
Cuchulain that fought night-long with the foam;
What says the clock in the great clock tower;
Niam that rode on it; Lad and Lass
That sat so still and played at the chess
Heart; deep heroic wantonness;
A slow low note & an iron bell;

III

Aleel, his countrymen; Hanrahan
That seemed but a wild wenching man;
What says the clock in the great clock tower

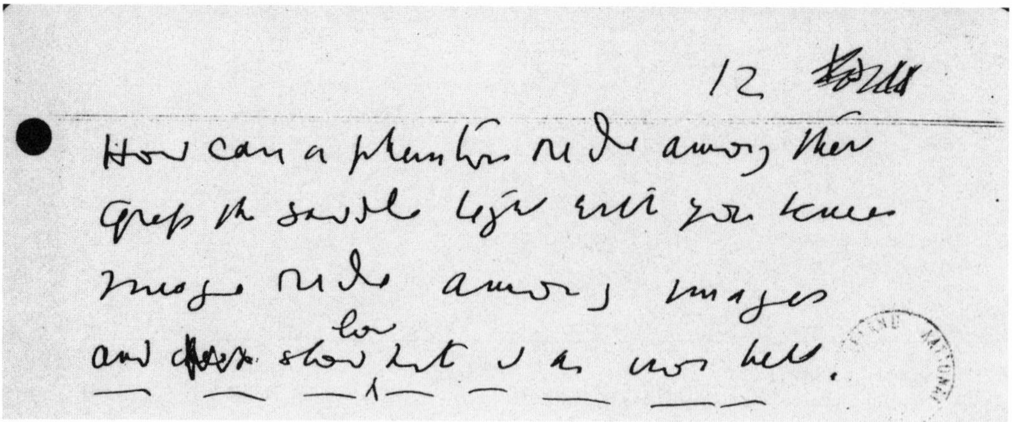

12

How can a phantom ride among them
Grip the saddle tight with your knees
Images ride among images
And slow low note & an iron bell.

ALTERNATIVE SONG FOR THE SEVERED HEAD IN
THE KING OF THE GREAT CLOCK TOWER

[NLI 8769, pp. 11 and 12]

[p. 11]

Images ride – I heard a man ~~sta~~ say –
Out of Ben Bulben and Knocknarea,
What says the clock in the Great Clock Tower.
Out of the grave, saddle & ride
But turn from the Rosses crawling tide
The meet's upon the mountain side,
A slow low note & an iron bell
II   come
What made them mount & what made them ~~ride~~
Cuchulain that fought night-long with the foam;
What says the clock in the Great Clock Tower;
Niam that rode on it; lad and lass
That sat so still and played at the ~~cle~~ chess
Heart's deep heroic wantonness;
A slow low note & an iron bell;
III
Aleel, his Countess; Hanrahan
That seemed but a wild wenching man;
What says the clock in the Great Clock Tower

[p. 12]

How can a phantom ride among these
Grip the saddle tight with your knees
Images ride among images
low
And ~~deep~~ slow note & an iron bell.
^

found in NLI 8769, pp. 11 and 12 *transcribed above*
BC, 4^{v} *transcribed below*
BC, 40^{r}
published in *Life and Letters*, November 1934, p. 145 *transcribed below*
KGCT'34
KGCT'35
FMM

19 As the first "t" of "tight" is uncrossed, possibly "light" is meant, but "tight" seems more likely.

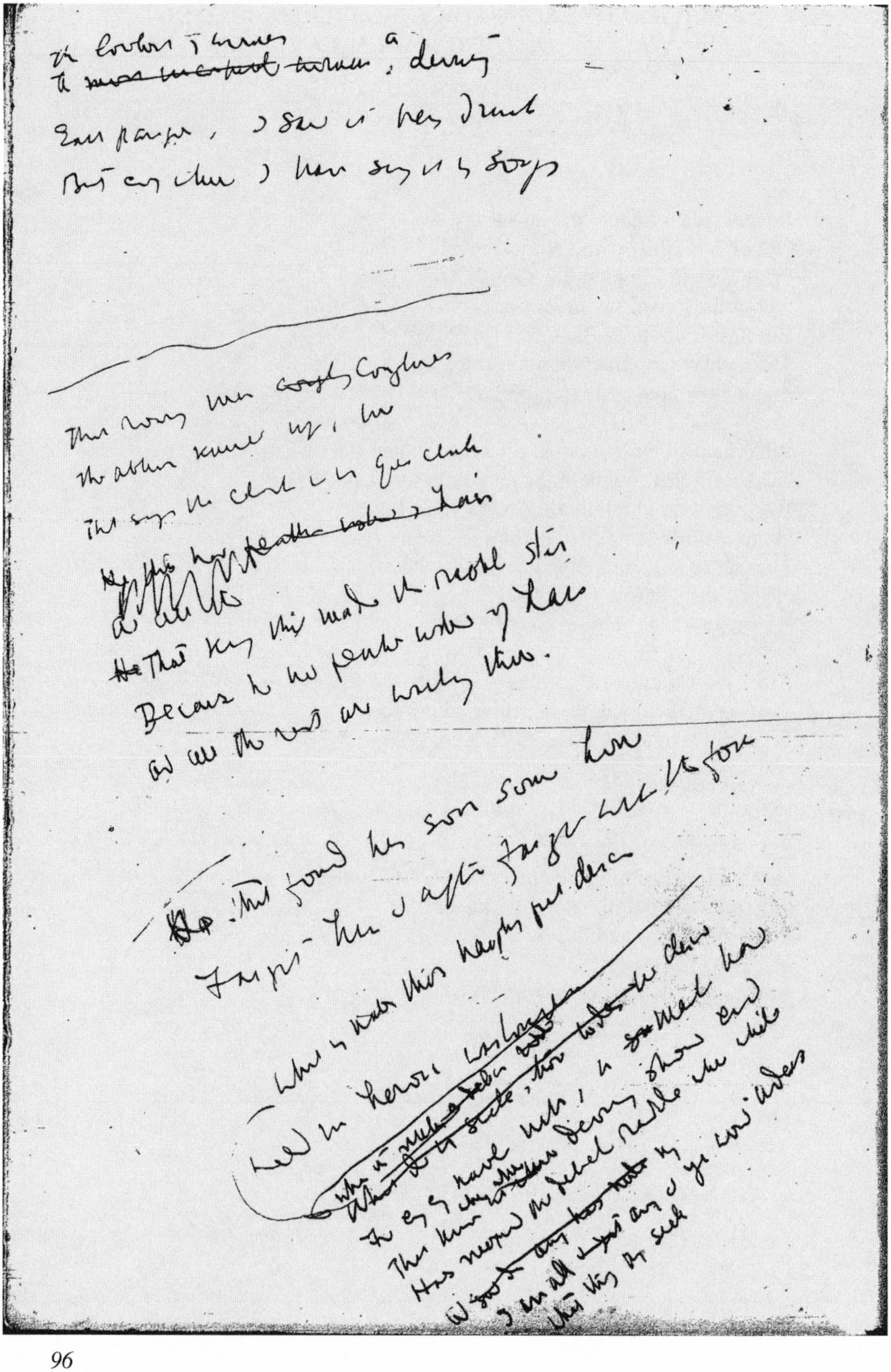

[BC, 4v]

That roaring man [?~~Congles~~] [?Conglures]
The ablest knight upon a time
That says the clock in the great clock
He that had ~~feathers instead of hair~~
And all the
~~He~~ That King that made the people stare
Because he had feathers instead of hair
And all the rest are waiting there.

He that found his son some home
Fought him & after fought with the foam

What is makes those haughty feet descend

Held in heroic wantonness

The text is in the middle of the page. Above it are a few lines of a draft of *The King of the Great Clock Tower*. Below it are some lines from the poem that ends *The King of the Great Clock Tower*.

3 For "That" read "What"?

9 For "some" read "come"?

11 This line is not part of the poem. It is clued in from the end of *The King of the Great Clock Tower* below.

Alternative Song for the Severed Head

[*Life and Letters* (London) 11 (November 1934):145]

[*untitled in text of play*]

Images ride, I heard a man say,
Out of Benbulben and Knocknareagh,
What says the Clock in the Great Clock Tower?
Out of the grave. Saddle and ride
But turn from Rosses' crawling tide,
The meet's upon the mountain side.
A slow low note and an iron bell.

What made them mount and what made them come,
Cuchulain that fought night long with the foam;
What says the Clock in the Great Clock Tower?
Niam that rode on it; lad and lass
That sat so still and played at the chess--
What but heroic wantonness.
A slow low note and an iron bell.

Aleel, his Countess; Hanrahan
That seemed but a wild wenching man;
What says the Clock in the Great Clock Tower?
And all alone comes riding there
The King that could make his people stare,
Because he had feathers instead of hair.
A slow low note and an iron bell.

---

title *untitled KGCT'34, KGCT'35* "ALTERNATIVE SONG FOR THE SEVERED HEAD IN *THE KING OF THE GREAT CLOCK TOWER*" *FMM*
1 SADDLE and ride, *FMM*
2 Ben Bulben and Knocknarea, *FMM*
4 All those tragic characters ride *FMM*
8 What brought them there so far from their home, *FMM*
9 foam, *FMM*
10 *Tower. KGCT'34, KGCT'35*
12 chess? *KGCT'34, KGCT'35, FMM*
13 wantonness *KGCT'35* wantonness? *FMM*
13/ Tune by Arthur Duff. *FMM*

At the foot of BC, 40^r (see p. 222, below) appears the following note in Yeats's hand:

Correction in Clock Tower Song – p. 9
sadl & ride' — I heard a man say
Out of ~~Ben Bul~~ Ben Bulben & Knocknarea
those
All ~~the~~ tragic characters ride
But turn from Ros
[?]
What brought them there, so far from their home

These corrections were made in *FMM*.

TWO SONGS REWRITTEN FOR THE TUNE'S SAKE

I

[*Plays in Prose and Verse* (New York, 1924), pp. 34–35]

My pretty Paistin is my heart's desire,
Yet I am shrunken to skin and bone
For all my toil has had for its hire
Is drinking her health when lone, alone—

Oh I would think that I had my fee,
Though I am shrunken to bone and skin,
Could I but drink, my love on my knee
Between two barrels at the inn.

Nine nights I lay in longing sore
Between two bushes under the rain;
Thinking to meet my love once more
I cried and whistled but vain, all vain.

---

found in NLI 30,547,8^{v} *transcribed below*
BC, 35^{r} *transcribed below*
FMM-HRC, pp. 56–57 *transcribed below*
published in *Plays in Prose and Verse* (New York, 1924), pp. 34–35 *transcribed above*
Collected Plays (London, 1934)
A Full Moon in March (1935)
Nine One-Act Plays (London, 1937)

The song is untitled in *The Pot of Broth*, from which I have excerpted it, providing new line numbers.

[NLI 30,547, 8v]

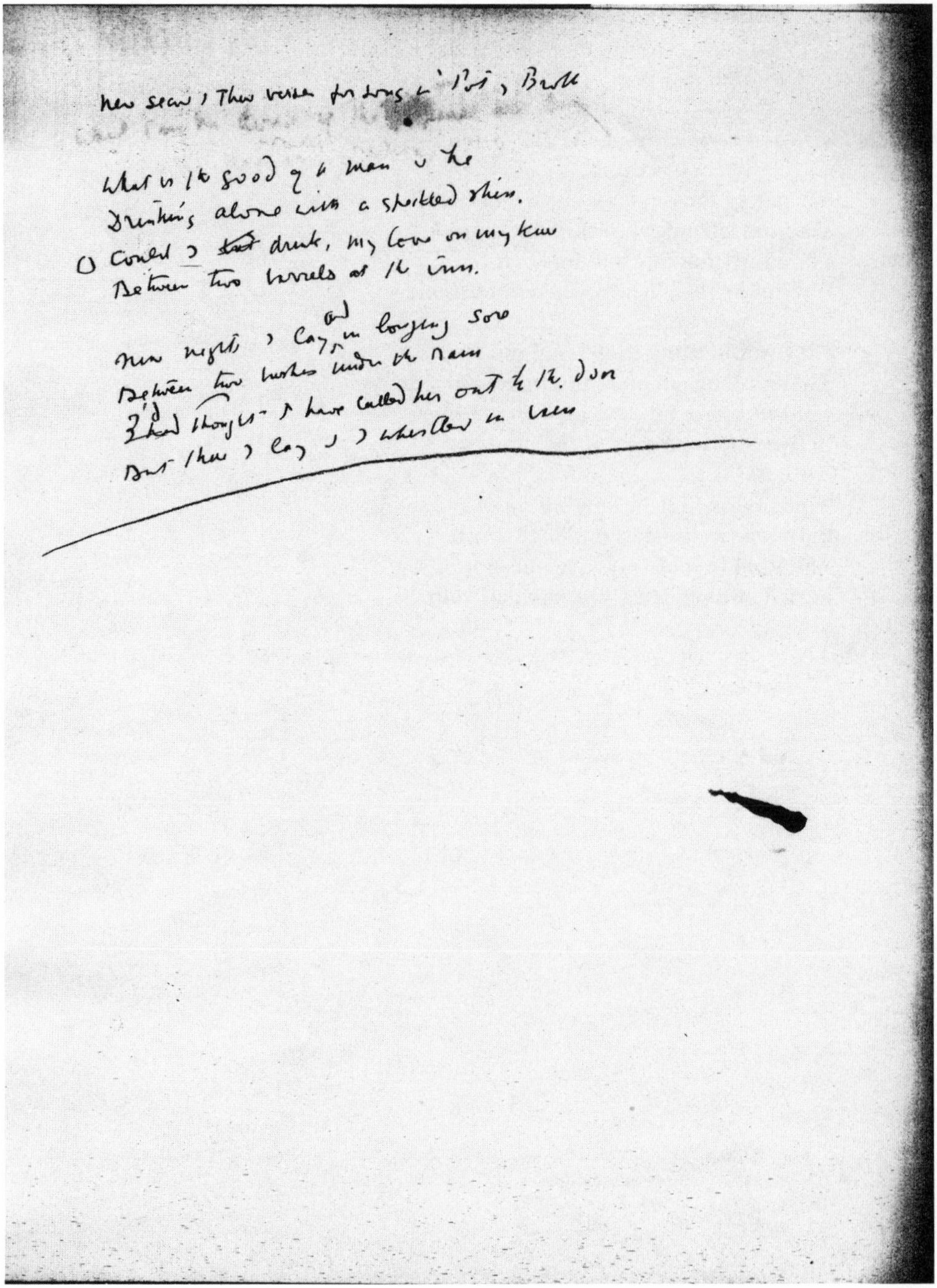

new scene / Three verses for song in 'Pot of Broth

What is the good of a man & he
Drinking alone with a speckled shin.
O could I ~~[illegible]~~ drink, my love on my knee
Between two barrels at the inn.

Nine nights I lay in longing sore
Between two bushes under the rain
I'd thought I have called her out to the door
But there I lay & I whistled in vain

[NLI 30,547, 8v]

New Second of Three Verses for Song in 'Pot of Broth

What is the good of a man & he
Drinking alone with a speckled shin.
O could I ~~but~~ drink, my love on my knee
Between two barrels at the inn.

                    and
Nine nights I lay ^ in longing sore
Between two bushes under the rain
I'd
~~I had~~ thought to have called her out to the door
But there I lay and I whistled in vain

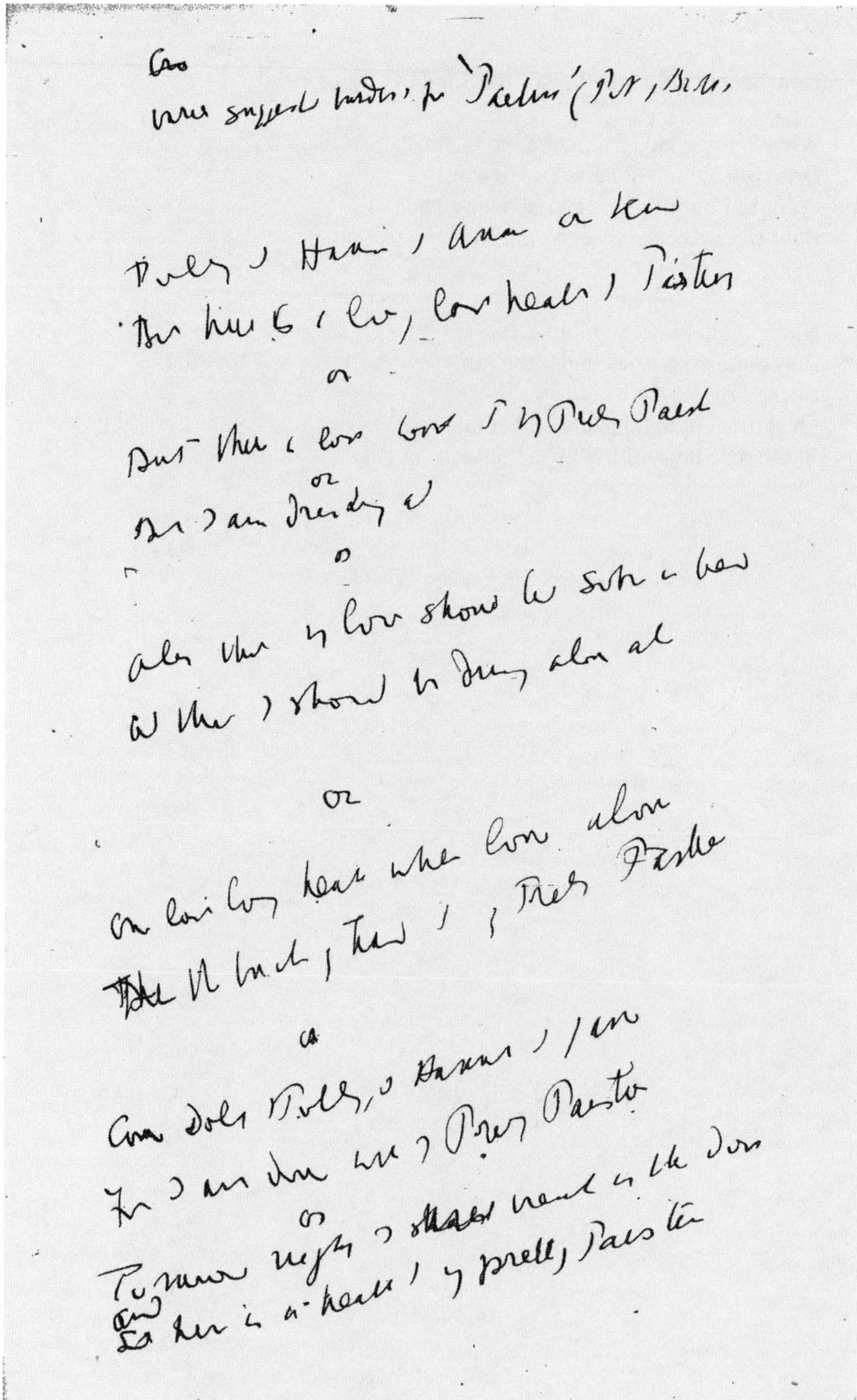

[BC, 35r]

~~[?]~~

Various suggested burdens for 'Paistin' (Pot of Broth)

1 Dolly & Hannah & Ann are kind
2 But here is a long last health to Paistin
3 or
4 But there a last word to my pretty Paistin
5 or
6 But I am drinking al
or
7 Alas that my love should be sick in bed
8 And that I should be drinking alone al
9 or
10 One last long health [?when] lone alone
{At
11 {[?] the touch of hand [?of] [?my] Pretty Paistin
12 or
13 Come Doll & Polly, & Hannah & Jane
14 For I am done with [?my] Pretty Paistin
15 or
{shall
16 Tomorrow night I {[?should] break in the door
And
17 So here is a health to my pretty Paistin

With "al" in lines 6 and 8 Yeats probably shortens "alone."

Two Songs Rewritten for the Tune's Sake

[*FMM*-HRC, pp. 56–57]

[p. 56]

I

A bright haired slut
~~That blonde girl~~ there is my heart's desire,
But I am shrunken to skin and bone,
For all my toil has had for its hire
Is drinking her health when lone, alone—
Aro, aro,
Tomorrow night I will break in the door.

What is the good of man if he
Live lone, alone with a speckled shin?
O could I drink, my love on my knee,
Between two barrels at the inn.
Aro, aro
Tomorrow night I will break in the door.

[p. 57]

Nine nights I lay and in longing sore
Between two bushes under the rain;
I had thought to have called her out to the door,
But there I lay and I whistled in vain.
Aro, aro,
Tomorrow night I will break in the door.

From *The Pot of Broth.*
Tune: Paistin Finn.

---

1 In probably the latest revision of this line Yeats has penciled in the change indicated. Obviously Yeats could not have meant this to be a revision of the play but only of the song. The purpose of the song in the play is for the Tramp to flatter the character Sibby, who could not be expected to accept "slut."

The version in *FMM* (1935) is the same as that in *FMM*-HRC (without the holograph revision) and with slight variants in punctuation in *Nine One-Act Plays* (London, 1937). In *Collected Plays* (1952), Mrs. Yeats, no doubt on the basis of some authorization from her husband, altered all three refrains, ll. 5–6, 11–12, and 17–18.

In *Collected Plays* (1934), p. 100, the equivalent of line 1 begins "My pretty Paistin is," as in *Plays in Prose and Verse*.

2 But I am] Yet am I *Collected Plays (1934)*

5–6, 11–12, 17–18 Oro, oro!
To-morrow night I will break down the door. *(all in italics) Poems (1949)*

8 Live lone, alone] Drinking alone *Collected Plays (1934)*

II

[*Plays in Prose and Verse* (New York, 1924), p. 399]

**O would that I were an old beggar
Without a friend on this earth
But a thieving rascally cur,
A beggar blind from his birth;
Or anything else but a man
Lying along on a bed
Remembering a woman's beauty
Alone with a crazy head.**

---

found in BC, 35^{v}, 36^{r} *transcribed below*
NYPL(1) *transcribed below*
published in *Plays in Prose and Verse* (New York, 1924), p. 399 *transcribed above*
Times

The song is untitled in *The Player Queen*, from which I have excerpted it, providing new line numbers.

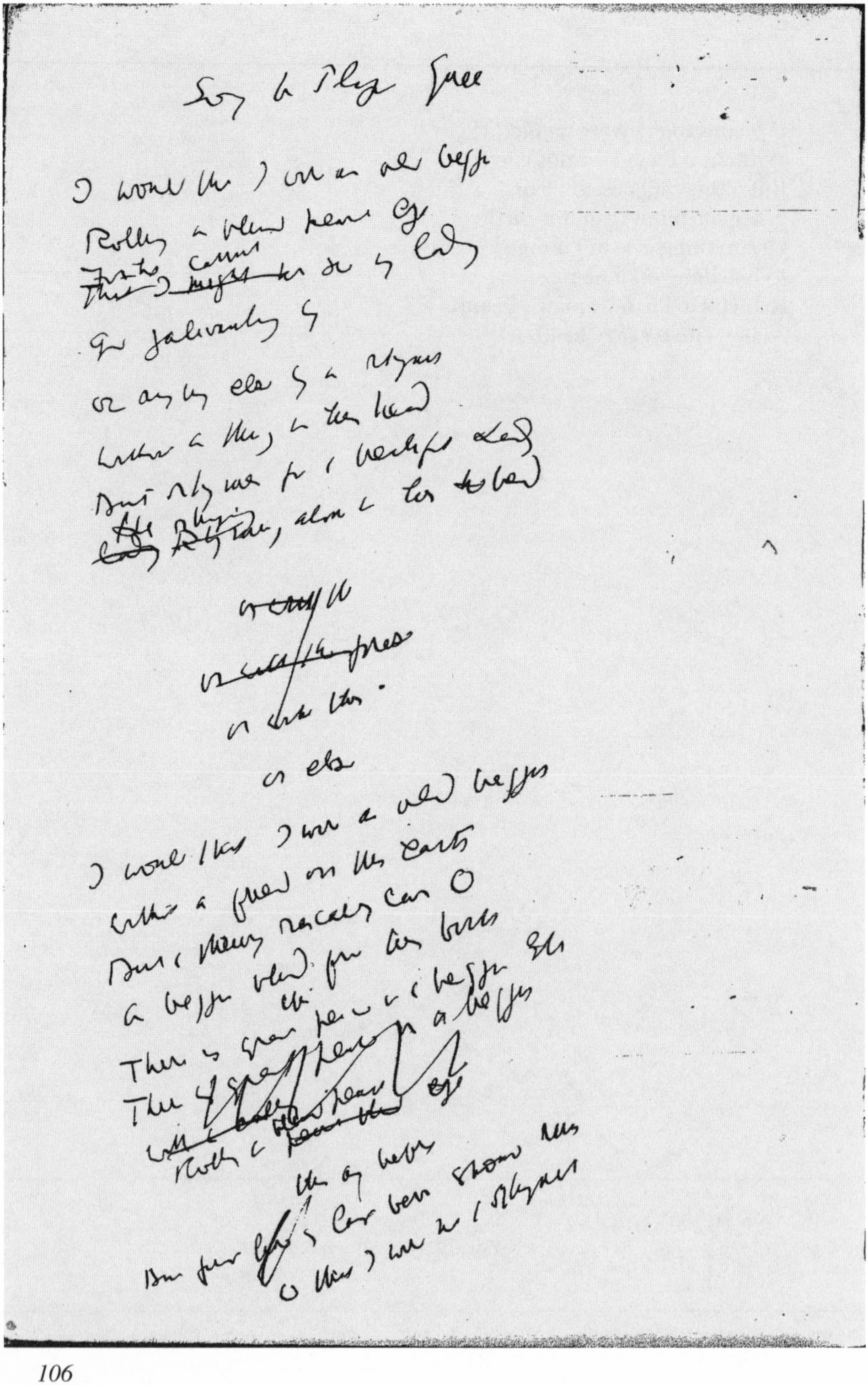
Song to Play Guee
I would that I were an old beggar
Rolling a blind pearl eye
~~That I might~~ For he cannot see my lady
Go gallivanting by
Or anything else but a rhymer
Without a thing in his head
But rhymes for a beautiful lady
~~Lady~~ He rhyming alone in his bed
or [illegible]
or [illegible]
or [illegible]
or else
I would that I were an old beggar
Without a friend on this earth
But a thieving rascally cur O
But a beggar blind from his birth
There is great pleasure in a beggar
Rolling a blind pearl eye
But few things can bear
O that I were but a rhymer

[BC, 35^{v}]

Song for Player Queen

I would that I were an old beggar
Rolling a blind pearl eye
For he cannot
~~That I might n~~ot see my lady
Go gallivanting by
or anything else but a rhymer
Without a thing in his head
But rhymes for a beautiful Lady
He rhyming
~~lady~~ ~~Rhyming~~ alone in his ~~h~~ bed

~~or with~~ the
~~or with the~~ [?pres]
or with [?this] –
or else

I would that I were an old beggar
Without a friend on [?this] earth
But a thieving rascally cur O
A beggar blind from his birth
etc.
There is a great peace in a beggar Etc
There is a great peace in a beggar
~~With a rolling~~
blind pearl
Rolling a ~~pearl blind~~ eye

then as before
But first ~~line of~~ last verse should run
O that I were not a rhymer

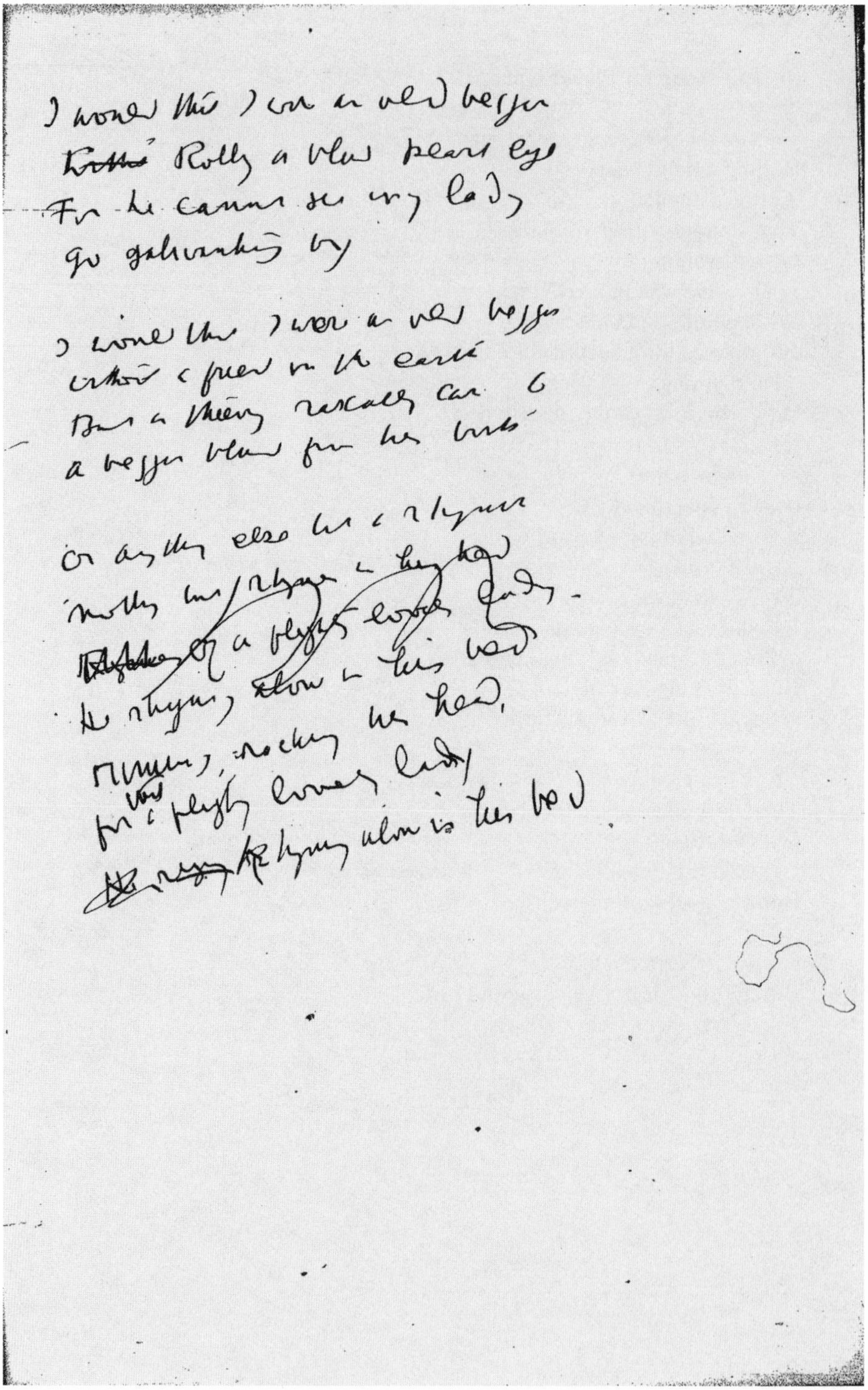
I would that I were an old beggar
~~Rolling~~ Rolling a blue bleary eye
For he cannot see any lady
go galivanting by

I would that I were an old beggar
without a friend on the earth
But a thieving rascally cur
a beggar blind from his birth

Or anything else but a rhymer
~~Nothing but / rhymer~~ a hungry head [?]
~~[illegible]~~ Of a plighted lovers lady
He rhymes alone in his bed
Rhymes, rocking his head,
for a plighted lovers lady
~~He rhymes~~ He rhymes alone in his bed

[BC, 36^{r}]

I would that I were an old beggar
[~~?Without~~] Rolling a blind pearl eye
For he cannot see my lady
Go galivanting by

I would that I were an old beggar
Without a friend on the earth
But a thieving rascally cur [?A]
A beggar blind from his birth

Or anything else but a rhymer
Nothing but rhymes in his head
~~Rymes~~ Of a flighty lovely lady –
He rhyming alone in his hed
Riming, racking his head,
that
For a flighty lovely lady
R
~~He rhyming~~ rhyming along in his bed

[NYPL(1), 1^{r}]

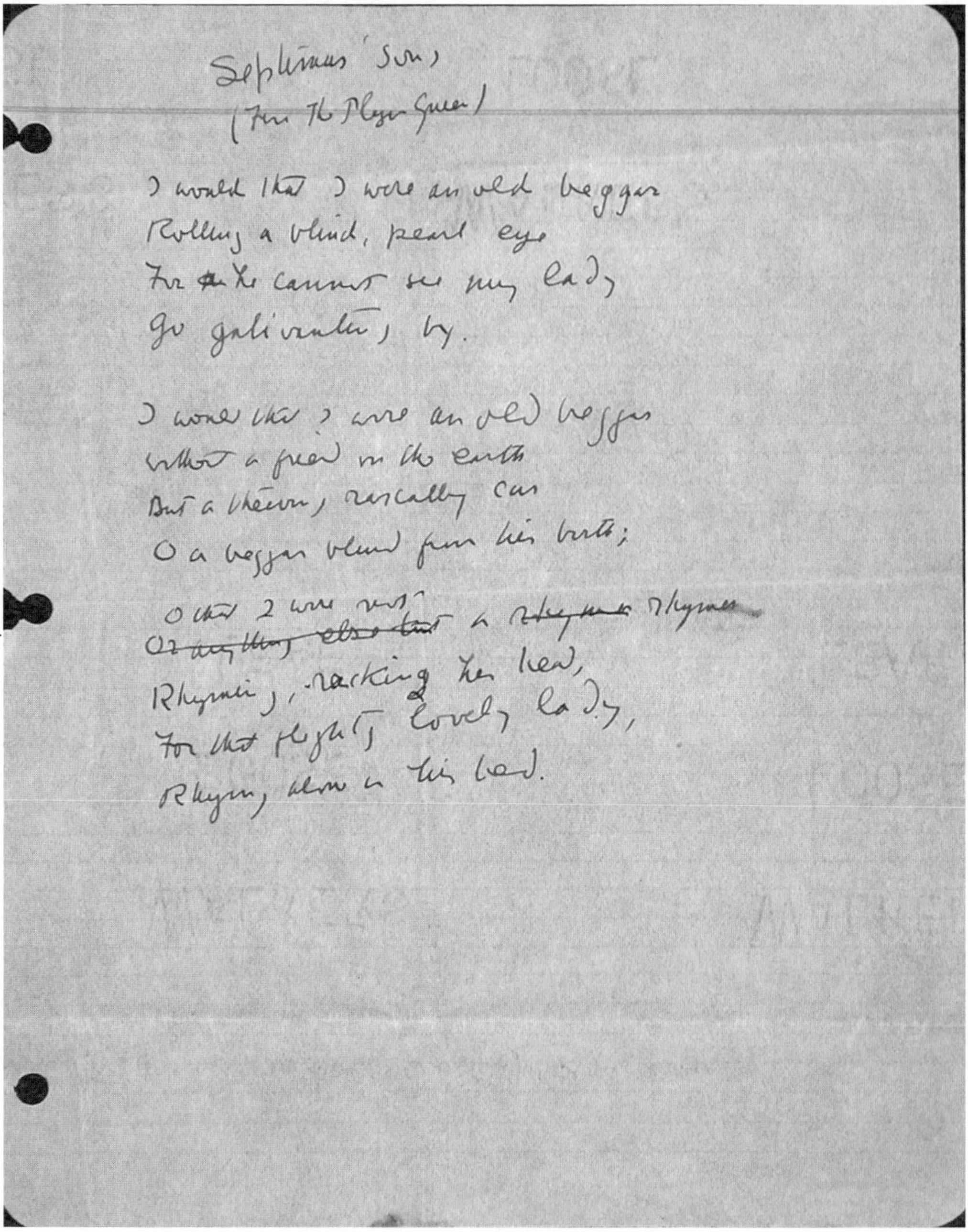
Septimus' Song
(For The Player Queen)

I would that I were an old beggar
Rolling a blind, pearl eye
For ~~he~~ he cannot see my lady
Go galivanting by.

I would that I were an old beggar
Without a friend on the earth
But a thieving, rascally cur
O a beggar blind from his birth;

O that I were not
~~Or anything else but~~ a ~~rhymer~~ rhymer
Rhyming, racking his head,
For that flighty lovely lady,
Rhyming alone in his bed.

[NYPL(1), 1^{r}]

Septimus' Song
(From The Player Queen)

I would that I were an old beggar
Rolling a blind, pearl eye
For ~~the~~ he cannot see my lady
Go galivanting by.

I would that I were an old beggar
Without a friend on the earth
But a theiving rascally cur
O a beggar blind from his birth;

O that I were not
~~Or anything else but~~ a ~~rhymer~~ rhymer
Rhyming, racking his head,
For that flighty lovely lady,
Rhyming alone in his bed.

---

title A Song *Times* II *FMM*
subtitle parentheses lacking Times, FMM
2 blind pearl eye, *Times, FMM*
4 by; *Times, FMM*
5 A dreary, dreepy beggar *Times, FMM*
7 thieving rascally cur— *Times, FMM*
9–10 Or anything else but a rhymer
Without a thing in his head *Times, FMM*
11 But rhymes for a beautiful lady *Times* But rhymes for a beautiful lady, *FMM*
12 He rhyming *Times, FMM*
12/ From *The Player Queen FMM*
signature W. B. Yeats *Times lacking FMM*

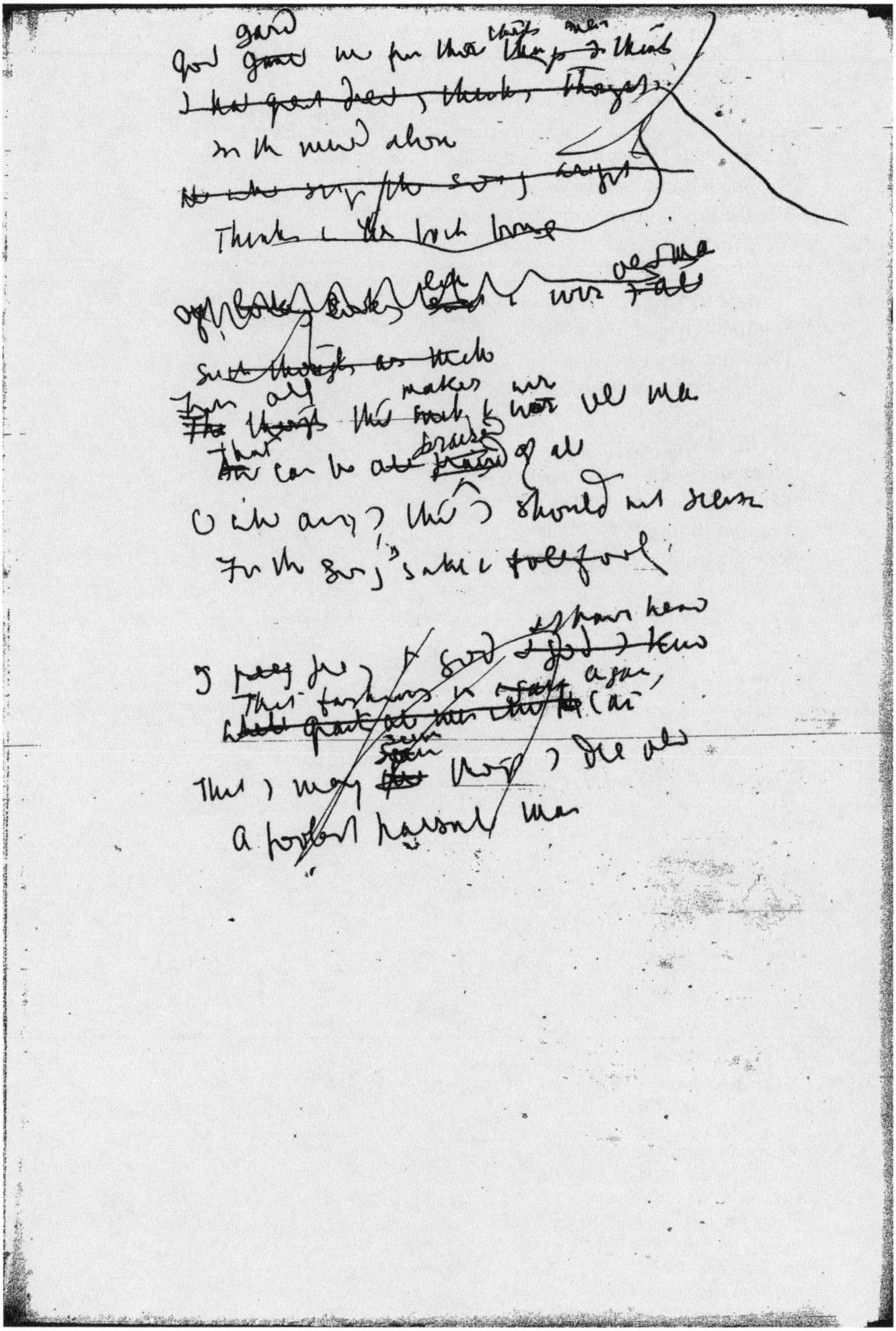

A PRAYER FOR OLD AGE

[BC, 7v]

gard   thoughts men
God ~~guard~~ me from those ~~things~~ ~~I~~ think
~~I had great dread of thinking thoughts~~
In the mind alone
~~He who sings the song aright~~
Thinks in his back bone

[~~?like~~]   ~~old man~~
~~Of looking looking [?such] a wise of all~~

~~Such thoughts as make~~
From all   makes   wise
~~The thoughts~~ that [~~?make~~] a [~~?wise~~] old man
That   praised
~~And~~ can be all [~~?praised~~] of all
O what am I that I should not seem
’s
For the song sake a ~~foll~~ fool

& I have hard
I ~~pey~~ prey to god ~~& god I know~~
That fashions in ~~again~~ again,
He
~~Whill grant all men what he~~ can
seem
~~seem~~
That I may [~~?the~~] though I die old
A foolish passionate man

---

found in BC, 7v, 8r *transcribed above and below*
published in *The Spectator*, November 2, 1934, p. 669 *transcribed below*
The King of the Great Clock Tower (1934)
The King of the Great Clock Tower (1935)
A Full Moon in March (1935)

Lines 1–5 above are clued in to lines 4–6 of BC, 8r.

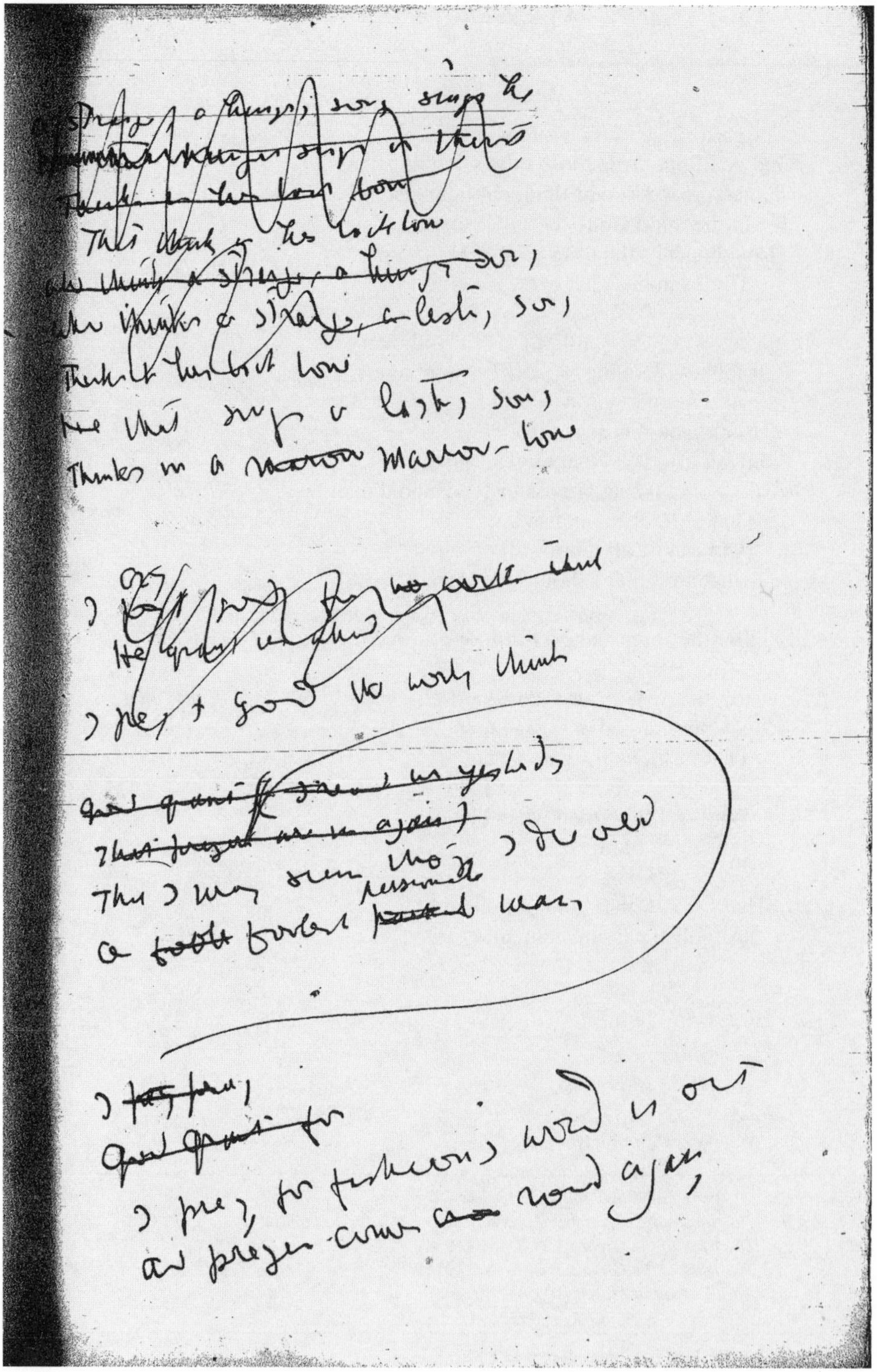
He that sings a lasting song,
Thinks in a marrow-bone
That I may seem though I die old
A foolish passionate man.
I pray, for fashion's word is out
And prayer comes round again,

[BC, 8^r]

A strange and hungry song sings he
~~[?] That hunger sings or thirst~~
~~Thinks in his back bone~~
  That thinks in his back bone
~~Who thinks a strange, a hungry song~~
Who thinks a strange, a lasting song
Thinks [?] his back bone
He that sings a lasting song
Thinks in a ~~marow~~ marrow-bone

  cry
I ~~pray~~ to god [?for] [?his] worthy thoughts
  He grant us what
I pray to god that worthy thinks

~~God grant~~ { (~~I read but yester~~day
~~That prayers are in again)~~
That I may seem though I die old
  passionate
A ~~fooli~~ foolish [~~?passionate~~] man

I ~~prey pray~~
~~God grant for~~
I prey, for fashions word is out
And preyer comes ~~cro~~ round again,

Lines 17–20 are clued in to lines 13–14.

[*The Spectator*, November 2, 1934, p. 669]

Old Age

God guard me from those thoughts men think
In the mind alone,
He that sings a lasting song
Thinks in a marrow bone;

From all that makes a wise old man
That can be praised of all;
O what am I that I should not seem
For the song's sake a fool.

I pray—for fashion's word is out
And prayer comes round again—
That I may seem though I die old
A foolish, passionate man.

W. B. Yeats

title *untitled in the text of the preface KGCT'34, KGCT'35* "A PRAYER FOR OLD AGE" *FMM*
2 alone; *FMM*
4 marrow-bone *FMM*
8 fool? *FMM*
11 seem, . . . old, *FMM*
12 *no signature FMM*

[NLI 30,795]

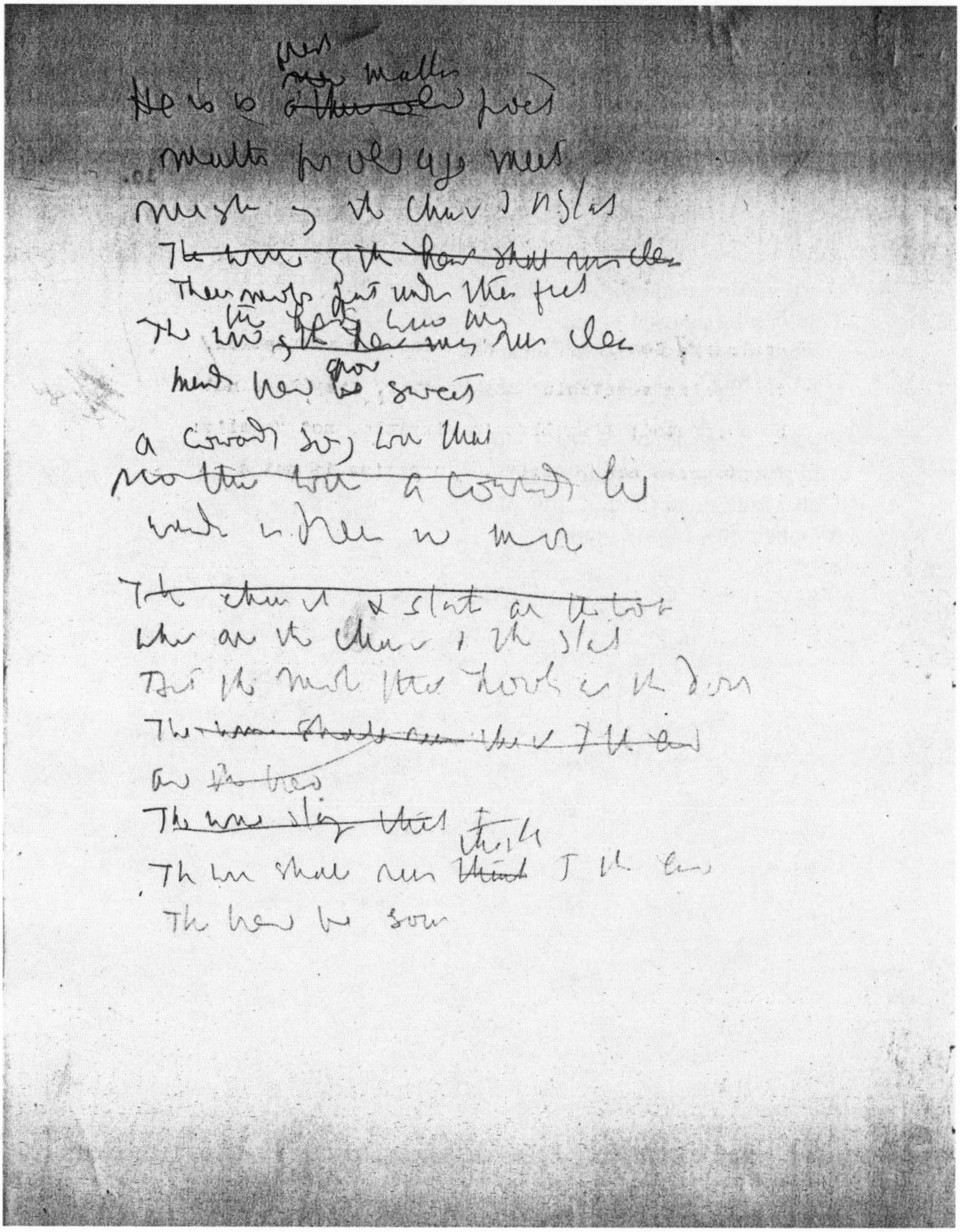

CHURCH AND STATE

[NLI 30,795]

fresh
~~new~~ matter
Here is ~~a theme old~~ poet
Matter for old age meet
Migh of the church and state
~~The wine of the heart shall run clear~~
Their mobs put under their feet
The hearts wine my
The wine ~~of the heart my~~ run clear
grow
Minds bread ~~be~~ sweet

A cowardly song were that
~~No that were a cowardly~~ lie
Wander in dream no more
~~The church & state are the bob~~
What are the church & the state
But the mob that howls at the door
The ~~wine shall run thick to the end~~
And ~~the bread~~
~~The wine stay thick t~~
thick
The wine shall run ~~think~~ to the end
The bread be sour

---

found in NLI 30,795 *transcribed above*
NLI 30,521 *transcribed below*
published in *The Spectator*, November 23, 1934, p. 788 *transcribed below*
Poetry (Chicago), December 1934
The King of the Great Clock Tower (1934)
The King of the Great Clock Tower (1935)
A Full Moon in March (1935)

---

3 For "migh" read "might"
5 For "my" read "may"?
9 For "bob" read "mob"?

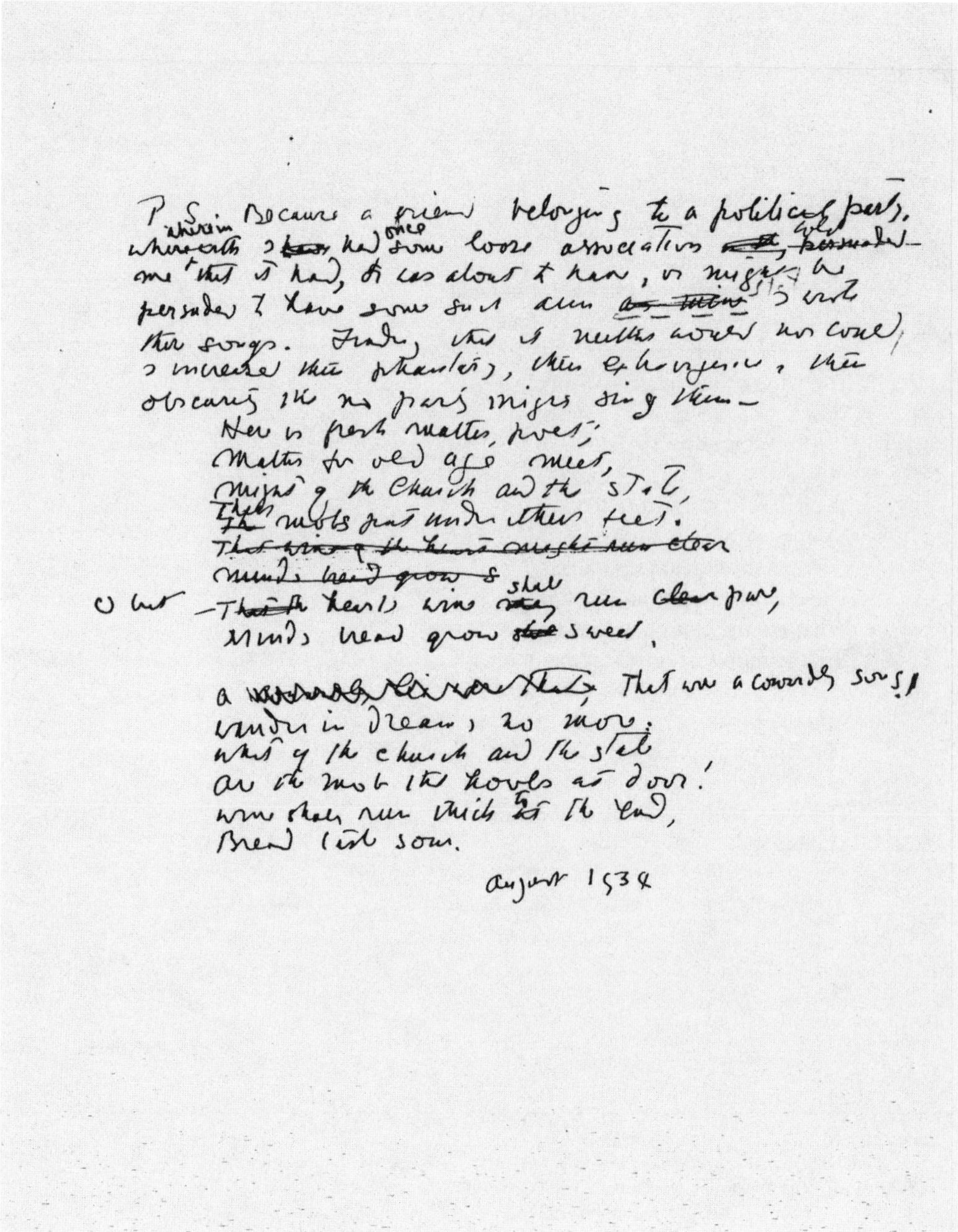

P.S. Because a friend belonging to a political party, ~~wherewith~~ wherein I ~~[illegible]~~ had once some loose association ~~[illegible]~~, ~~persuaded~~ who persuaded me that it had, or was about to have, or might be persuaded to have some such aim ~~as these~~ as I wrote these songs. Finding that it is neither would nor could increase their followers, their enthusiasm, their obscurity, I know no party might sing them—

Here is fresh matter, poet;
Matter for old age meet,
Might of the Church and the State,
~~The~~ Their mobs put under their feet.
~~That wine of the heart might run clear~~
~~Mind's bread grow s~~
O but ~~That the~~ hearts wine ~~stay~~ shall run ~~clear~~ pure,
Minds bread grow ~~stale~~ sweet.

A ~~[illegible]~~, That were a cowardly song!
Wander in dreams no more.
What if the church and the state
Are the mob that howls at door!
Wine shall run thick to the end,
Bread taste sour.

August 1934

Above the text in NLI 30,521 is the postscript that appears over the poem in *The King of the Great Clock Tower*.

[NLI 30,521 and *The Spectator,* November 23, 1934, p. 788]

[NLI 30,521]

Here is fresh matter, poet;
Matter for old age meet,
Might of the Church and the state,
Their
~~The~~ mobs put under their feet.
~~That wine of the heart might run clear~~
~~Minds bread grow s~~
shall
O but – ~~That the~~ hearts wine ~~may~~ run ~~clear~~ pure,
Minds bread grow swe sweet.

A ~~cowardly lie were that;~~ That were a cowardly song . /
Wander in dreams no more:
What if the church and the state
Are the mob that howls at door!
to
Wine shall run thick ~~at~~ the end,
Bread taste sour.
August 1934

[*The Spectator*, November 23, 1934, p. 788]

A Vain Hope

Here is fresh matter, poet,
Matter for old age meet;
Might of the Church and the State,
Their mobs put under their feet.
O but heart's wine shall run pure
Mine's bread grow sweet.

That were a cowardly song,
Wander in dreams no more;
What if the Church and the State
Are the mob that howls at the door?
Wine shall run thick to the end,
Bread taste sour. **W. B. Yeats**

---

title *untitled in text of postscript to* COMMENTARY ON THE THREE SONGS *in P, KGCT'34, KGCT'35*; "CHURCH AND STATE" *FMM*

5 pure, *FMM*

10 door! *P*, *KGCT'34*, *KGCT'35*, *FMM*

11 Wind shall *P*

date and signature August, 1934 / William Butler Yeats *(in italics) P*; August 1934. *KGCT*'34, *KGCT*'35, *FMM*

[MBY 673, letter 1, 1v]

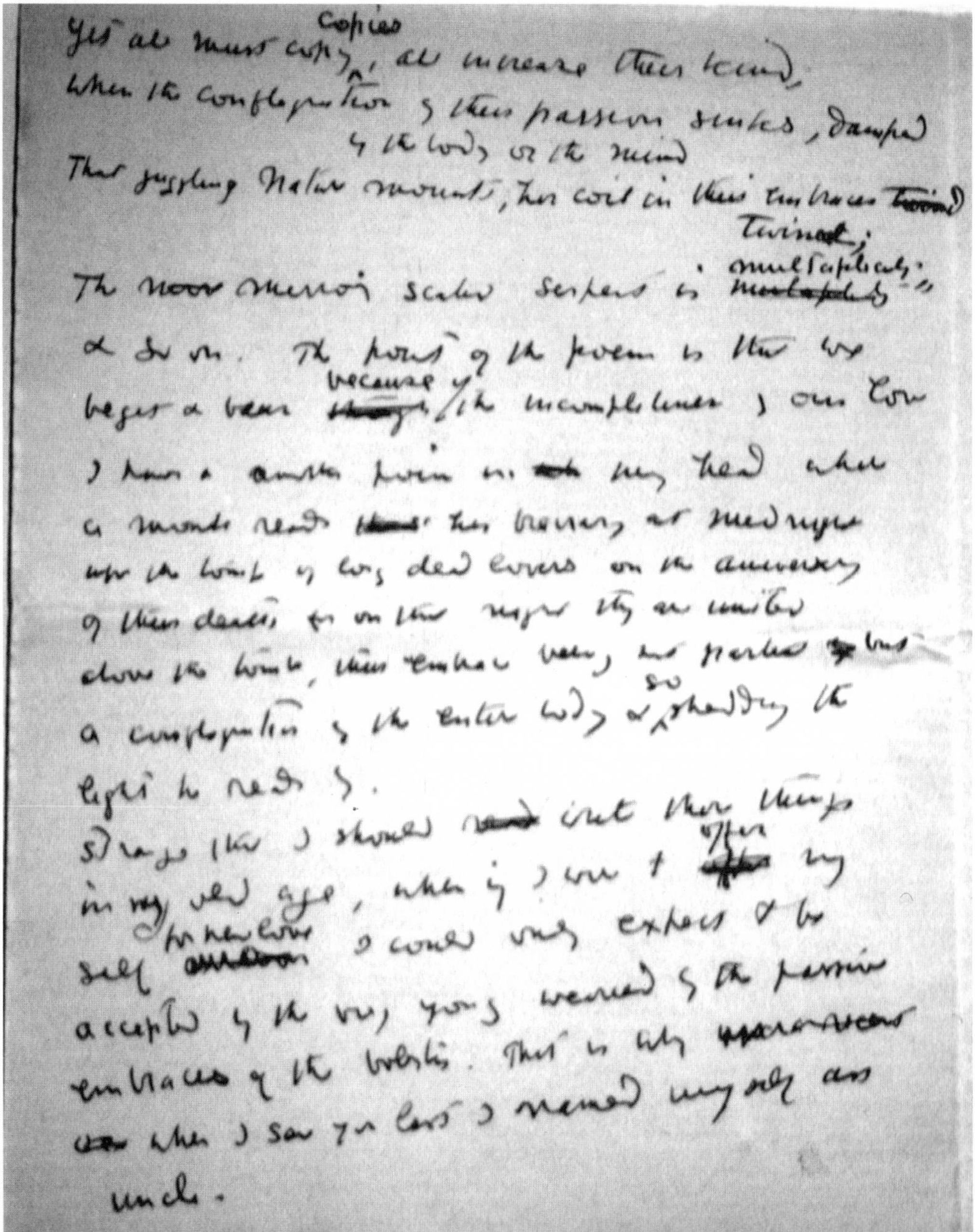

Yet all must copy copies, all increase their kind;
When the conflagration of their passion sinks, damped
by the body or the mind
That juggling Nature mounts, her coil in their embraces twined;
The mirror-scaled serpent is multiplicity"

& so on. The point of the poem is that we beget & bear because of the incompleteness of our love.

I have a another poem in my head where a monk reads his breviary at midnight upon the tomb of long dead lovers on the anniversary of their death, for on that night they are united above the tomb, their embrace being not partial but a conflagration of the entire body & so shedding the light he reads by.

Strange that I should write these things in my old age, when if I were to offer my self for new love I could only expect to be accepted by the very young wearied of the passive embraces of the bashful. This is why when I saw your look I named myself only as uncle.

SUPERNATURAL SONGS

1. Ribh at the Tomb of Baile and Ailinn

[MBY 673, letter 1, 1^{v}]

I have another poem in [?~~mi~~] my head where
a monk reads [?~~the b~~] his breviary at midnight
upon the tomb of long dead lovers on the anniversary
of their death, for on that night they are united
above the tomb, their embrace being not partial [~~?~~] but
so
a conflagration of the entire body and^shedding the
light he reads by.

---

found in MBY 673, letter 1, 1^{v} *transcribed above*
BC, 16^{r}, 17^{r}, 18^{r} *transcribed below*
Chicago(1), pp. 38–40 *transcribed below*
published in *Poetry* (Chicago), December 1934
The London Magazine, December 1934
The King of the Great Clock Tower (1934)
The King of the Great Clock Tower (1935)
A Full Moon in March (1935)

From a letter to Olivia Shakespear, July 24 [postmark July 25, 1934] from Riversdale. Transcribed from SB 3.4.58. See *Letters*, p. 824.

[BC, 16r]

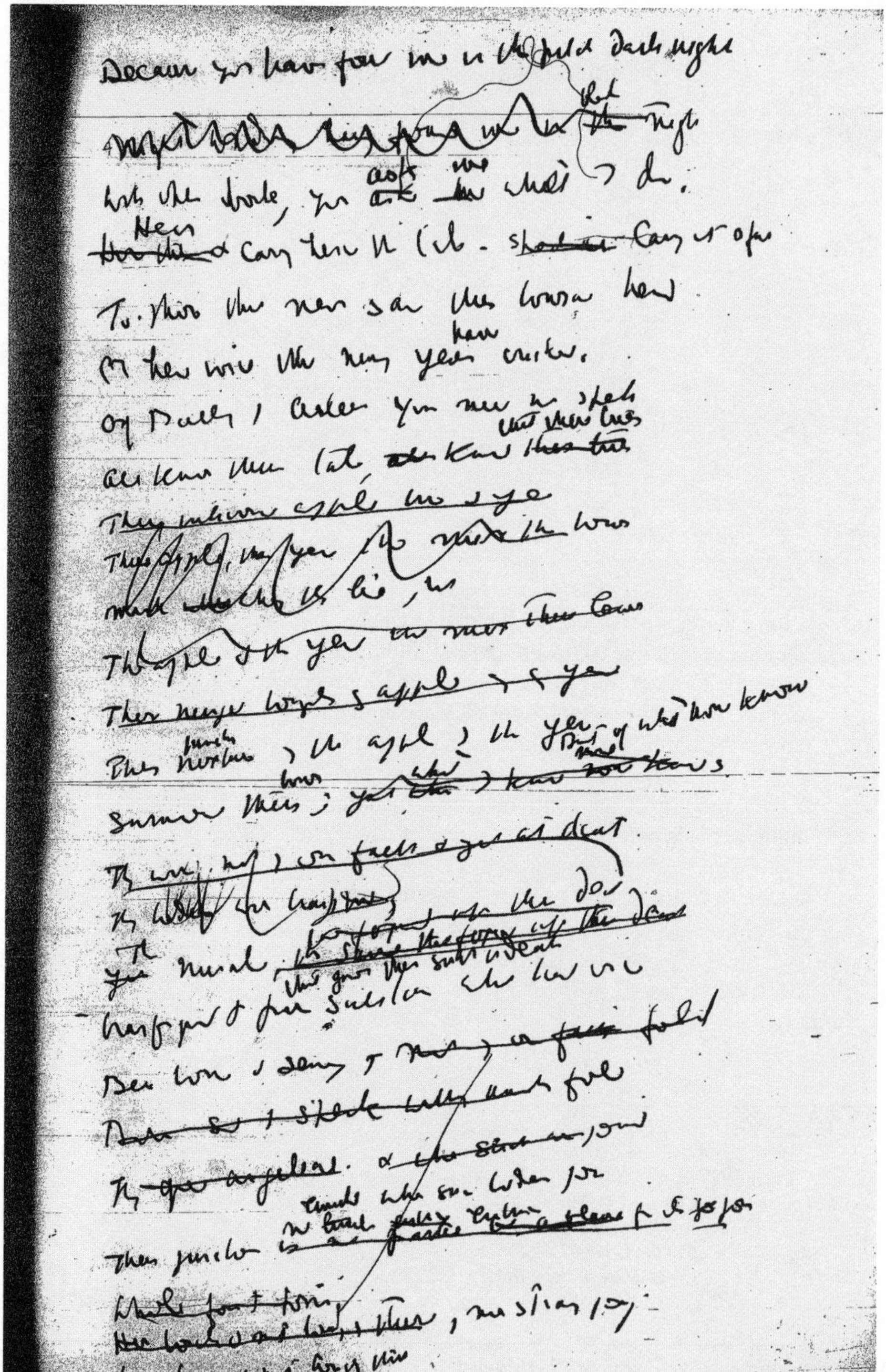

[BC, 16r]

black
2 ~~Night wandering having found me in the night~~
ask me
3 With open book, you ~~ask~~ ~~me~~ what I do.
Hear
4 ~~Here then~~ & carry hence the tale. ~~Speak it~~ Carry it afar
5 To those that never saw this tonsured head
have
6 Nor heard voice that ninety years cracked.
7 Of Bally and Aileen you need not speak
that these trees
8 All know their tale, ~~all~~ know ~~these trees~~
9 ~~These interwind apple tree & yew~~
10 Their apple, there yew that mix their boughs
11 Mark where where they lie, but
12 ~~The apple & the yew that mix their leaves~~
13 ~~Those merged boughs of apple & of yew~~
juncture
14 This mixture of the apple & the yew
But of what none knows
bones what ~~none~~
15 Surmount their; ~~yet what I know none knows~~
16 ~~They were not of one faith & yet at death~~
17 Their bodies were [?transfigured]
The ~~transformed after their death~~
18 ~~Yet~~ miracle ~~they share that form after their death~~
that gave them such a death
19 Transfigured to pure substance what had once
20 Been bone & sinew, ~~not of one faith fold~~
21 ~~Born so to speak within another~~ fold
22 ~~They grew angelical~~. ~~& when such are~~ joined
limited when such bodies join
no ~~limit~~ ~~entire~~ entire
23 Their junction ~~is not parted but a flame for its jo joins~~
24 ~~Whole form to form~~
25 ~~Here touch & not touch & there~~, nor straining joy
26 Here touch & not touch there

9 For "interwind" read "interwinding"?

[BC, 17r]

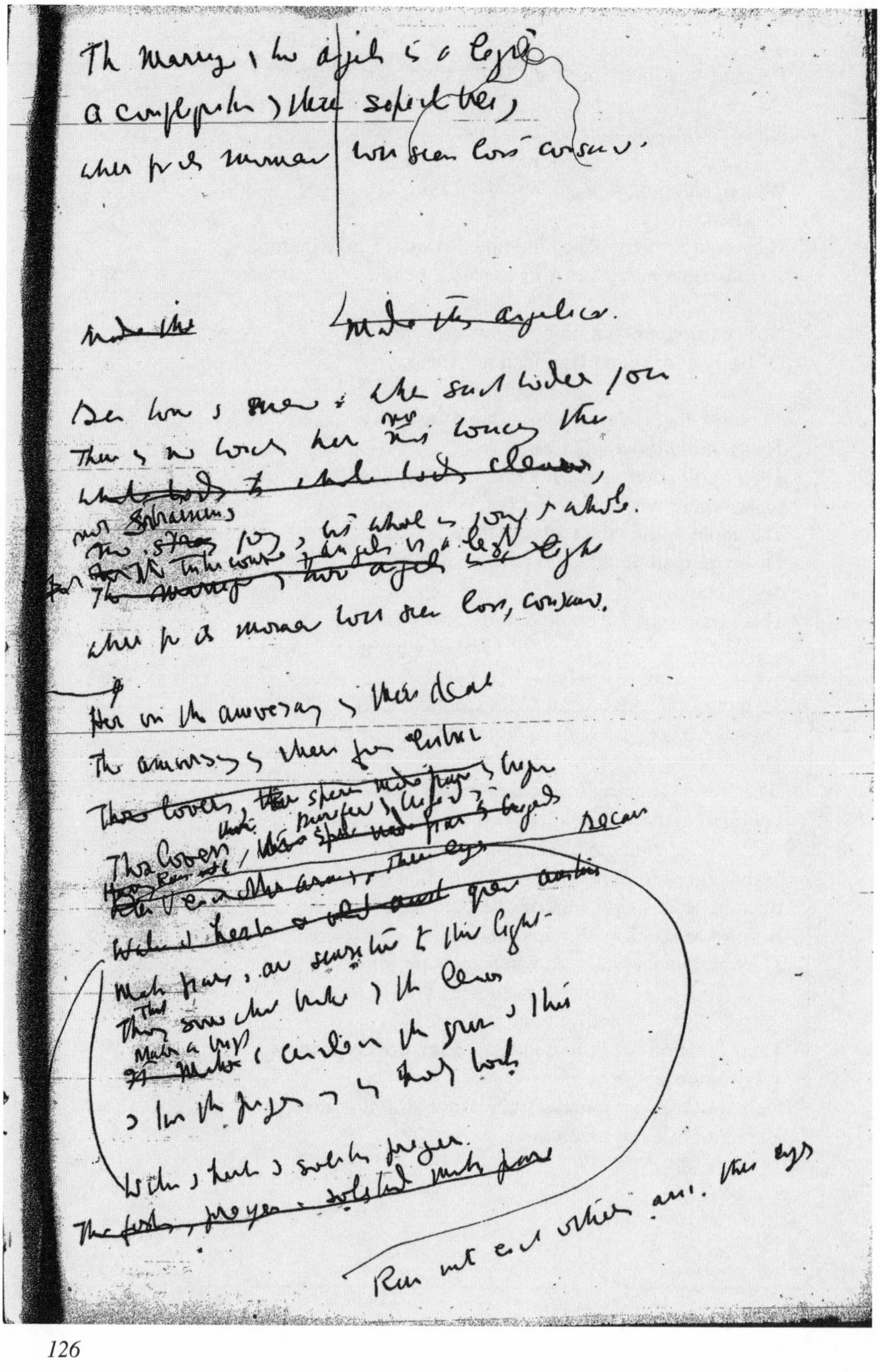

[BC, 17[r]]

The marriage of the angels is a light
A conflagration of their separate being
Where for the moment both seem lost consumed

~~Made the~~ ~~Made them angelical~~

Been bone & sinew; when such bodies join
nor
There is no touching here ~~not~~ touching there
~~Whole body to whole body cleaves,~~
Nor straining
No ~~straining~~ joy, but whole is joined to whole
For ~~For~~ The intercourse of angels is a light
The marriage of two angels is a light
Where for the moment both seem lost, consumed.

Here on the anniversary of their death
The anniversary of their first embrace
~~Those lovers, their spirits made pure by tragedy~~
~~their~~ purified by tragedy
Those lovers, ~~their spirits made pure by tragedy~~
~~Hurry~~ ~~Run into~~
~~[?Run] [?to] each others arms, these eyes~~ ~~Because~~
~~Water & herb & old aust great [?austerities]~~
Make pure, are sensitive to that light
That
Though somewhat broken by the leaves
Makes a bright
~~It makes~~ a circle on the grass & there
I turn the pages of my holy book

Water & herb & solitary prayer
~~That fasting, prayer & solitude make pure~~

Run into each others arms. These eyes

10 The following lines are clued in at the arrow from the left-hand page, fol. 16[v]:
atmosphere
Here in the pitch dark ~~night~~ above
The trembling of the apple & the yew
15 The line is clued to line 23.
16 The line is clued separately to lines 22 and 21. The word "aust" is incomplete for "austerities."

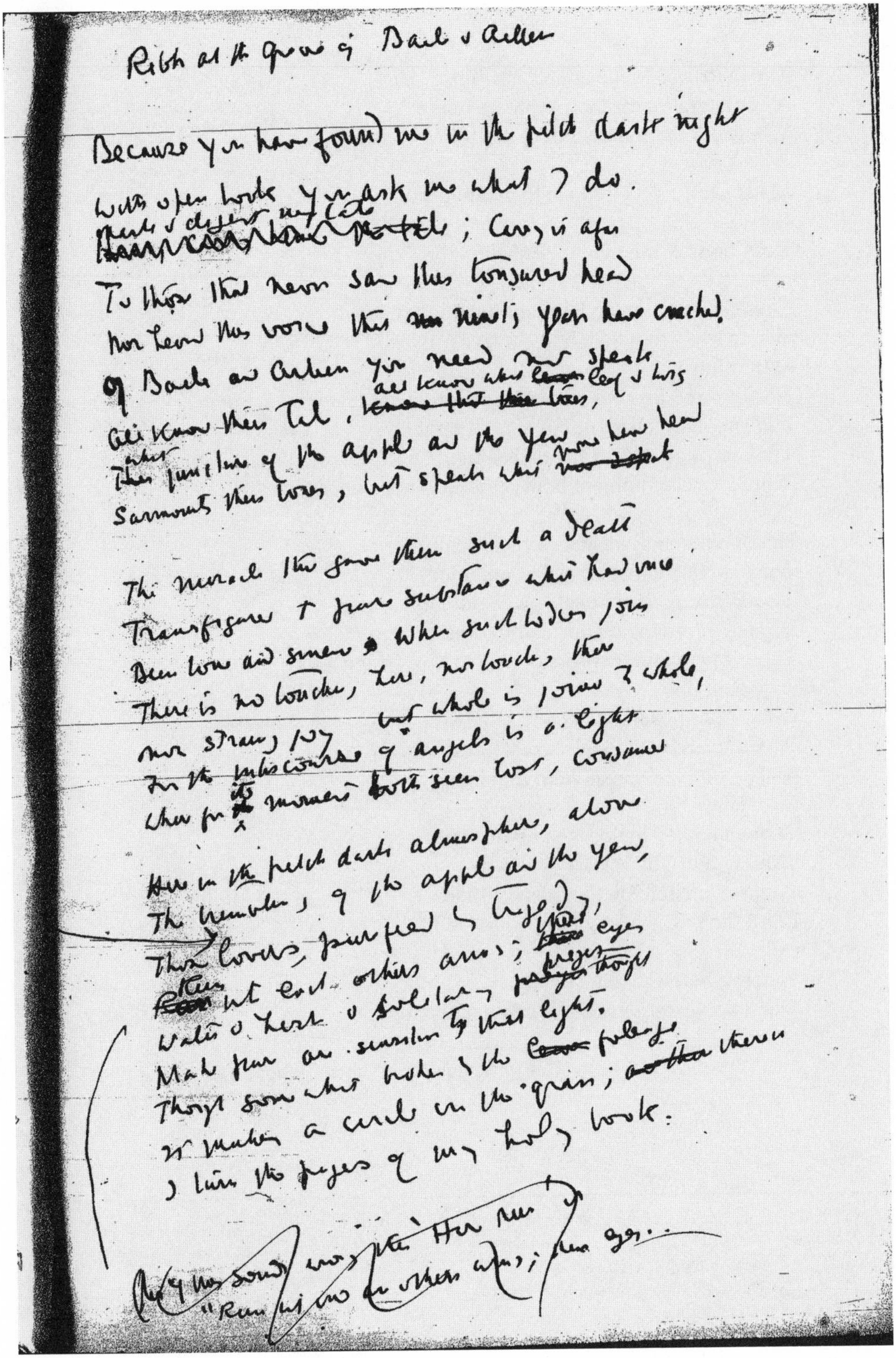
Ribh at the grave of Baile & Aillinn

Because you have found me in the pitch dark night
With open book you ask me what I do.
speech & [illegible] ; Lovers is after
To those that never saw this tonsured head
Nor heard this voice that ninety years have cracked.
Of Baile and Aillinn you need not speak,
All know their tale, all know what leaf & twig
What juncture of the apple and the yew
Surmount their bones, but speak what none have heard

The miracle that gave them such a death
Transfigured to pure substance what had once
Been bone and sinew; when such bodies join
There is no touching here, nor touching there
Nor straining joy but whole is joined to whole,
For the intercourse of angels is a light
Where for its moment both seem lost, consumed

Here in the pitch dark atmosphere, above
The trembling of the apple and the yew,
Those lovers, purified by tragedy,
Hurry into each others arms; these eyes
Water & heart & solitary pages thought
Made pure and sensitive by that light,
Though somewhat broken by the foliage thereon
Or making a circle on the grass;
I turn the pages of my holy book.

[BC, 18r]

Ribh at the Grave of Baile & Aillen

Because you have found me in the pitch dark night
With open book you ask me what I do.
Mark & digest my tale
~~Hear, carry hence the tale~~ ; Carry it afar
To those that never saw this tonsured head
Nor heard this voice that nin ninety years have cracked.
Of Baile and Aileen you need not speak
all know what leaves leaf & twig
All know their tale, ~~know that these trees,~~
What
~~This~~ juncture of the apple and the yew
none have heard
Surmounts their bones, but speak what ~~now I speak~~

The miracle that gave them such a death
Transfigured to pure substance what had once
.
Been bone and sinew, } When such bodies join
There is no touching here, nor touching there
Nor straining joy but whole is joined to whole
For the intercourse of angels is a light
its
Where for ~~the~~ moment both seem lost, consumed

Here in the pitch dark atmosphere, above
→ The trembling of the apple and the yew,
Those lovers, purified by tragedy,
Run these
~~Run~~ into each others arms; ~~these~~ eyes
prayer
Water & herb & solitary ~~prayer~~ ~~thought~~
Make pure are sensitive [?to] that light.
Though somewhat broken by the ~~leaves~~ foliage
It makes a circle on the grass; ~~and there~~ therein
I turn the pages of my holy book.

(Or if this sounds wrong then 'Here run' or
"Run into one anothers arms . .

---

18 Clued in at the arrow are two from the facing page, fol. 17v:
Here on the anniversary of their death,
The anniversary of their first embrace, ...

1. Ribh at the Tomb of Baile and Ailinn

[Chicago(1), pp. 38–40]

SUPERNATURAL SONGS
RIBH AT THE TOMB OF BAILE AND
~~AILEEN~~ AILLINN

Because you have it in the pitch dark night
With open book you ask me what I do:
Mark and digest my tale, carry it afar
To those that never saw this tonsured head
Nor heard this voice that ninety years have cracked.
Of Baile and ~~Aileen~~ you need not speak, Aillinn
All know their tale, all know what leaf and twig,
What juncture of the apple and the yew,
Surmounts their bones; but speak what none have heard.

The miracle that gave them such a death
Transfigured to pure substance what had once
Been bone and sinew; when such bodies join
There is no touching here, nor touching there,
Nor straining joy, but whole is joined to whole;
For the intercourse of angels is a light
Where for its moment both seem lost, consumed.

38

---

title unnumbered P I *KGCT'34, KGCT'35* I. *LM, FMM*
1 you have found me *LM, KGCT'34, KGCT'35* you have found me in the pitch-dark *FMM*
2 do. *FMM*
3 cracked *KGCT'35*
9 Surmount *KGCT'34, KGCT'35, FMM*

[Chicago(1), pp. 38–40 continued]

Here in the pitch dark atmosphere above
The trembling of the apple and the yew,
Here on the anniversary of their death
The anniversary of their, first embrace
Those lovers, purified by tragedy
Hurry into each other's arms; these eyes,
By water, herb and solitary prayer
Made acquiline, are open to that light.
Though somewhat broken by the leaves, that light
Lies in a circle on the grass; therein
I turn the pages of my holy book.

---

17 Pitch-dark *FMM*

19 death, *FMM*

20 their first embrace *KGCT'34, KGCT'35* their first embrace, *FMM*

21 tragedy, *KGCT'34, KGCT'35, FMM*

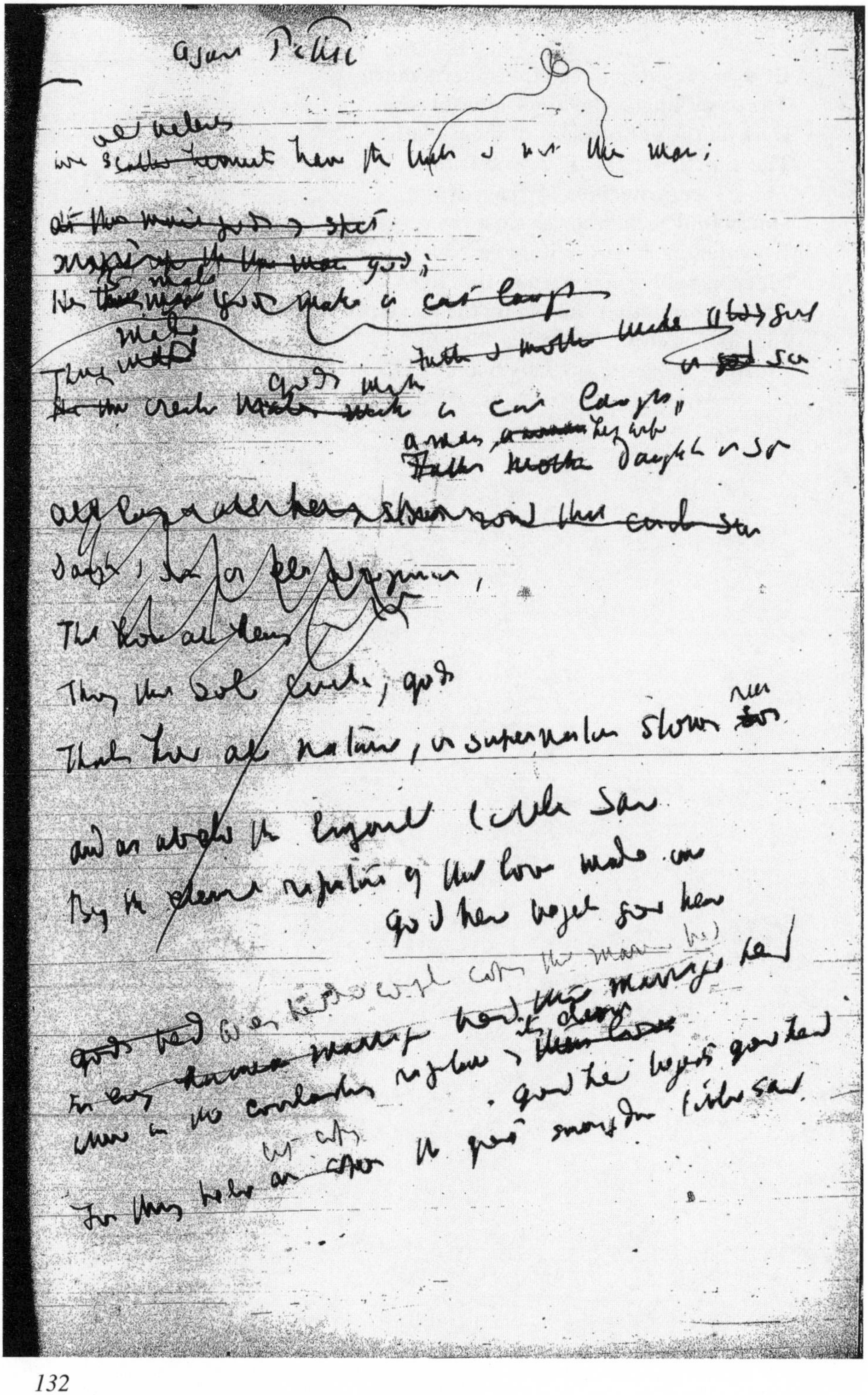

SUPERNATURAL SONGS

2. Ribh denounces Patrick

[BC, 13r]

Against Patrick

old believers
1 We ~~scattered hermits~~ have the truth & not this man;
2 ~~At those mail gods I spit~~
3 ~~I spit upon the three man god~~;
3 male
4 His three ~~mail~~ gods make a ~~cat laugh~~
male
5 Three ~~mail~~ ~~Father & mother made a~~ ~~boy~~ girl
gods make ~~or girl son~~
6 His three created ~~males~~ make a cat laugh,
a man ~~a woman~~ his wife
~~Father~~ ~~Mother~~ Daughter or Son

---

found in BC, 13r, 12v, 14r, 13v, 15r, 14v, 15v *transcribed above and below*
MBY 673, letter 1, 1r, 1v *transcribed below*
Chicago(1), p. 40 *transcribed below*
Houghton

published in *Poetry* (Chicago), December 1934
The London Mercury, December 1934
The King of the Great Clock Tower (1934)
The King of the Great Clock Tower (1935)
A Full Moon in March (1935)

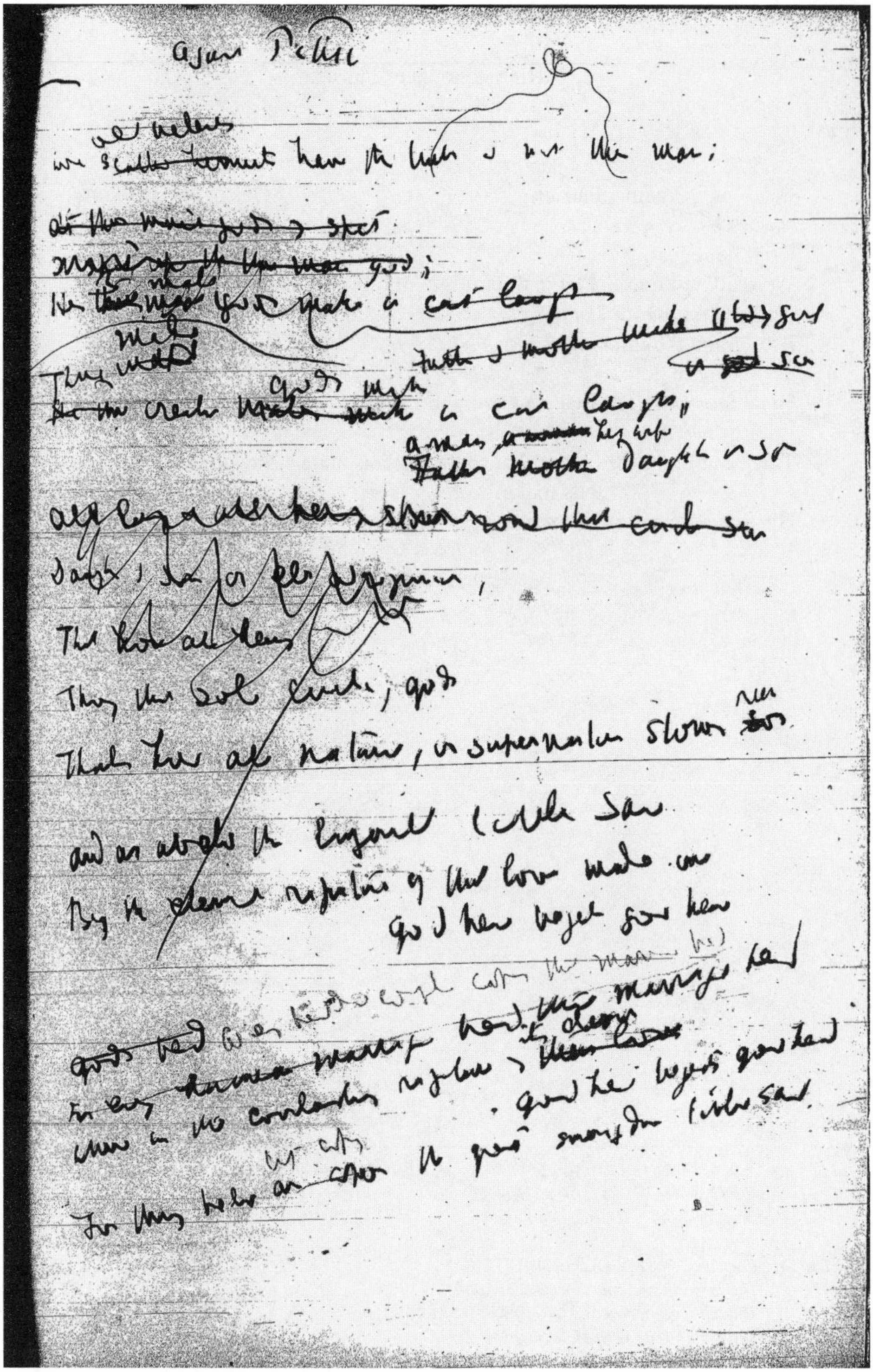

[BC, 13r continued]

7 ~~All [?earthly] & all [?heavenly] stories round that circle sun~~
8 Daughter & son or else androgynous,
9 Thats how all heavenly
10 Through that sole circle, gods
run
11 Thats how all natural, or supernatural stories ~~son~~
12 And as abelow the Emerald Tablet Said
13 By the element rapture of that love made one
14 Godhead begets godhead
15 ~~gods bed~~ *And as bedded couples copy the marriage bed*
16 ~~For every human marriage bed that marriage~~ bed
its desire
17 Where in the everlasting rapture of ~~their love~~
godhead begets godhead
but copy
18 For things below ~~are copies~~ the great smaragdine tablet said

---

12 "Abelow" may be a slip for "above-below."
13 For "element" read "elemental"?
16 Canceled in pencil.
18 "are copies" is canceled in pencil.

[BC, 12^v]

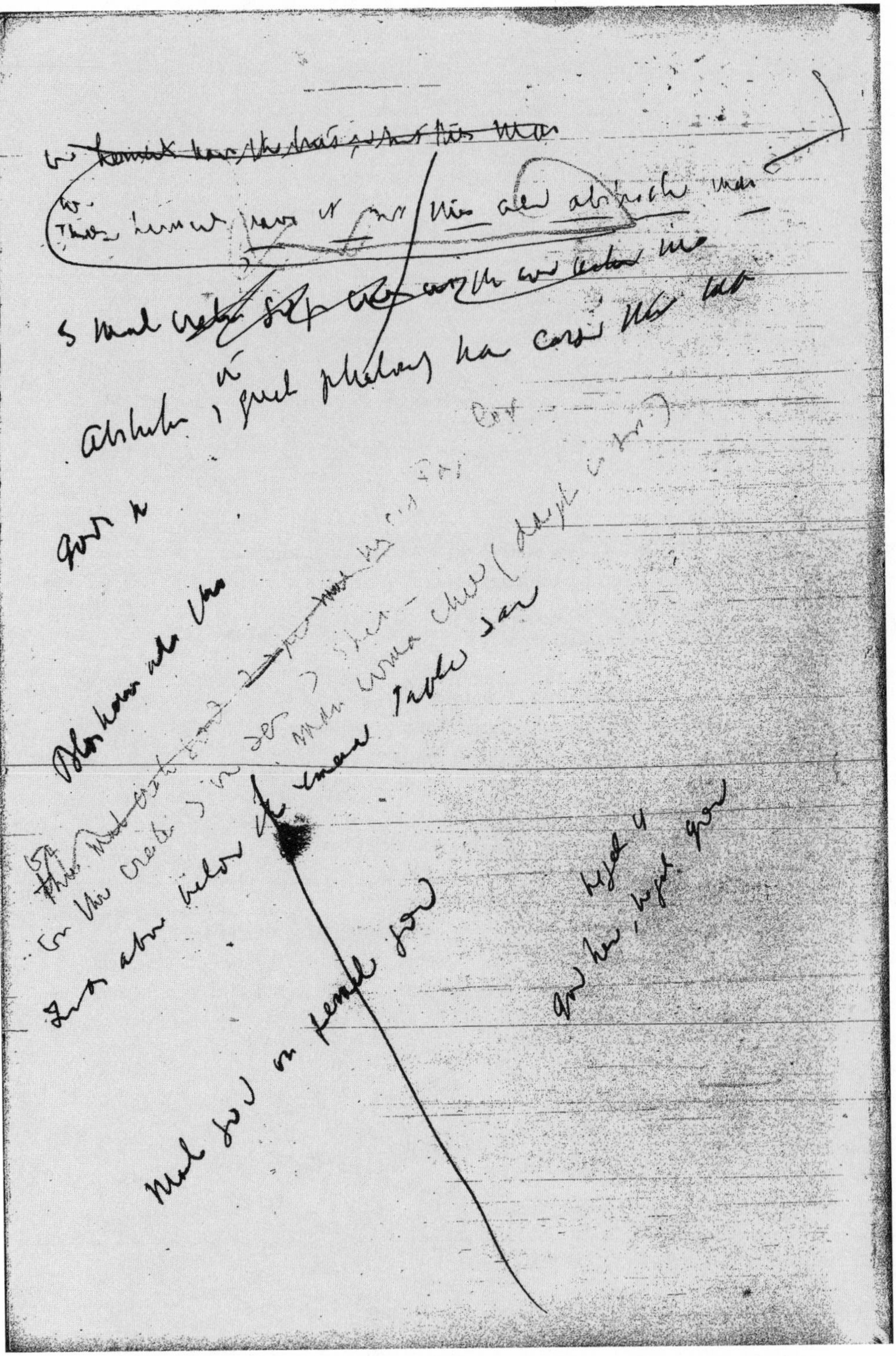

[BC, 12ᵛ]

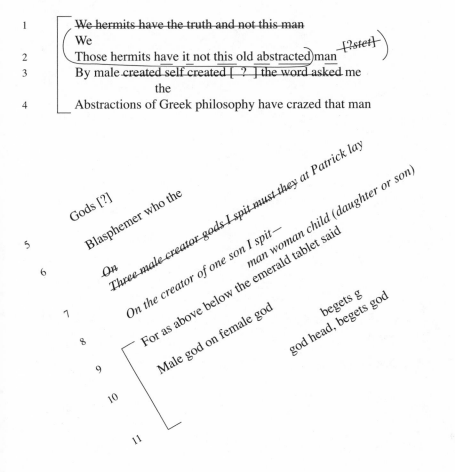

~~We hermits have the truth and not this man~~
We
Those hermits have it not this old abstracted man ~~[?stet]~~
By male ~~created self created [?] the word asked~~ me
the
Abstractions of Greek philosophy have crazed that man

Gods [?]
Blasphemer who the
~~On~~ ~~*Three male creator gods I spit must they*~~ *at Patrick lay*
man woman child (daughter or son)
On the creator of one son I spit—
For as above below the emerald tablet said
begets g
Male god on female god god head, begets god

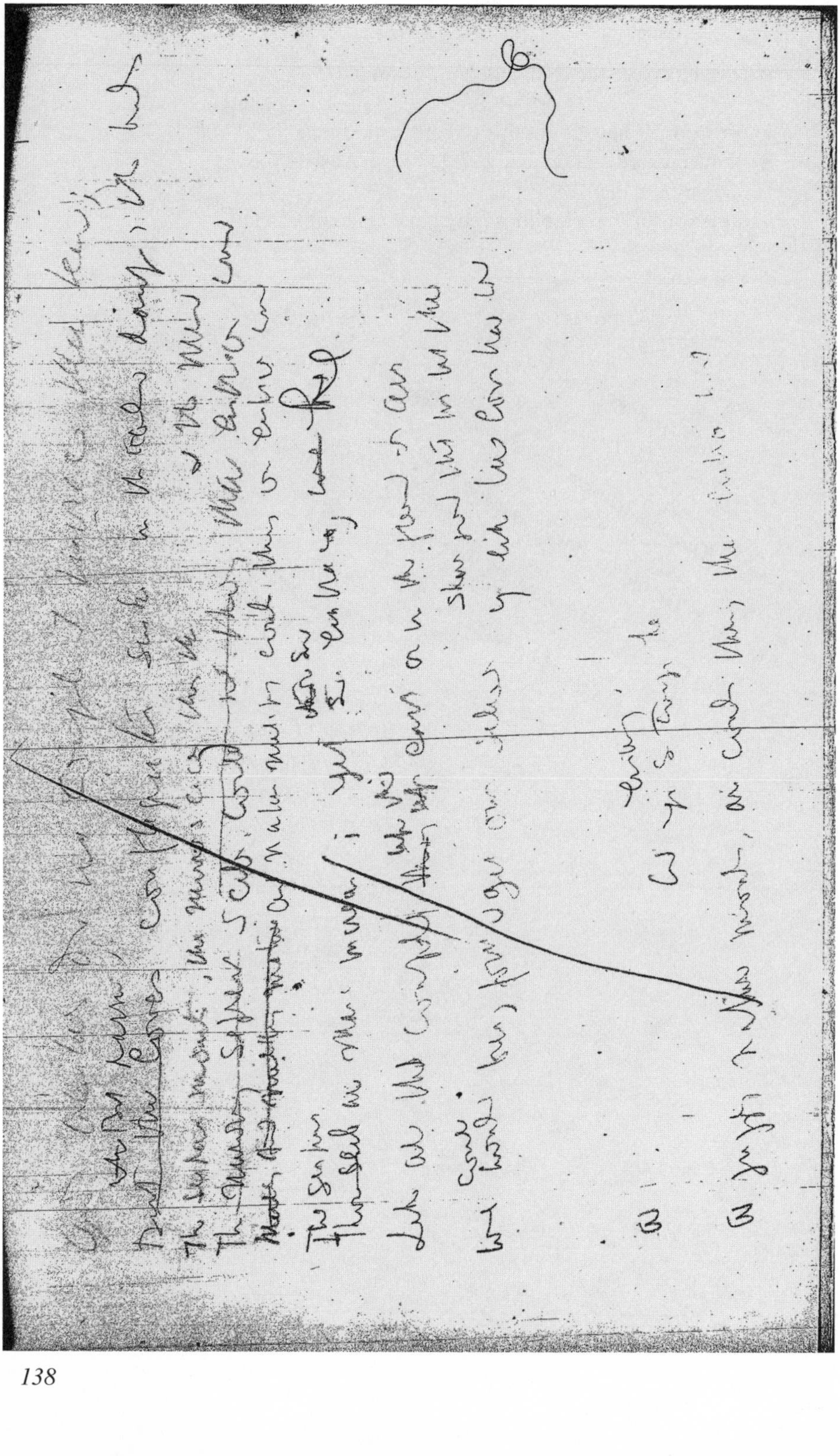

[BC, 14r]

Gods creatures do not couple to increase their kind;
~~Wh~~ But passion
~~But their loves~~ conflagration sinks in the cold damp of the body
& the mind
The serpents mouth, the mirror scales through the
The ~~mirroring serpent~~ ~~scales could not through~~ their embraces wind
~~Multy~~ ~~And multiply Natures~~ And Natures multiply coils through [?*our*] *embraces wind*
The Serpent
~~those~~ so {s
Those scales are mans increase; yet ~~so~~ embrace ~~we~~ he
upon this
[?*Let*] *all that couple ~~thus upon~~ earth or in the flood or air*
share god that is but three
could
We would bring forth & get our selves if like true love had we

embraces
As *And yet so* [?] *he*

As juggling Nature mounts, are coils through the embraces wind

Canceled in pencil.
5 For "multiply" read "multiplying" both times?
11 For "the" read "their"?

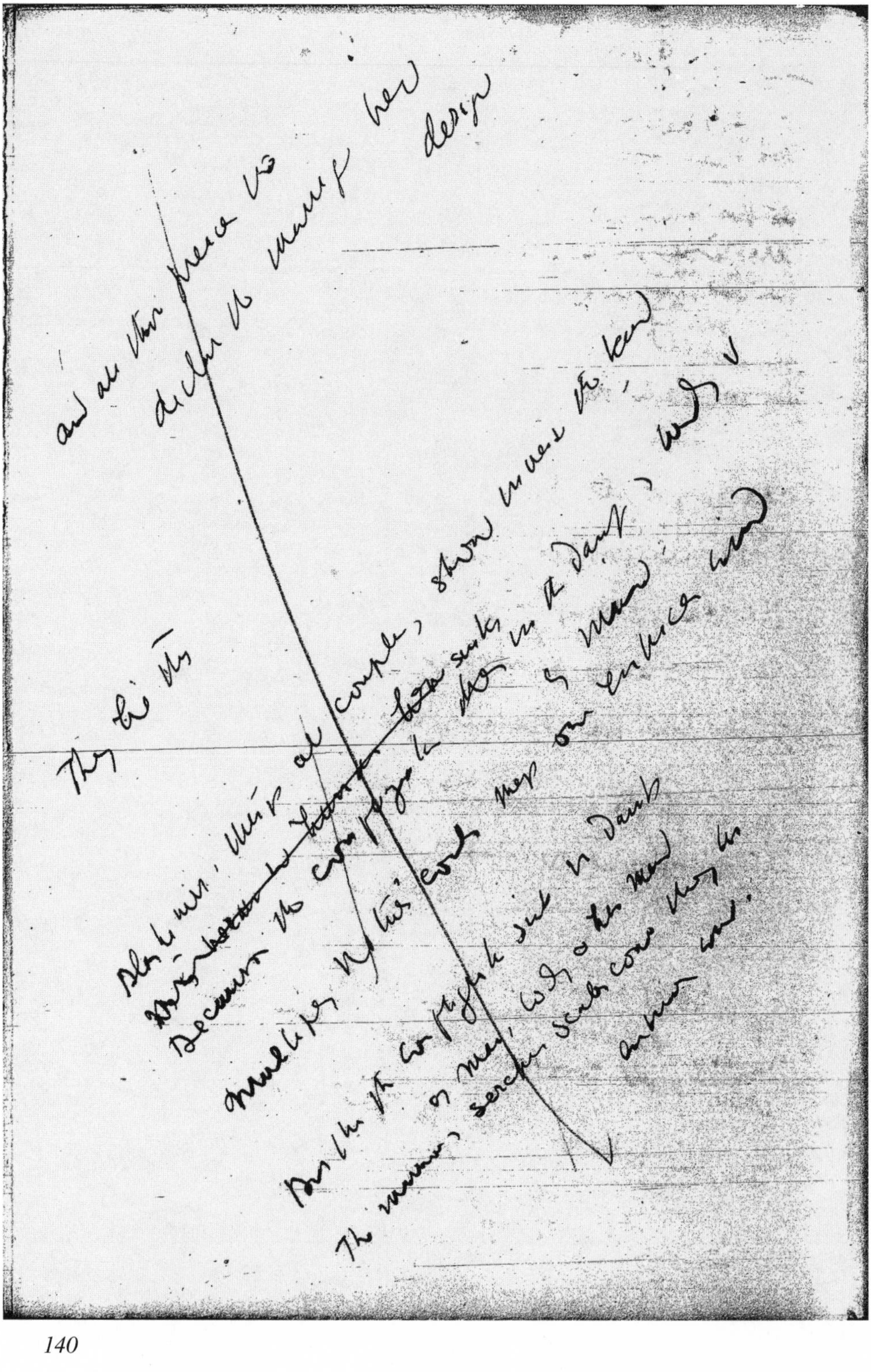

[BC, 13v]

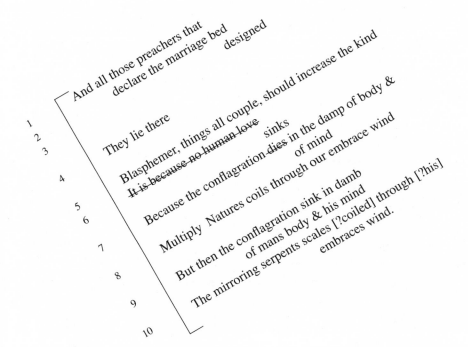

And all those preachers that
declare the marriage bed
designed
They lie there
Blasphemer, things all couple, should increase the kind
~~It is because no human love~~
sinks
Because the conflagration ~~dies~~ in the damp of body &
of mind
Multiply Natures coils through our embrace wind
But then the conflagration sink in damb
of mans body & his mind
The mirroring serpents scales [?coiled] through [?his]
embraces wind.

The entire draft is canceled in pencil.

5 For "the" read "their"?

9 For "sink in damb" read "sinks in damp"?

[BC, 15r]

1

Abstractions of the Greek philosophers have crazed the man
A father, mother child (daughter or son)
Upon his three male gods I spit. ~~*A man, a*~~
Thats how all natural or supernatural stories run

2

And every bedded couple copies the marriage bed
Where in the everlasting rapture of desire, god head begets god head
For things below are copies the great {*S* / *smaragdine*} {*T* / *tablet said*}

~~An Irish Monk~~

---

9 Black ink.

[BC, 14v]

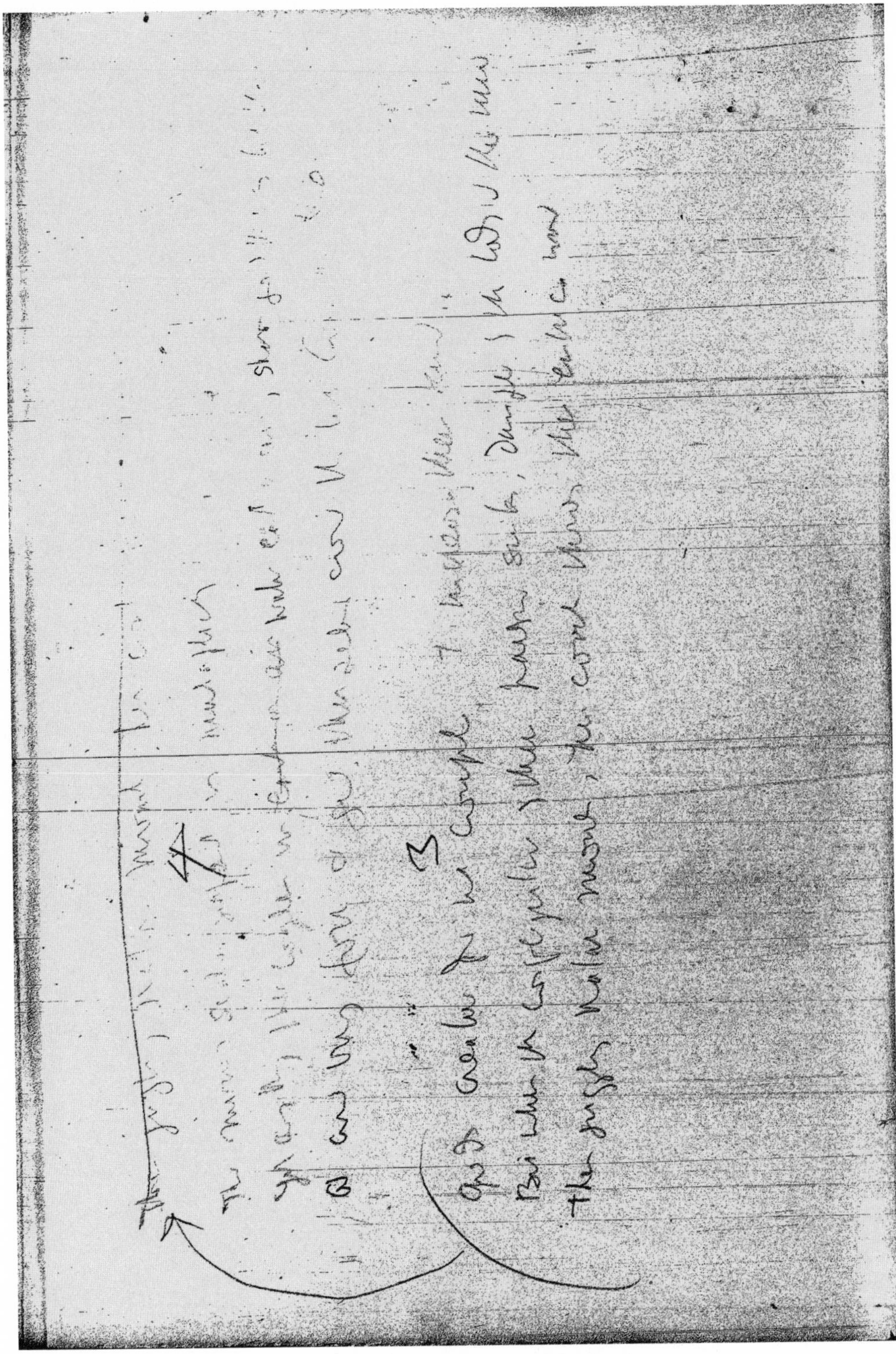

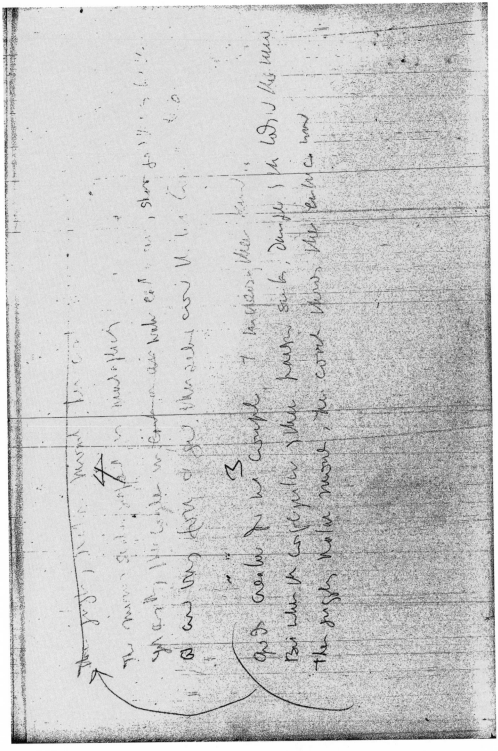

[BC, 14[v]]

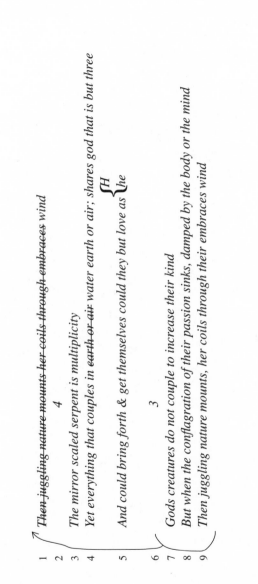

~~Then juggling nature mounts her coils through embraces~~ wind
4
The mirror scaled serpent is multiplicity
Yet everything that couples in ~~earth or air~~ water earth or air; shares god that is but three
And could bring forth & get themselves could they but love as {*H* / *he*}

3
Gods creatures do not couple to increase their kind
But when the conflagration of their passion sinks, damped by the body or the mind
Then juggling nature mounts, her coils through their embraces wind

---

2 The 4 goes through "serpent" and was obviously added afterwards.
6 Stanza 3 is clued in before stanza 4.

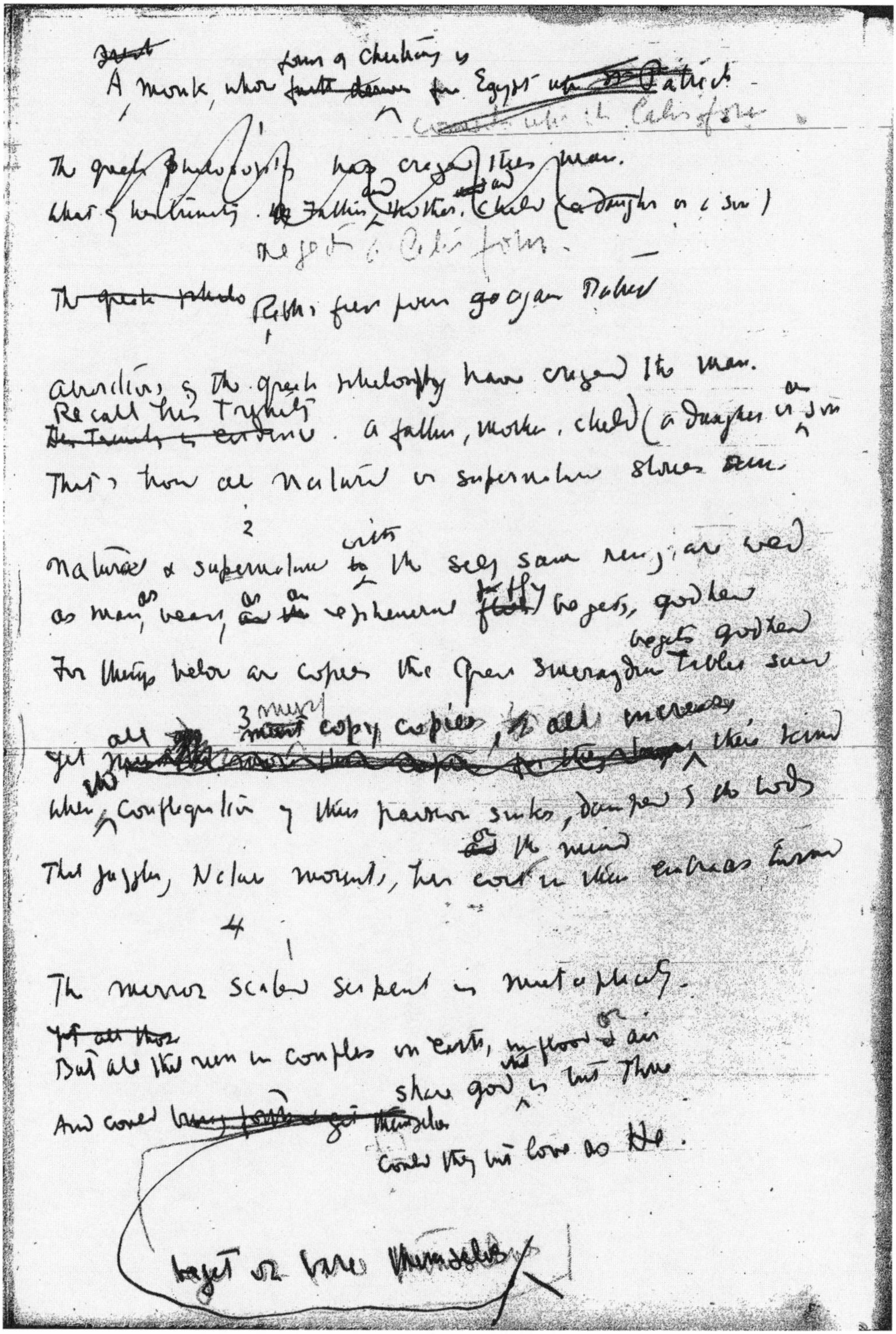
~~Saint~~
A monk, whose ~~faith drew~~ form of chastity is from Egypt ~~[illegible]~~ Patrick
came when the Californian

The great philosophy has crazed this man.
What of [illegible] . ~~He~~ Father, and Mother, Child (a daughter or a son)
the god of California.

~~The great philo~~ Ribh [illegible] from [illegible]

abstractions of the great philosophy have crazed the man.
Recall this Trinity
~~The Trinity of [illegible]~~ a father, mother, child (a daughter or a son)
That's how all natural or supernatural stories run.

2

Natural & supernatural ~~to~~ with the self same ring are wed
as man, as beast, as an ~~the~~ ephemeral ~~[illegible]~~ fly begets, godhead begets godhead
For things below are copies the great Smaragdine Tablet said

3 must
~~must~~ copy copies, all increase
yet all ~~[illegible]~~ their kind
When the conflagration of their passion sinks, damped by the body or the mind
That juggler, Nature mounts, her coil in their embraces twined

4

The mirror scaled serpent is multiplicity.
~~Yet all those~~
But all that run in couples on earth, in flood or air
share god that is but three
And could ~~[illegible]~~ themselves
could they but love as He.

beget or bear themselves

[BC, 15v]

~~Irish~~ form of Christianity is
A monk, whose ~~faith descends~~ from Egypt ~~upon St Patrick~~
^
comments upon its Celtic form

1
The Greek philosophy has crazed the man
and ~~and~~ and
What of matrimony. ~~[?]~~ Father ^Mother, child (a daughter or a son)
rejects a Celtic form
The Greek philo
Ribh's first poems ~~go~~ against Patrick

1
Abstractions of the Greek philosopy have crazed the man.
Recall his Trinity a
~~The Trinity is evidence~~. A father, mother, child (a daughter or ^son)
That's how all natural or supernatural stories run.

2
with
Natural & supernatural ~~in~~ the self same ring are wed
as as an ^ ~~f~~ fly
As man, beast, ~~and~~ ~~the~~ ephemeral ~~flies~~ begets, godhead
begets godhead
For things below are copies the Great Smaragdine Tablet said

1 The cancellations are in pencil.

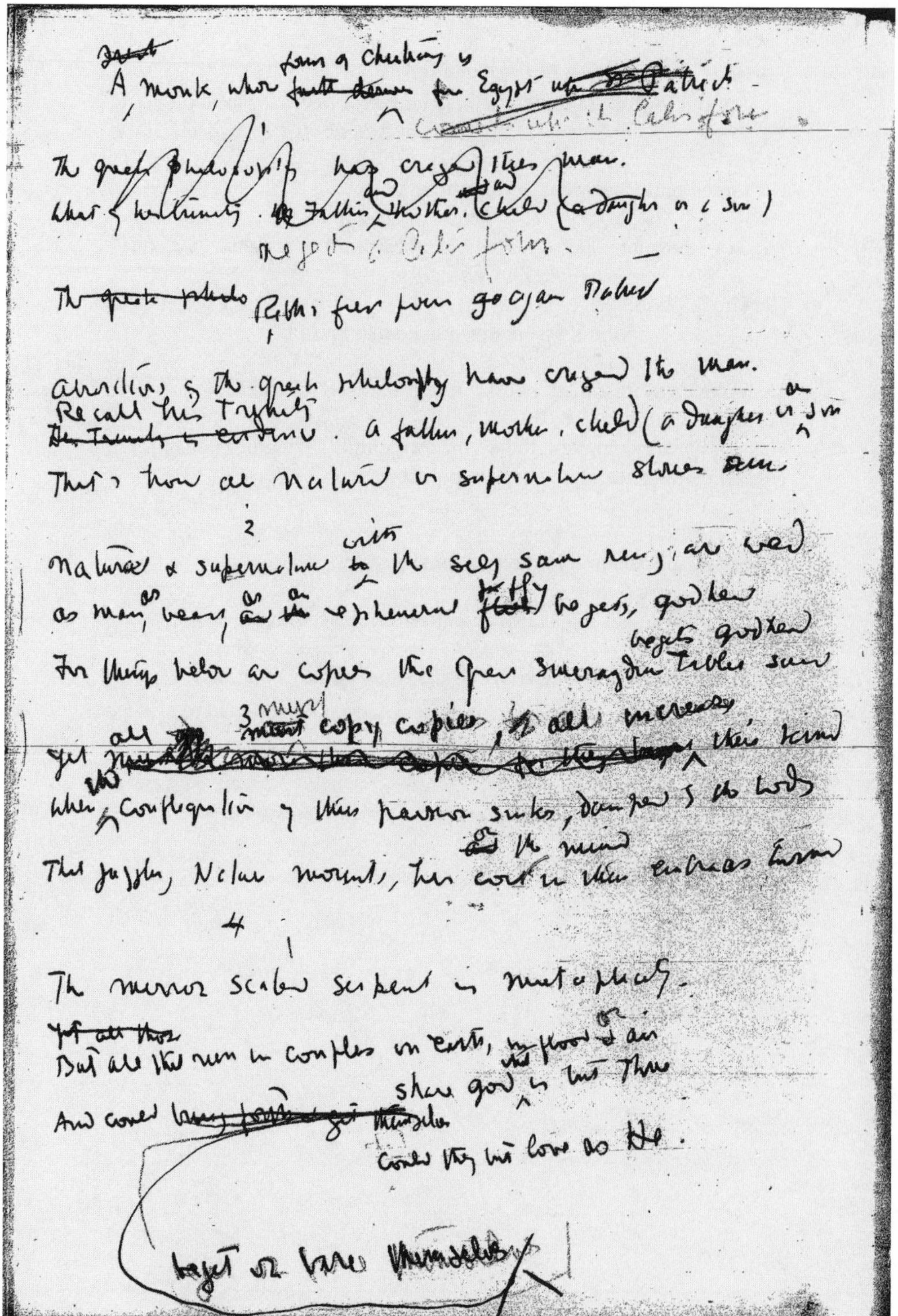
A monk, whose form of chicken is for Egypt ...
whom the Celts for ...

The greek philosophy has crazed this man.
What is [illegible]. Father and mother, child (a daughter or a son)
The god of Celtic form.

Ribh's fear from god again [illegible]

abstraction of the greek philosophy have crazed the man.
Recall this Trinity . a father, mother, child (a daughter or son)
That's how all natural or supernatural stories run.

2

Natural & supernatural with the self same ring are wed
as man, as beast, as an ephemeral fly begets, godhead
For things below are copies the Great Smaragdine Tablet said
begets godhead

3

yet all must copy copies, all increase their kind
When the conflagration of their passion sinks, damped by the body or the mind
That juggling Nature mounts, her coil in their embraces twined

4

The mirror scaled serpent is multiplicity.
But all that run in couples on earth, in flood or air
share god that is but three
And could beget or bear themselves
could they but love as He.

[BC, 15ᵛ continued]

3
must
all ~~must~~ copy copies all increase
~~Yet [?Nature] [?] more than copies for they beget~~ ^their kind
the
When^ conflagration of this passion sinks, damped by the body
or
~~and~~ the mind
That juggling Nature mounts, her coil in their embraces twined
4
The mirror scalèd serpent is multiplicity.
~~Yet all these~~
or
But all that run in couples on earth, in flood ~~&~~ air
that
share God ^ is but three
And could ~~bring forth & get themselves~~
could they but love as He.
beget or bare themselves ^

---

15 The lower "must" is in ink, the higher in pencil, "copy copies" and "all increase" in ink over pencil.

16 The inserted "the" is in ink over pencil.

19 A mark above the "e" of "scaled" is probably a grave accent to indicate that the word is pronounced with two syllables.

21 The "or" is in pencil.

22 The cancellation and the words "beget or bare themselves" are ink over pencil.

[MBY 673, letter 1, 1r and 1v]

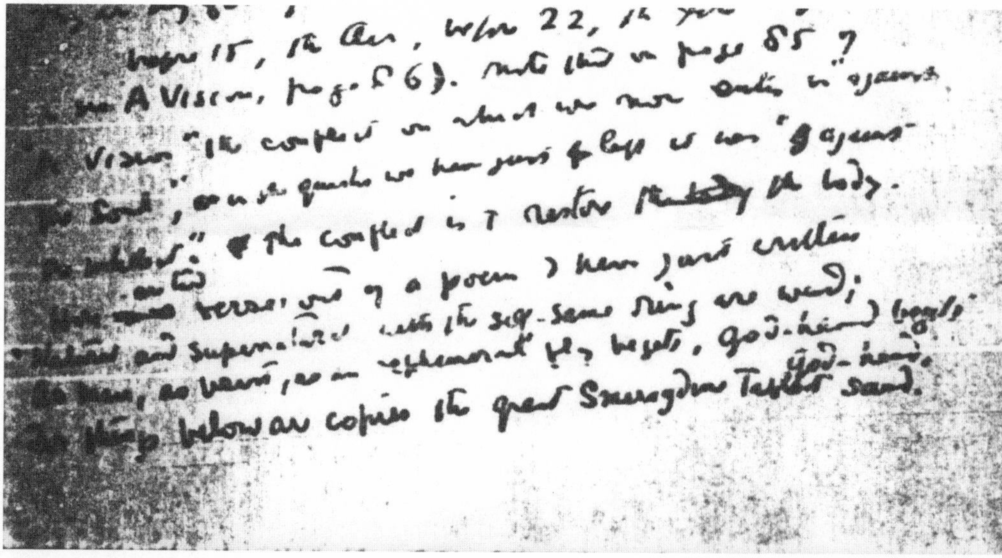

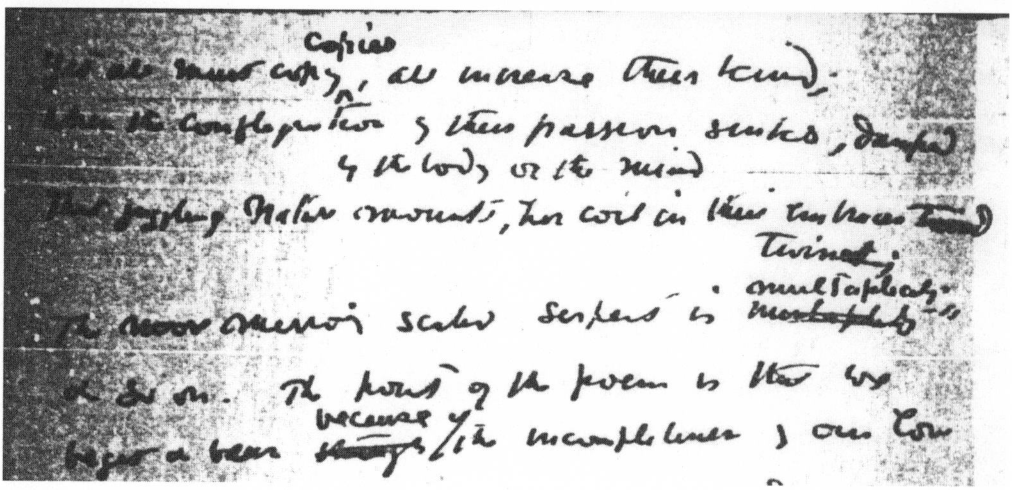

[MBY 673, letter 1, 1ʳ and 1ᵛ]

[1ʳ]

are two
Here ~~is a~~ verses out of a poem I have just written

“Natural and supernatural with the self-same ring are wed;
As man, as beast, as an ephemeral fly begets, God-head begets
God-head, ^
For things below are copies the great Smaragdine Tablet said.

[1ᵛ]

copies
Yet must all copy^, all increase their kind;
When the conflagration of their passion sinks, damped
by the body or the mind
That juggling Nature mounts, her coil in their embraces ~~twined~~
twined;
multaplicity.
The ~~mir~~ mirror scaled serpent is ~~multaplity~~”

and so on. The point of the poem is that we
because of
beget and bear ~~through~~ the incompleteness of our love

From a letter to Olivia Shakespear, July 24 [postmark July 25, 1934] from Riversdale. Transcribed from SB 3.4.57. See *Letters*, p. 824.

[Chicago(1), p. 40]

2 RIBH PREFERS AN OLDER THEOLOGY

Abstractions of the Greek Philosophy have crazed the man,
Recall his Trinity. A father, mother, child, (a daughter or a son),
That's how all natural or supernatural stories run.

Natural and supernatural with the self-same ring are wed
As man, as beast, as an ephemeral fly begets, Godhead begets Godhead,
For things below are copies the Great Smaragdine Tablet said.

Yet all must copy copies, all increase their kind,

---

title *unnumbered Houghton, P* 2 *KGCT'34, KGCT'35* 2. *LM* 2. RIBH DENOUNCES PATRICK *FMM*

1 An abstract Greek absurdity has crazed the man— *FMM*

2 child,] child *Houghton, P, LM, KGCT'35* Recall that masculine Trinity. Man, woman, child *FMM* A Trinity that is wholly masculine[.] Man, woman, child (daughter or son), *FMM-HRC*

4 wed. *Houghton, LM, KGCT'34, KGCT'35, FMM*

5 Godhead,] Godhead. *Houghton*

6 copies, *FMM*

7 kind; *Houghton, LM, KGCT'34, KGCT'35, FMM*

2–3 On p. 63 of *FMM*-HRC, lines 2 and 3 are revised as follows in black ink:

An abstract Greek absurdity has crazed the
man ≠
~~all together~~
A Trinity ~~that would be masculine~~ that is wholly masculine
~~Recall that masculine Trinity~~ Man, Woman,
child (~~a~~ daughter or ~~a~~ son),

[Chicago(1), p. 40 continued]

8 **When the conflagration of their passion sinks, damped**
by the body or the mind,
9 **That juggling nature mounts, her coil in their embraces twined.**
10 **The mirror scalèd serpent is multiplicity,**
11 **But all that run in couples, on carth, in flood or air, share**
God that is but three,
12 **And could beget or bear themselves could they but love as He.**

---

10 mirror scalèd *Houghton* mirror-scalèd *FMM*
11 carth] earth, *Houghton, P, LM, KGCT'34, KGCT'35, FMM*

[BC, 48^{v}]

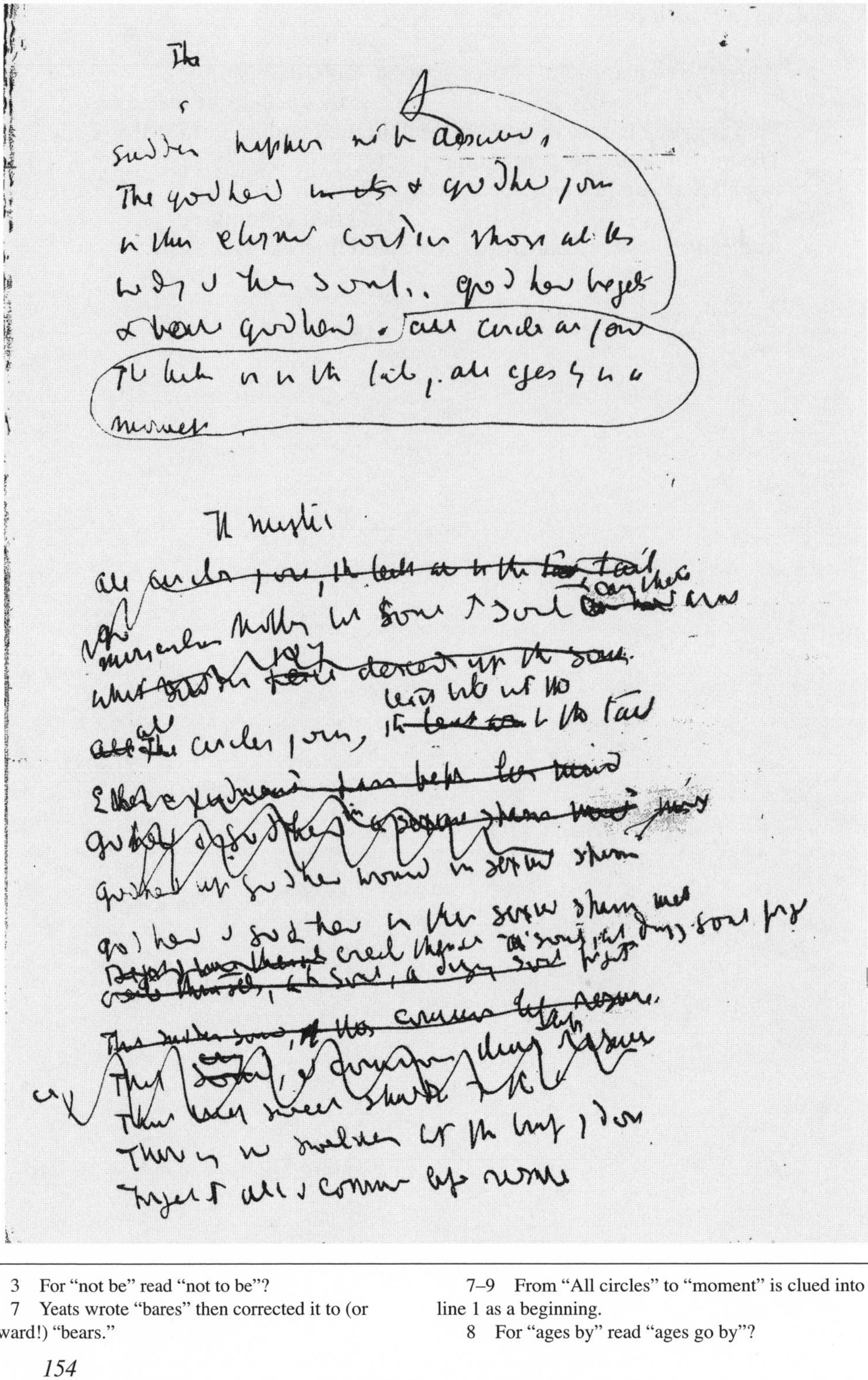

3 For “not be” read “not to be”?

7 Yeats wrote “bares” then corrected it to (or toward!) “bears.”

7–9 From “All circles” to “moment” is clued into line 1 as a beginning.

8 For “ages by” read “ages go by”?

3. Ribh in Ecstasy

[BC, 48v]

1 ~~The~~
2 ,
3 Sudden happiness not be described,
4 The godhead in its & godhead join
5 in their eternal coition through all [?his]
6 body & soul.. God head begets
{ear / ere}
7 & ba{ear/ere}s godhead, All circles are joined
8 The teeth are in the tale [?]. All ages by in a
9 moment.

The Mystic

10 All ~~circles join, the teeth are in the tale tail~~
can there
11 [~~?go~~] Nothing but Soul t Soul ~~can now~~ avail
miraculous ~~joy~~
12 ~~What sudden peace descends upon the soul~~
All teath bite into the
13 ~~All~~ ~~The~~ circles join, the teath are in the tail
14 ~~Eden & judgement pass before his mind~~
in
15 ~~Godhead & godhead a sexual spasm must mix~~
16 Godhead upon godhead wound in sexual spasm

17 Godhead & godhead in their sexual spasm met
18 ~~Beget & bare themselves~~ Create themselves – ~~[?]~~ Soul ah dizzy soul forget
19 ~~Create themselves, ah soul, a dizzy soul~~ forget
20 ~~That sudden sound, [?] this common life resume~~
~~cry~~ life
21 cry That ~~sound~~, & common [?daily] resume.
22 That brief sweet [?shudder] & the [?]
23 There is no sweetness but the trump of doom
24 Forget it all & common life resume

found in BC, 48v, 50r, 49v, 51r, 50v, *transcribed above and below*
NLI 30,519 *transcribed below*
BC, 52r *transcribed below*
published in *A Full Moon in March* (1935)

[BC, 50r]

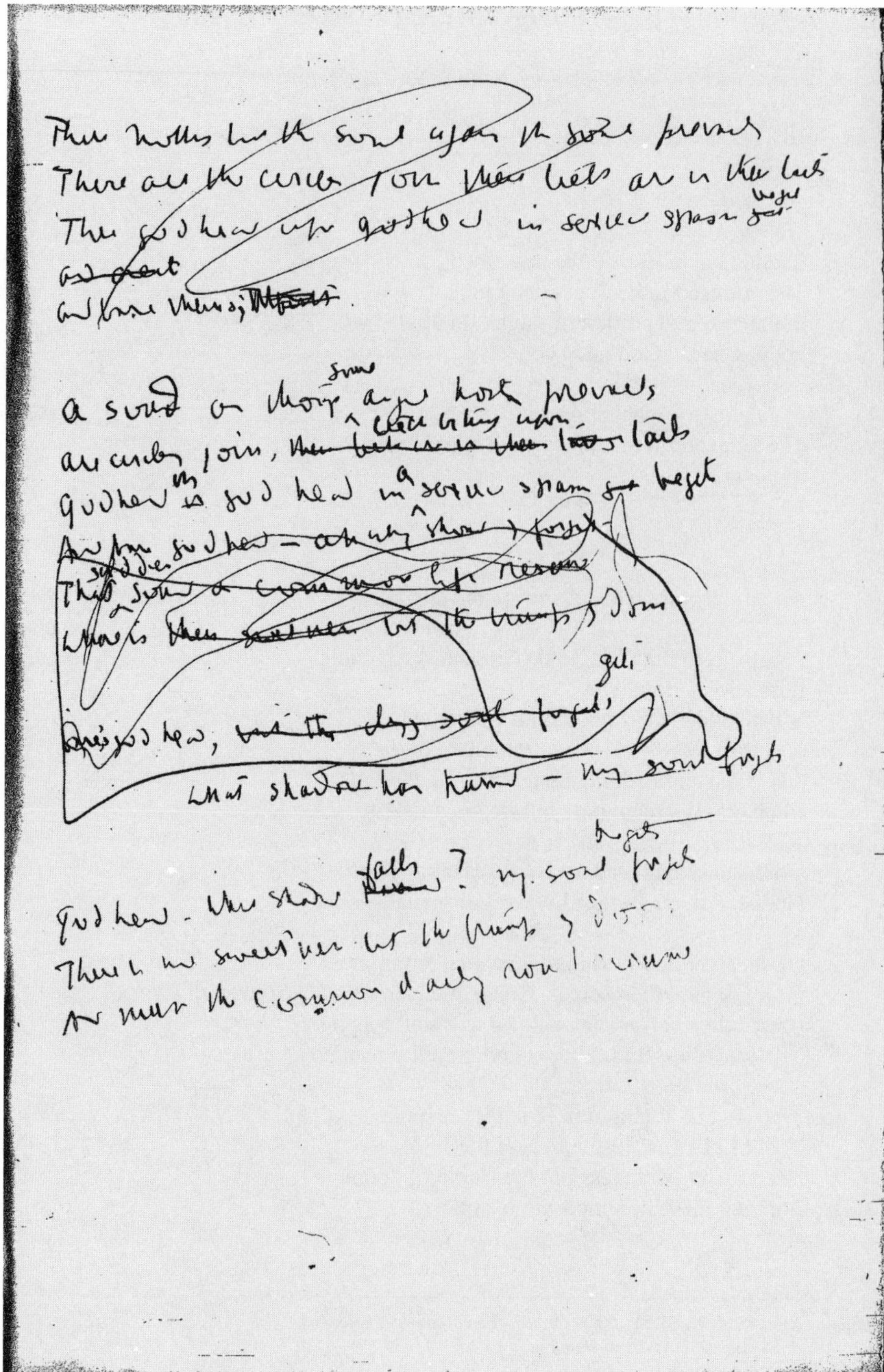

[BC, 50r]

There is nothing but the soul against the soul prevails
There all the circles join there teeth are in there tails
beget
There godhead upon godhead in sexual spasm ~~get~~
~~And create~~
And bare thems; ~~[?] birth~~

some
A sound as though ^ angel host prevails
teeth biting upon
All circles join, ~~their teeth are in their tales~~ tails
on a
Godhead ~~in~~ god head in ^ sexual spasm ~~get~~ beget
And bare godhead – ah why should I forget
sudden
That ^ sound & common life resume
Where is there sweetness but the trump of doom

gets
bares god head, ~~but the [?dizzy] soul forgets~~
What shadow has passed – ~~My soul forgets~~

~~begets~~
falls
Godhead – what shadow ~~passed~~? My soul forgets
There is no sweetness but the trump of doom
And must the common daily round resume

---

9 For "bare" read "bear"?

14–15 I think Yeats put "begets" at the end of otherwise blank line 14 as he intended to make a couplet, rhyming with "forgets," out of lines 14 and 15. See lines 8–9.

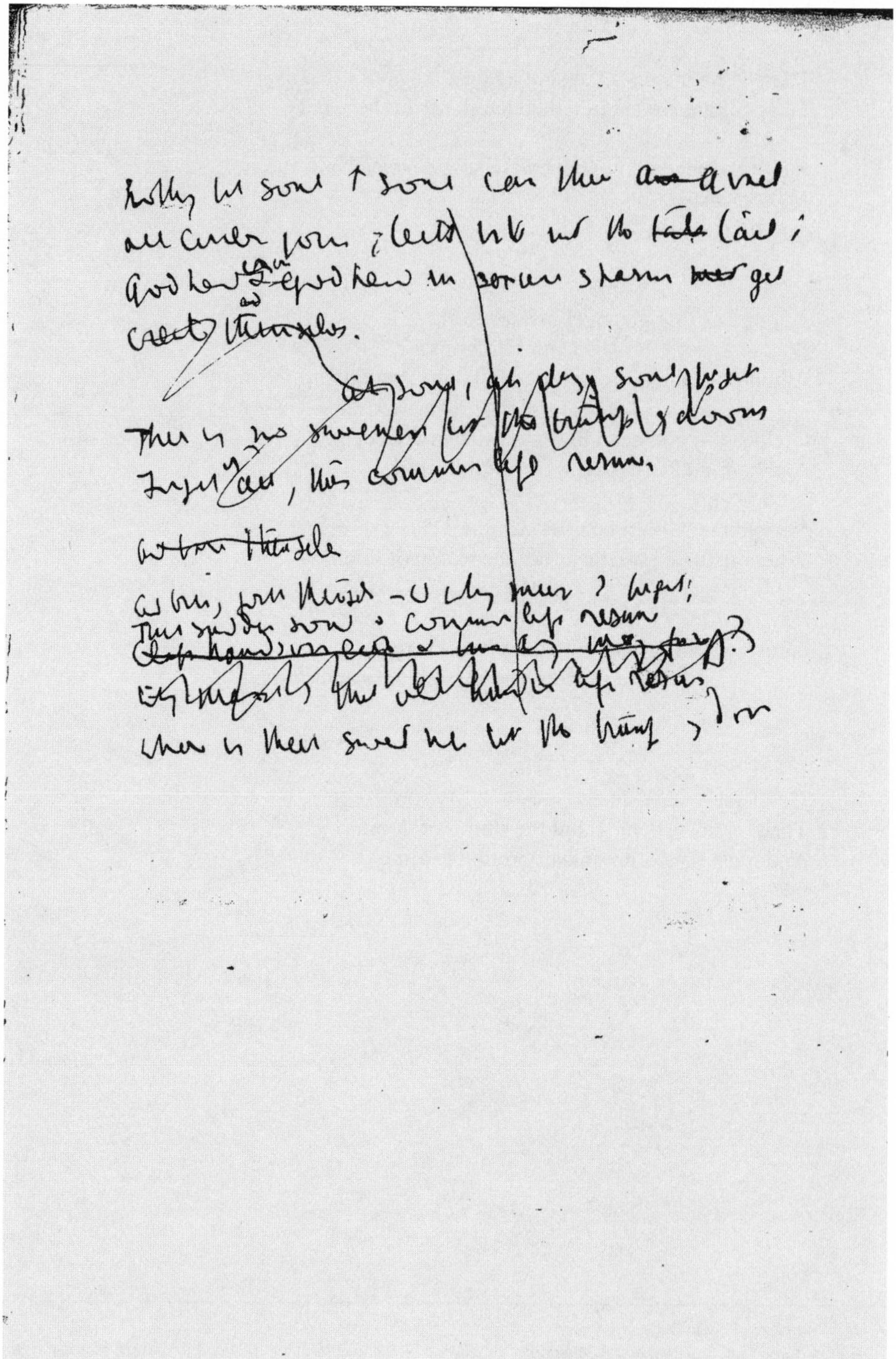

[BC, 49v]

Nothing but soul t soul can there ~~av~~ avail
All circles join & teeth bite into the ~~tale~~ tail;
~~upon~~
God head & god head in sexual spasm ~~met~~ get
~~and~~
Create themselves.
Ah soul, ah dizzy soul forget
There is no sweetness but the trump of doom
it
Forget all, this common life resume.

~~And bare themselves~~

And bring forth themselves – O why must I forget,
That sudden sound & common life resume
~~Clap hands on [?earth] & turn away my face?~~
Why must I that old humdrum life resume
Where is there sweet ness but the trump of doom

7 For "bare" read "bear"?

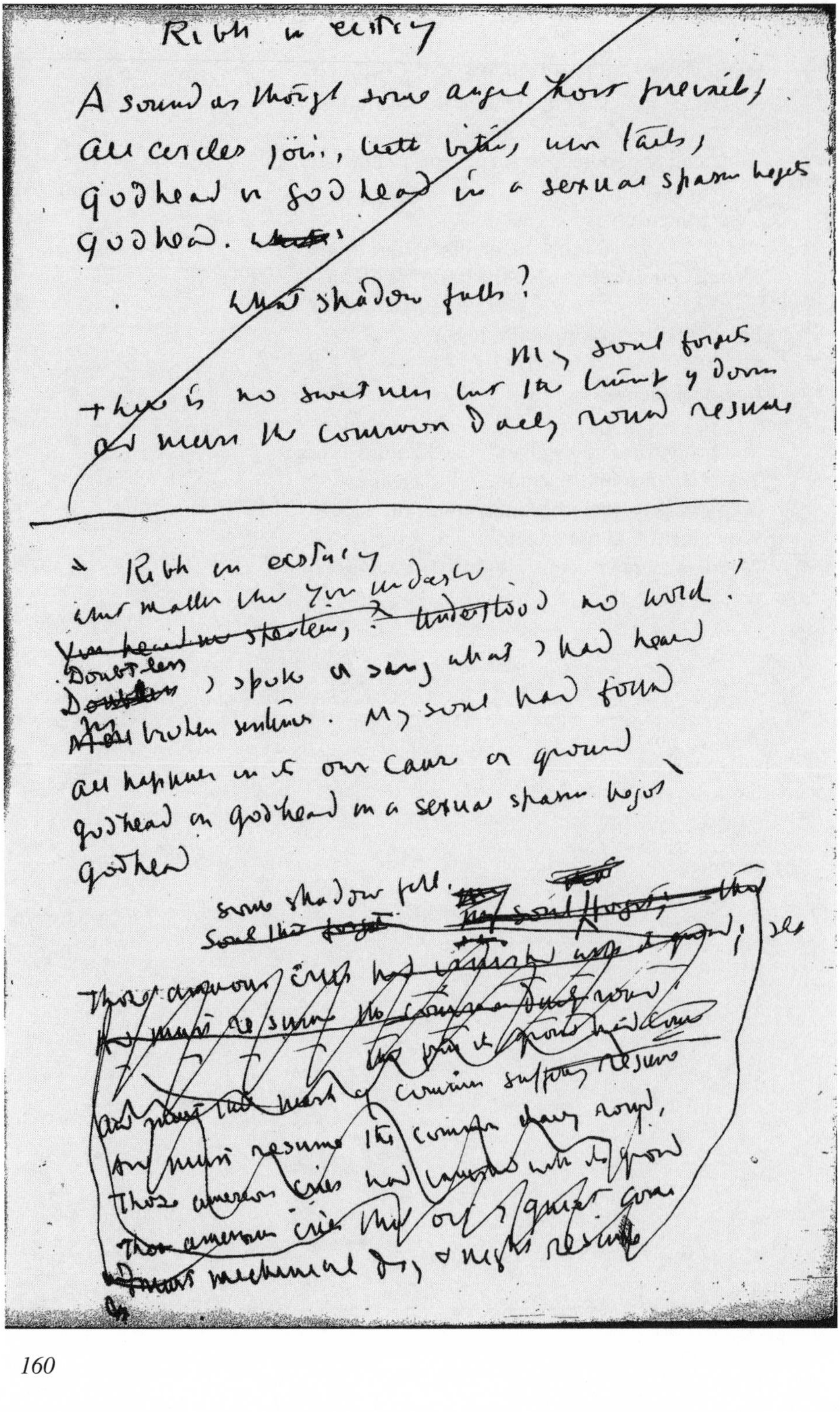

Ribh in ecstasy

A sound as though some angel horn prevails;
All circles join, begin, end fails,
Godhead on godhead in a sexual spasm begets
Godhead.

What shadow falls?

My soul forgets
There is no sweetness but the living of doom
And must the common daily round resume

Ribh in ecstasy
What matter that you understood no word!
~~You heard me stutter,~~
Doubtless I spoke or sang what I had heard
In broken sentences. My soul had found
All happiness in its own cause or ground
Godhead on godhead in a sexual spasm begot
Godhead

Some shadow fell. ~~My soul forgot;~~
~~Soul that forgot~~

~~Those amorous cries had vanished into the ground~~
~~And must resume the common daily round~~
~~And must the mask of common suffering resume~~
And must resume the common daily round,
Those amorous cries had vanished into the ground
~~Those amorous cries~~ that out of quiet come
~~Must~~ mechanical day & night resume

[BC, 51r]

Ribh in ecstasy

A sound as though some angel host prevails;
All circles join, teeth biting upon tails;
Godhead on godhead in a sexual spasm begets
Godhead. ~~What~~ s
What shadow falls?

My soul forgets
There is no sweetness but the trump of doom
And must the common daily round resume

Ribh in ecstasy

What matter that you understood
~~You heard me speaking? Unders~~tood no word?
Doubtless
~~Doubtless~~ I spoke or sang what I had heard
In
~~Mere~~ broken sentences. My soul had found
All happiness in its own cause or ground
Godhead on godhead in a sexual spasm begot
Godhead
Some shadow fell. ~~My~~ ~~that~~
~~Soul that forgot~~ ~~My soul forgot; that~~
Those amorous cries ~~had vanished with its ground;~~ stet
~~And must resume the common daily round~~
that from its ground had come
And must that mark of common suffering resume
And must resume the common daily round,
Those amorous cries had vanished with its ground
Those amorous cries that out of quiet come
And
Must mechanical day & night resume
[?]

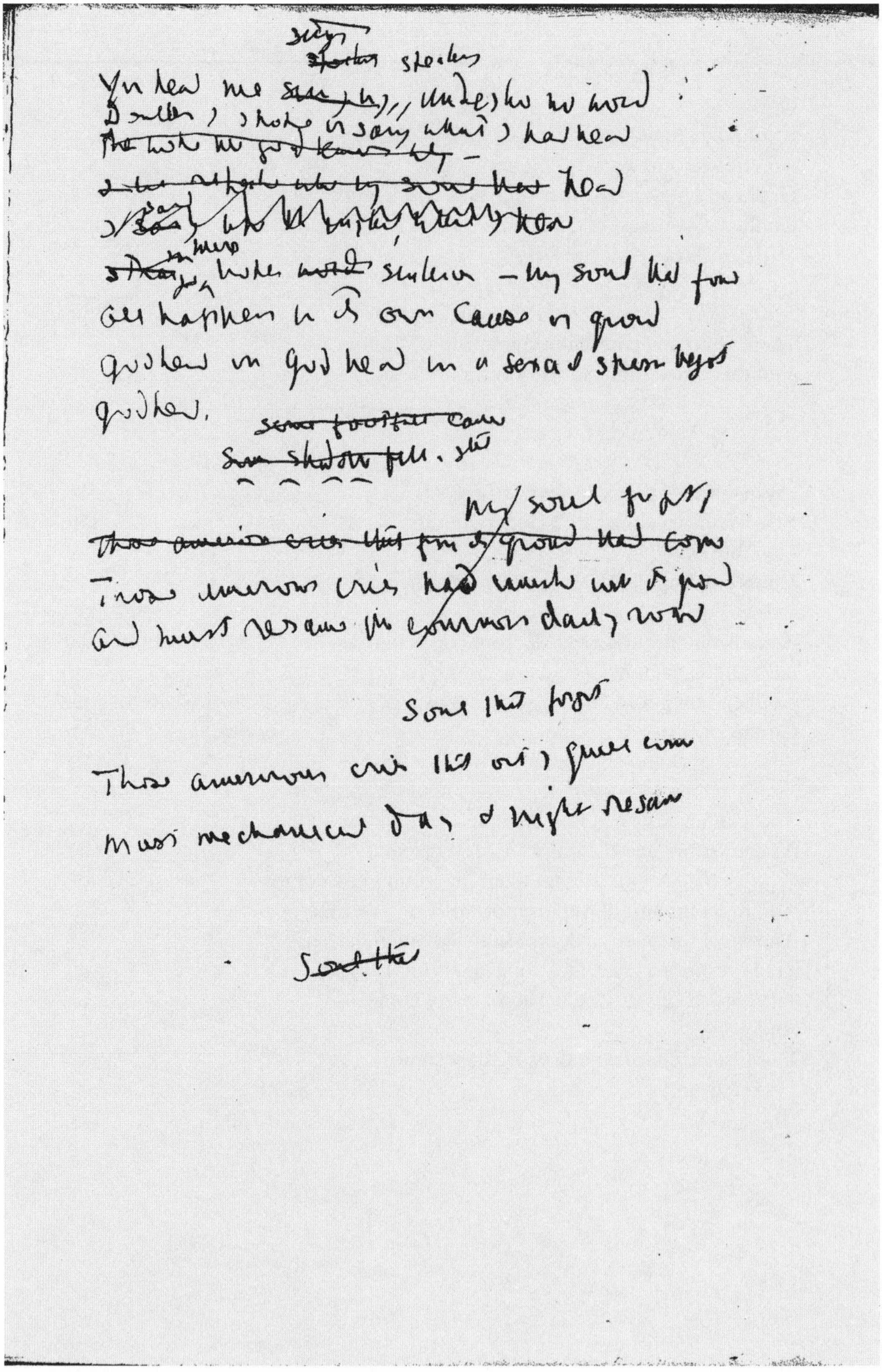
speaking
You hear me say it, understand no word
Doubtless I spoke or sang what I had heard
heard
in broken sentences — My soul had found
All happiness in its own cause or ground
Godhead on Godhead in a sexual spasm begot
Godhead.
Some footfall came
Some shadow fell. etc
My soul forgot
Those amorous cries that out of quiet come
Must mechanical day & night resume

[BC, 50v]

~~singing~~
~~speacking~~ speaking
You heard me ~~singing~~,, understood no word
Doubtless I spoke or sang what I had heard
~~Then woke me god knows why~~
~~I but repeated what my soul had~~ heard
~~said~~
~~I sang upon the instant, what I heard~~
In Mere
~~Strange~~ ^ broken ~~words~~ sentences – My soul had found
All happiness in its own cause or ground
Godhead on godhead in a sexual spasm begot
Godhead.
~~some footfall came~~
~~Some shadow fe~~ll. stet

My soul forgot;
~~Those amorous cries that that from its ground had come~~
Those amorous cries had vanished with its ground
And must resume the common daily round

Soul that forgot
Those amorous cries that out of quiet come
Must mechanical day & night resume

~~Soul that~~

[NLI 30,519]

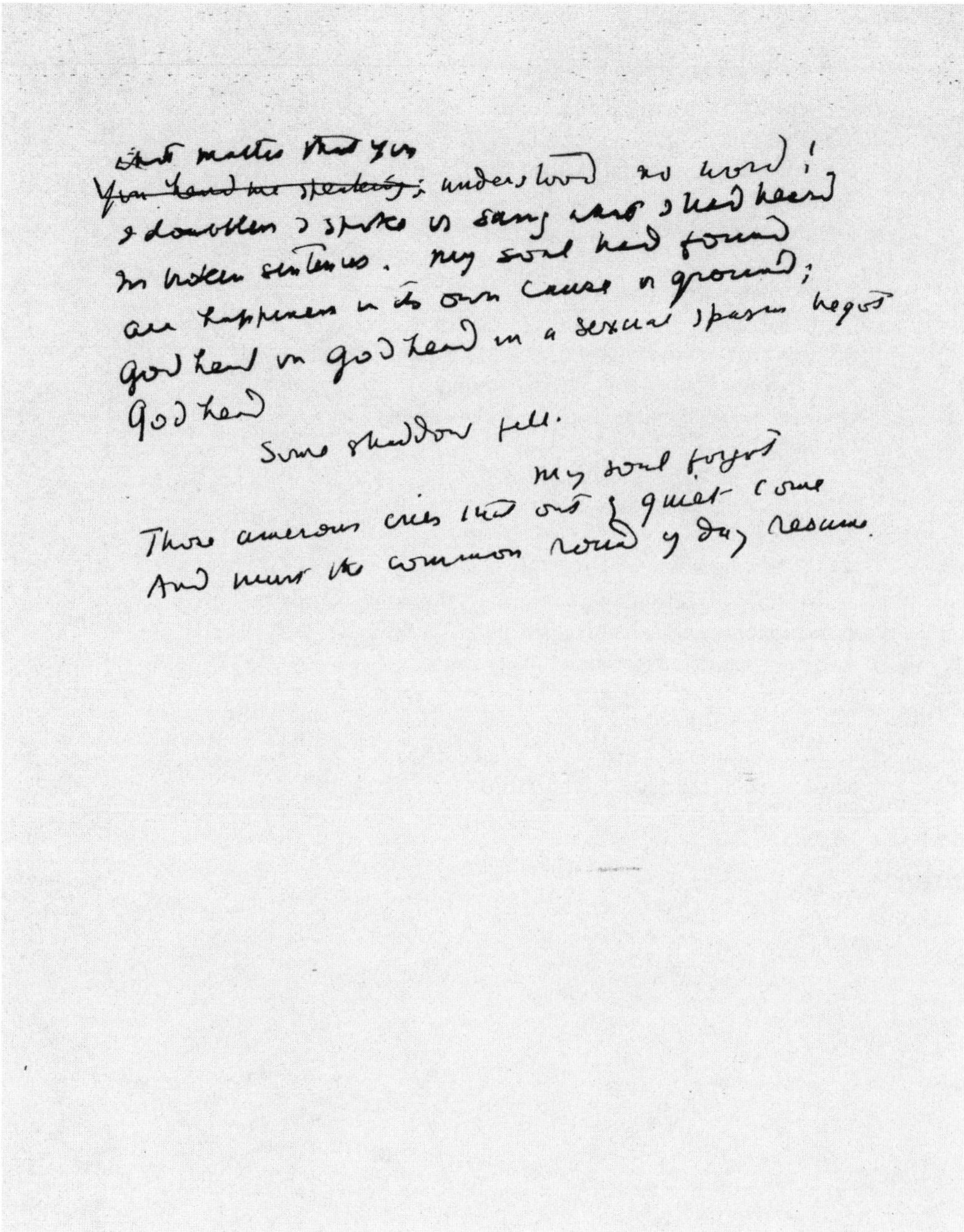
What matter that you
~~You heard me speaking~~; understood no word!
& doubtless I spoke or sang what I had heard
In broken sentences. My soul had found
all happiness in its own cause or ground;
God head on God head in a sexual spasm begot
God head
Some shadow fell.
my soul forgot
Those amorous cries that out of quiet come
And must the common round of day resume.

[NLI 30,519]

What matter that you
~~You heard me speaking~~; understood no word!
I doubtless I spoke or sang what I had heard
In broken sentences. My soul had found
All happiness in its own cause or ground;
Godhead on Godhead in a sexual spasm begot
Godhead
Some shaddow fell.
My soul forgot
Those amerous cries that out of quiet come
And must the common round of day resume.

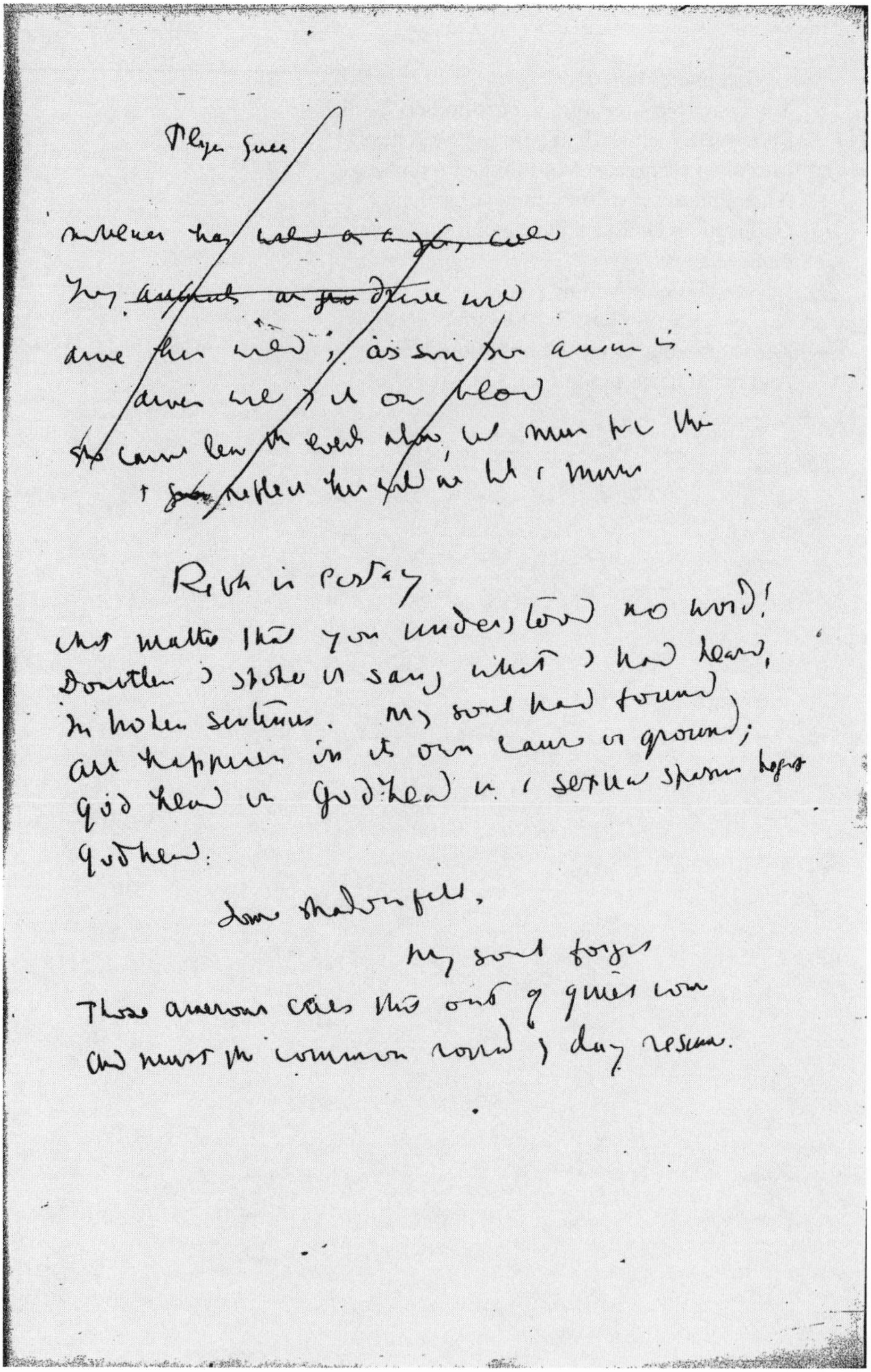

Ribh in Ecstasy

What matter that you understood no word!
Doubtless I spoke or sang what I had heard,
In broken sentences. My soul had found
All happiness in its own cause or ground;
God head on God head in sexual spasms begot
Godhead:
Some shadow fell.
My soul forgot
Those amorous cries that out of quiet come
And must the common round of day resume.

[BC, 52^{r}]

Ribh in ecstasy

What matter that you understood no word!
Doubtless I spoke or sang what I had heard,
In broken sentences. My soul had found
All happiness in its own cause or ground;
God head on Godhead in a sexual spasm begot
Godhead.
Some shadow fell.
My soul forgot
Those amorous cries that out of quiet come
And must the common round of day resume.

---

title numbered 3. RIBH IN ECSTASY *FMM*
2 heard *FMM*
4 ground. *FMM*
5 Godhead on Godhead in sexual *FMM*
6 *all printed on one line FMM*

Above the draft is a draft of lines for *The Player Queen*.

At this point Yeats, having finished “Ribh in Ectasy,” writes “There” on 51^{v} with ideas he has developed in these manuscripts but not finally used.

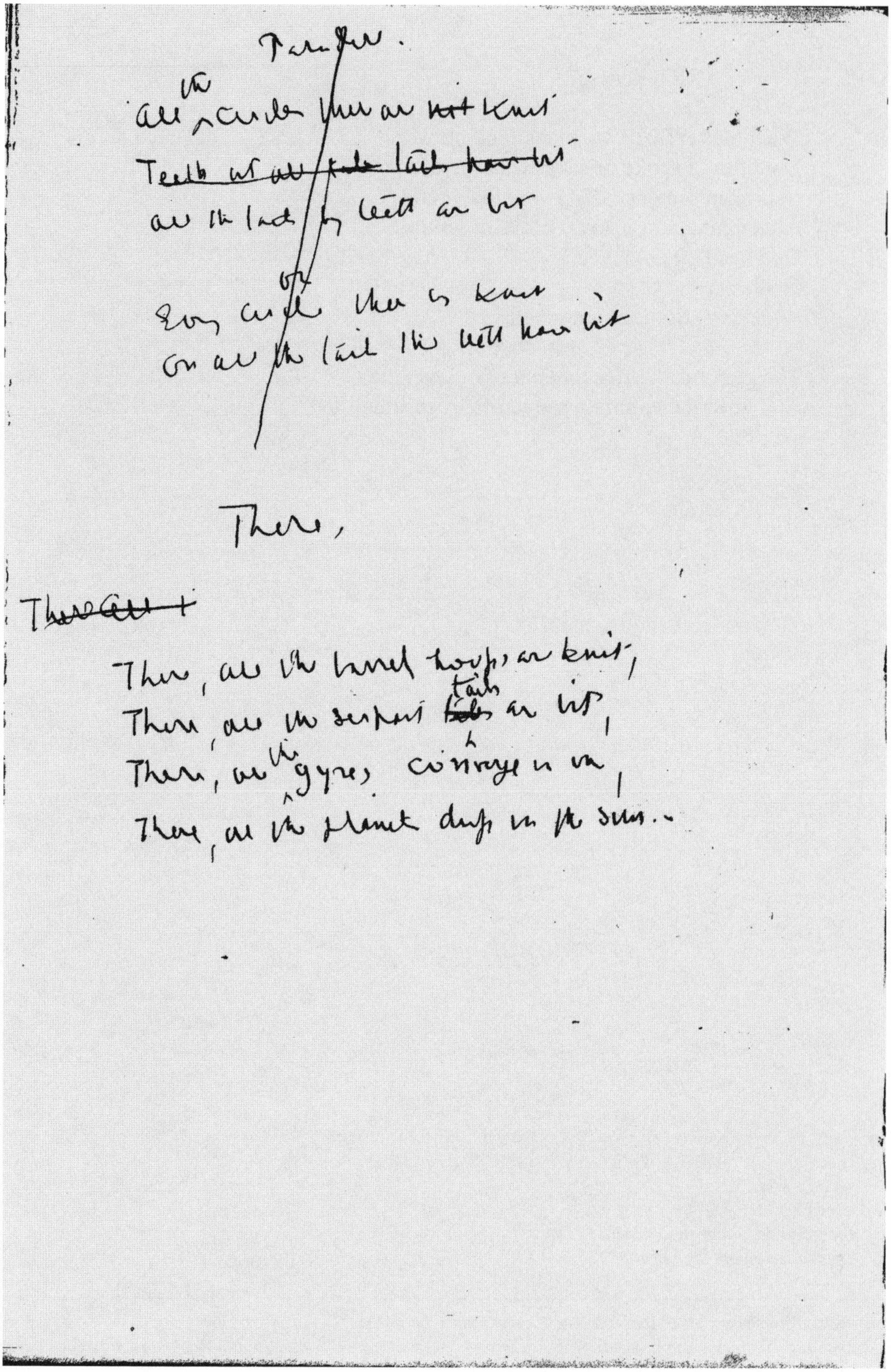
Parnell.
All the circles that are knit
All the tails by teeth are bit
Every circle that is knit
On all the tail the teeth have bit
There,
There all the barrel hoops are knit,
There all the serpent tails are bit,
There all the gyres converge in one,
There all the planets drop in the sun.

SUPERNATURAL SONGS

4. There

[BC, 51^{v}]

Paradise.

the
All‸circles there are ~~nit~~ knit
~~Teeth into all tales tails have bit~~
All the tails by teeth are bit

or
Every circle there is knit ,
On all the tails the teeth have bit

There.

~~There all [?]~~

There, all the barrel houps are knit,
tails
There, all the serpent ~~tales~~ are bit,
the
There, all‸gyres converge in one,
There, all the planets drop in the sun.

---

found in BC, 51^{v} *transcribed above*
published in *A Full Moon in March* (1935)

---

title *numbered* 4. THERE *FMM*
8 There all the barrel-hoops *FMM*
9 There all the serpent-tails *FMM*
10 There all *FMM*
11 There all . . . Sun. *FMM*

See also "3. Ribh in Ecstasy," 51^{r}, pp. 160–161, and note to 52^{r} on p. 167.

[NLI 30,546, 3r]

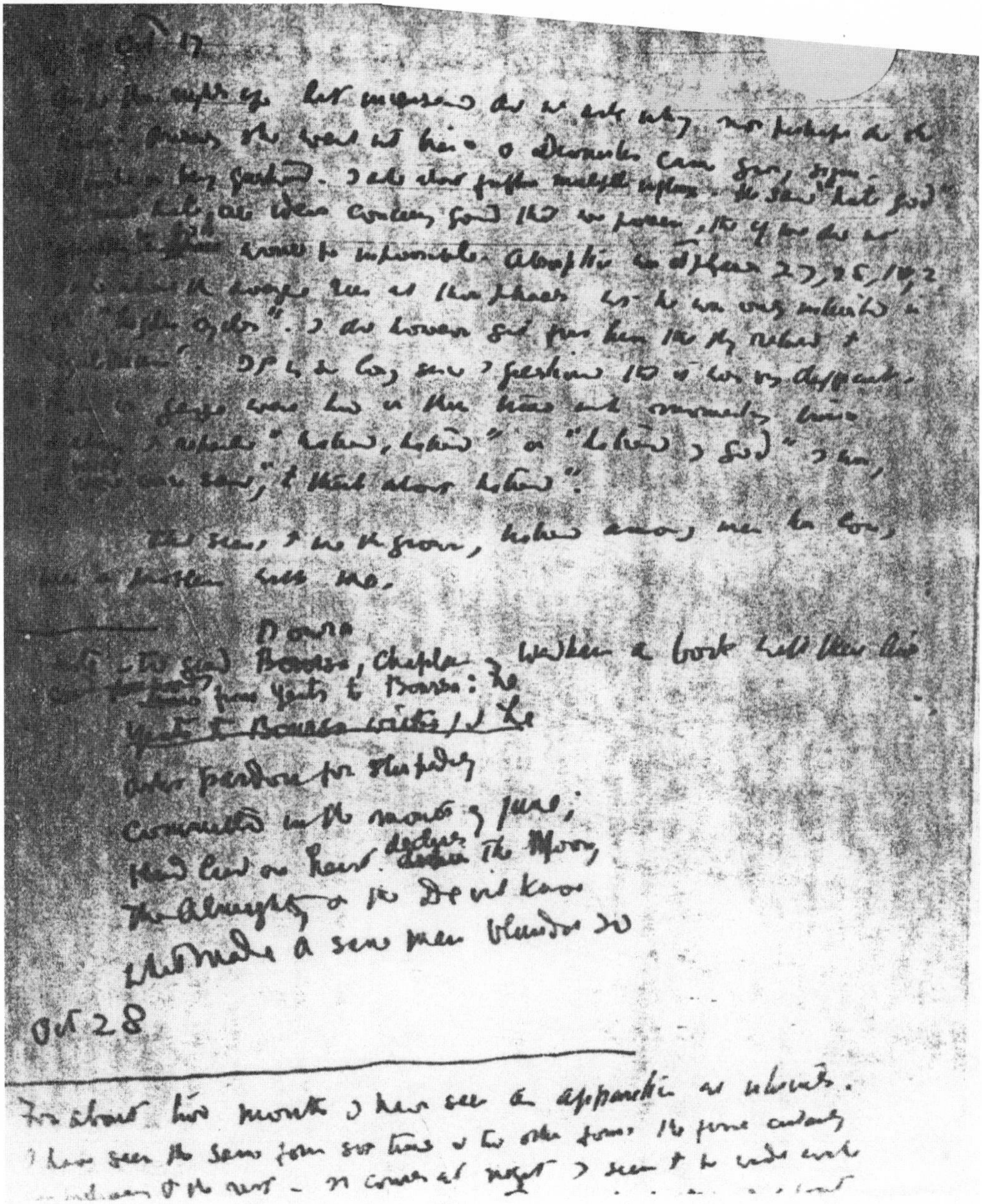

Oct 28

For about two months I have seen an apparition as [illegible]

SUPERNATURAL SONGS

5. Ribh considers Christian Love insufficient

[NLI 30,546, 3^{r}]

Oct 17

George three nights ago lit incense - I did not ask why nor perhaps did she
know. Presently she went into trance & Dionertes came giving signs.
He [?insisted] on being questioned. I asked about [?fifteen} multiple influx. He said "hate god"
We must hate all ideas concerning god that we possess, that if we did not
in god
absorption ~~[? ?]~~ would be impossible. Absorption was at phases 27, 28, 1 & 2
I asked about the average man at those phases but he was only interested in
the "higher cycles". I did however get from him that they returned to
"equilibrium". [?It] is so long since I questioned that it was very difficult.
Later on George went two or three times into momentary trance
& always to repeated, "hatred, hatred" or "hatred of god" I was,
voice
the ~~[?]~~ once said, "to think about hatred".
That seems to me the growing hatred among men has long
been a problem with me.

---

found in NLI 30,546, 3^{r} *transcribed above*
BC, 18^{v}, 20^{r}, 19^{v}, 21^{r}, 20^{v}, 22^{r}, 40^{r}, 21^{v} *transcribed below*
Chicago(1), pp. 41–42 *transcribed below*
NLI $30{,}020_{2}$

published in *Poetry* (Chicago), December 1934
The London Mercury, December 1934
The King of the Great Clock Tower (1934)
The King of the Great Clock Tower (1935)
A Full Moon in March (1935)

Transcribed from SB 21.6.159.

1 The year is 1933.

4 "He [?insisted]": "insisted" is Curtis Bradford's reading, *Yeats at Work* (Carbondale: Southern Illinois University Press, 1965), p. 135.

11 For "to repeated" read either "repeated" or "to repeat"?

13 For "That" read "What"?

Below the text is a verse apology, dated October 28, to "Bowra, Chaplain of Waldham" College (C. M. Bowra, an Oxford don and author of *The Heritage of Symbolism*), and below that is a note beginning "For about two months I have such an apparition at intervals."

[BC, 18ᵛ]

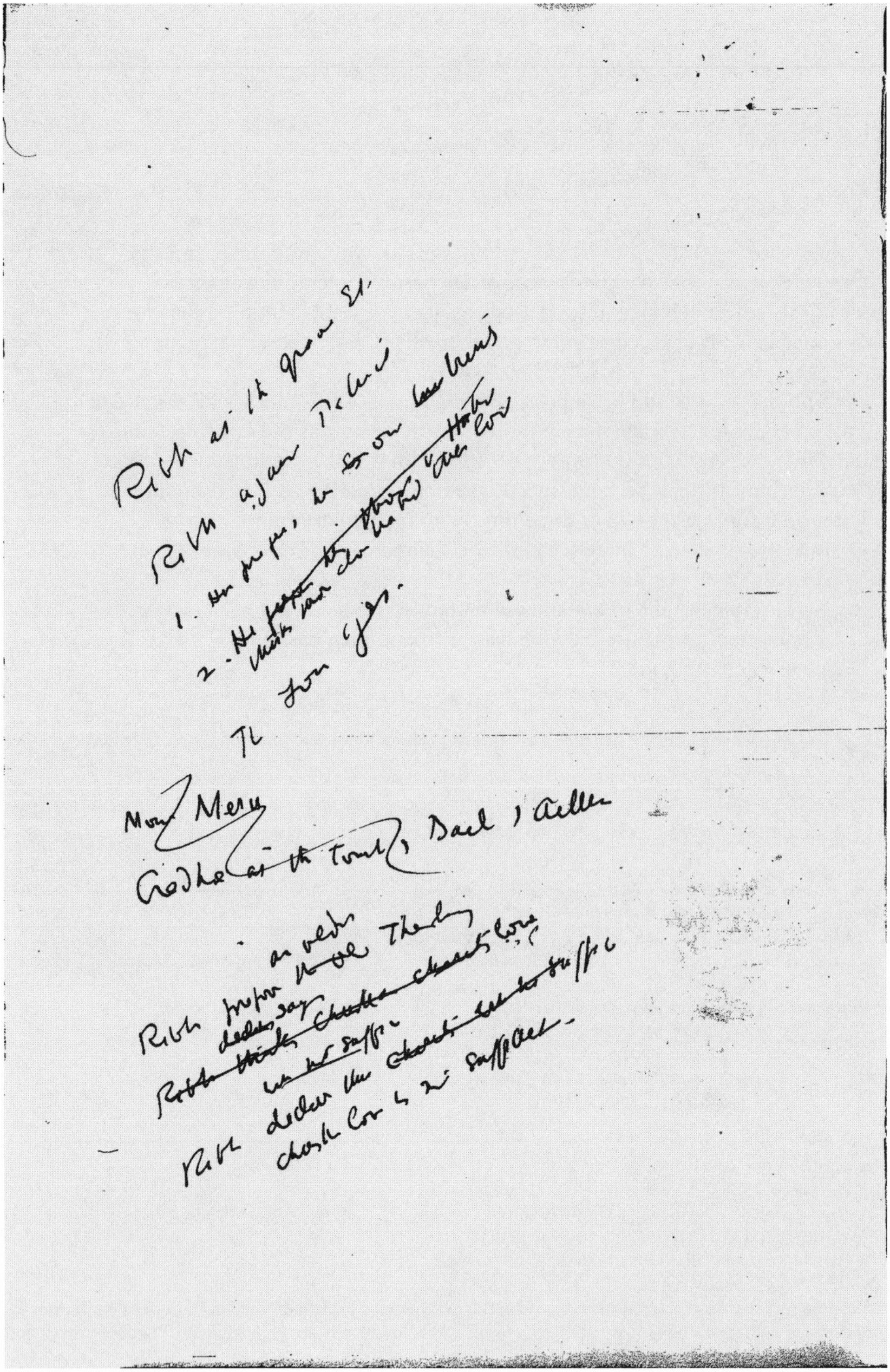

[BC, 18v]

1 Ribh at the grave Etc
2 Ribh against Patrick
3 1. He prefers his ~~Ete~~ own ~~tri~~ Trinity
4 2. He ~~fixes his thought on Hatred~~
thinks more about hatred than love

5 The Four Ages

6 Mount Meru
7 Aedhe at the tomb of Baile and Aillin

an older
8 Ribh proposes ~~the old~~ theology
~~declares~~ says
9 ~~Ribh thinks Christian charity~~ love
~~will not suffice~~
10 Ribh declares that ~~charity will not suf~~fice
christian love is not sufficient.

On this page Yeats puts down some order for the "Supernatural Songs," mentioning six poems, but then seems occupied with "Ribh considers Christian Love insufficient" in lines 4, 9, and 10.

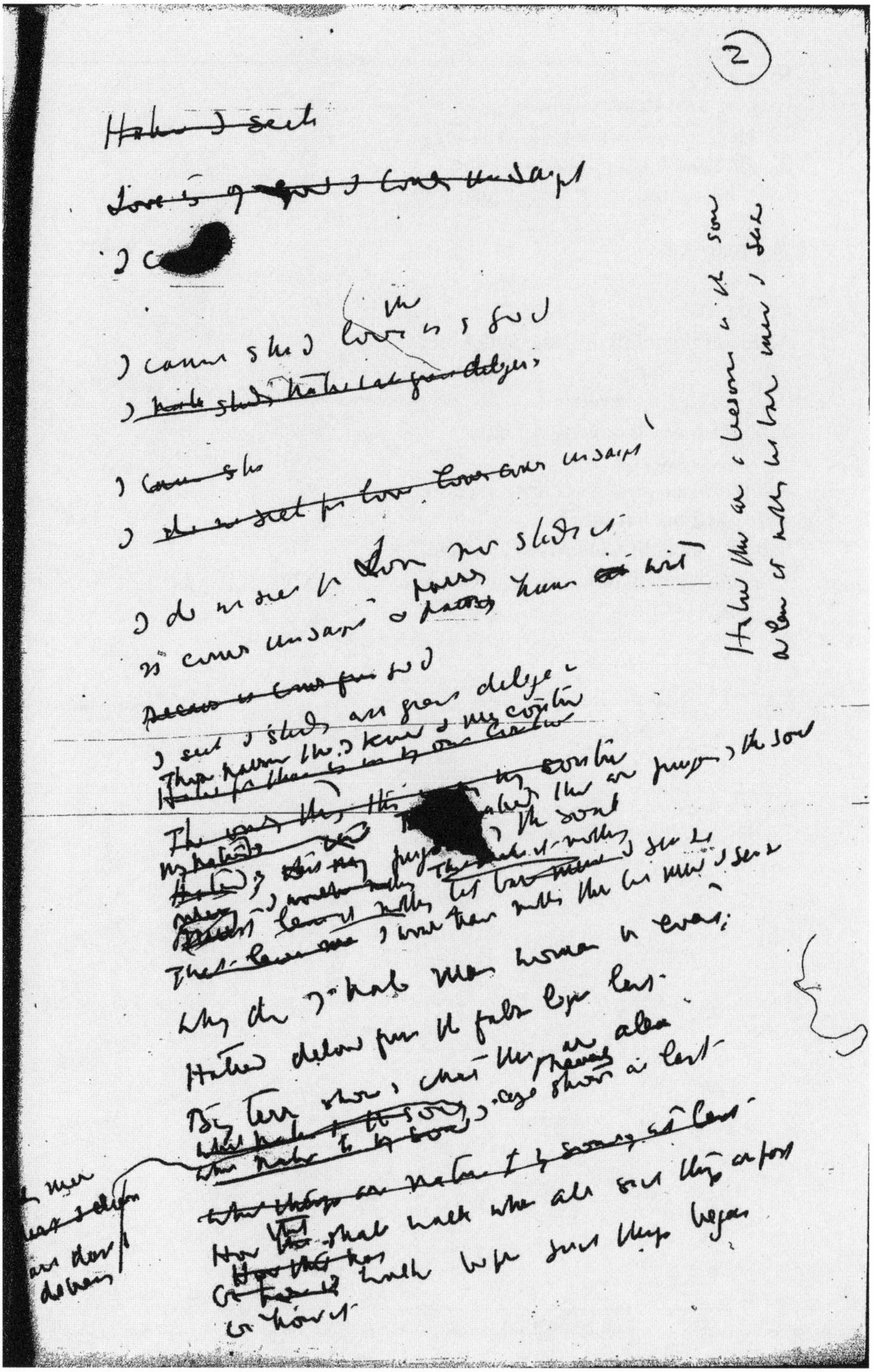

[BC, 20r]

~~Hatred I seek~~ (2)
~~Love is of God & comes unsought~~
I [?]

that
I cannot stud love is of god
~~I hate study hatred with great diligence~~
~~I can stu~~
I ~~do not seek for love love c~~omes unsought
{L
I do not seek for {love nor study it
passes
It comes unsought & ~~passes~~ human ~~uit~~ wit
~~Because it comes from~~ god
I seek and study with great diligence
Those passions that I know & may control
~~Hatred for that is in my own control~~
~~The only thing [?this] [?is] [?in] my control~~
~~My hatred, that~~ [?] [?hatreds] that are purges of the soul
~~Hatred; that may~~ purg[?] of the soul
~~[?May]~~ –I ~~[?] nothing~~ that [?make] it nothing
Must leave it nothing but bare mind & sense
~~That leave me~~ I would have nothing there but mind & sense
Why do I hate man woman or event;
Hatred delivered from the false logic lent
By terror shows what things are alea
reveals
[?] Mere ~~What native to the soul~~ Age shows at last
~~dirt & dun~~ ~~What native to my soul~~
[?Dirt] dust & [?debris] ~~What things are native to my soul; at last~~
that
How ~~tht~~ shall walk when all such things are past
~~How that has~~
~~Or how it~~ walked before such things began
Or how it

Hatred that are a besom to the soul
And leave it nothing but bare mind & sense.

The circled "2" at top right is in pencil.
In the first line in the right margin, for "Hatred" read "Hatreds"?
4 For "stud" read "study"?
13 For "this" read "that"?
13–16 A large ink blot makes it impossible to read these lines accurately.
21 For "alea" read "alien"?

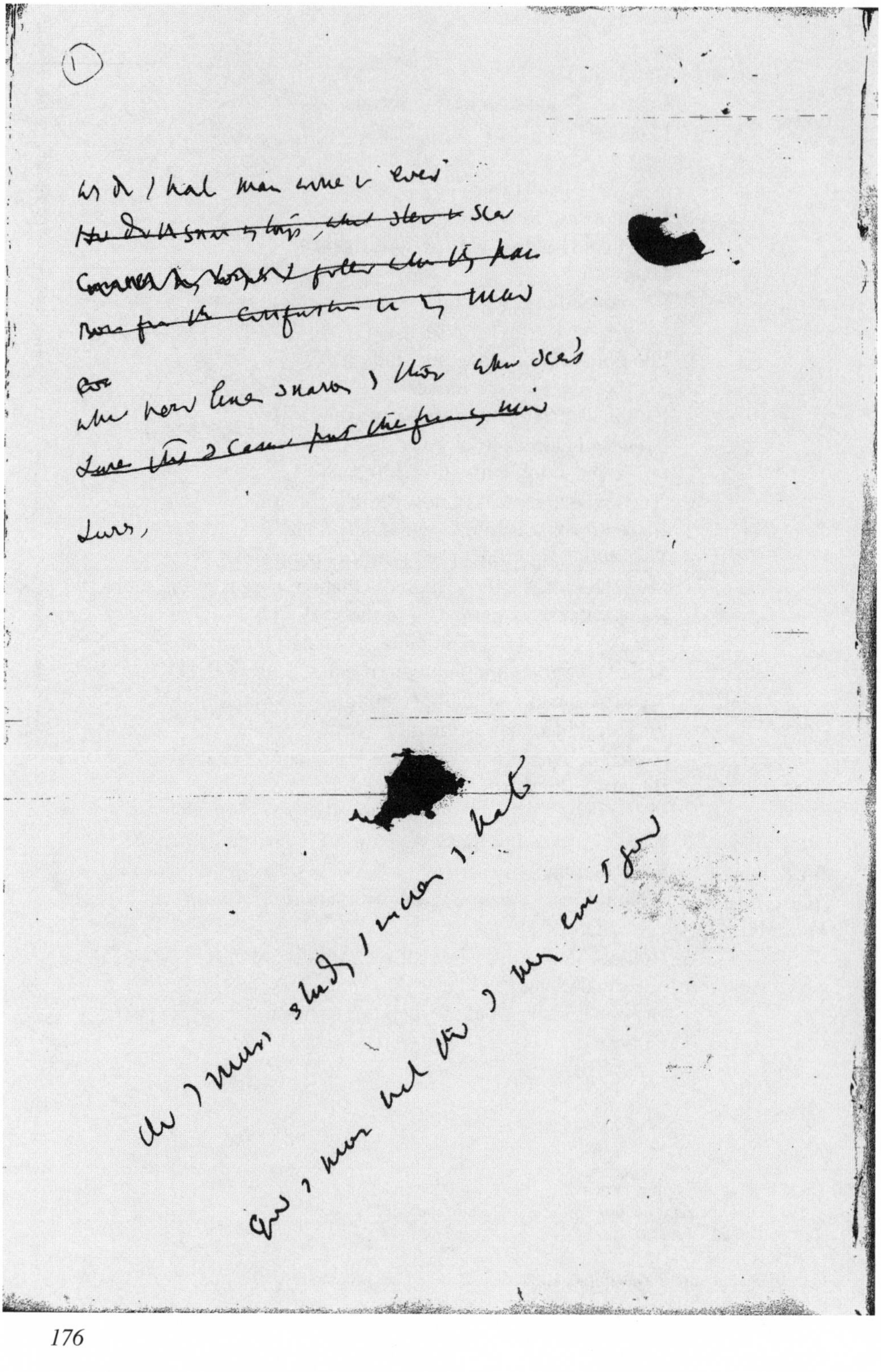

[BC, 19ᵛ]

①

Why do I hate man woman or event
~~How do they snap my trap, what [?stench] or~~ scent
~~Compels my [?hounds] to follow where they pass~~
~~Born from the confusion in my mi~~nd
~~Con~~
What hound lives [?snared] by those whose scent
~~Lures that I cannot put them from my mi~~nd
[?Lures]

And I must study to increase my hate
God must I hate that I may come to god

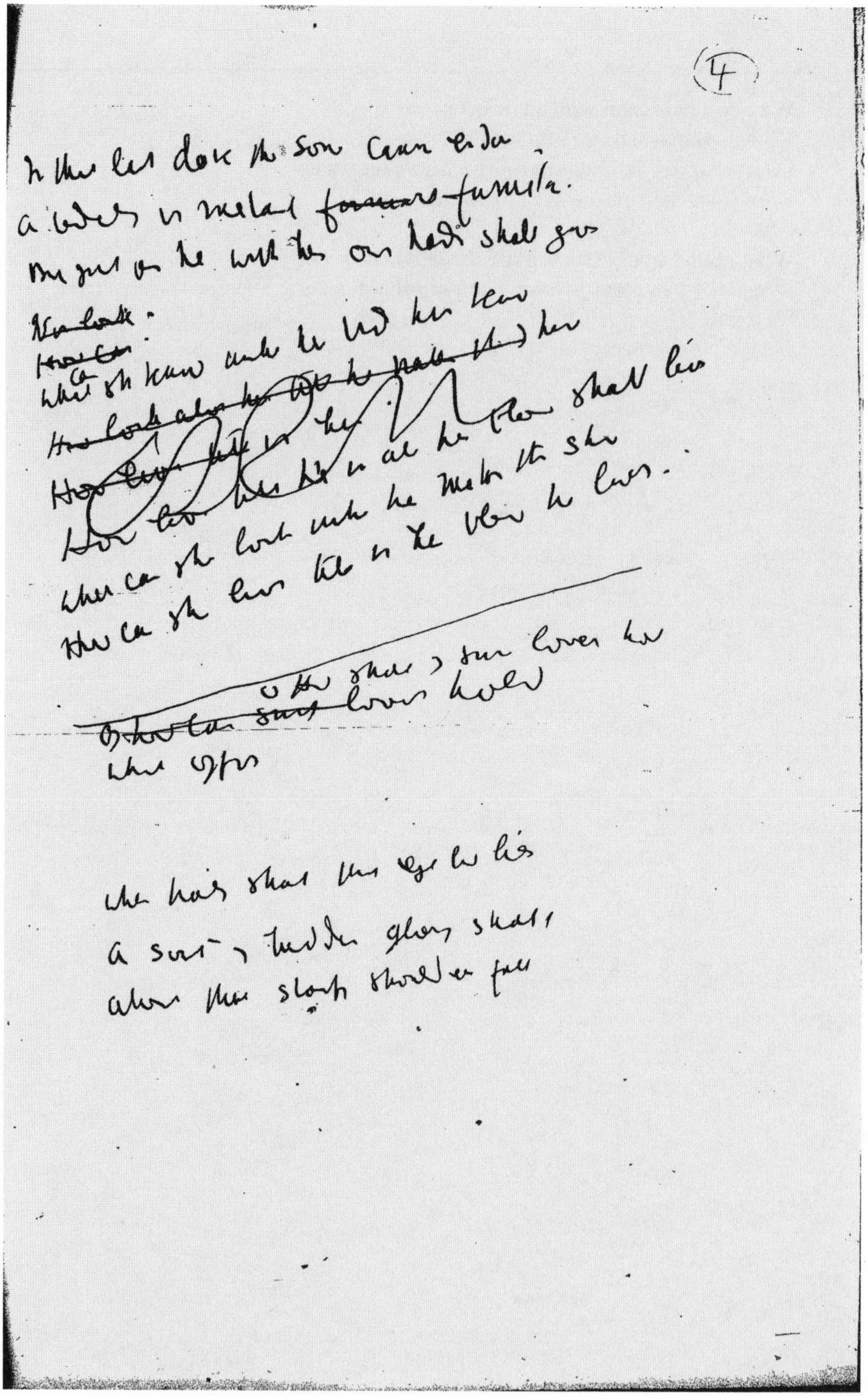
(4)

In the last dark the sun came [illegible]
a [illegible] is melted ~~[illegible]~~ familiar.
But yet on the with his own hands shall grow

~~[illegible]~~:
~~[illegible]~~
What can she know until he hid her tears
~~[illegible]~~
~~[illegible]~~ shall [illegible]
~~[illegible]~~ all the [illegible] the shoe
~~[illegible]~~ till he [illegible] the lover.
What can she [illegible] until he [illegible]
How can she [illegible] till he [illegible]

~~[illegible]~~ lovers hold
[illegible]

When [illegible] shall [illegible] lie
A [illegible] glory shall
[illegible] should [illegible] fall

[BC, 21r]

(4)

In that last dark the soul cannot endure
A bodily or [?mental] ~~furniure~~ furniture
But [?yet] as he with his own hands shall give
~~Nor look~~
~~How can~~
    can
What she know until he bid her know
~~How look about her till he make the s~~how
~~How live till~~ in her
How live till he in all her blood shall live
Where can she look until be makes the show
How can she live till in her blood he lives.

At the bottom of the page is a draft of an unpublished poem, "Margot." For a full version of this poem addressed to Margot Ruddock, see *Ah, Sweet Dancer,* opposite p. 80.

[BC, 20^{v}]

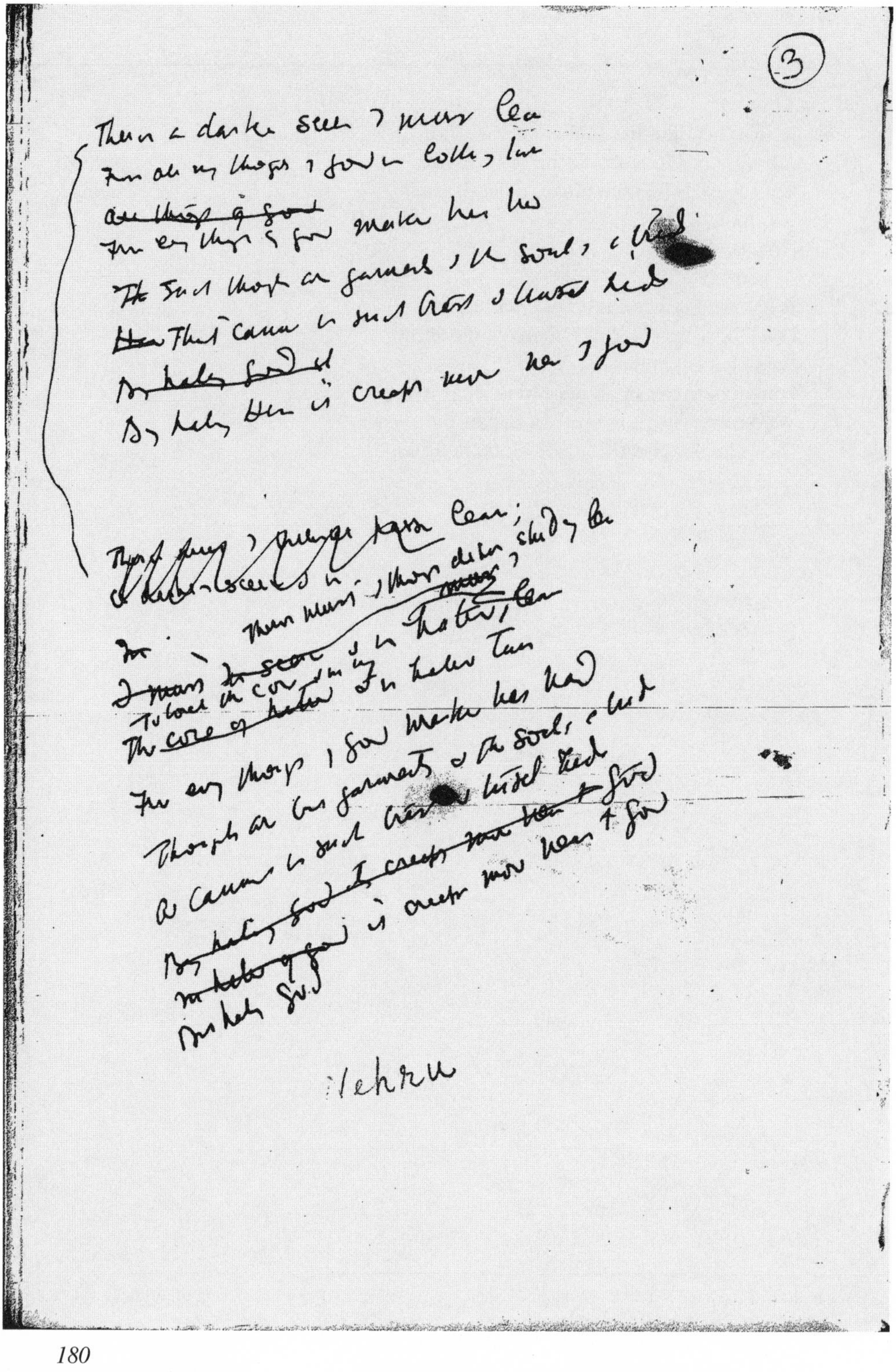

[BC, 20v]

3

Thereon a darker science I must learn
From all my thoughts of god in loathing turn
~~All thought of god~~
From every thought of god mankind has had
~~The~~ Such thoughts are garments & the souls a bride
~~How~~ That cannot in such trash & tinsel hide
~~By hating god it~~
By hating Him it creeps more near to god

Thereon must I [?bitterest] passion learn;
A darker [?science] & in
~~In~~ Thereon must I through [?darker] study learn
~~must~~
~~I must in scorn & in hatred, learn~~
To touch the core & in my
~~The core of hatred~~ & in hatred turn
From every thought of god mankind has had
Thoughts are but garments & the souls a bride
And cannot in such trash & tinsel hide
~~By hating god [?it] creeps more near to god~~
~~In hatred of god~~ it creeps more near to god
[?By] hating god

Lines are numbered top to bottom. However, line 1 is clued into line 9, and lines 1–8 seem to be a rewriting of 9–19. If true, Yeats began by entering lines 9–19 halfway down the page but did not delete this original entry when he made the second.

Below the draft, in pencil, is "Nehru," probably in Mrs. Yeats's hand.

[BC, 22r]

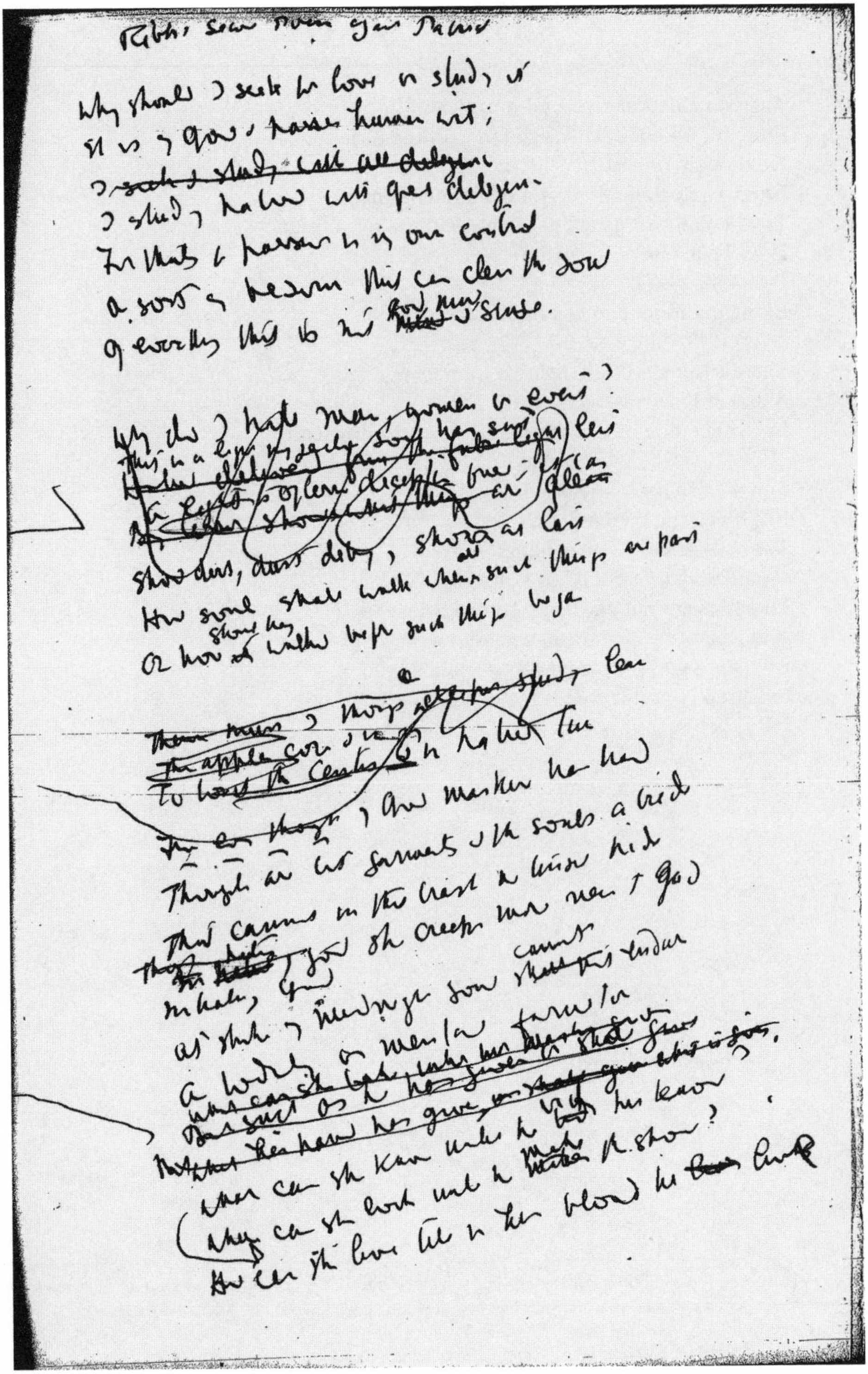

[BC, 22r]

Ribhs Second Poem against Patrick

Why should I seek for love or study it
It is of god & passes human wit;
~~I seek to study with all diligence~~
I study hatred with great diligence
For that's a passion in my own control
A sort of besom that can clear the soul
god, mind,
Of everything that is not ~~mind~~ & sense.

Why do I hate man, women, or event?
That is a light my jealous soul has sent
~~Hatred delivered from the false li~~ght lent
A light Of terror deception freed
~~By terror shows what things are~~ alean
Show dirt, dust debris, shows at last
all
How soul shall walk when^such things are past
Showed how
Or how ~~it~~ walked before such things began

a
~~Then must I through^deeper study~~ learn
The apple core & in my
~~To touch the centre &~~ to hatred turn
For every thought of god mankind has had

10 For "terror deception" read "terror & deception"? For "alean" read "alien"?
11 For "Show" read "Shows"?

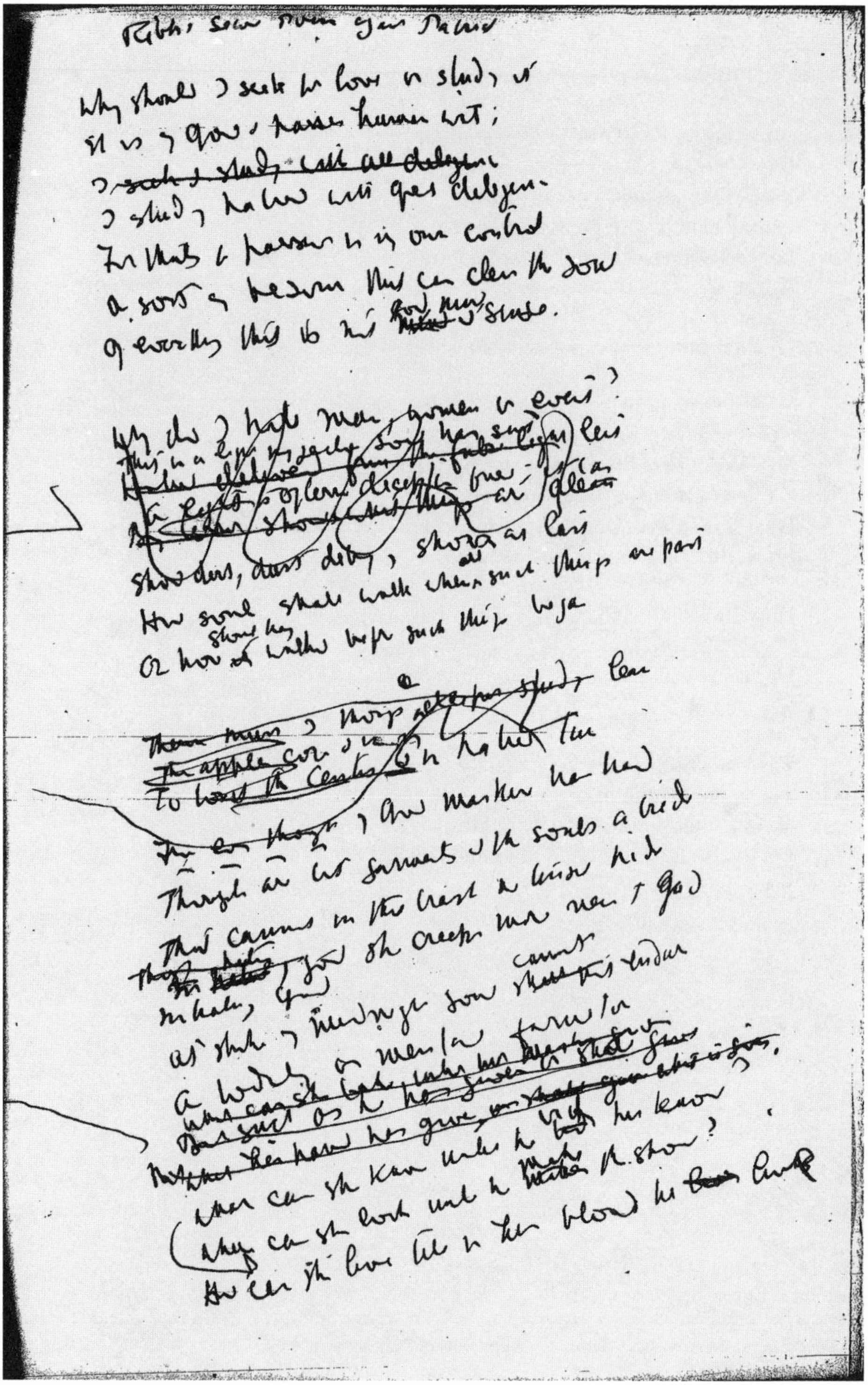

[BC, 22ʳ continued and 40ʳ]

[22ʳ continued]

18 Thoughts are but garments and the souls a bride
19 That cannot in that trash and tinsel hide
~~Through hating~~ {G
20 ~~In hatred of g~~od she creeps more near to {god
In hating god

cannot
21 At stroke of midnight soul ~~shall not~~ endure
22 A bodily or mental furniture
~~What can she take until her master gi~~ve
23 ~~But such as he has given or shall give~~
24 ~~But What his hand has given, or shall give what is given.~~
bid
25 What can she know until he ~~bids~~ her know
make
26 Where can she look until he ~~makes~~ the show?
{e
27 How can she live till in her blood he ~~lives~~ liv{es

[BC, 40ʳ]

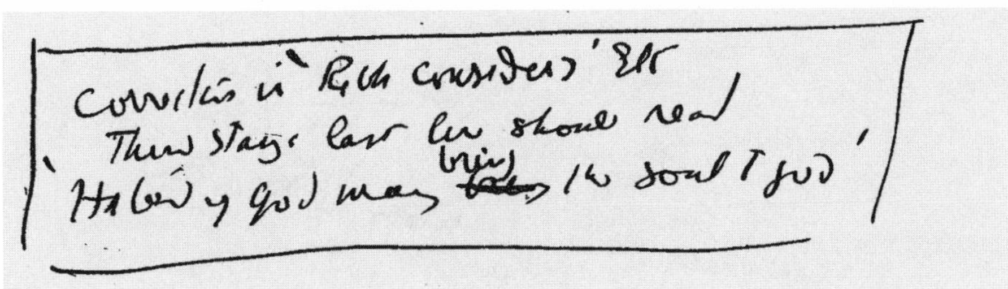
Correction in 'Ribh considers' Etc
Third stanza last line should read
bring
'Hatred of God may ~~bring~~ the soul to god'

22ʳ, l. 20 On 40ʳ (shown above) appears this note:
Correction in 'Ribh considers' Etc
Third stanza last line should read
bring
'Hatred of God may ~~bring~~ the soul to god'

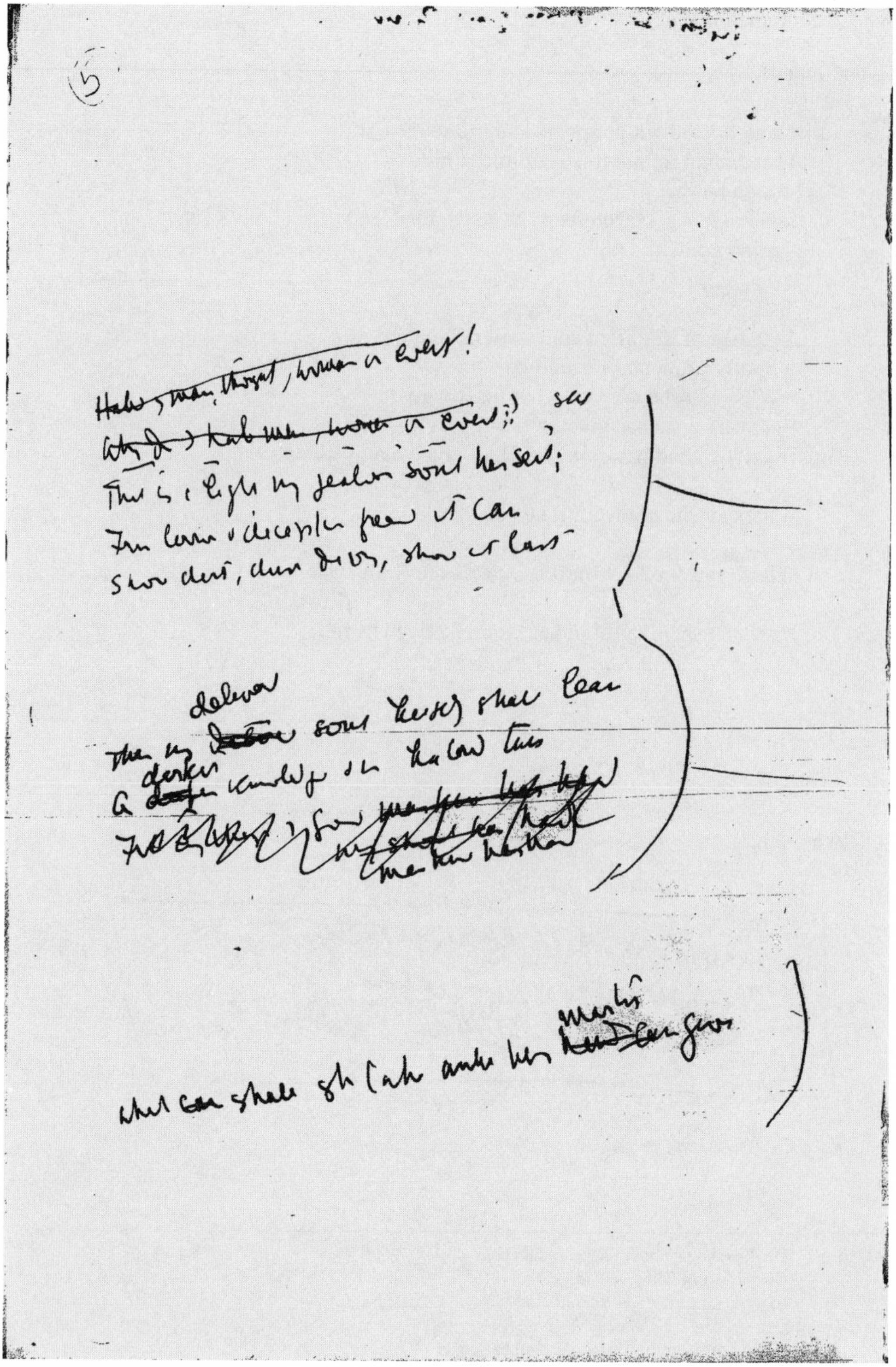

[BC, 21v]

~~Hatred of man, thought, woman or event~~
~~Why do I hate man, woman or eve~~nt;? stet
That is a light my jealous soul has sent;
From terror & deception freed it can
Show dirt, dust debris, show at last

delivered
Then my ~~delivered~~ soul herself shall learn
darker
A ~~deeper~~ knowledge & to hatred turn
For every thought of god ~~mankind has ha~~d
~~my shoul has~~ had
mankind has had

master
What can shall she take until her ~~hands~~ can give

1–5 These lines are clued in to correct canceled lines 8–11 on facing folio 22r.
6–8 These lines are clued in to correct canceled lines 14–17 on facing folio 22r.
9 This line is clued in to correct canceled lines 23–24 on facing folio 22r.

5. Ribh considers Christian Love insufficient

[Chicago(1), pp. 41–42]

3 RIBH CONSIDERS CHRISTIAN LOVE INSUFFICIENT.

Why should I seek for love or study it,
It is of God and passes human wit;
I study hatred with great diligence
For that's a passion in my own control,
A sort of besom that can clear the soul
Of everything that is not mind or sense.

Why do I hate man, woman or event?
That is a light my jealous soul has sent.
From terror and deception freed it can
Discover ~~impurities~~ impurities
Sweep all things alien out, can show at last
How soul may walk when all such things are past,
How soul has walked before such things began.

Then my delivered soul herself shall learn
A darker knowledge and in hatred turn
From every thought of God mankind has had,

---

title *unnumbered P* 3 *KGCT'34, KGCT'35* 3. *LM* 5. INSUFFICIENT *FMM*
1 it? *P, LM, KCGT'34, KCGT'35, FMM*
3 diligence, *FMM*
10 Sweep all things alien and can *rev to* Discover impurities and can *NLI 30,020*$_2$
12 has walked] could walk *LM, KCGT'34, KCGT'35, FMM*
15 had. *FMM*

---

15 No stanza break after this line.

[Chicago(1), pp. 41–42 continued]

Thought is a garment and the soul's a bride
That cannot in that trash and tinsel hide:
In hating God she may creep close to God.

At stroke of midnight soul cannot endure
A bodily or mental furniture.
What can she take until her Master give!
Where can she look until He make the show!
What can she know until He bid her know!
How can she live till in her blood He live!

18 Hatred of God may bring the soul to God. *FMM*

[BC, 23r]

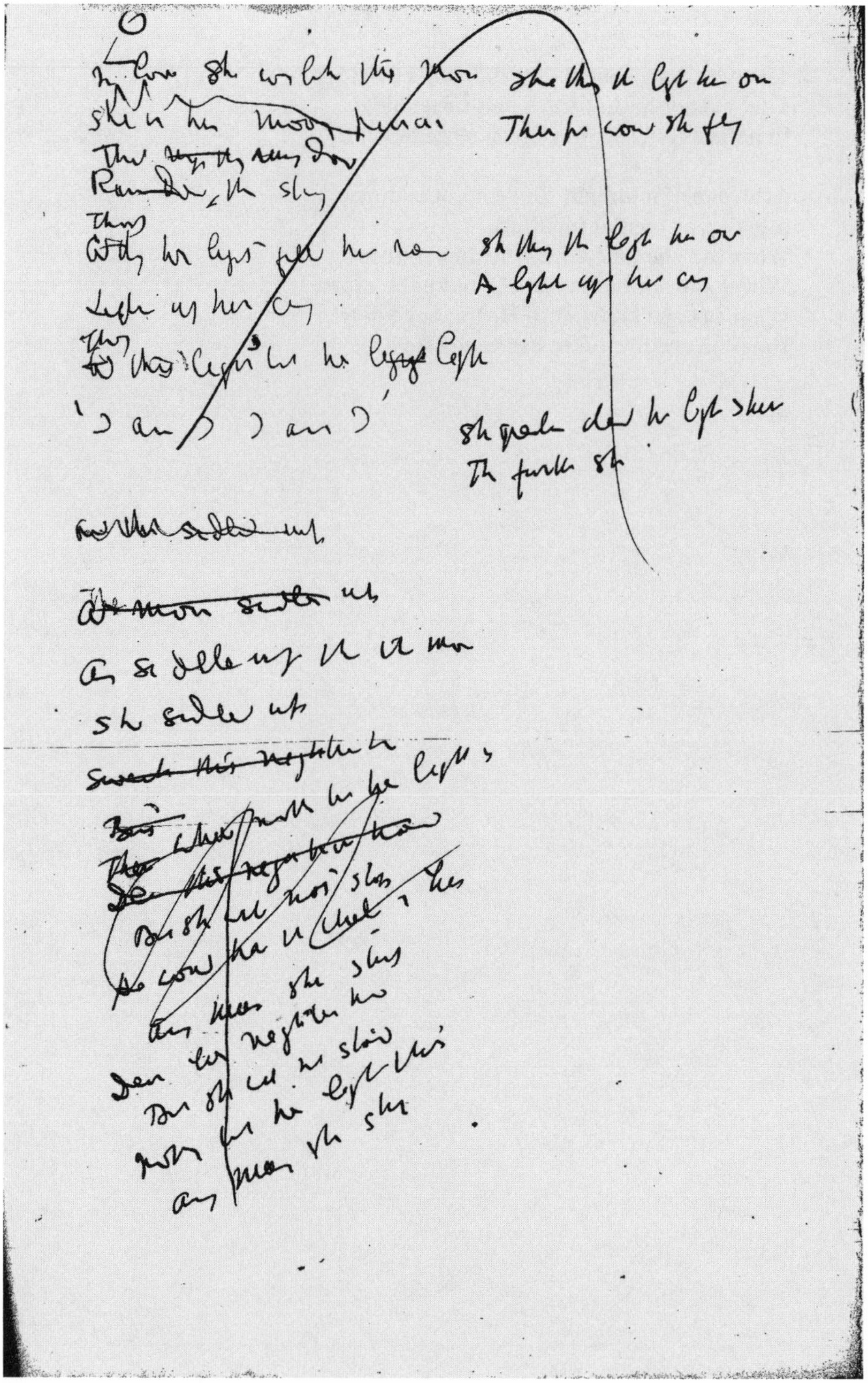

SUPERNATURAL SONGS

6. He and She

[BC, 23^{r}]

O
~~In love~~ she was like the moon
~~She in her moon~~ purity
That ~~sings [?through]~~ runs down
Ran down, the sky
Though
And though his light filled her ran
Lifted up her cry
Though s
~~And~~ that light but his [?ligyt] light
'I am I I am I'

~~And she sidled up~~

~~And moon sidles up~~

As she sidles up the the moon
She sidled up
~~Sweet this neigh~~borhood
~~But~~
~~There Where~~ nothing but his light [?]
~~[?Sweet] tht neighborhood~~
But she will not stop
He would have the whole of her
Away must she [?stray/?skip]
Dear his neighborhood
But she will not stand
Nothing but his light there
Away must she skip

She thought the light her own
Therefore would she fly

She thought the light her own
A lighted up her cry

The greater did her light shine
The further th

---

found in BC, 23^{r}, 22^{v}, 24^{r}, 23^{v}, 25^{r}, 24^{v}, 26^{r} *transcribed above and below*
MBY 673, letter 3, 2^{r}, 2^{v} *transcribed below*
Chicago(1), p. 42 *transcribed below*
published in *Poetry* (Chicago), December 1934
The London Mercury, December 1934
The King of the Great Clock Tower (1934)
The King of the Great Clock Tower (1935)
A Full Moon in March (1935)

In line 4 of the revision on the right, for "A lighted" read "And lifted"?

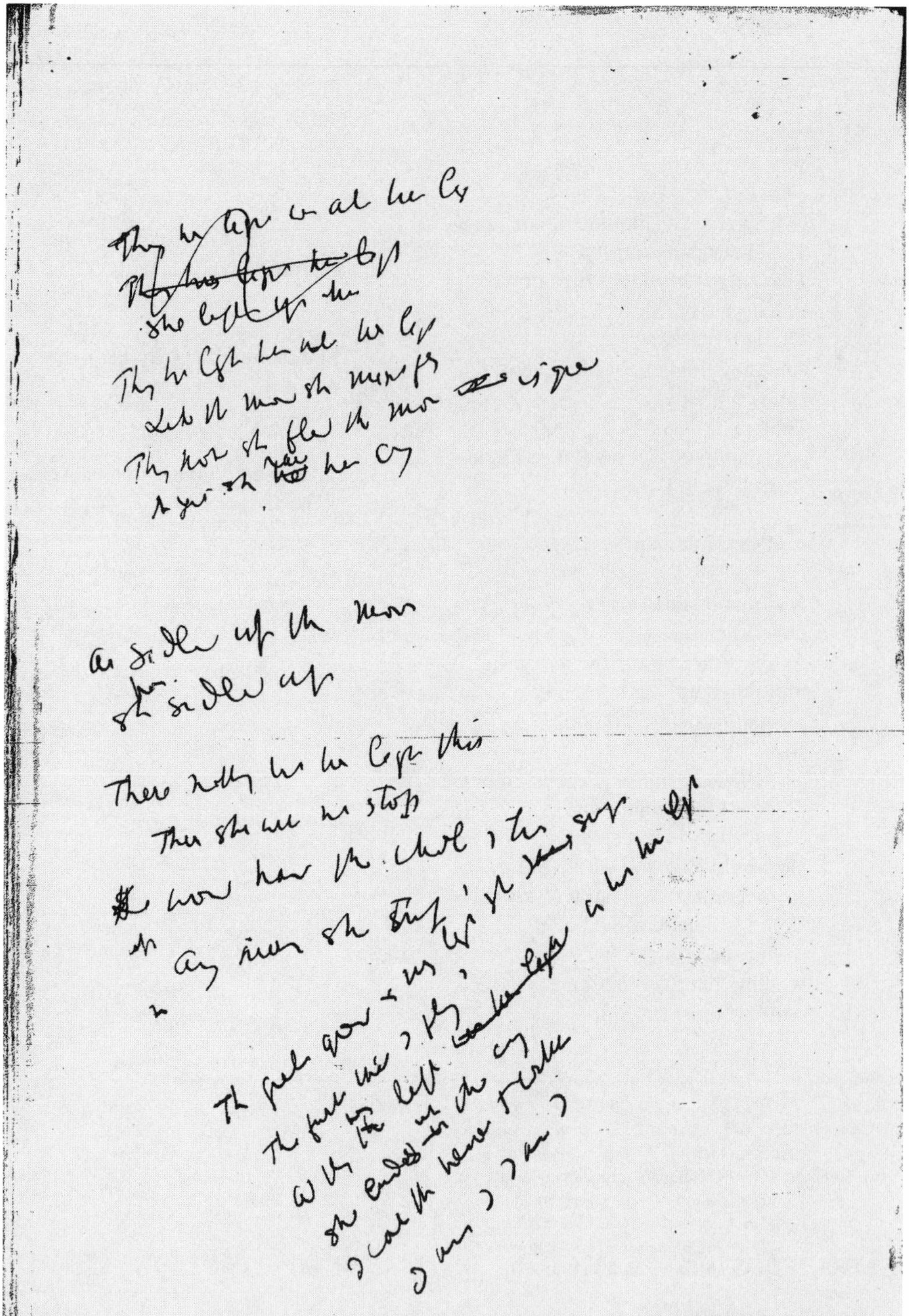

[BC, 22v]

Though his light was all her lig
~~Though his light her light~~
She lifts up her
Though his light was all her light
Like the moon she must fly
The more she fled the more ~~it s~~ it grew
rais
An yet she ~~he~~ her cry

As sidled up the moon
has
She sidled up

There nothing but [?his] light there
There she will not stop
{He
{S would have the whole of her
[?up]
{trip
Away must she {s

The greater grows [?] my light' she ~~sang~~ sings
The further that I fly'
my
And though ~~the~~ light ~~was his light~~ is but his light
{s upon
She end {ed ~~with~~ the cry
I call the heavens to witness
I am I I am I

1 For "lig" read "light"?
7 For "rais" read "raised"?

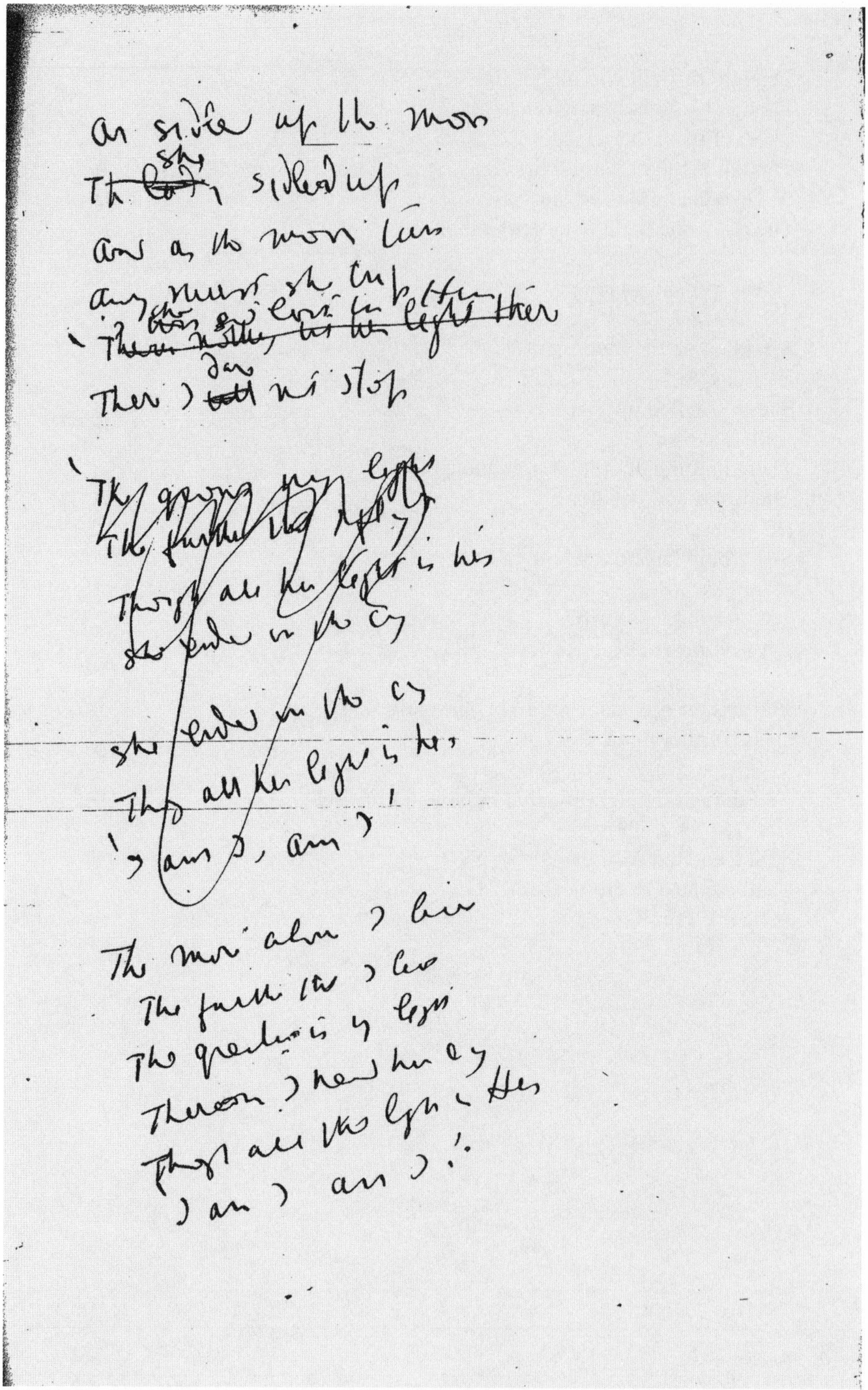

[BC, 24^{r}]

As sidled up the moon
she
~~The lady~~ sidled up
And as the moon [?turns]
Away must she trip
[?she]
~~Was~~ so lost in Him
~~'Theres nothing but [?his] light there~~
dare
There I ~~will~~ not stop

'The grows my light
The further that I fly
Though all her light is his
She ended [?in] [?the] cry

She ended [?in] [?the] cry
[?Though] all her light is his
'I am I, am I'

The more alone I live
The further that I [?live]
The greater is my light
Thereon I heard her cry
Though all the light is His
'I am I am I.'

[BC, 23v]

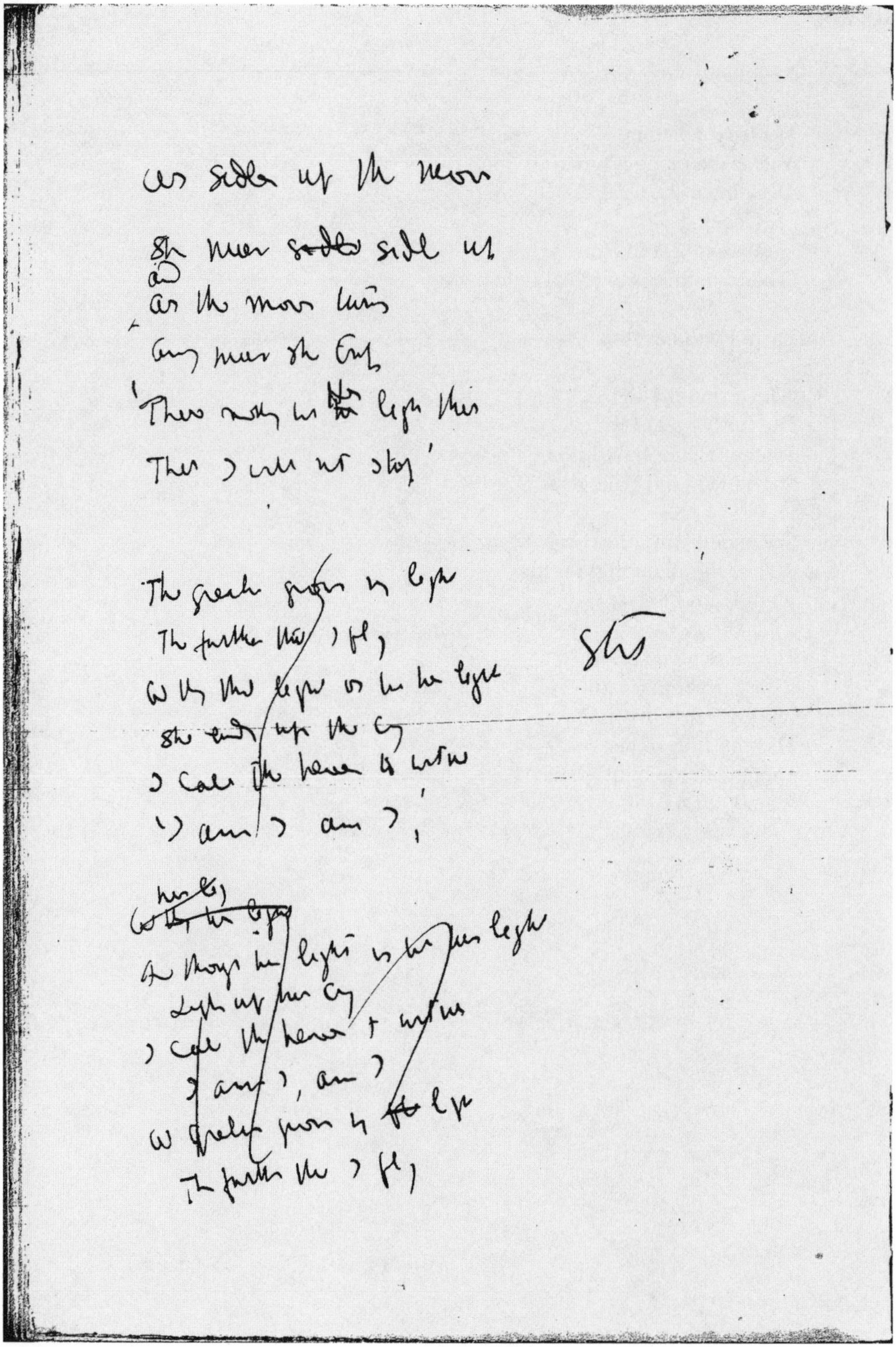

[BC, 23v]

As sidles up the moon
She must ~~sidls~~ sidle up
And
^As the moon turns
Away must she trip
His
'Thers nothing but ~~his~~ light ther
Ther I will not stop'

The greater grows my light
  The further that I fly
And though that light is but his light Stet
  She ends up the cry
I call the heavens to witness
  'I am I am I.'

[? ~~her] lig~~
And ~~though his light~~

And though her light is but his light
  Lifted up her cry
I call the heavens to witness
  I am I, am I
And greater grows my ~~fli~~ [?light]
  The further that I fly

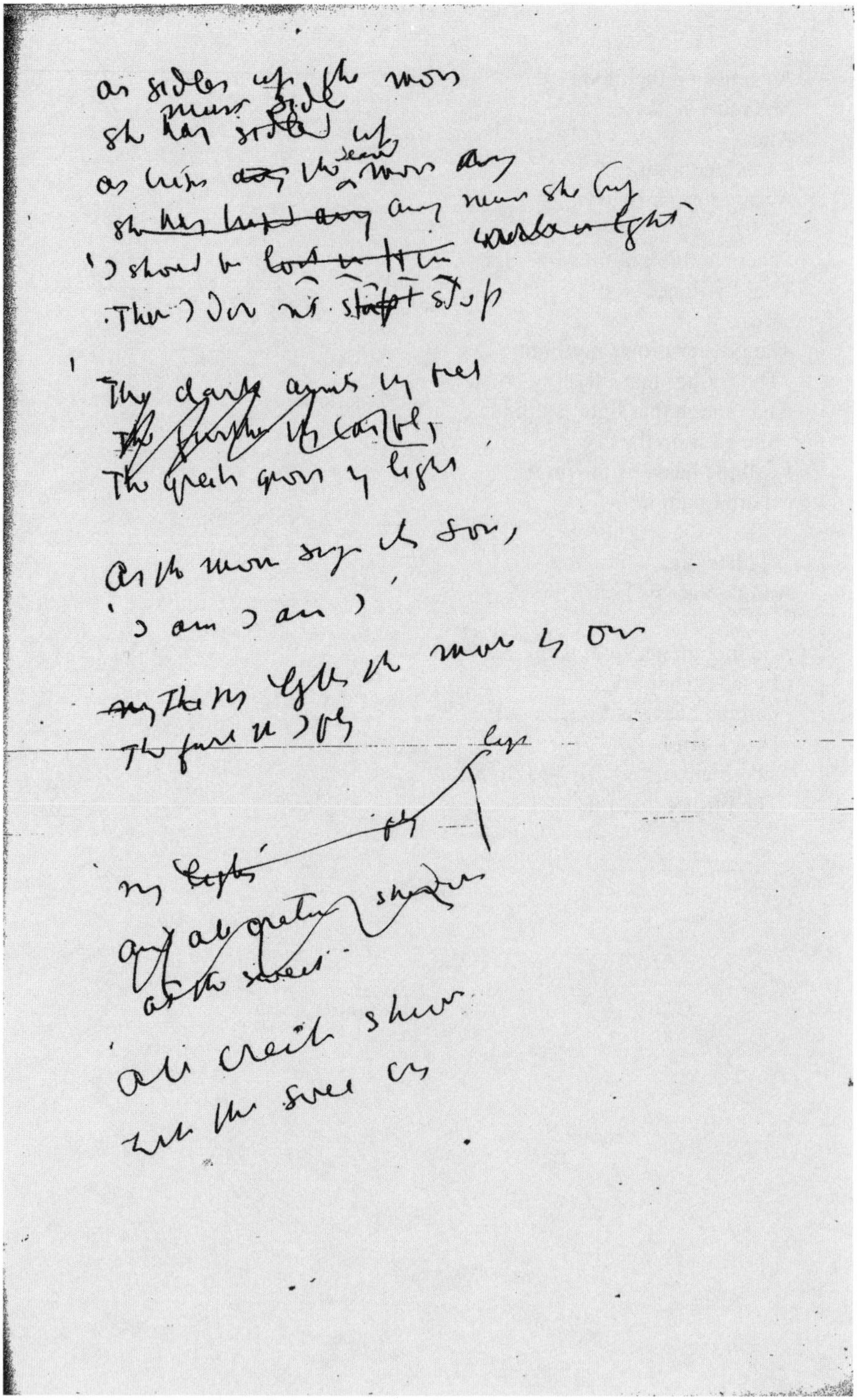

[BC, 25r]

As sidles up the moon
    must sidle
She has ~~sidled~~ up
                    scared
As trips ~~away~~ the ^ moon away
~~She has triped away~~ Away must she trip
‘ I should be ~~lost in Him~~ ~~veiled in light~~
There I dare not ~~stopt~~ stop

‘ The dark awaits my feet
The further they can fly
The greater grows my light

As the moon sings the song
‘I am I am I’

~~My~~ ~~The~~ My lights the more my own
The furt th I fly

                              ~~light~~
                    ~~fly~~
My ~~lights~~
And all creation shivers
  At the sweet

All creation shivers
With that swee cry

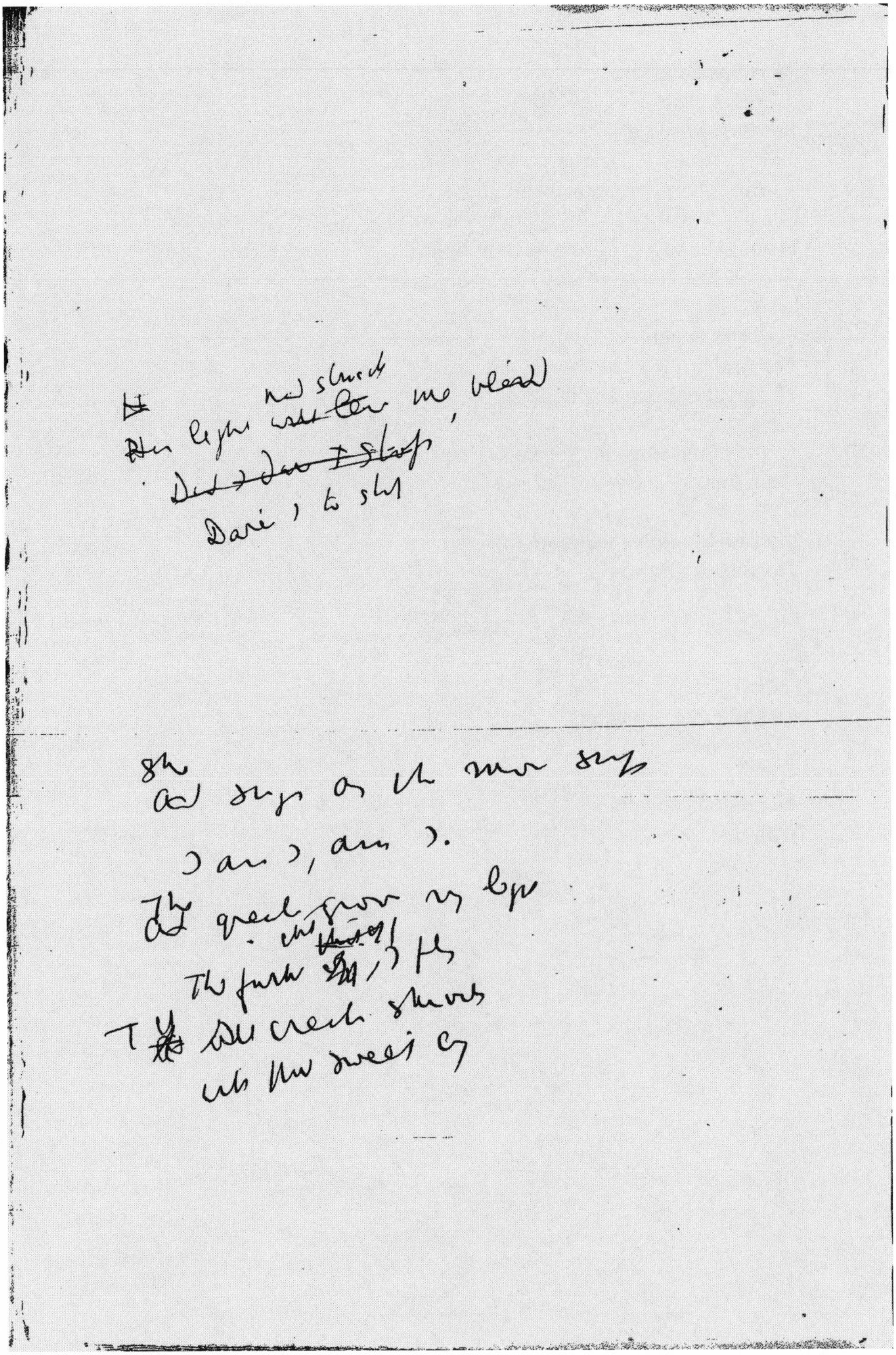

[BC, 24v]

~~H~~ had struck
His light ~~will leave~~ me blind
~~Did I dare to stop~~
Dare I to stop

She
~~And~~ sings as the moon sings
I am I, am I.
The
~~And~~ greater grows my light
that
~~that~~ off
The further ~~off~~, I fly
Till {A
~~And~~ {all creation shivers
With that sweet cry

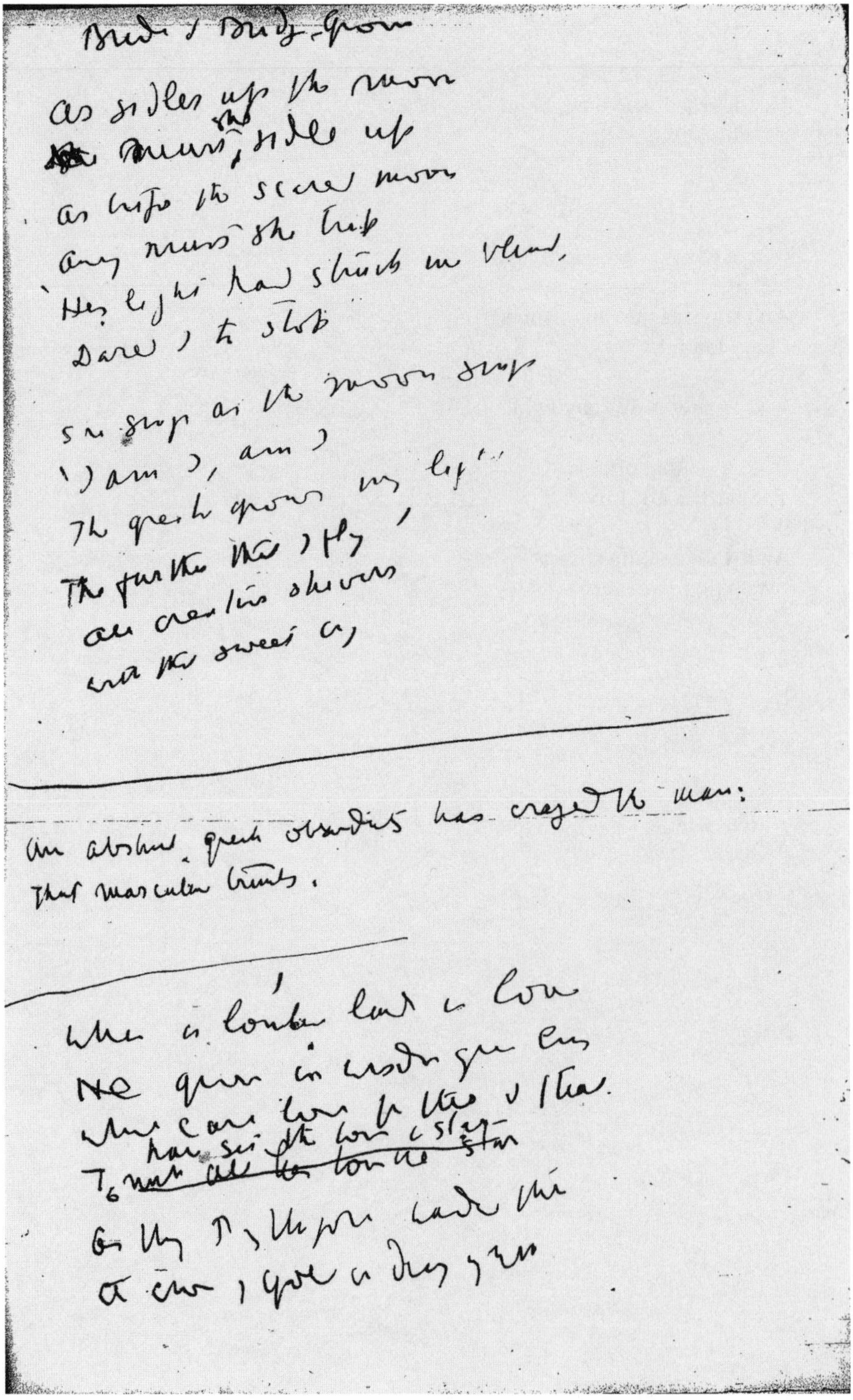

[BC, 26^{r}]

Bride & Bridg-Groom

As sidles up the moon
{M she
~~She~~ {must ^ sidle up
As trips the scared moon
Away must she trip
'His light had struck me blind,
Dared I to stop'

She sings as the moon sings
'I am I, am I
The greater grows my light
The further that I fly'
All creation shivers
With that sweet cry

Drafts of lines for "Ribh denounces Patrick" (*Poems*, p. 290), from "Supernatural Songs," and for "[Every loutish lad in love]" (*Poems*, p. 587), from *A Full Moon in March*, appear farther down on this page.

title For "Bridg-Groom" read "Bride-Groom."

[MBY 673, letter 3, 2r and 2v]

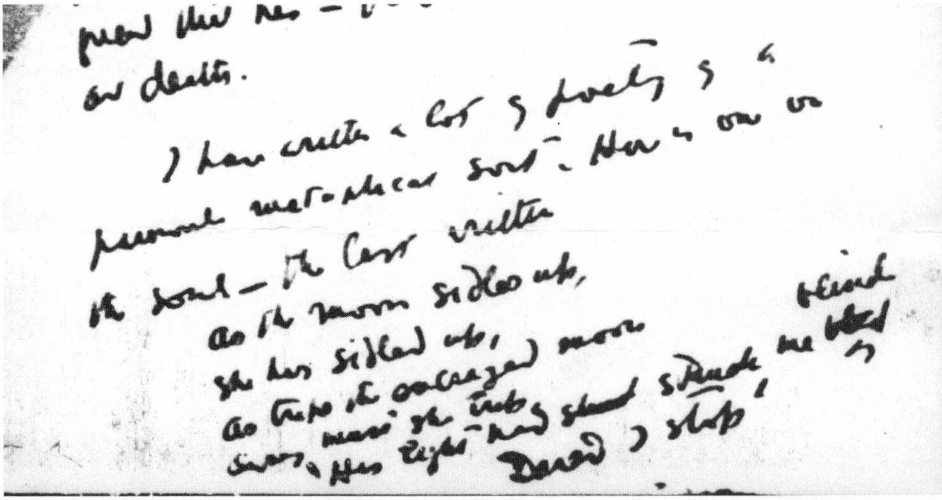

[illegible] — on death.

I have written a lot of poetry of a personal metaphysical sort. Here is one on the soul — the last written

As the moon sidles up,
She has sidled up,
As trips the scared moon
Away must she trip:
'His light had struck me blind
Dared I stop'

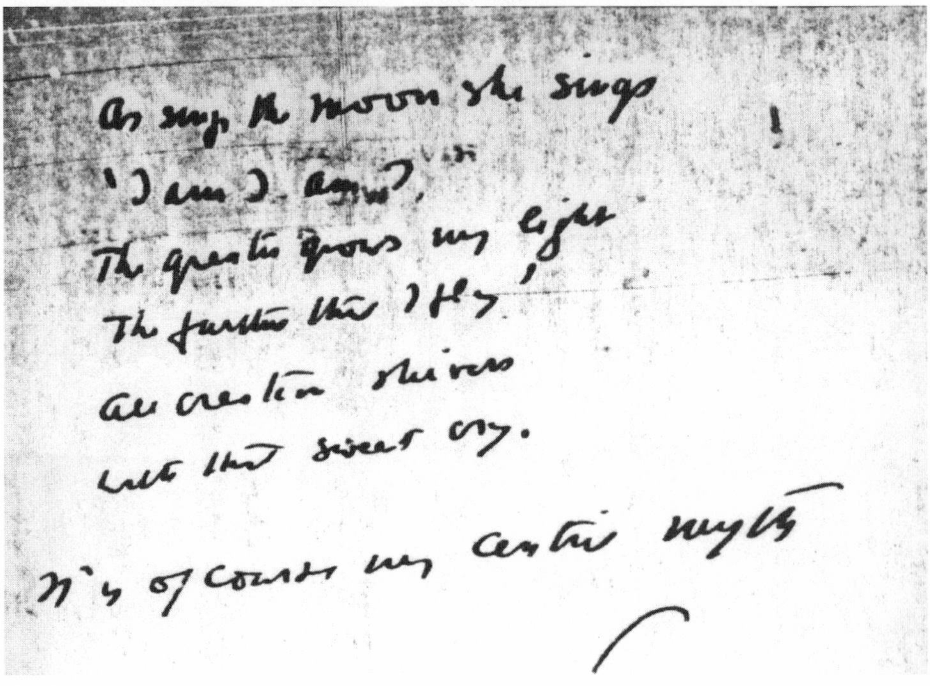

As sings the moon she sings
'I am I, am I;
The greater grows my light
The further that I fly.'
All creation shivers
With that sweet cry.

It is of course my central myth

Variants for *Chicago(1)*, p. 42, opposite

title unnumbered *P* 4. *LM* 6. *FMM*

4 trip: *FMM*

6 stop'. *FMM*

7 sings: *FMM*

10 fly'. *FMM*

[MBY 673, letter 3, 2^{r} and 2^{v}; Chicago(1), p. 42]

[MBY 673, letter 3, 2^{r}]

I have written a lot of poetry of a personal metaphysical sort. Here is one on the soul — the last written

As the moon sidles up,
She has sidled up,
As trips the [~~?mo~~] crazed moon
Away must she trip.
blind
'His light had [~~?stru~~] struck me ~~blid~~ ^
Dared I stop'

[2^{v}]

As sings the moon she sings
'I am I am I,
The greater grows my light
The further that I fly'
All creation shivers
With that sweet cry.

It is of course my centric myth.

[Chicago(1), p. 42]

4 HE AND SHE

As the moon sidles up
Must she sidle up,
As trips the scared moon
Away must she trip,
'~~Her~~ light had struck me blind His
Dared I stop'

She sings as the moon sings
'I am I, am I;
The greater grows my light
The further that I fly.'
All creation shivers
With that sweet cry.

MBY 673 From a letter to Olivia Shakespear, August 25 [postmarked August 28, 1934] from Riversdale. Transcribed from SB 3.4.46. See *Letters*, pp. 828–829.

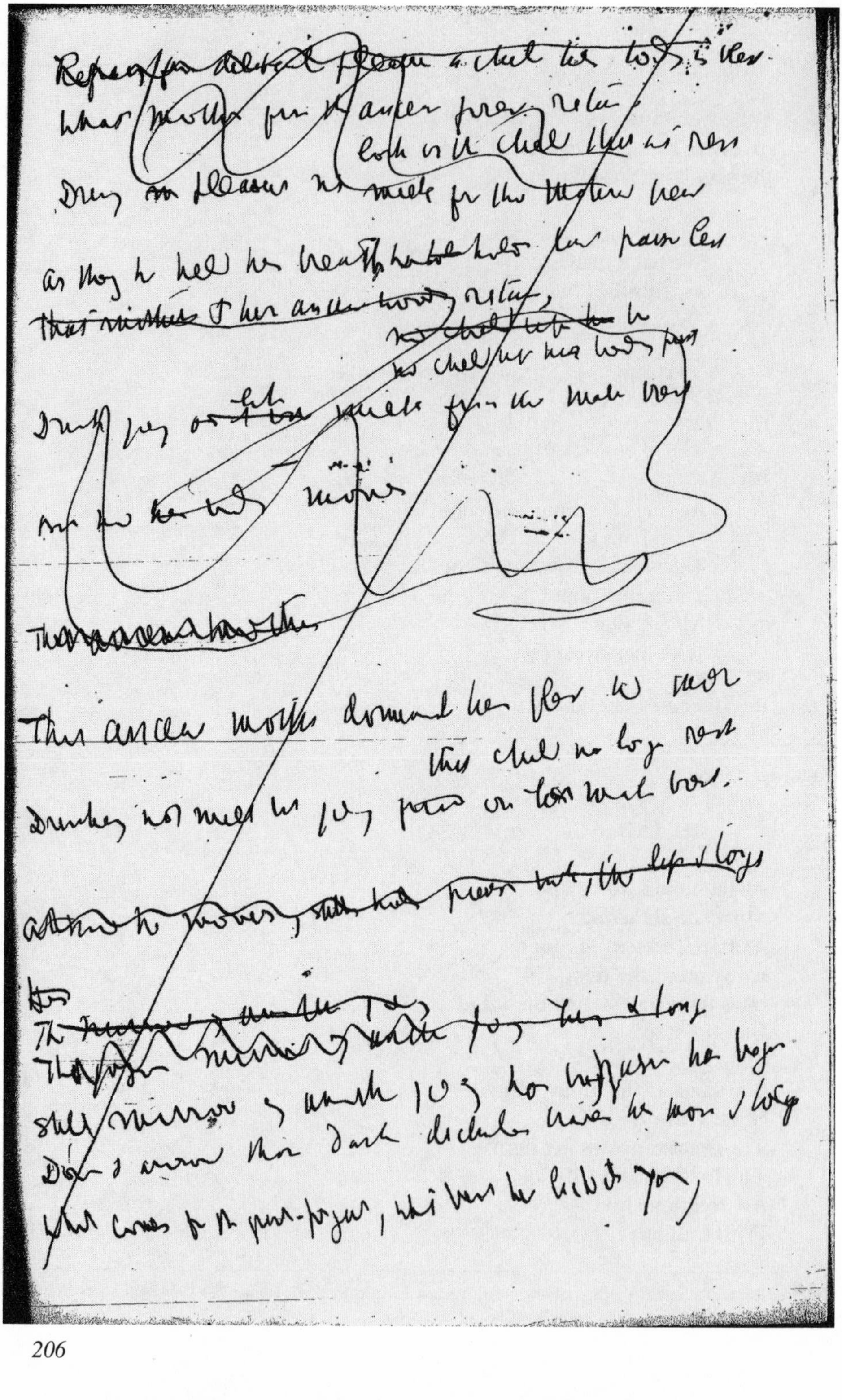

SUPERNATURAL SONGS

7. What Magic Drum?

[BC, 38^{r}]

1 ~~Refraining from deliberate pleasure a while his body is blest~~
2 What mother from the ancient forest returns
look on the child there at rest
3 Drinking ~~no~~ pleasure not milk from that maternal breast
4 As though he held his breath he ~~hol~~ holds back passion lest
5 That mother to her ancient woods return,
~~no child upon him pr~~
no child upon hi{r s body prest
like
6 Drink joy ~~as it were~~ milk from that maternal breast
7 But now his body moves

8 ~~The Ancient Mother~~
9 That Ancient Mother dominate his flesh no more
that child no longer rest
10 Drinking not milk but joy ~~from~~ on [?her] maternal breast.
11 ~~Although he moves, still holding passion back, the lips & tongue~~
12 ~~His~~
13 The ~~Mirrored by another joy~~
14 The joyous mirror of another joy lips & tongue
15 Still mirrored by another joy has begg passion has begun
16 Down & around those dark declivities travel his mouth & tongue
17 What comes from the great forgest, what beast has licked its young

---

found in BC, 38^{r}, 37^{v}, 39^{r}, 38^{v}, 39^{v}, 40^{r} *transcribed above and below*
NLI 30,178 *transcribed below*
published in *A Full Moon in March* (1935)

---

5 Since Yeats seldom dots an "i" one cannot always distinguish "his" from "her," a crucial distinction in this poem: "upon him" could be "upon her." Here, "No child upon his body prest" is clearly emended by an overwriting to "No child upon her body prest".

6 The "it" in "Drink joy as it were milk" could alternatively be a caret pointing up to "like." What looks like "male" is, I think, meant to be "maternal."

10 "Maternal" is incomplete and could conceivably be "male." Partly because of meter, I think the word is shorthand for "maternal."

15 For "begg" read "begun"?

16 The woman in Yeats's poem "Parting" refers to her "dark declivities."

17 For "forgest" read "forest"?

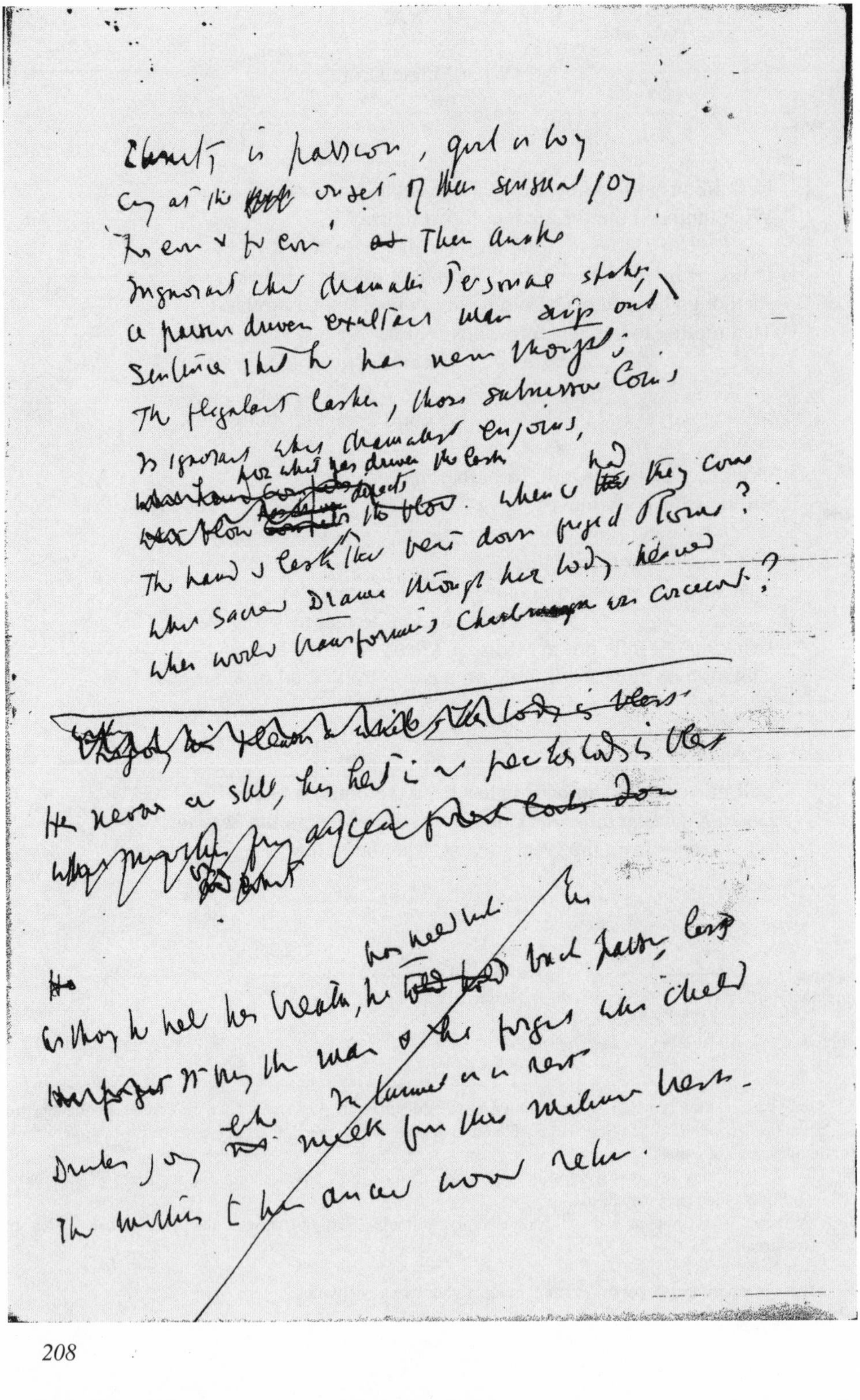
Chastity is passion, girl or boy
Cry at the [illegible] onset of their sensual joy
"For ever & for ever" — then awake
Ignorant what dramatis personae spake;
A passion driven exultant man sings out
Sentences that he has never thought;
The flagrant lover, those submissive loins
Is ignorant what dramatist enjoins,
[illegible] for what has driven the lark [illegible] directs
[illegible] blow [illegible] the blow. Whence had they come
The hand & lark that beat down pagan Rome?
What sacred drama through her body heaved
When world transforming Charlemagne was conceived?

[illegible]
He knows a skill, his heart is [illegible]
[illegible]

[illegible]
Although he held her breath, he [illegible] back [illegible]
[illegible] the man [illegible]
Drunken joy [illegible] [illegible] for the [illegible] breast.
The [illegible] ancient [illegible]

[BC, 37v]

~~Wi~~thing
~~Forgoing his pleasure a while, his body is blest~~
His nerves are still, his heart is at peace his body is blest
What mother from ancient forest looks down
or
and what

~~He~~
has held back
As though he held his breath, he ~~told holds~~ back passion, lest
~~He forget~~ It bring the man & he forget what child
like In turmoil or in rest
Drinks joy ~~not~~ milk from that maternal breast –
That Mother to her ancient wood return.

Above the draft of "What Magic Drum?" is a draft of "Whence had they Come?" (see p. 227 below).
1 For "withing" read "witholding"?

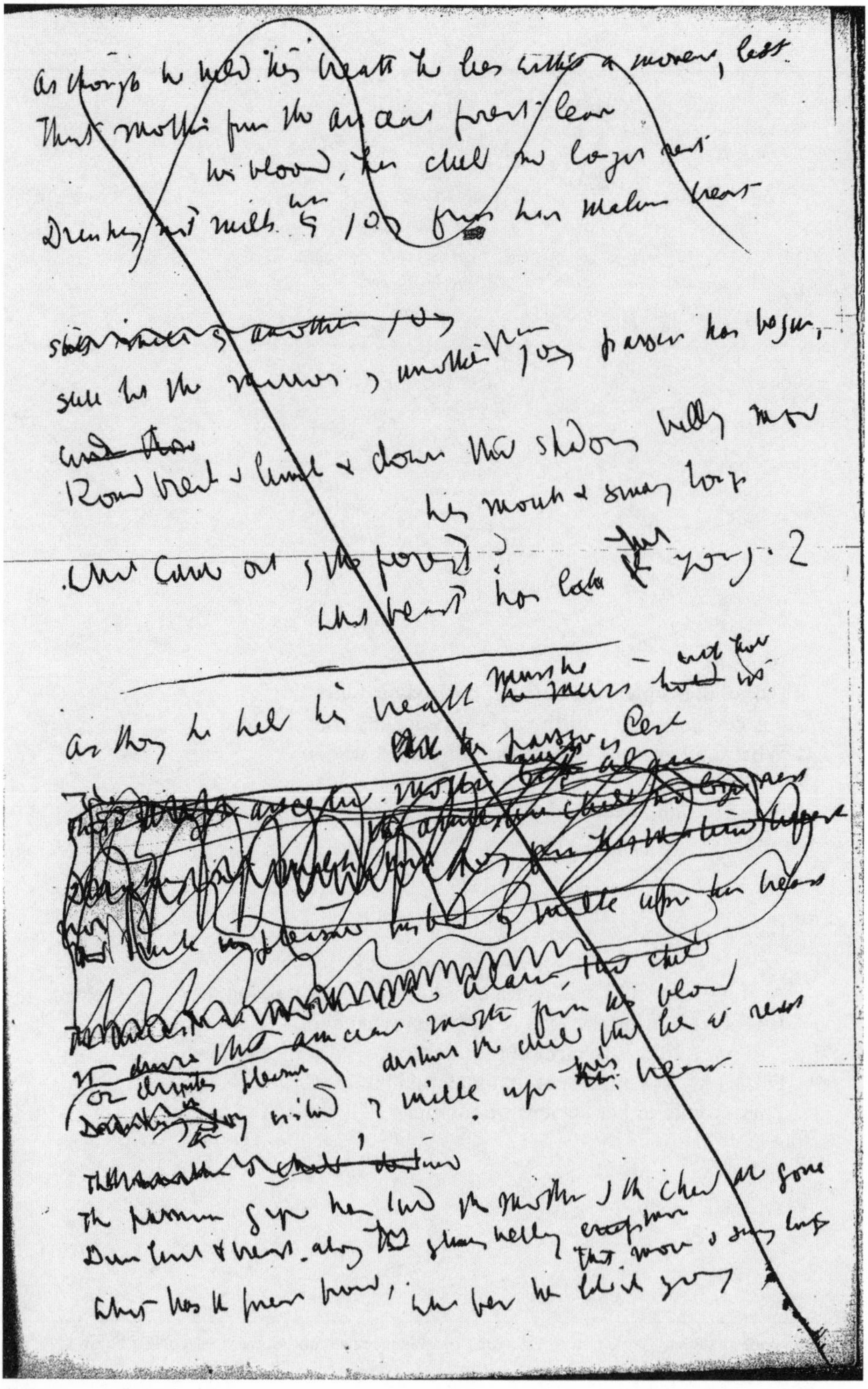

[BC, 39^{r}]

1 As though he held his breath he has withheld a movement, lest
2 That mother from the ancient forest leave
his blood, her child no longer rest
but
3 Drinking not milk ~~by~~ joy from her maternal breast

4 ~~Still mirr of another joy~~
pass
5 Still but the mirror of another ~~joy~~ passion has begun,
6 ~~And those~~
7 Round breast & limb & down that shadowy belly move
his mouth & sinewy tongue
8 What came out of the forest?
his
What beast has licked ~~its~~ young?

Yeats has struck out entire page, top and bottom.

2, 3, 8 Unless the "i" is dotted, one cannot usually tell "his" from "her" except by context. Or, even if one thinks one can tell the difference (sometimes the tail of an "s" hooks in a bit to the left at the end of a word, while that of the "r" comes straight down or heads to the right), one cannot prove or be absolutely sure of the accuracy of one's reading. The phrase "his breast" occurs in line 3 of the published poem. One cannot be sure in the drafts whether it is "his" or "her" breast.

4 For "mirr" read "mirror".

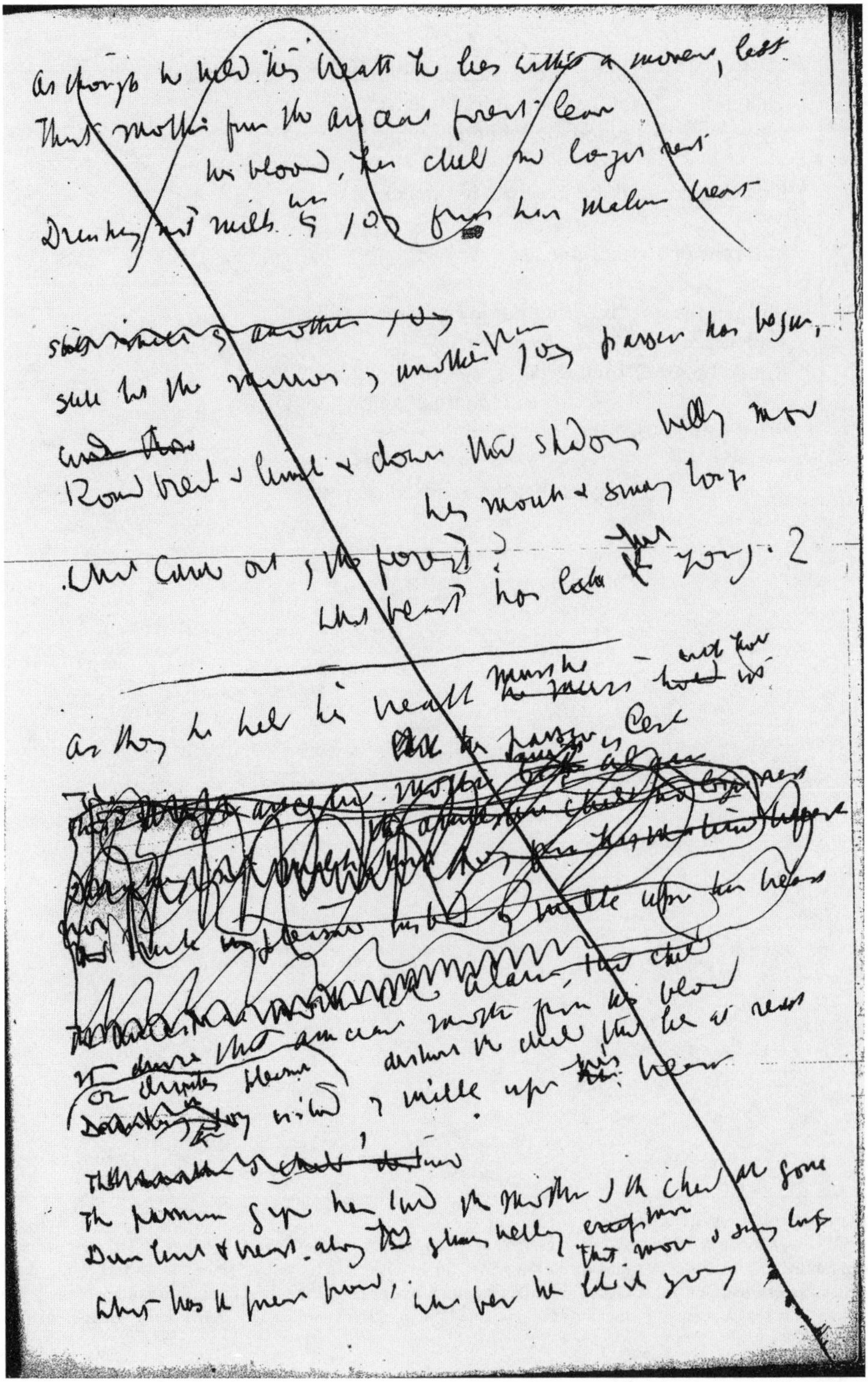

[BC, 39r continued]

must he — with ~~hold~~

9 As though he held his breath ~~he must hold~~ ~~out~~

~~[?]~~ his passion lest

The vanish in

10 ~~That~~ strange ancestral Mother take alarm

the ancestral child no longer rest

11 Drinking not milk but joy from her maternal breast

Nor

12 ~~And~~ milk but pleasure instead of milk upon his breast

13 The Ancient Mother take alarm, that child

14 It drive that Ancient Mother from his blood

Disturb the child that lies at rest

Or drinks pleasure

~~in~~ her

15 ~~Drinking~~ ^ ~~joy~~ instead of milk upon ~~his~~ breast

16 ~~The mother & child disturbed~~

17 The passionate gyre has turned the mother & the child are gone

her

18 Down limb & breast along ~~that~~ glimmering belly ~~creep~~ move

that mouth & sinewy tongue

19 What has the forest [?found].

What beast has licked its young

9 Yeats draws a line to separate two drafts.

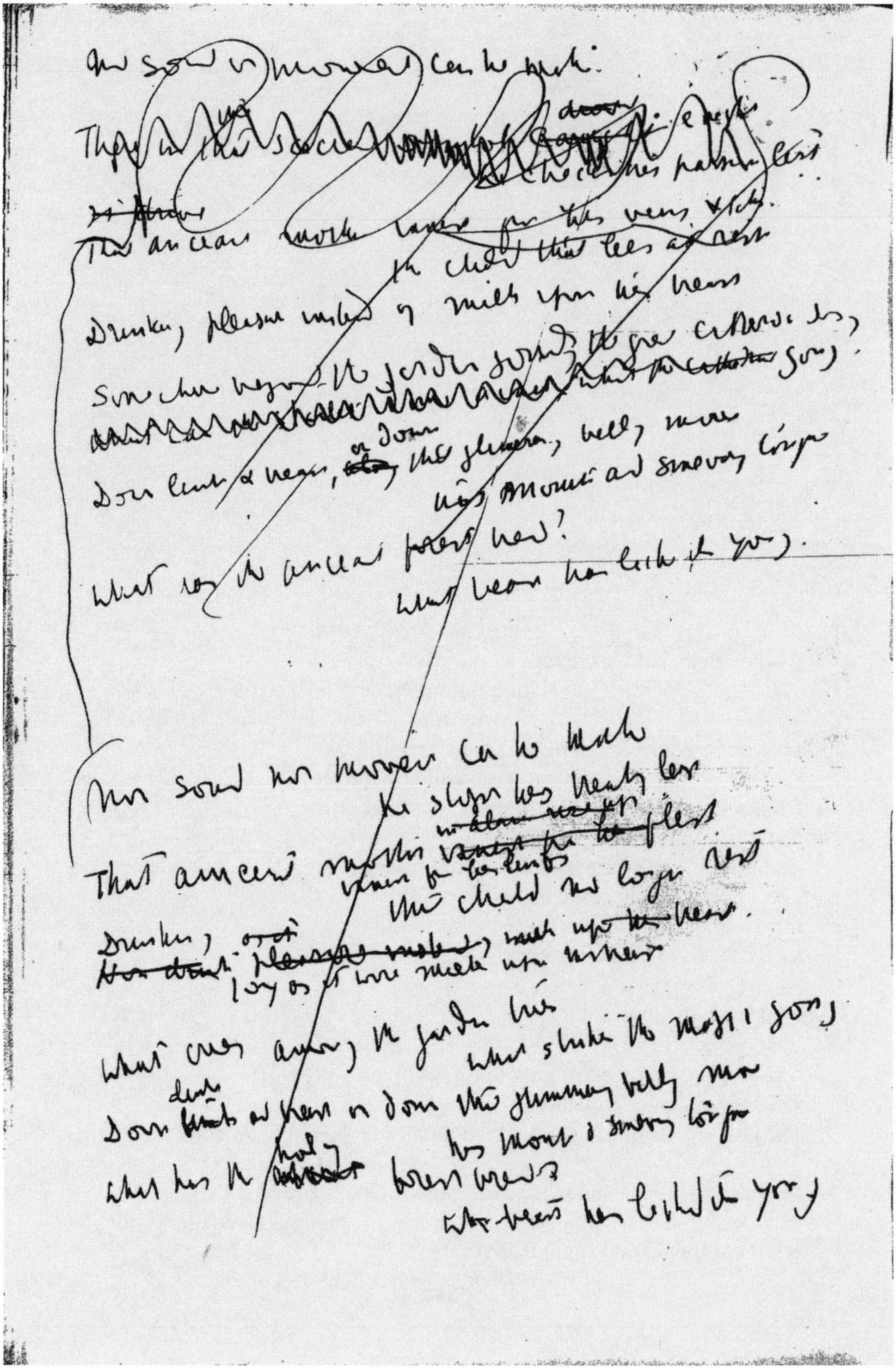

[BC, 38^v]

1 No sound or movement can he make
the drowned
2 There in that secret symbol ~~caught~~ caught
he checks his passion lest
3 ~~It drive~~
4 That Ancient Mother vanish from his veins & take
the child that lies at rest
5 Drinking pleasure instead of milk upon his breast
6 Somewhere beyond the garden sounds the great cathedral gong
7 ~~What can the starlit dome await, what the cathedral~~ gong.
or down
8 Down limb & breast, ~~along~~ that glimmering belly move
his mouth & sinewy tongue
9 What has the ancient forest bred?
What beast has licked its young.

Yeats has struck out the entire page, top and bottom.

4 I capitalize "Ancient Mother" but cannot really tell whether Yeats has done so or not. The arrow leads from line 10 of the draft below.

5, 8 Yeats has dotted the "i" of "his" in both instances.

7 The "starlit dome" and "cathedral gong" occur in "Byzantium."

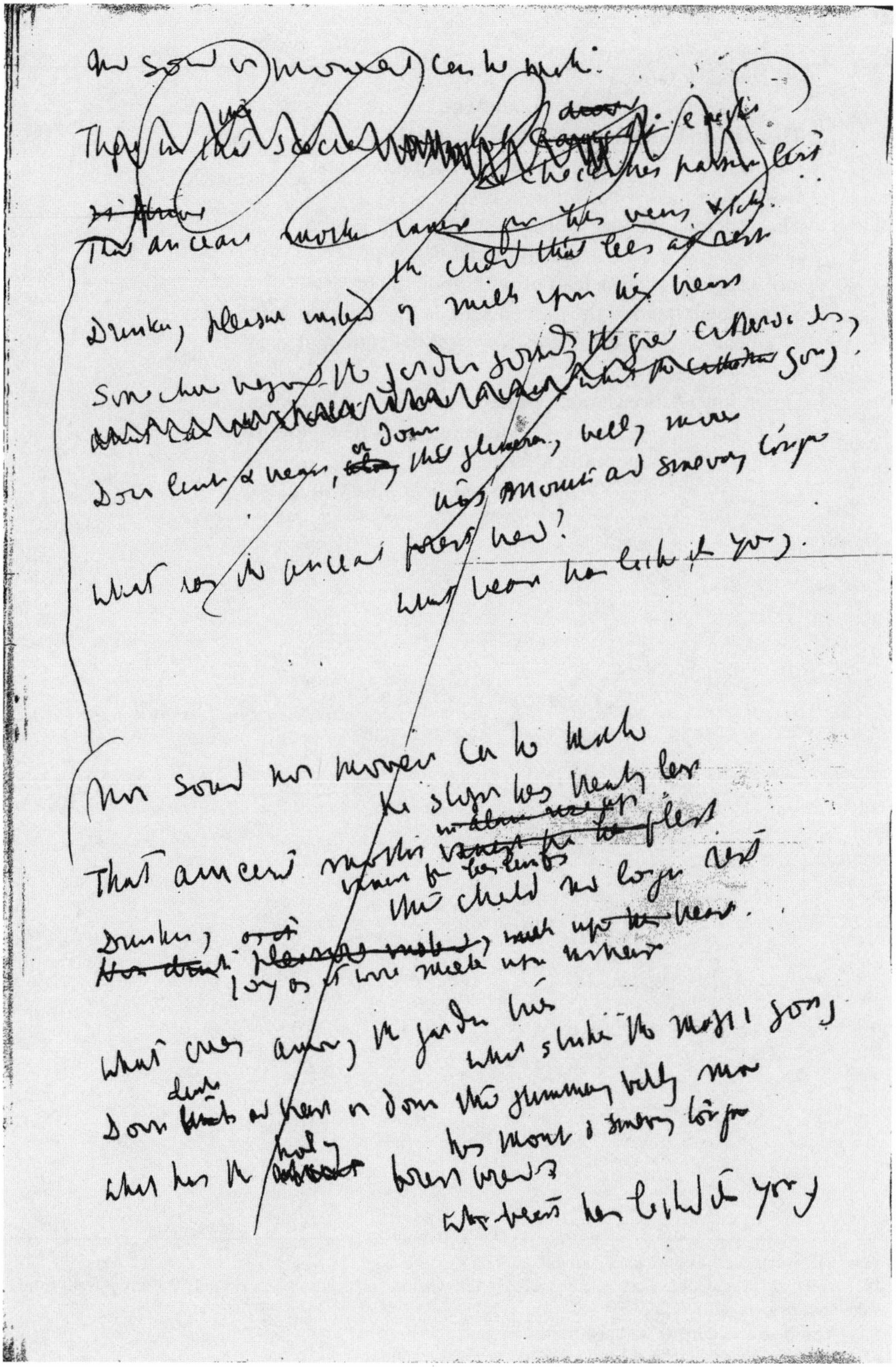

[BC, 38v continued]

10 Nor sound nor movement can he make
he stops his breathing lest

~~in alarm rise up~~
11 That Ancient Mother ~~vanish from his~~ flesh
vanish from his limbs

that child no longer rest
Drinking ~~as it~~
12 ~~Have drun~~k ~~pleasure instead~~ of milk upon his breast
joy as it were milk upon hisbreast
13 What cries among the garden trees
What strikes the magic gong
limb
14 Down ~~limbs~~ and breast or down that glimmering belly move
his mouth & sinewy tongue
holy
15 What has the ~~ancient~~ forest bred?
What beast has licked its young

Yeats has struck out entire page, top and bottom.

10 Yeats has clued this line into line 4 above and apparently wishes lines 10–15 to replace 4–9.

12 "Drinking as it" was perhaps to be "Drinking as it were pleasure."

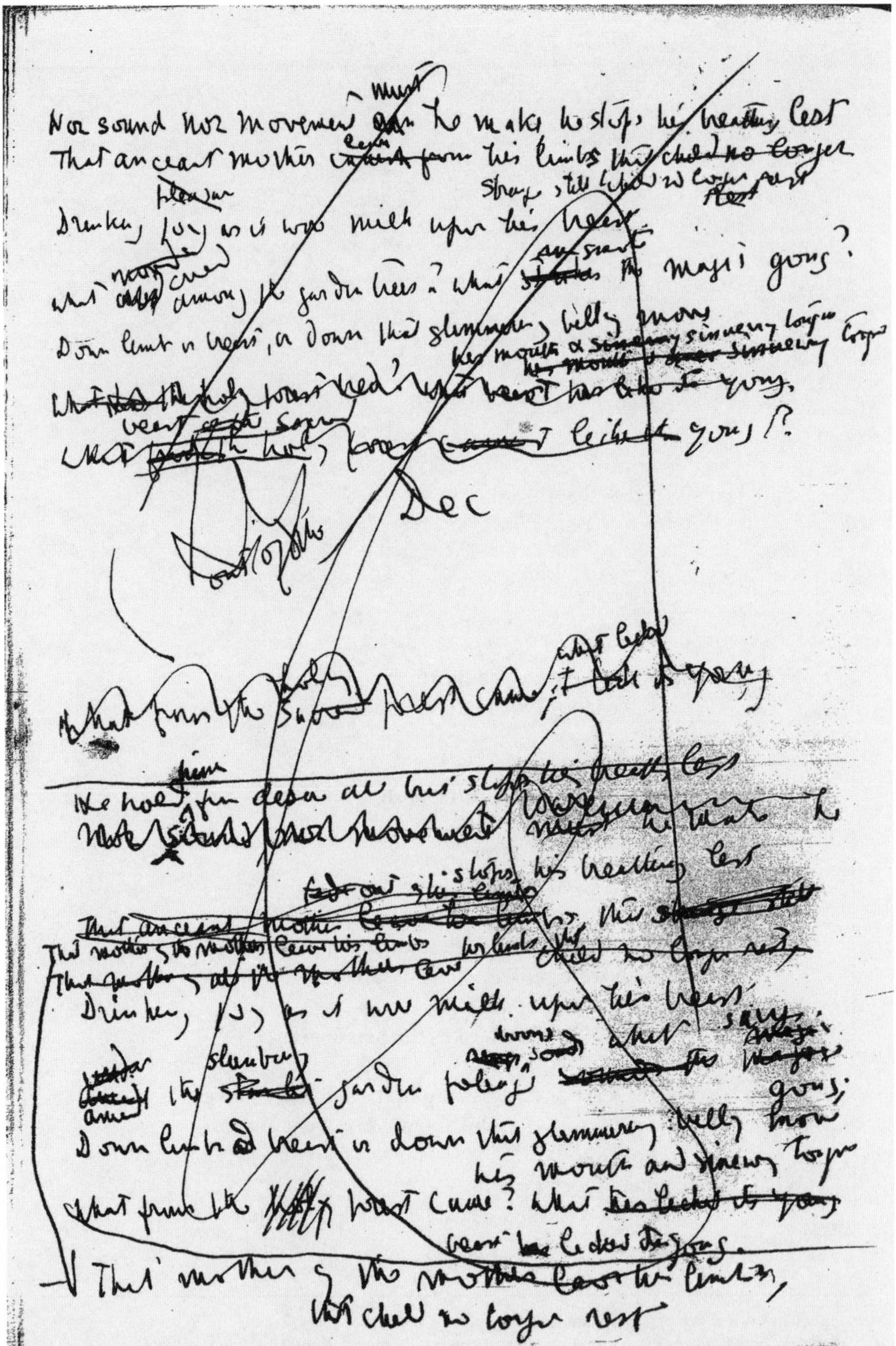

[BC, 39v]

must
1 Nor sound nor movement ~~can~~ he make he stops his breathing lest
leave
2 That Ancient Mother ~~vanish~~ from his limbs, that ~~child no longer~~
Strange still child no longer rest
~~rest~~
~~pleasure~~
3 Drinking joy as it were milk upon his breast
~~moved~~ cried ~~[?]~~ smote
4 What ~~cried~~ among the garden trees? What ~~strikes~~ the magic gong?
5 Down limb or breast, or down that glimmering belly move
his mouth & ~~sinewy~~ tongue
~~his mouth & sinew~~ sinewy tongue
6 ~~What has the holy forest bred? What beast has licked its young.~~
beast of the sacred
7 What ~~from the holy~~ forest ~~came~~ to lick its young?

Dec
8 ~~out of the~~

holy what licked
9 What from the ~~sacred~~ forest came; ~~to lick~~ its young

---

Yeats has struck out entire page, top and bottom.

7 On writing this draft Yeats imagined the poem finished and dated it "Dec." The year was 1934.

8 The phrase "out of the" is attached to line 7 by one clue line and to line 9 by another. Both lines 7 and 9 are short a metrical foot. This lack would be filled by substituting "out of the," "of the," or "from the."

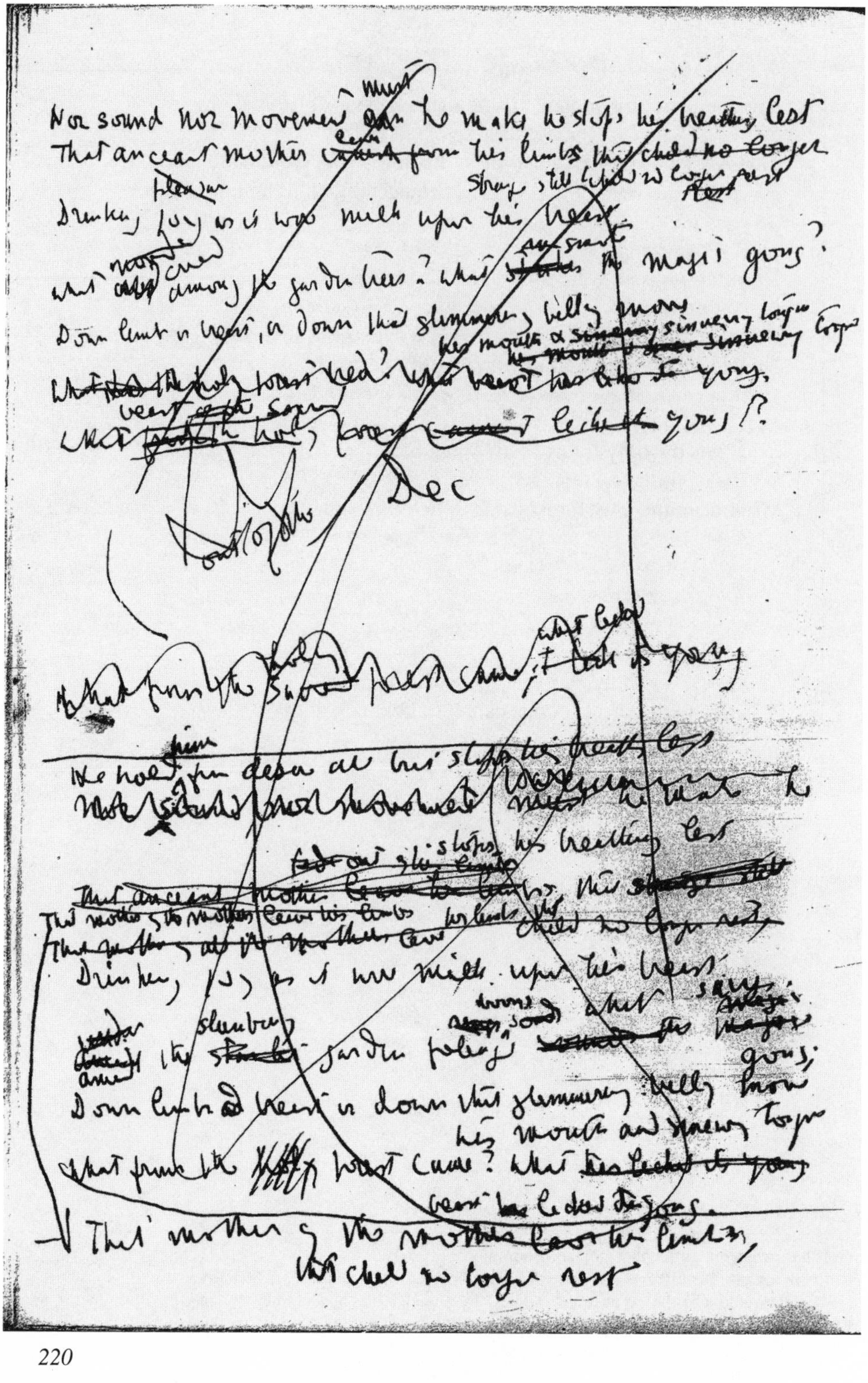

[BC, 39v continued]

him
10 He holds ^ from desire all but stops his breathing lest
dare
11 Nor ^ sound, nor movement ~~must~~ he make he

stops his breathing lest
~~fade out of his limbs~~
12 ~~That Ancient Mother leave his limbs~~, that ~~strange still~~
13 That ~~mother of all the mothers leave his limbs~~
his limbs that
14 ~~That mother of all the mothers leave child no longer rest,~~
15 Drinking of joy as it were milk upon his breast
booms [?sings].
~~Under~~ slumbering ~~rings~~ ^ ~~sounds~~ what ~~magic~~
16 ~~Amid~~ the ~~star lit~~ garden foliage ~~sounds the magic~~
gong;
17 Down limb and breast or down that glimmering belly move
his mouth and sinewy tongue
18 What from the ~~holy~~ forest came? What ~~has licked its young~~
beast ~~has~~ licked its young.
19 That mother of the mothers leave his limbs,
that child no longer rest

Yeats has struck out entire page, top and bottom.
10 Yeats draws a line to separate two drafts.
19 This line is set off by a rule and clued in as a substitute for lines 13 and 14.

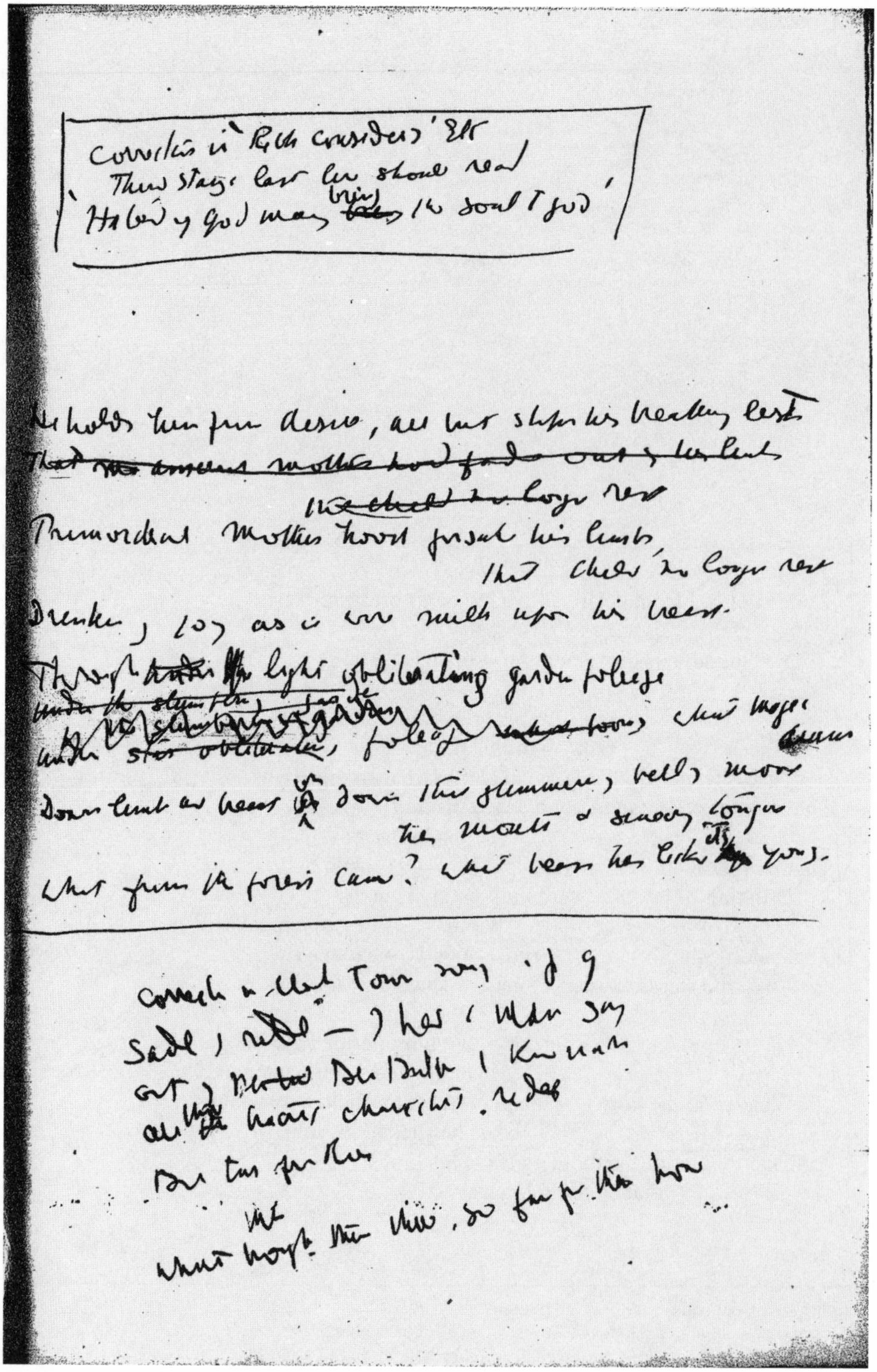
Primordial Mother hood forsook his limbs

That child no longer rest

Drinking joy as it were milk upon his breast.

What from the forest came? what beast has licked its young.

[BC, 40^{r} and NLI 30,178]

[BC, 40^{r}]

1 He holds him from desire, all but stops his breathing lest
2 ~~That mo ancient motherhood fade out of his limbs~~
~~that child no longer~~ rest
3 Primordial Mother hood forsake his limbs,
that child no longer rest
4 Drinking joy as it were milk upon his breast
5 Through ~~under the~~ light obliterating garden foliage
6 ~~Under the slumbering garden~~
the slumbering garden
7 Under ~~star obliterating~~ foliage ~~what booming~~ what magic
drum
or
8 Down limb and breast ~~[?]~~ down that glimmering belly move
^ his mouth & sinewy tongue
its
9 What from the forest came? What beast has licked ~~[?]~~ young.

[NLI 30,178]

1 He holds him from desire, all but stops his breathing lest
2 Primordial Motherhood forsake his limbs, the child no longer rest
3 Drinking joy as it were milk upon his breast.

4 Through light obliterating garden foliage what magic drum?
5 Down limb and breast or down that glimmering belly move his mouth and
sinewy tongue
6 What from the forest came? What beast has licked its young.

Above the draft is a correction for "Ribh considers Christian Love insufficient" (see p. 185); below it is a draft of "Alternative Song for the Severed Head" in *The King of the Great Clock Tower* (see p. 98).

---

title 7. WHAT MAGIC DRUM? *FMM*
2 rest, *FMM*
5 tongue, *FMM*
6 young? *FMM*

[BC, 36v]

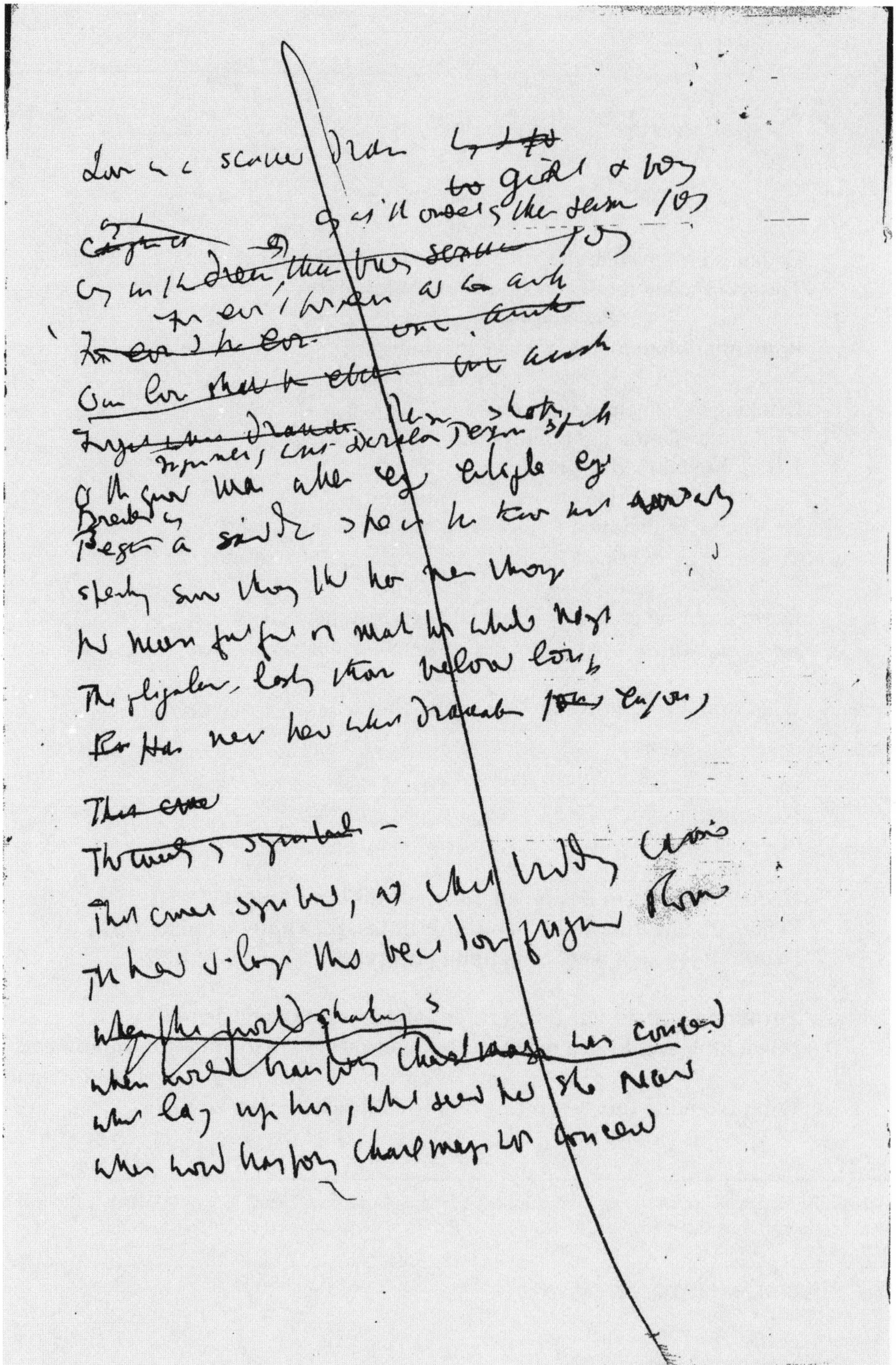

8. Whence had they Come?

[BC, 36v]

Love is a scacred drama ~~[? ? ?]~~
                    rl
~~bo~~ gi{ l & boy
~~Cry~~
~~Caught~~ Cry at the onset of their sexual joy
~~of~~
Cry in the ~~dream, their brief sexual joy~~
For ever & forever and ~~aw~~ awake
‘ ~~For ever & for ever once awake~~
~~Our love shall be eternal once~~ awake
~~Forget what Dramatis~~ Personae spake
[?Ignorer] of what Dramatis Personae spake
O the grown man when eye entangles eye
Breaks into
Begins a sudden speech he knows not ~~how~~ why
Speaking some thought that has never thought
But must fulfil or make his whole naught
The flagalant, lashing those beloved loins
~~R[?e]~~ Has never heard what dramatist ~~joins~~ enjoins
~~That cruel~~
~~The cruelty of symbols~~ —
That cruel symbol, at what bidding came
The hand & lash that beat down [?frigid] Rome
~~When the world shaking s~~
When world transforming Charlemagne was conceived
What lay upon her, what seed had she received
When world transforming Charlemagne was conceived

---

found in BC, 36v, 37r, 37v *transcribed above and below*
NLI 30,167 *transcribed below*
published in *A Full Moon in March* (1935)

---

1 For "scacred" read "sacred."
10 For "that has" read "that he has"?
11 For "whole naught" read "whole life naught"?

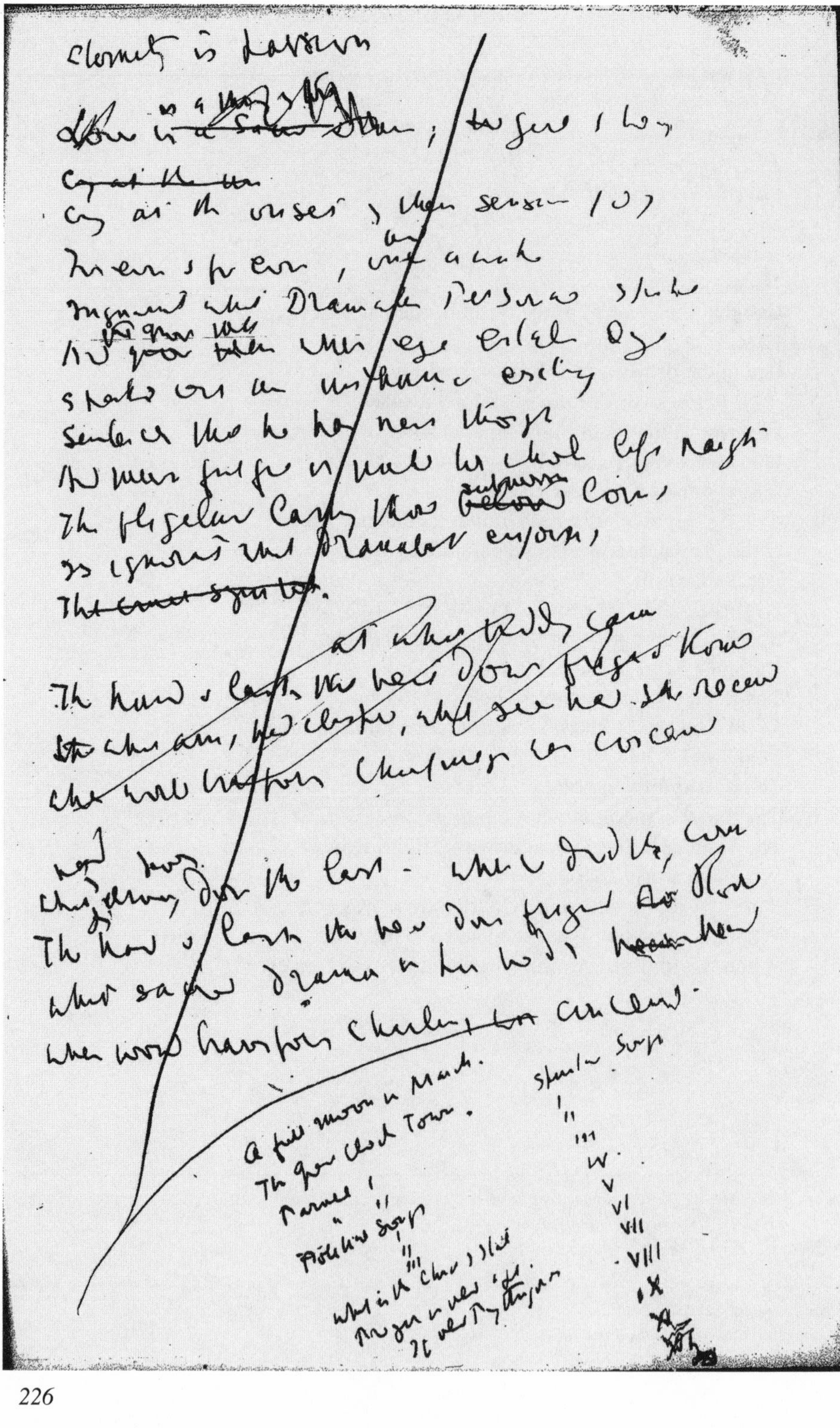

[BC, 37r]

1 Eternity is passion
        is a ~~thing of [?Art]~~
2 Love is ~~a Sacred Drama~~; ~~bo~~ girl & boy
3 ~~Cry at the un~~
4 Cry at the onset of their [?sexual] joy
                                        and
5 For ever & for ever, once awake
6 Ignorant what Dramatis Personae spake
      the grown man
7 And ~~grown men~~ when eye [?entangles] eye
8 Speaks out an [?unknown] ecstasy
9 Sentences that he has never thought
10 And must fulfil or make his whole life naught
                                        submissive
11 The flagelant lashing those ~~beloved~~ loins
12 Is ignorant what dramatist enjoins
13 ~~That cruel symbol~~.

14   At what bidding came
15 The hand & lash that beat down frigid Rome
16 ~~[?The]~~ What arms had clasped, what [?see] had she received
17 When world transforming Charlemagne was conceived

    [?hand] [?fever]
18 What^driven, down the lash – Whence did they come
19 The hand & lash that beat down frigid ~~ro~~ Rome
20 What sacred drama in her body ~~heav~~ heaved
21 When world transforming Charlemagne was conceived

---

16 For "[?see]" read "seed"?
Below the draft the following notes appear in black ink:

A full moon in March.	
The Great Clock Tower.	Spiritual Songs
Parnell I	I
II	II
Political Songs	III
I	IV
II	V
III	VI
What is the Church & State	VII
Prayer in Old Age.	VIII
If old Pythagoras	IX
	X
	XI
	~~[?]~~

The roman numerals IX, X, and XI under "Spiritual Songs" were revised from X, XI, and XII.

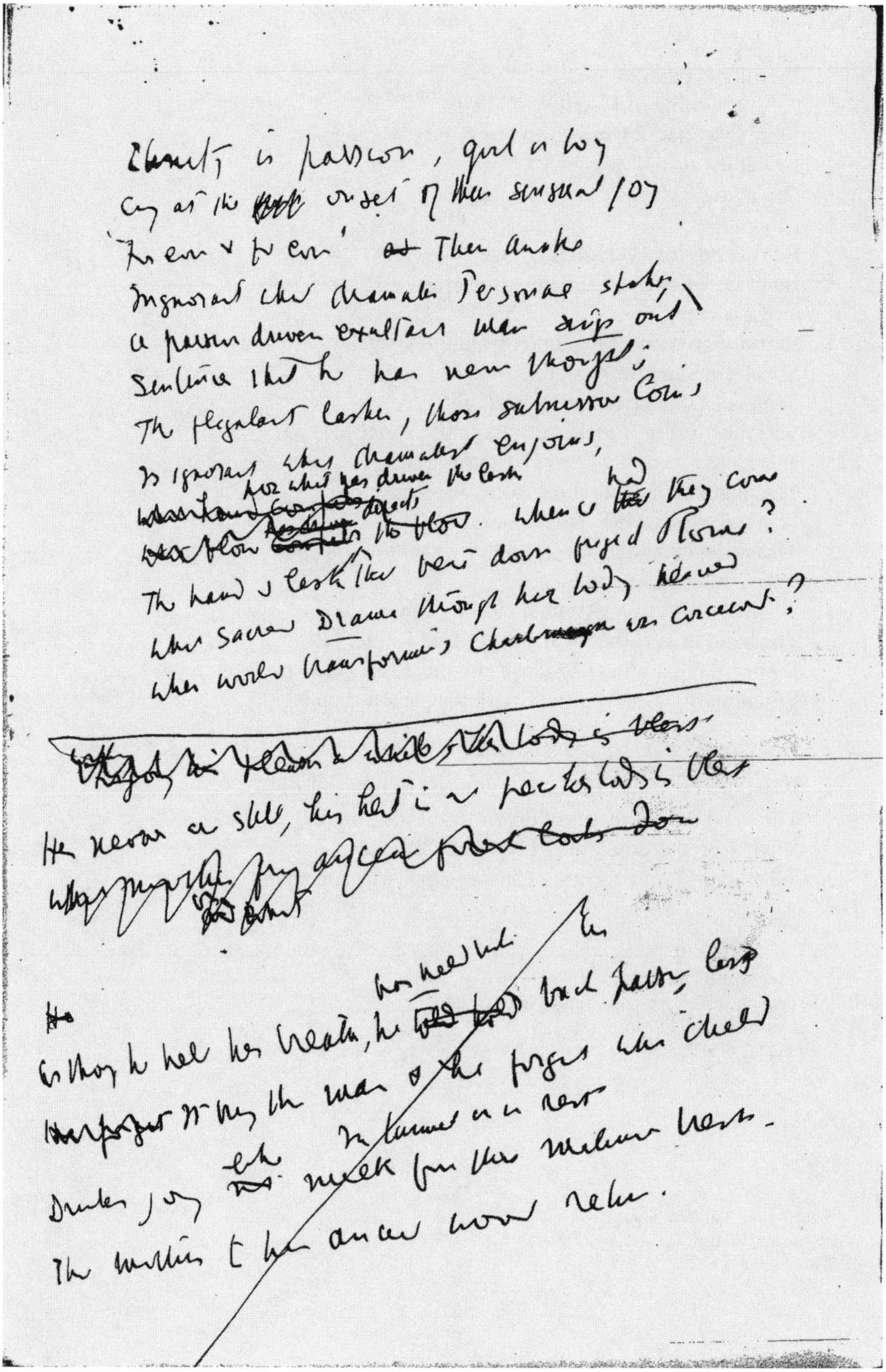
Chastity is passion, girl or boy
Cry at the ~~[illegible]~~ onset of their sensual joy
'For ever & for ever' ~~at~~ Then awake
Ignorant what dramatis personae spake;
A passion driven exultant man sings out
Sentences that he has never thought;
The flagrant lover, those submissive come[?]
Is ignorant what dramatist enjoins,
for what has driven the lash
~~[illegible]~~ ~~[illegible]~~ the blow. whence had they come
The hand & lash that beat down frigid Rome?
What sacred Drama through her body heaved
When world transforming Charlemagne was conceived?

~~[illegible]~~
He [illegible] [illegible], his [illegible] [illegible]
~~[illegible]~~

Although he had her breath, he [illegible] back [illegible]
[illegible] the man & the [illegible] [illegible]
Drunken joy [illegible] [illegible]
The mother [illegible] [illegible]

[BC, 37^{v} and NLI 30,167]

[BC, 37^{v}]

Eternity is passion, girl or boy
Cry at the ~~first~~ onset of their sensual joy
'For ever & for ever' ~~and~~ Then awake
Ignorant what dramatis Personae spake;
A passion driven exultant man sings out
Sentences that he has never thought;
The flagalant lashing those submissive loins
Is ignorant what dramatist enjoins,
[?Nor] what has driven the lash
~~What hand compels~~
~~has driven~~ directs had
~~What blow compels the blow~~ Whence ~~had~~ they come
The hand & lash that ^ beat down frigid Rome?
What Sacred Drama through her body heaved
When world transforming Charlemagne was conceived?

[NLI 30,167]

Eternity is passion, girl or boy
Cry at the onset of their sexual joy
"Forever and forever;" then awake
Ignorant what Dramatis Personae spake;
A passion driven exultant man sings out
Sentences that he has never thought;
The Flagellant lashes those submissive loins
Ignorant what that dramatist enjoins
Nor what has driven the lash. Whence had they come
The hand and lash that beat down frigid Rome?
What sacred drama through her body heaved
When world-transforming Charlemagne was conceived.

Below the draft of "Whence had they Come?" on BC, 37^{v}, is a draft of "What Magic Drum?" (see p. 209).

---

title numbered 8. WHENCE HAD THEY COME? *FMM*
3 'For ever and for ever'; *FMM*
5 passion-driven *FMM*
8 enjoins, *FMM*
9 What master made the lash. Whence had they come, *FMM*
12 conceived? *FMM*

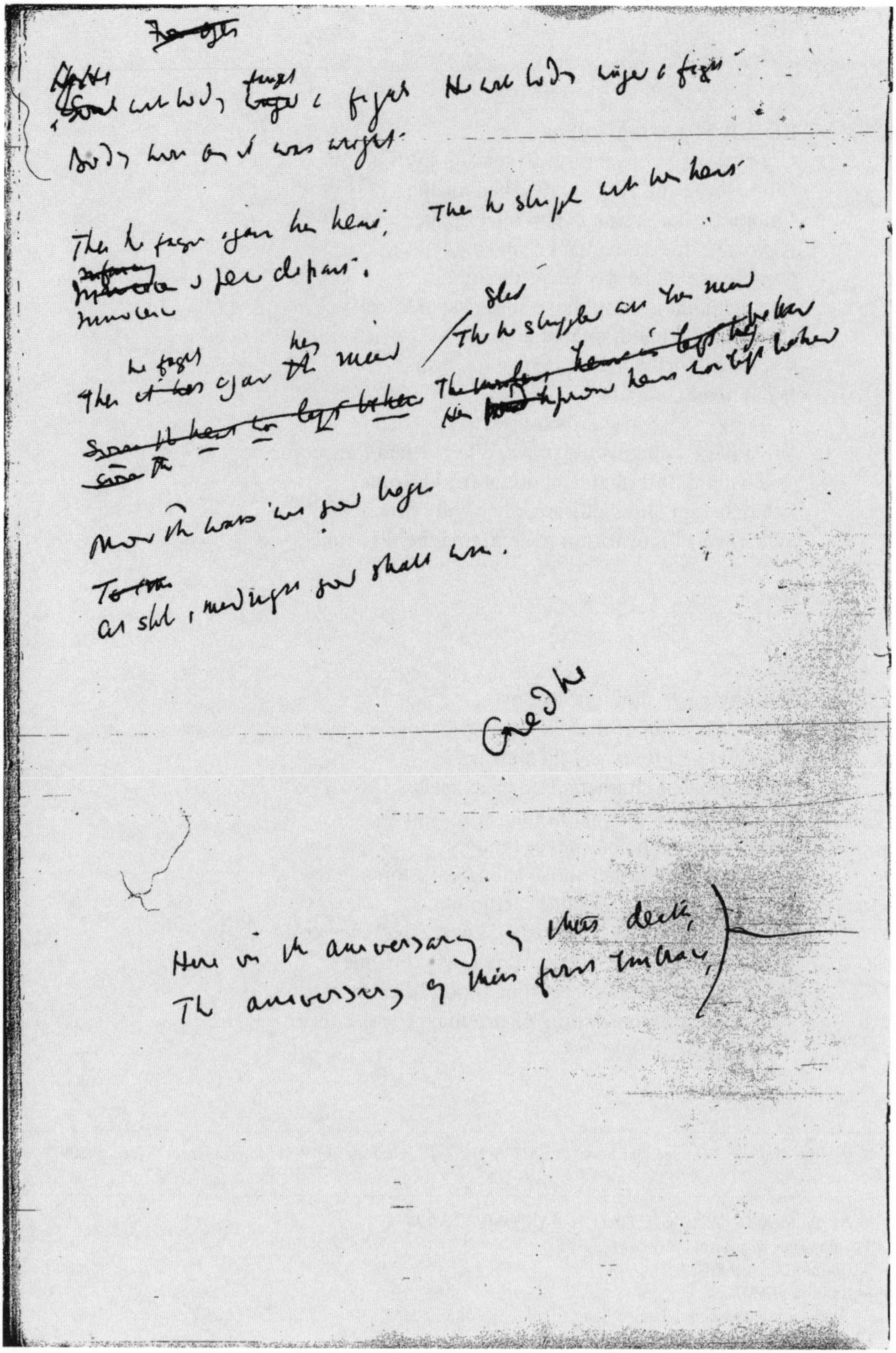

SUPERNATURAL SONGS

9. The Four Ages of Man

[BC, 17v]

~~Four Ages~~

~~He~~ He fought
~~Soul~~ with body ~~waged~~ a fight He with body waged a fight
Body won as it walks [?upright]

Then he fought against his heart, Then he struggles with his heart
~~Infancy~~
~~Innocence~~ & peace depart.
Innocence

stet
he fought his
Then ~~it war~~ against ~~the~~ mind / Then he struggled with his mind
~~Soon the heart was left behind~~ ~~The insolent heart is left beg~~ behind
proud
~~Soon~~ the his ~~[?]~~ } his proud heart was left behind

Now the wars with god begin

~~To me~~
At stroke of midnight god shall win.

---

found in BC, 17v, 19r *transcribed above and below*
MBY 673, letter 2, 1r *transcribed below*
Chicago(1), pp. 42–43 *transcribed below*
published in *Poetry* (Chicago), December 1934
The London Mercury, December 1934
The King of the Great Clock Tower (1934)
The King of the Great Clock Tower (1935)
A Full Moon in March (1935)

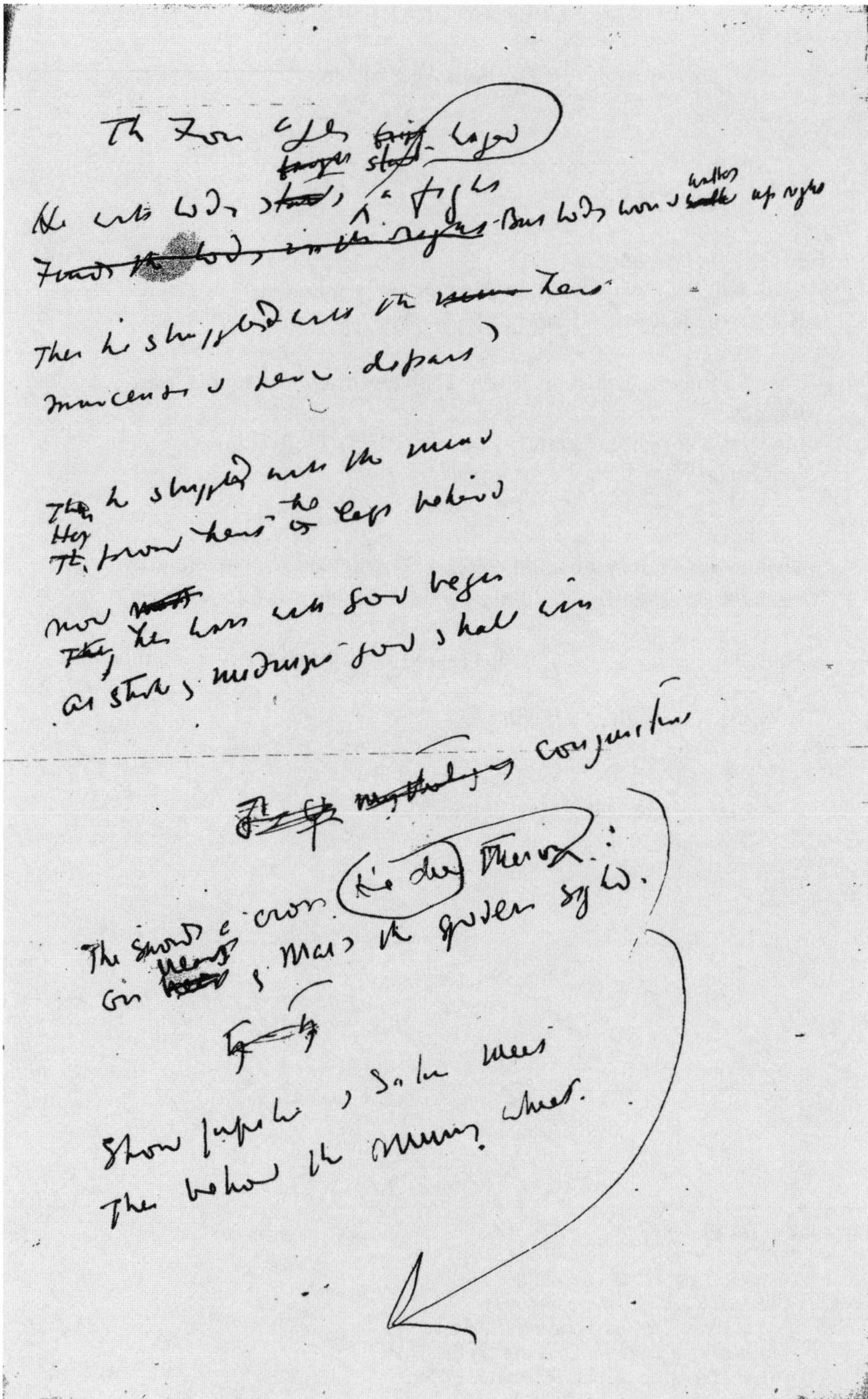

[BC, 19r]

The Four Ages

~~fought~~ waged
~~fought~~ ~~start~~
He with body ~~starts~~ ^ a fight
walks
~~Finds the body in the right~~ But body won & ~~walked~~ up right

Then he struggled with the ~~mind~~ heart
Innocence & peace depart

Then he struggled with the mind
His he
~~The~~ proud heart ~~is~~ left behind

Now ~~must~~
~~Then~~ ^ his wars with god begin
At stroke of midnight god shall win

Below the draft is a draft of "Conjunctions" (see p. 237).

[MBY 673, letter 2, 1r]

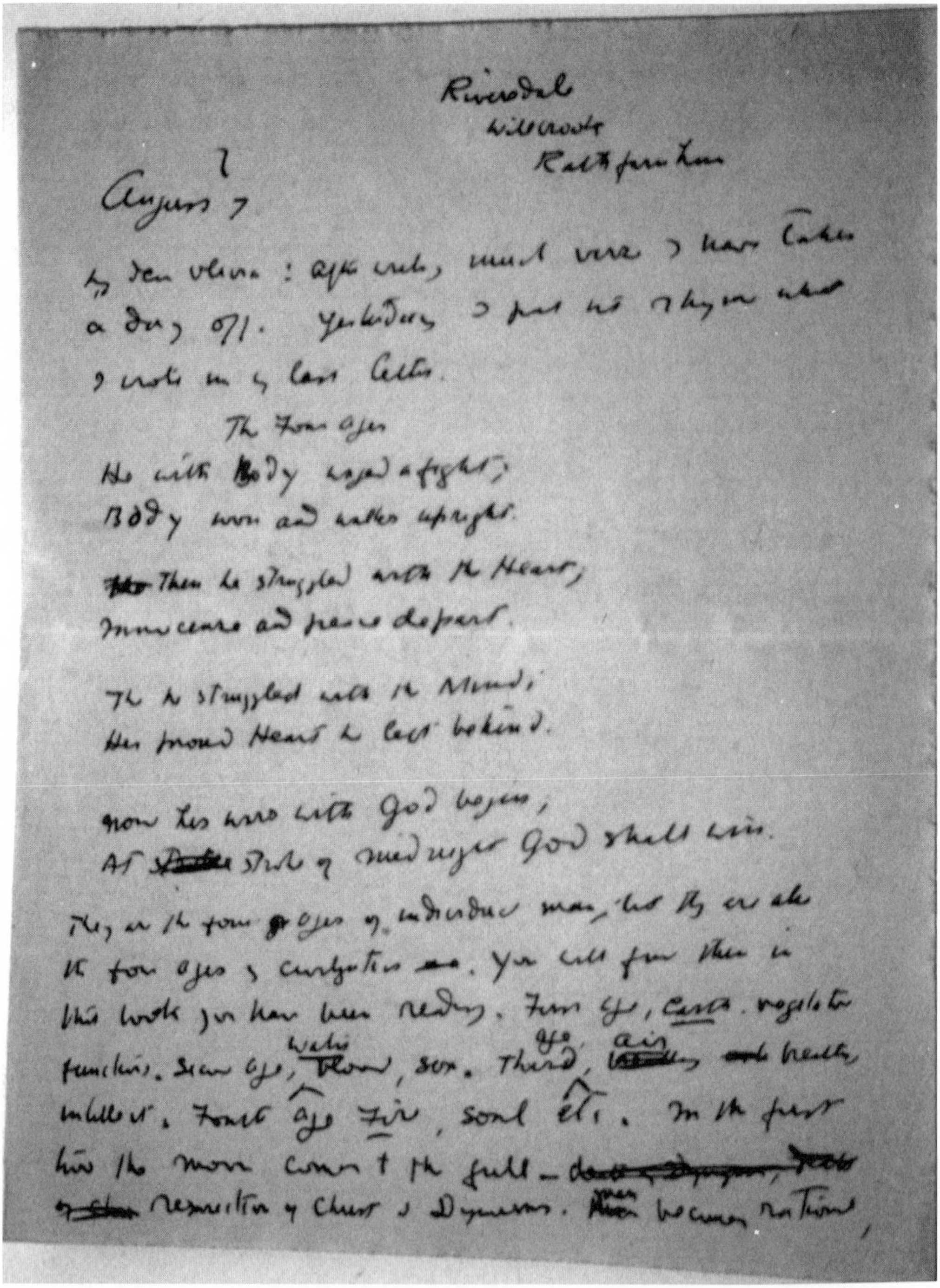

Riversdale
Willbrook
Rathfarnham

August 7

My dear Olivia: after weeks, much verse I have taken a day off. Yesterday I put into rhyme what I wrote in my last letter.

The Four Ages

He with body waged a fight;
Body won and walks upright.

Then he struggled with the heart;
Innocence and peace depart.

Then he struggled with the mind;
His proud heart he left behind.

Now his wars with God begin,
At stroke of midnight God shall win.

They are the four ages of individual man, but they are also the four ages of civilization. You will find them in the book you have been reading. First age, earth, vegetative functions. Second age, water, blood, sex. Third age, air, breath, intellect. Fourth age fire, soul etc. In the first the moon comes to the full — resurrection of Christ & Dionysus. Man becomes rational,

[MBY 673, letter 2, 1r, and Chicago(1), pp. 42–43]

[MBY 673, letter 2, 1r]

The Four Ages

He with Body waged a fight;
Body won and walks upright.

~~The~~ Then he struggled with the Heart;
Innocence and peace depart.

Then he struggled with the Mind,
His proud Heart he left behind.

Nor his wars with God begin,
At ~~stroke~~ stroke of midnight God shall win

[Chicago(1), pp. 42–43]

5 THE FOUR AGES OF MAN

He with body waged a fight,
But body won; it walks upright.

Then he struggled with the heart,
Innocence and peace depart.

Then he struggled with the mind;
His proud heart he left behind.

Now his wars on God begin,
At stroke of midnight God shall win.

MBY 673 From a letter to Olivia Shakespear dated August 7 [postmark August 9, 1934]. Transcribed from SB 3.4.63. See *Letters*, p. 386.

Variants for Chicago(1), pp. 42–43:
title unnumbered P 5. *LM* 5 *KGCT'34, KGCT'35* 9. *FMM*
3 heart; *FMM*
7 begin; *FMM*

[BC, 19r]

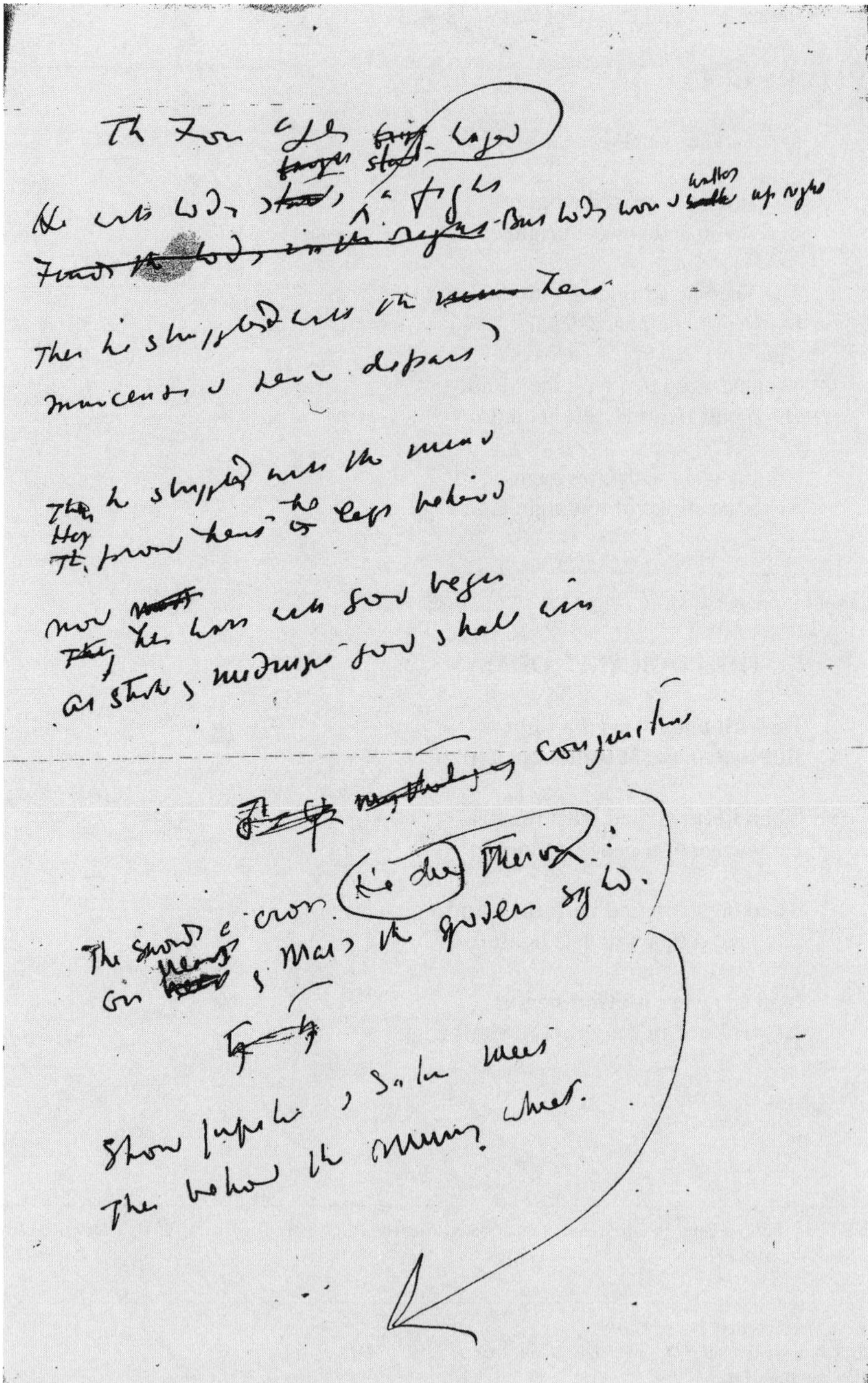

SUPERNATURAL SONGS

10. Conjunctions

[BC, 19r]

~~♂ ♀~~ ~~mythology~~ Conjunctions

The swords a cross (He died) thereon^:
heart
On [~~?heart~~] of Mars the goddess sighed.
~~5 – 5~~
Should Jupiter & Saturn meet
Then behold the mummy wheat.

---

found in BC, 19r *transcribed above*
MBY 673, letter 3, 1v *transcribed below*
Chicago(1), p. 43 *transcribed below*
published in *Poetry* (Chicago), December 1934
The London Mercury, December 1934
The King of the Great Clock Tower (1934)
The King of the Great Clock Tower (1935)
A Full Moon in March (1935)

Above the draft is a draft of "The Four Ages of Man" (see p. 233).

1 "He died" is clued in after "thereon."

1–2 Clued in to follow lines 3–4.

2–3 "5 – 5" is written, and canceled, between the stanzas.

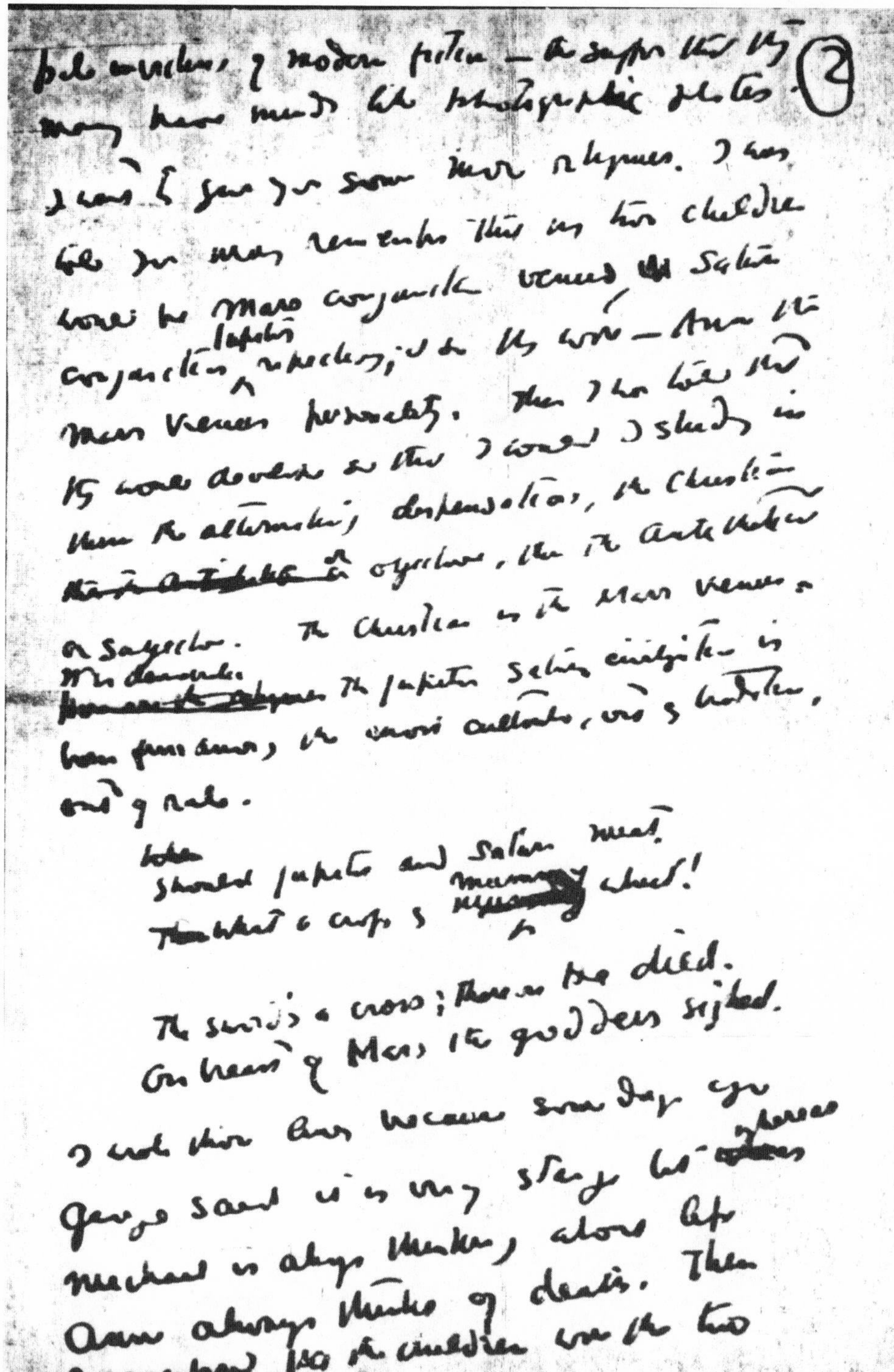
full analysis of modern fiction — a suggestion that they
may have minds like photographic plates. (2)

I want to give you some more rhymes. I was
told you may remember that as two children
would be Mars conjunct Venus and Saturn
conjunction Jupiter, [illegible] they would — then the
Mars Venus personality. Then I was told that
they would develop so that I would I should in
them the alternating dispensations, the Christian
~~[illegible]~~ or objective, then the Antithetical
[illegible] the Christian is the Mars Venus — a
a subjective. The Christian is the Mars Venus — a
~~[illegible]~~ the Jupiter Saturn civilization is
[illegible], the [illegible], one of [illegible],
end of rule.

When
~~Should~~ Jupiter and Saturn meet,
~~Then~~ What a crop of ~~[illegible]~~ mummy wheat!

The sword's a cross; thereon he died.
On breast of Mars the goddess sighed.

I wrote these lines because some days ago
George said it is very strange but whereas
Michael is always thinking about life
Anne always thinks of death. Then
I remember that the children were the two

[MBY 673, letter 3, 1^{v}, and Chicago(1), p. 43]

[MBY 673, letter 3, 1^{v}]

~~Whe~~
Should Jupiter and Saturn meat,
mummy
~~Then~~ What a crop of [?~~mumy~~] wheat!
∧
The sword's a cross; thereon He died.
On breast of Mars the goddess sighed.

[Chicago(1), p. 43]

6 CONJUNCTIONS

If Jupiter and Saturn meet,
What a crop of mummy wheat;

The sword's a cross; thereon He died:
On breast of Mars the goddess sighed.

MBY 673 From a letter to Olivia Shakespear August 25, 1934 [postmark August 28, 1934] from Riversdale. Transcribed from SB 3.4.47. See *Letters*, pp. 827–828.

Variants for Chicago(1), p. 43:
title unnumbered P 6. *LM* 6 *KGCT'34, KGCT'35* 10. *FMM*

[O'Shea 2039A]

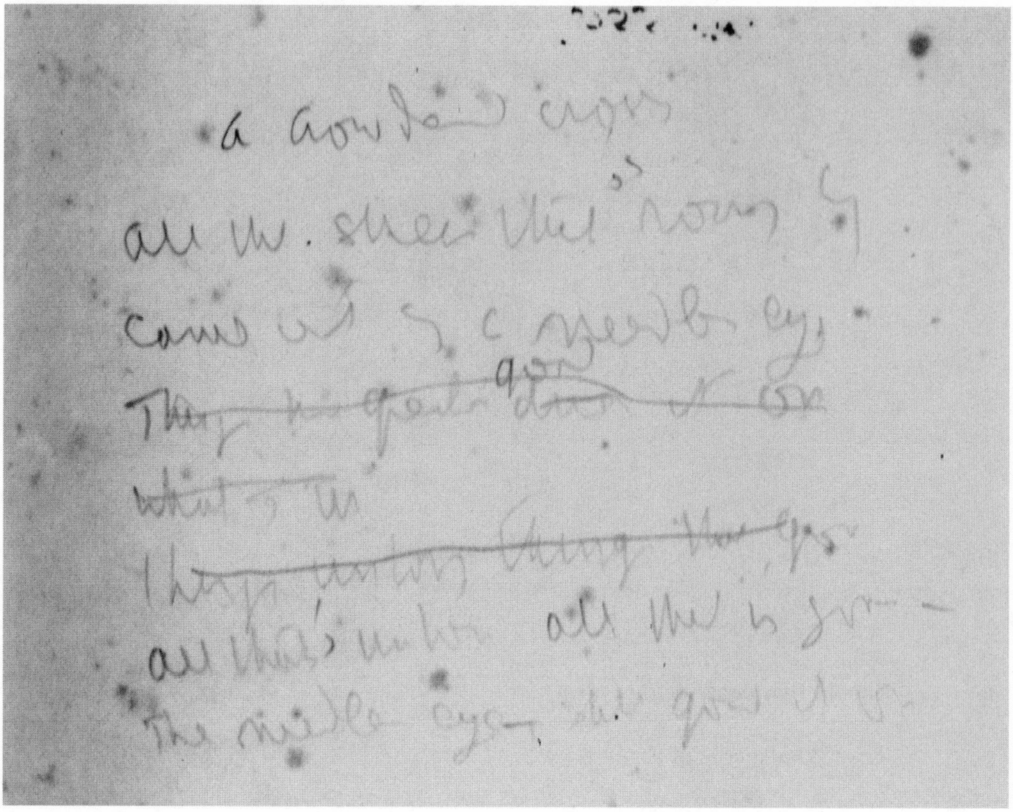

11. A Needle's Eye

[O'Shea 2039A and Chicago(1), p. 43]

[O'Shea 2039A]

A Crowded Cross
All the stream that's roaring by
Came out of a needle's ~~eye~~
——— goad
~~Things [? ?] drive it on~~
What is un
Things unborn things that [?gone/?goad]
All that's unborn, all that is gone
The needle's eye – still goad it on.

[Chicago(1), p. 43]

7 A NEEDLE''S EYE

All the stream that's roaring by
Came out of a needle's eye;
Things unborn, things that are gone,
From ~~the~~ needle's eye still goad it on.
7

---

found in O'Shea 2039A *transcribed above*
Chicago(1), p. 43 *transcribed above*
published in *Poetry* (Chicago), December 1934
The London Mercury, December 1934
The King of the Great Clock Tower (1934)
The King of the Great Clock Tower (1935)
A Full Moon in March (1935)

Variants for Chicago(1), p. 43:
title *unnumbered P* 7. *LM* 7 *KGCT'34, KGCT'35* 11. *FMM*

[MBY 545, p. 379]

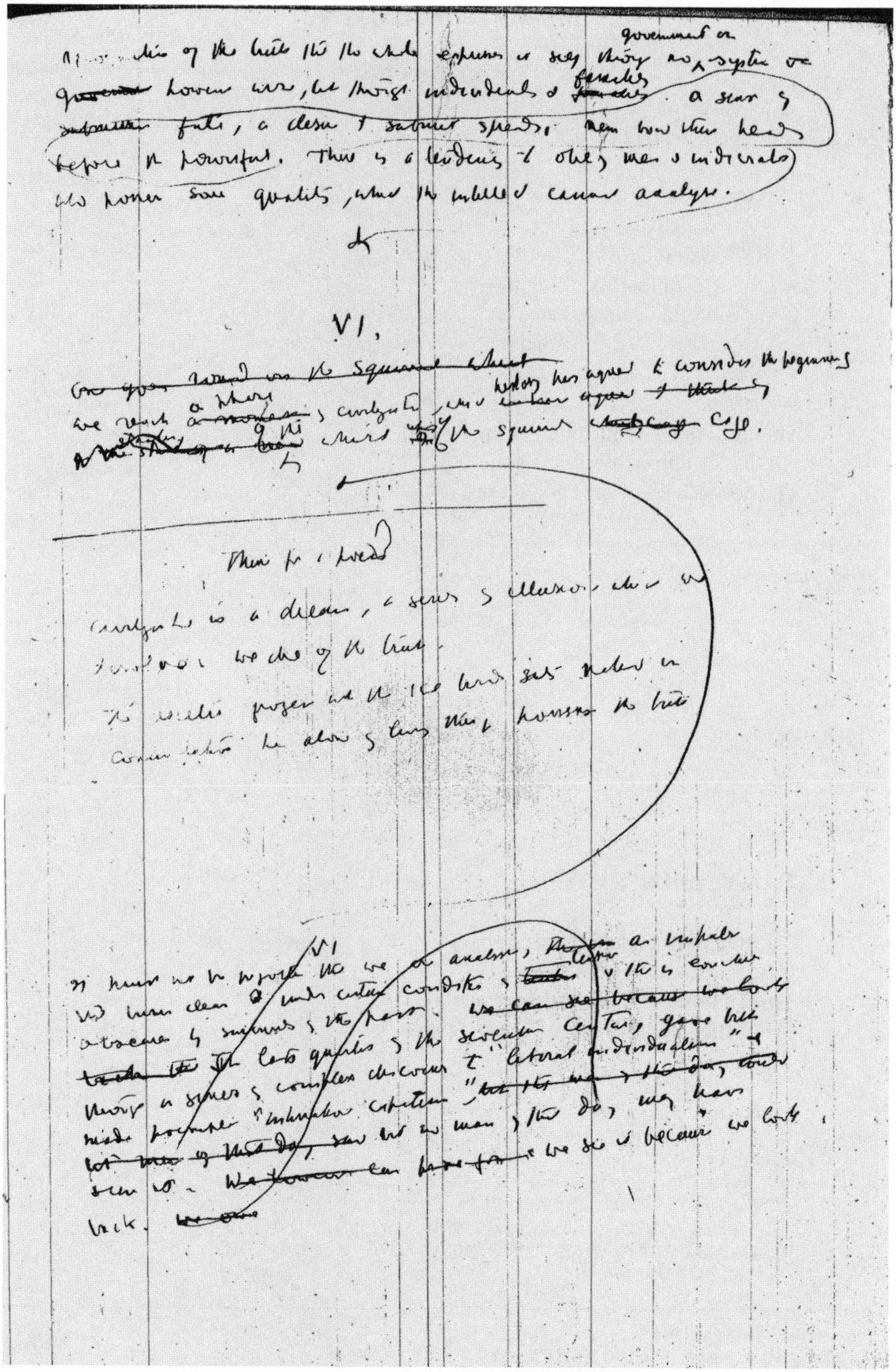
[illegible] of the truth that the whole experience is seen through a government or system or government however wise, but through individuals & families. A sense of [illegible] fate, a desire to submit spreads; men bow their heads before the powerful. There is a tendency to obey men & individuals who possess some quality which the intellect cannot analyse.

VI.

we reach a theory of conjugation, [illegible] history has agreed to consider the beginnings of [illegible] which [illegible] the squirrel cage.

There for a period

conjugation is a dream, a series of illusions which we [illegible] [illegible] [illegible] of the truth.

[illegible]

VI

It must not be [illegible] that we [illegible] analysis, [illegible] an impulse [illegible] clear [illegible] under certain conditions of [illegible] & this is [illegible] obscured by [illegible] of the past. [illegible] The last quarter of the seventeenth century, gave birth through a series of complex discoveries to "liberal individualism" & made possible "individual creation" [illegible] but the men of that day, [illegible] have [illegible] we see it because we look back.

12. Meru

[MBY 545, p. 379]

Theme for a Poem

Civilization is a dream, a series of illusions which we
dissolve as we die of the truth.
The ascetic frozen into the ice bird sits naked in
contemplation he alone of living things possesses the truth

---

found in MBY 545, pp. 379, 380, 381 *transcribed above and below*
NLI 30,111 *transcribed below*
Chicago(1), p. 44

published in *Poetry* (Chicago), December 1934
The London Mercury, December 1934
The King of the Great Clock Tower (1934)
The King of the Great Clock Tower (1935)
A Full Moon in March (1935)

The arrow circling the text on the right connects the passage below it to that above. For "ice bird" one is undoubtedly meant to read "ice berg." A new sentence begins with "he alone."

I have transcribed "Meru" from MBY 545 (pp. 379, 380, and 381) as it appears in the microfilm at SUNY Stony Brook. I have been helped by a transcription of p. 379 by Curtis Bradford in his index to MBY 545. Near the poem, on pp. 374–375, appears a draft of "Parnell's Funeral" dated April 1933. This "Theme for a Poem" was probably written about that time.

[MBY 545, p. 380]

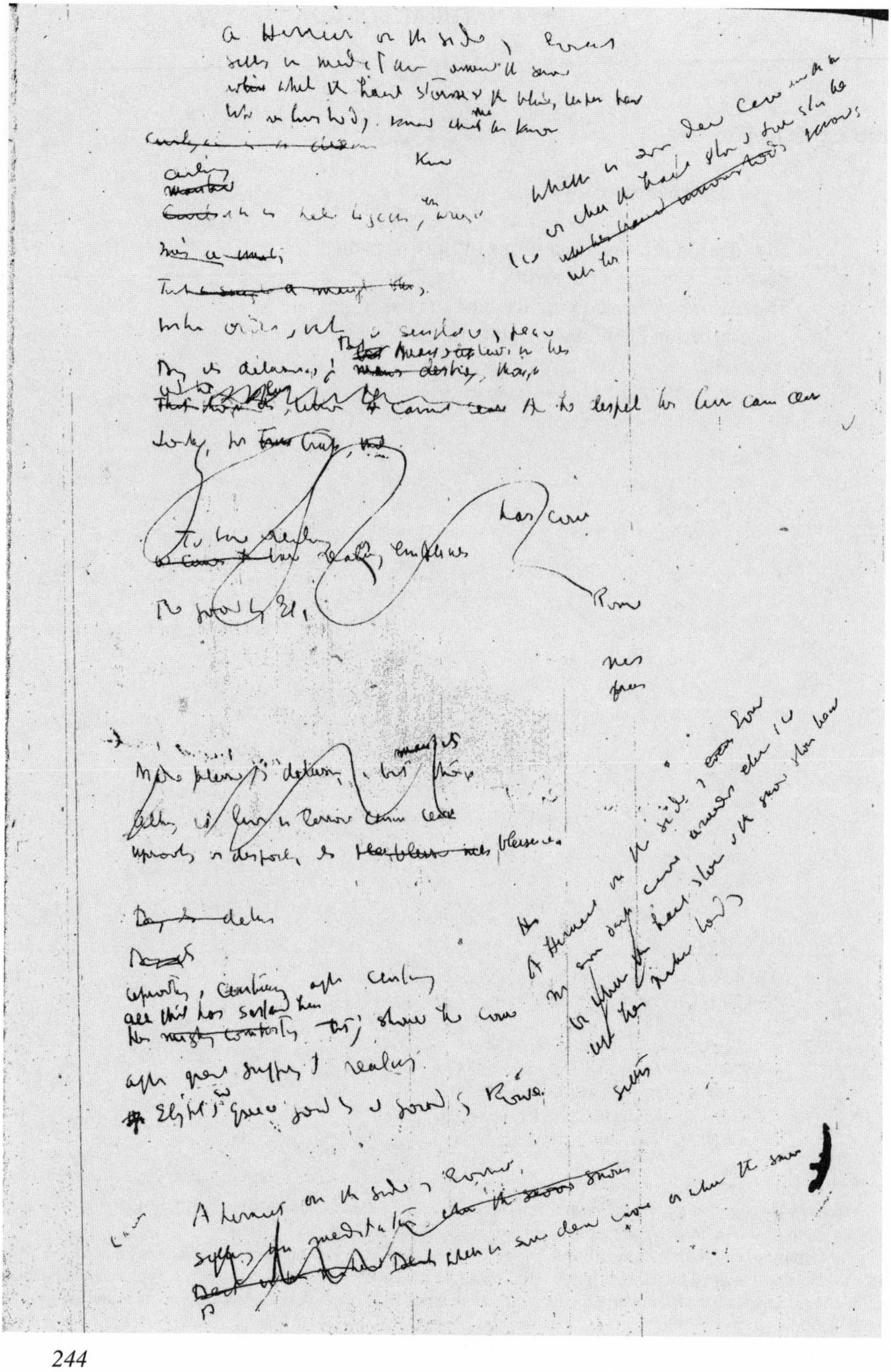

[MBY 545, p. 380]

A Hermit on the side of Everest
[?Sitting] in meditation amidst the snow
~~While~~ While the [?hail] storm & the blinding tempest beat
[?that]
Upon his living body [?know] what he knows

~~Civilization is a dream~~
Know
[?Civilization]
~~Mankind~~ en
~~Civilization~~ is held together, wrought
~~[?] a [?unity]~~
~~T[?aken] [?singly] a [?] they~~

Whether in some dim cave in [?]
Or where the hail storm & snow storm be
Ice
upon ~~his hard unconscious body~~ [?knows]
upon his

Make order, make a semblance of peace
But
~~but~~ Mans ~~lif~~ live for his
By its delusions [?] [?of] ~~mirror darkly~~, though

~~And he~~ [?~~slay~~]
~~That [?hope] [?or] & terror cannot cease~~ And he despite his terror cannot cease

Looking for ~~true~~ truth, that

has come
To bare reality or
~~And comes to~~ bare reality emblemes
Rome
Then good by Etc.

Transcribed from SB 21.5.216.
11 For "be" read "beat"?
15 For "though" read "thought"?

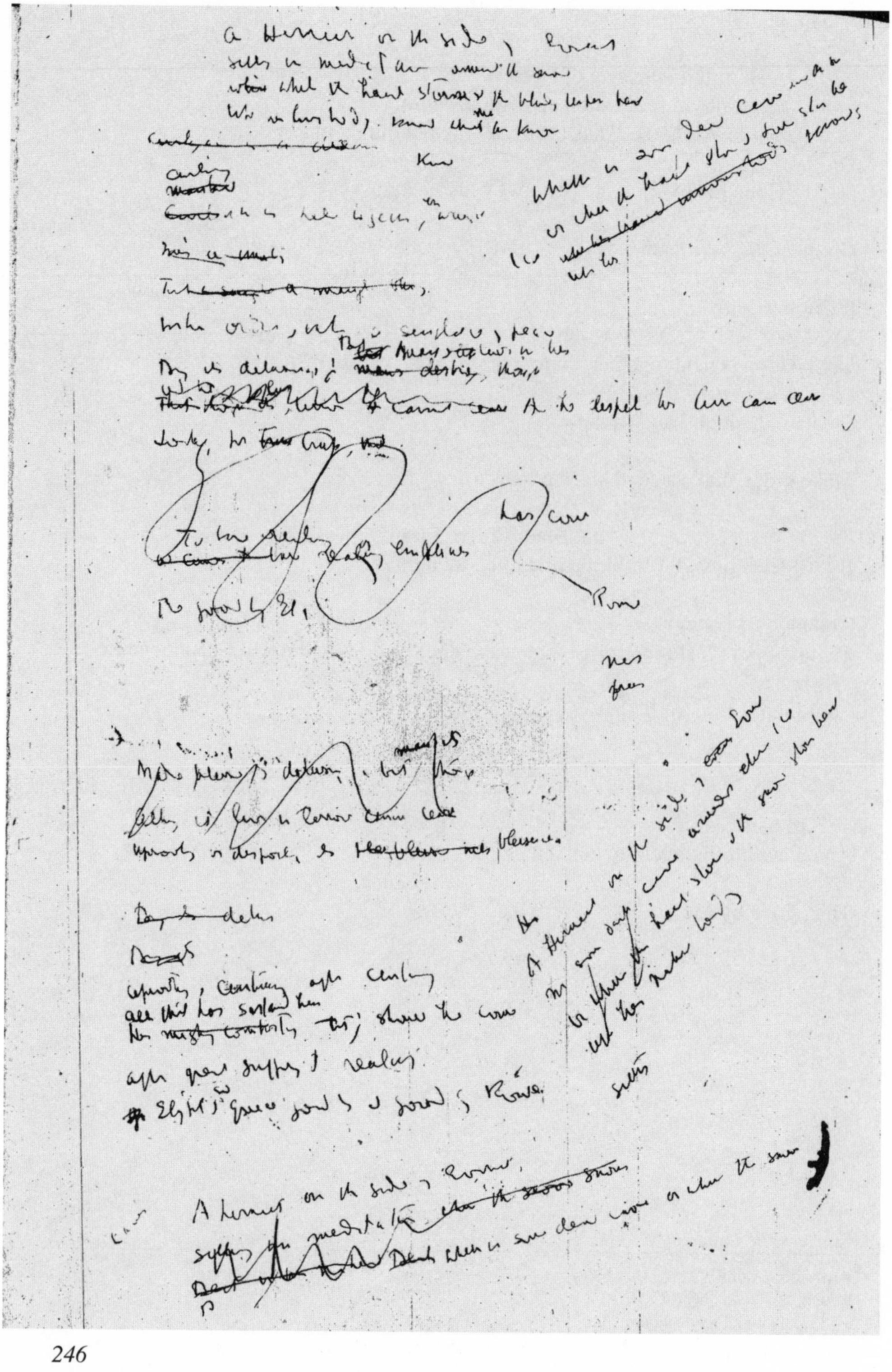

[MBY 545, p. 380 continued]

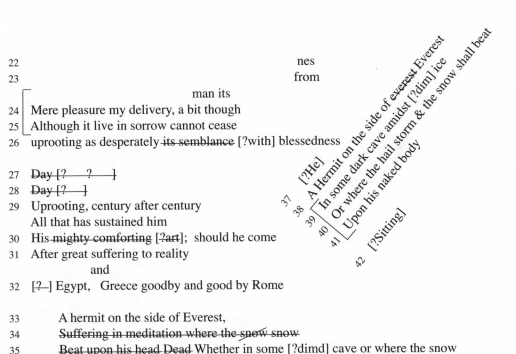

nes
from
man its
Mere pleasure my delivery, a bit though
Although it live in sorrow cannot cease
uprooting as desperately ~~its semblance~~ [?with] blessedness

~~Day [? ?]~~
~~Day [?]~~
Uprooting, century after century
All that has sustained him
His ~~mighty comforting~~ [~~?art~~]; should he come
After great suffering to reality
and
[~~?~~] Egypt, Greece goodby and good by Rome

A hermit on the side of Everest,
~~Suffering in meditation where the snow snow~~
~~Beat upon his head Dead~~ Whether in some [?dimd] cave or where the snow
[?]

[?He]
A Hermit on the side of ~~everest~~ Everest
In some dark cave amidst [?dim] ice
Or where the hail storm & the snow shall beat
Upon his naked body
[?Sitting]

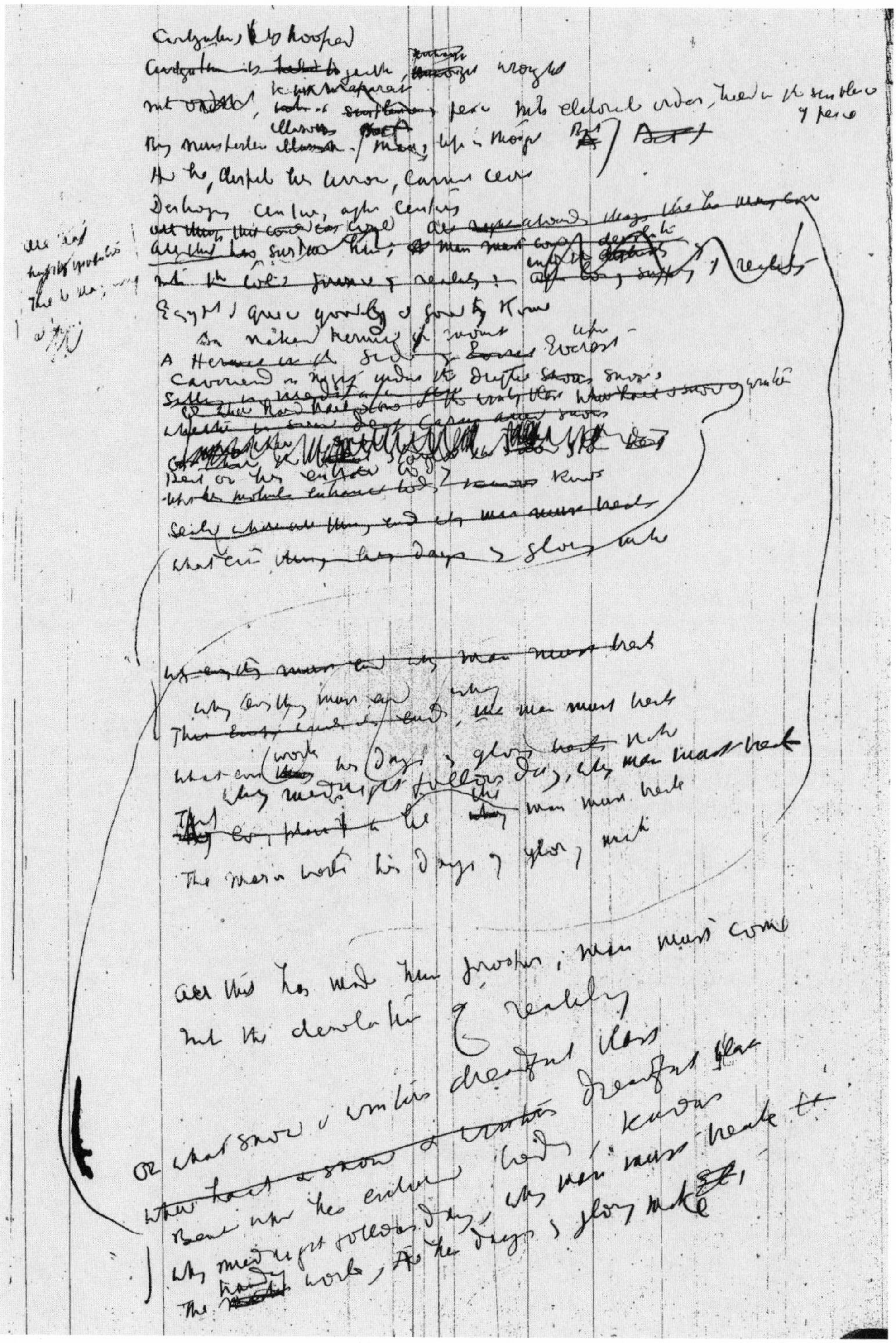
Civilization, hooped
And he, despite his terror, cannot cease
Destroying century after century
Egypt & Greece goodbye & goodbye Rome
Caverned in night under the drifted snows
All this has made him ...; man must come
Into the desolation of reality
Or what snow & winter's dreadful blast

[MBY 545, p. 381]

Civilization [?] is hooped
~~wrought~~
1 Civilization is held together, ~~wrought~~ wrought
[? ?in ?apparent]
2 Into order [?into a] semblance of peace Into elaborate order, held in the semblance of peace
illusions ~~But A~~ But/
3 By numberless ~~illusions.~~ / man's life is thought ~~A~~/ ~~But~~/
4 And he, despite his terror, cannot cease
5 Destroying century after century
~~All things that could can~~ could ~~All [?ample] abounding things that he may come~~
6 ~~All that has sustained him; A man must come~~ ~~desolate~~
~~into the desolation of~~
7 ~~Into the cold [?presence] of reality~~; ~~after long suffering of reality~~
8 Egypt & Greece goodby & goodby Rome

An naked hermit ~~on~~ Mount upon
9 A ~~Hermit in the~~ side ~~of Everest~~ Everest
Caverned in night under the drifted ~~snows~~ snows
10 ~~[?Sitting] in meditation [?in]~~
~~Or where [?hard] hail stones & the wintry blast~~ ~~Where hail & snow &~~ winter
11 Whether in some deep cavern [?wind] [?moans]
~~[?Or whether]~~
12 ~~Or where the [?] storms the snow storm beat~~
Beat on his ~~entran~~ body
13 ~~[? ? ?] entranced body knows knows~~
14 ~~[?] where all things end why man must break~~
15 Whatever ~~thing his days of glory make~~

Transcribed from SB 21.5.216.

6 Line 6 is rewritten corrected in lines 20 and 21. In the left margin next to 6 is written, then canceled,

All tha
has supported
that he may come
desolat
~~[?].~~

11–15 These lines are revised in lines 23–27.

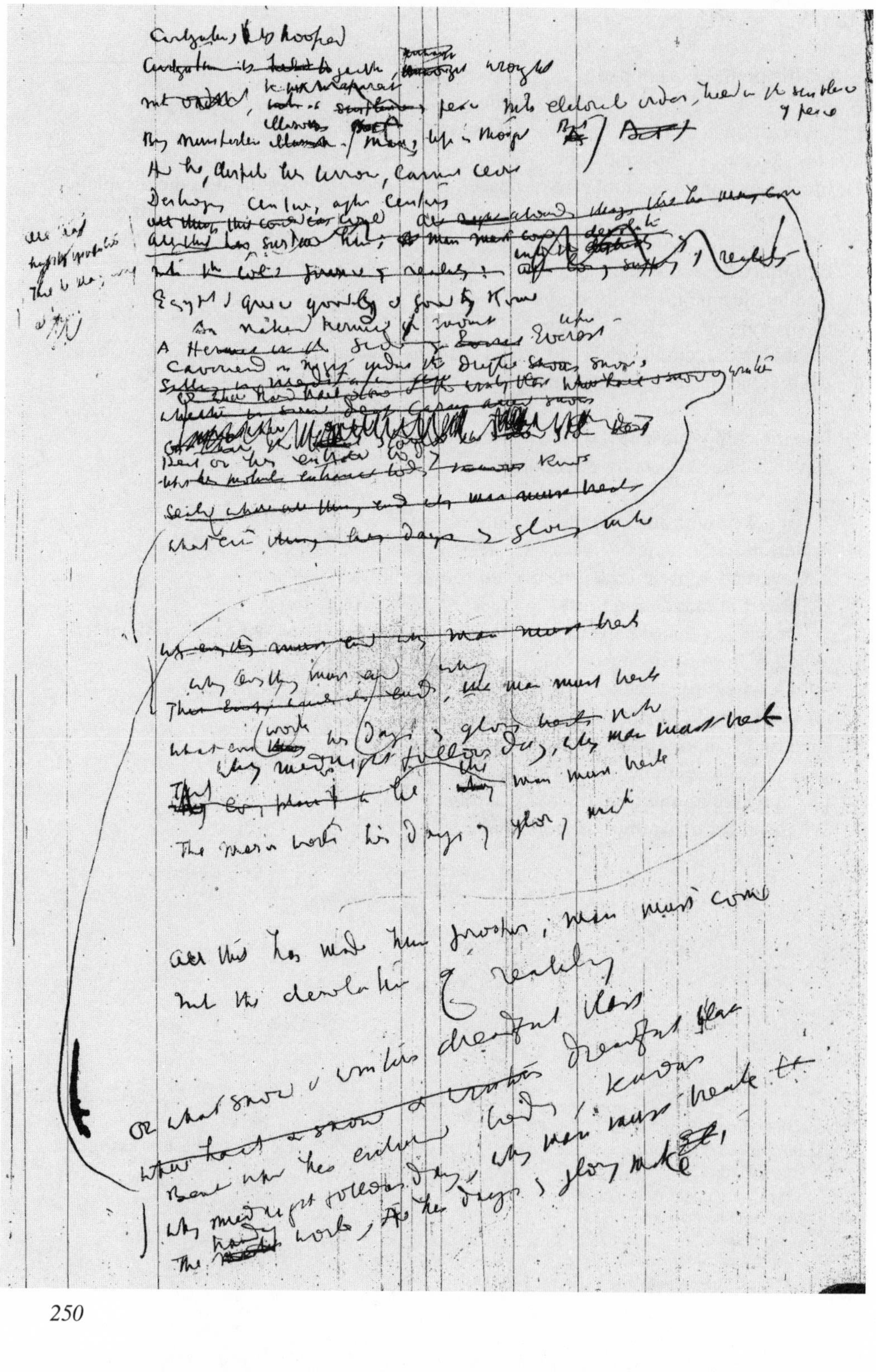

[MBY 545, p. 381 continued]

~~Why everything must end why man must break~~
Why everything must end   why
~~This body meets its end~~, ~~that~~ man must break
work
Whatever ~~thing~~ his days of glory [?~~break~~] make
why midnight follows   day, why man must break
That   [?that]
~~Why every [?plan] is a [?lie]   why~~ man must break
The master work his days of glory make

All that has made him prosper; man must come
Into the desolation of reality

Or what snow & winters dreadful blast
~~When hail & snow & winters~~ dreadful blast
Beat upon his entranced body, knows
Why midnight follows day, why man must break Etc.
handy   ~~Etc.~~
The ~~master~~ work, All his days of glory make

21–22   These lines are linked to lines 19–20.
25–27   These lines are linked to lines 10–12.

[NLI 30,111]

The summons up

civilization is hooped together, brought
Under a rule, ~~under~~ under the semblance of peace
By manifold illusion; but man's life is thought
And he, despite his terror, cannot cease
Ravening through century after century,
Ravening, raging & uprooting, that he may come
into the ~~desolation~~ desolation of reality:
Egypt & Greece good bye & good bye Rome.

Hermits upon Mount Meru or Everest
Caverned in night under the drifted snow,
Or where that snow and winter's dreadful blast
Beat down upon their naked bodies, know
That day brings round the ~~dark~~ night, that before dawn
His glory & his monuments are gone.

[NLI 30,111]

The summing up

Civilisation is hooped together, brought
~~[?a]~~ the
Under a rule, ~~under~~ or under^semblance of peace
By manifold illusion; but mans life is thought
And he, despite his terror, cannot cease
Ravening through century after century,
raging
Ravening ^ & uprooting that he may come
Into the [?~~desolation~~] of desolation of reality:
Egypt & Greece good by & goodby Rome.

Hermits upon Mount Meru or Everest
Caverned in night under the drifted snow,
Or where that snow and winters dreadful blast
Beat down upon their naked bodies, know
~~dark~~
That day brings round the ~~night,~~ that before dawn
His glory & his monuments are gone.

---

title *unnumbered* MERU *Chicago(1), P, LM, KGCT'34, KGCT'35* 12. MERU *FMM*
3 man's *Chicago(1), P, LM, KGCT'34, KGCT'35, FMM* thought, *FMM*
6 Ravening, *P, LM, KGCT'34, KGCT'35, FMM* raging, *FMM*
8 Greece good-bye . . . good-bye Rome. *P, LM, KGCT'34, KGCT'35* Greece good-bye, . . . good-bye, Rome! *FMM*
9 Everest, *FMM*
11 winter's *Chicago(1), P, LM, KGCT'34, KGCT'35, FMM*

Transcribed from SB subgroup I, series I, subseries A, box 4, folder 77.